Ebony and Ivy

EBONY & IVY

Race, Slavery, and the Troubled History
of America's Universities

CRAIG STEVEN WILDER

BLOOMSBURY PRESS
NEW YORK · LONDON · NEW DELHI · SYDNEY

Published by Bloomsbury Press, New York

All papers used by Bloomsbury Press are natural, recyclable products made from
wood grown in well-managed forests. The manufacturing processes conform to
the environmental regulations of the country of origin.

LIBRARY OF CONGRESS CATALOGING-IN-PUBLICATION DATA
HAS BEEN APPLIED FOR.

ISBN: 978-1-59691-681-4

First U.S. edition 2013

3 5 7 9 10 8 6 4

Designed by Rachel Reiss

Typeset by Westchester Book Group
Printed and bound in the U.S.A. by Thomson-Shore Inc., Dexter, Michigan

TO

Gloria Wilder

Contents

There is no drama like the drama of history.

—C. L. R. JAMES, *THE BLACK JACOBINS* (1938)

[Henry] Watson's behavior merely showed that
Connecticut tutors could become Alabama cotton
planters in a single generation.

—HERBERT GUTMAN, *THE BLACK FAMILY
IN SLAVERY AND FREEDOM* (1976)

A catastrophe occurred which was so great that it is
little discussed. Else it would dominate all discourse
about the human story in the Western Hemisphere.
Plymouth Rock and Pilgrims, Columbus and Captain
John Smith would shrink to footnotes. Even the losses
of the American Civil War of 1861–1865 were trifling
when compared to the Great Dying.

—ROGER G. KENNEDY, *HIDDEN CITIES* (1994)

A Connecticut Yankee at an Ancient Indian Mound

"Remember me to all my friends and relations—I wish you and others of the family as many as can write to write to me often and tell me about every thing and any thing," Henry Watson begged his father, "about every body and thing I care any thing about." Written from New York in November 1830, where the young man had booked passage on the schooner *Isabella* to Mobile, Alabama, the letter mixed a premature homesickness with a sense of youthful expectation. Watson was from East Windsor, Connecticut, just north of Hartford, and he was heading south to find work as a teacher in an academy or on a plantation. He carried a packet of introductory letters from his professors at Washington College (Trinity) in Hartford and Harvard College in Cambridge, family friends including Professor Benjamin Silliman of Yale College, and his father's business acquaintances. After graduating from Yale, Silliman had considered a job in the South, and his brother Selleck did leave Yale to become a tutor in Charleston, South Carolina.[1]

College initiated Henry Watson into the slave regimes of the Atlantic world. The founding, financing, and development of higher education in the colonies were thoroughly intertwined with the economic and social forces that transformed West and Central

Africa through the slave trade and devastated indigenous nations in the Americas. The academy was a beneficiary and defender of these processes.

College graduates had exploited these links for centuries. They apprenticed under the slave traders of New England, the Mid-Atlantic, and Europe. They migrated to the South and to the West Indies for careers as teachers, ministers, lawyers, doctors, politicians, merchants, and planters. The end of the slave trade and the decline of slavery in the North did not break these ties. The antebellum South represented a field of opportunity, where the wealth of the cotton planters was funding the expansion of the educational infrastructure.

The *Isabella* could carry a handful of passengers, and Watson had a small, comfortable cabin. He stored his trunk on board and then explored New York City while he waited for departure. He detailed his spending, documented his efforts to be frugal wherever possible, and sent weekly updates on his progress to his father. Those communications were also filled with complaints about things like the cost of the books that he needed to further his education. Like Selleck Silliman, Watson did not intend to spend his life as a plantation teacher. He wanted to earn a salary for a year, improve his health in a warmer climate, and then study law. Later that month, this twenty-year-old aspiring tutor boarded the schooner for the voyage south.[2]

An education in Hartford and Cambridge was reasonable preparation for living among the slaveholders of Alabama. The presidents of Connecticut's colleges and universities led one of the most extreme branches of the American Colonization Society—founded in 1817 to transplant free black people outside the United States. New England's colonizationists cast African Americans as a threat to democracy and social order, encouraged campaigns to halt the development of free black communities, and even destroyed schools for African American children. They silenced debate about slavery and vehemently attacked abolitionism as the cause of political tensions between the slave and free states.[3]

Harvard was approaching its two hundredth anniversary, which meant that it was also nearing the bicentennial of its intimate engagement with Atlantic slavery. Beginning with the first graduating class, boys from Cambridge had been seeking fortunes in the plantations. By the time Henry Watson matriculated, Harvard's history was inseparable from the history of slavery and the slave trade.

College had armed Watson with theories of racial difference and scientific claims about the superiority of white people. The academy refined these ideas and popularized the language of race, providing intellectual cover for the social and political subjugation of non-white peoples. In a class with the Harvard anatomist John Collins Warren, Watson learned that in physical development, cultural accomplishment, and intellectual potential, black people sat at the bottom of humanity. Professor Warren also revealed that the most advanced scientific research confirmed the biological supremacy of the boys in that room. It is likely that Henry Watson Jr. already believed in the natural dominion of white people, and that the scientific certainty with which most of his professors argued the primacy of Europeans and the backwardness of Africans only confirmed his views. Harvard, like Washington College, was a pillar of the antebellum racial order. Not only were the students, the faculties, the officers, and the trustees white, but people of color came to campus only as servants and objects.[4]

From Mobile, Watson traveled north toward Greensboro, through territories where "plantations are very thick." It was now December and he was focused on securing a salary. "These regions seem to be a fine place for *female* teachers, they are in great demand," he reported despondently to his father. He still could not find a teaching job at an academy or on a plantation, and an opening at the public school "would but little more than pay my board." While in Greensboro, he called upon Dr. John Ramsey Witherspoon—a South Carolina relative of the Reverend John Witherspoon, president of the College of New Jersey (Princeton) and signer of the Declaration of Independence—who was rumored to be in need of a teacher. The six months since Watson left home had been spent to little profit, which was all the more disappointing and insulting in a place he believed to be dominated by greedy planters, and where "the people are almost ignoramuses on some things. The Doctors are miserable, the Lawyers are not much better." To make matters

Professor John Collins Warren of Harvard
SOURCE: Countway Library, Harvard Medical School

worse, he lost his purse from a torn coat pocket. "It was one of the Christmas holidays and the streets were full of negroes," he explained, "so that I hardly expect to hear from it again." He went out with his host in search of the wallet but found nothing. The next morning, apparently unconscious of irony, he dispatched "a negro to hunt for it but unsuccessfully."[5]

"I PASSED AN INDIAN MOUND"

In May 1831 this would-be tutor packed his belongings and prepared to leave Alabama on horseback. The idea of returning to New England by horse likely had come from Caleb Mills, a New Hampshire resident who graduated from Dartmouth College in 1828. The two men passed near Northampton, Massachusetts, as

Watson was beginning his trip south. Mills later became professor of Greek and Latin at Wabash College and superintendent of education in Indiana. Watson took note of a particular piece of information during the exchange: "He said he had rode that same horse 5 or 6000 miles at the rate of 40 & 50 miles a day. Had just come from Kentucky." Short on cash, the young tutor chose that same method for his return. It was the perfect way to learn the geography and history of the region. "I passed an Indian mound different from most. . . . It appeared like a pyramid with a square base cut of about 15 ft. high. It is a regular square," Watson excitedly jotted while outside Tuscaloosa. He had already seen Indian mounds, and had stopped to carefully examine one near Carthage. He began searching for mounds and artifacts. The very next day, Watson rode through a portion of the "lands of the Cherokee nation" near the Tennessee border, but he "saw no indians or indian relics."[6]

Travelers at a Chattanooga Indian Mound
SOURCE: Library of Congress

That area was part of an enormous expanse of territory—tens of millions of acres—that the state and federal governments seized from Native nations and tribes, the most recent in a succession of human tragedies that transformed the demography of North America. Prior to the "Great Dying," an estimated four million people lived in the greater Mississippi Valley. New waves of death had come with the expansion of European outposts two centuries before Watson's journey. Violent raids into the interior from the Carolina colonies transferred microbes inland, forced flights and migrations that upset the socioeconomic order of indigenous societies, altered age distributions, and caused abrupt changes in diet and health that made the new diseases more deadly. Watson's attention had been drawn to the remnants of these civilizations—monumental architecture constructed at least a millennium before Stonehenge. The largest ruins in the Mississippi and Ohio valleys, equal in size and crafting to the pyramids of Egypt, could hold St. Peter's Basilica and its gardens. These sites were once the centers of civilizations supported by trading networks that stretched across the continent.[7]

There is a background to Watson's interest in these archaeological remains. As an undergraduate he had lived on campuses that were decorated with Indian bones and artifacts and that hosted lively discussions of the impending extinction of Native peoples, legacies of a long relationship between colleges and conquest. European nations founded academies to secure their colonial interests, and they supported these schools by exploiting the decline of Indian nations and the rise of African slavery.

A young college graduate riding horseback over ethnically cleansed lands carved into slave plantations had plenty to ponder. Watson's mind was quite busy. He marveled at the beauty and richness of the region. He saw planters driving Indians from the path of cotton, and took notes on the crop economy, hauling distances, and regional markets. At the home of a man whom he met on the road, he watched forty enslaved black people working 350 acres. "Cotton plantations go as far as the eye can reach. Corn, rye, and wheat abound. Large bodies of Negroes at work," he recorded as he passed from Alabama to Tennessee through Cherokee country.

He was, it is fair to note, impressed with the rewards of human slavery. When he reached Kentucky in June, he used his letters of recommendation to gain an audience with Henry Clay. "Said to be well off but not rich," Watson added after a lengthy and pleasant visit with the Great Compromiser, the senator and colonizationist who for a generation managed the political conflicts between the slave and free states.[8]

Henry Watson's generation had begun to wrestle, albeit poorly, with the moral and social implications of this history. In September 1831—shortly after Watson had returned to Connecticut—James Kent delivered the Phi Beta Kappa lecture during Yale's commencement. In 1793 Kent had become the first law professor at Columbia College in New York City. He bought a house, purchased an enslaved woman, and became a colonizationist and a prominent opponent of extending suffrage to free black people in New York State. Kent celebrated his chapter's fiftieth anniversary with a lecture that used science, theology, and history to proclaim the inevitable rise of the Europeans. It was the will of God that "the red men of the forest have . . . been supplanted by a much nobler race of beings of European blood," he began. It would have been a sin and "a perversion of the duties and design of the human race" to permit "roving savages of the forest" to maintain these lands as "a savage and frightful desert."[9]

YANKEES AND PLANTERS

Henry Watson was quite happy to get back to northern soil, but he was also allured by the wealth that he had seen in the South. He studied law under Henry Barnard, a Yale graduate who later served as a state and federal education commissioner. Although he claimed to hate slavery, Watson left Connecticut for Greensboro, Alabama, after just a couple of years, set up a law practice, and became a slave owner—a "sin," he confessed, but one that promised great benefits. Shrewd investments following the Panic of 1837 increased his wealth. He snatched up plantations and slaves in what once had been the home of the Creek. He referred to his enslaved black people as his children and discovered the "charm" of mastery. He spent his summers in New England, where cotton traders were dominating the commodities markets and massive cotton works were catalyzing an industrial revolution. Within a decade Watson owned more than fifty people. Letters to his parents show that his motive was money. He disdained southerners: their religious practices were noisy and rude, their company was unenlightening, and their culture was organized around avarice. For all his harsh judgments about the region and its people, he had become an excellent southern planter. Within two decades he counted more than a hundred black people as property, became a founder and the president of the Planters Insurance Company, and emerged as a staunch defender of human slavery. On the eve of the Civil War, this Connecticut Yankee belonged to the planter elite.[10]

Long after the collapse of slavery in the Mid-Atlantic and New England, northern colleges continued sending young men like Watson to the South and the Caribbean. The most successful cotton planter in the antebellum era was born, raised, and educated in Pennsylvania. Dr. Stephen Duncan moved to Mississippi after his undergraduate and medical training in Carlisle, Pennsylvania. He had graduated from Dickinson College, which was founded by Benjamin Rush—an opponent of slavery and a signer of the Declaration of Independence—to democratize education. Duncan married into a Mississippi family, and, by the outbreak of the Civil War, owned several cotton plantations, two sugar plantations, and more than a thousand human beings.[11]

EBONY AND IVY

Henry Watson Jr.'s career as master of a "degraded race" forced to work the lands of a "vanished people" embodies central themes in the history of the American college. It provides glimpses into the complexity of that past. The course of Watson's life flowed through grooves that were carved across the society by emotionally wrenching and brutal historical events. Watson likely never appreciated the intimacy of his connections to Native and African peoples—the ways that their lives unfolded into his and his into theirs, but his choices reflect that reality. His college education helped him access the rewards of centuries of violent conflicts and demographic upheavals, and afforded him the privilege of turning the physical reminders and cultural legacies of those events into objects of tourism and fascination.

Ebony and Ivy expands upon this history. The book is organized into two parts with chapters that advance fairly chronologically from the early colonial era to the nineteenth century. The chapter themes explore the relationships between colonial colleges and colonial slavery and the legacies of slavery in American intellectual cultures.

Part I, "Slavery and the Rise of the American College," examines how and why the earliest American academies became rooted in the slave economies of the colonial world. Colleges arrived in the Americas in response to European nations' attempts to seize territories and hold off rivals. European powers deployed colleges to help defend and regulate their colonial possessions and they turned to African slavery and the African slave trade to fund these efforts. Chapter 1, "The Edges of the Empire," focuses on the strategic and cultural functions of the first colleges in New Spain, New France, and the British American colonies. Chapter 2, "'Bonfires of the Negros,'" looks at the socioeconomic environment that transformed slave traders and slave owners into college founders and trustees in the British colonies. The high point of the African slave trade also marked, not coincidentally, the period in which higher education in the colonies expanded most rapidly. Chapter 3, "'The Very Name of a West-Indian,'" reveals how college governors nurtured their academies upon the slave economy—a pursuit encouraged by the demands of colony building and the sources of wealth in the Atlantic world. College administrators struggled for the loyalty and patronage of wealthy colonial families, and the survival of colonial schools often depended on their success in tapping the fortunes of American merchants and planters.

Chapter 4, "Ebony and Ivy," explores the ties between colleges and the regional slave economies. Radical demographic shifts in the colonial world changed the culture of the campus and the purpose of education. In the decades before the American Revolution, money from slave traders and planters transformed colleges into playgrounds for wealthy boys and drew these institutions further into the service of the colonial elite.

Part II, "Race and the Rise of the American College," examines the influence of slavery on the production of knowledge and the intellectual cultures of the United States. College founders and officers used enslaved people to raise buildings, maintain campuses, and enhance their institutional wealth. However, the relationship between colleges and slavery was not limited to the presence of slaves on campus. The American college trained the personnel and cultivated the ideas that accelerated and legitimated the dispossession of Native Americans and the enslavement of Africans. Modern slavery required the acquiescence of scholars and the cooperation of academic institutions. Faculties and officers embraced the benefits of human slavery and extrapolated from the enslavement of Africans and the destruction of Native civilizations predictions of a future in which vast populations of the world would be eternally subjected or inevitably eradicated.

Chapter 5, "Whitening the Promised Land," analyzes the colleges' role in crafting and propagating a determinist and widely held vision that white people would become the sole possessors of the North American mainland. Colleges stopped being instruments for Christianizing Native people and became a means of effacing the religious and national divisions between European colonists. The popular belief in the divine promise of a white continent combined with an insatiable hunger for land to help American colonists invent themselves as a single people and cast Native Americans as barriers to progress.

The pernicious social ideas of the colonial era informed equally destructive intellectual obsessions in the new nation. Chapter 6, "'All Students & All Americans,'" explains the origins of racial science in the Atlantic world. Race research brought the political and social ascent of the college. On both sides of the Atlantic, university faculties collected and processed information about human difference from which they forged theories of biological supremacy and inferiority. Scholars from the American colonies were central actors in the emergence of this racial science. Chapter 7, "'On the Bodily and Mental Inferiority of the Negro,'" examines an early nineteenth-century trial that included testimony from many of the leading race researchers in the nation. Race science raised the prestige of the academy and allowed scholars to challenge the authority of the church by asserting a new, secular expertise over human affairs. However, the growing authority and influence of science also reflected scholars' willingness and ability to defend the social order of slavery. The final chapter, "'Could They Be Sent Back to Africa,'" studies the resulting rise of the academy and academics as a distinct political constituency within the antebellum United States. Significantly, their claims to authority over race became scholars' route to the public sphere. Their first appearance as a force in the national political culture came as they articulated the social danger of free black people, whom they advocated relocating to Africa. This chapter offers an explanation for why college officers and professors were so dramatically overrepresented in movements to identify "racial" threats to the society and devise methods to homogenize the population.

In short, American colleges were not innocent or passive beneficiaries of conquest and colonial slavery. The European invasion of the Americas and the modern slave trade pulled peoples throughout the Atlantic world into each others' lives, and colleges were among the colonial institutions that braided their histories and rendered their fates dependent and antagonistic. The academy never stood apart from American slavery—in fact, it stood beside church and state as the third pillar of a civilization built on bondage.

PART I

Slavery and the Rise of
the American College

Coupling these men in Synods God hath blest,
By his word truth is found, error confest.
As helpfull unto godly learning they,
With Schooles and Colledge, finde out learnings way.

—EDWARD WINSLOW, 1647

To give a young Gentleman right Education;
The Army's the very best School in the Nation.
My School-master call'd me a Dunce and a Fool;
But at Cuffs, I was always the Cock of the School.
. . . Now, Madam, you'll think it a strange thing to say,
But the Sight of a Book, makes me sick to this Day.

—JONATHAN SWIFT, *A SOLDIER AND
A SCHOLAR* (1732)

CHAPTER I

The Edges of the Empire

Colleges in the Arsenal of European Imperialism

In 1704 Jonathan Belcher, Harvard College class of 1699, traveled to Europe, where he was received at the court of Sophia, Dowager Electress of Hanover, through whom England, Ireland, and Scotland were to be united under one crown. She presented Belcher with her portrait for the colonies. Humbled in the presence of this intellectually talented and generous lady, the young man promised to send back from America "some small matters," including candles original to New England. Belcher later decided to bring his gifts personally, returning to Europe in 1708 to fulfill his oath. The future colonial governor begged forgiveness for taking so long to keep his commitment and delivered salutations from Joseph Dudley, the royal governor of Massachusetts and New Hampshire. He delivered the candles. Belcher also presented Sophia with "an Indian Slave, A native of my Countrey, of which I humbly ask your Royal Highness's Acceptance." Io, the child whom Jonathan Belcher gave away, remained at court in Hanover, and Belcher drew rewards from this exchange for much of his life by exploiting the fantasies

*Sophia, Dowager Electress of Hanover, painted in Indian costume by
her sister, Luise Hollandine, in 1644*

about America's aboriginal peoples that had been circulating in
Europe for more than two centuries.[1]

Jonathan Belcher was a child of colonialism. He came of age in a
colony in which Christian hegemony went unchallenged. Disease
had devastated the Native populations of New England and the
militarization of the Christian settlements held the remaining Indian nations in submission. The African slave trade and its dependent commerce contributed to a robust New England economy that
further marginalized Native communities. In 1680 Andrew Belcher
and four other Boston businessmen sent the *Elizabeth,* under Captain William Warren, on a slaving mission that killed at least
twenty-two people and brought more than a hundred enslaved Africans to market in Rhode Island. Andrew Belcher was "a very great
Merchant" who amassed "a considerable Estate," reads his obituary.
That fortune afforded his son an education at Boston's Latin School,
then a preparatory ritual for entrance into Harvard College, where
he took two degrees. Jonathan Belcher worked as the European liai-
son for his father's merchant house, and solidified his social status by
marrying Mary Partridge, the daughter of New Hampshire lieutenant governor William Partridge. Jonathan Belcher sat on the Massachusetts Council for more than a decade. In 1729 King George II,

Sophia's grandson, appointed Belcher governor of Massachusetts, which made him an ex officio trustee of Harvard and brought the Indian missions of New England under his authority.[2]

Colleges supplied the administrations of the colonies, supported domestic institutions, and advanced Christian rule over Native peoples. After he was replaced as governor of Massachusetts in 1741, Belcher traveled to England in search of another appointment. He was granted the governorship of New Jersey, a significant demotion. Unable to secure a more attractive post, he reluctantly settled among a people in "a Wretched State of Ignorance[,] Unpolisht and of bad Manners." He chose Burlington, which was a short horse ride to more cosmopolitan Philadelphia. Governor Belcher reissued the charter of the College of New Jersey (Princeton), authorized lotteries to raise an endowment, promoted a European fund-raising campaign, donated a library of nearly five hundred volumes and a small art collection, and encouraged the admission of students from John and David Brainerd's mission among the Lenape (Delaware) Indians. In response to this generosity, the trustees decided to dedicate the first campus building to him, calling it Belcher Hall. The governor declined, suggesting instead that it be named Nassau Hall, in tribute to King William III of the royal House of Nassau, "the great Deliverer of the British Nation, from those two Monstrous Furies,—Popery & Slavery."[3]

Like his present to Sophia, Jonathan Belcher's generosity toward Harvard and the College of New Jersey was rooted in the oppression of other people. The first five colleges in the British American colonies—Harvard (established 1636), William and Mary (1693), Yale (1701), Codrington (1745) in Barbados, and New Jersey (1746)[4]—were instruments of Christian expansionism, weapons for the conquest of indigenous peoples, and major beneficiaries of the African slave trade and slavery.

ESCOLARES Y CONQUISTADORES

Diverse personnel patrolled Europe's American possessions, and a range of structures marked and secured the edges of its empires.

Missionaries, explorers, merchants, traders, and soldiers extended
the borders of the colonial world, and churches, forts, storehouses,
docks, and ships announced the permanence of the European
invasion. Scholars and schools were a less obvious but no less significant presence. Spain's conquests in the Americas were followed
by intensive periods of institution building. Universities catalyzed
cultural shifts in the capitals and hinterlands of the defeated Taino,
Carib, Aztec, Mayan, and Incan empires.

Dominican priests organized the Universidad de Santo Tomás
de Aquino (Universidad Autónoma de Santo Domingo), the first
college in the Americas. They began a seminary shortly after the
Spanish invasion, and a 1538 papal decree raised that academy to a
university. As early as the 1530s, Dominicans, Franciscans, and
Augustinians had seminaries in Mexico, where the Dominicans
laid the foundations of the Pontificia Universidad (1551). Jesuits
in Lima, Peru, founded the Universidad de San Marcos (1551) to
instruct *indios* and record and codify the Quechua language.
Franciscans built the Universidad de Antioquia (1554) in Colombia *"para ilustrar a los aborígenes."* Ordered priests established universities in Mexico City, Santo Domingo, Lima, and Medellín
modeled on those of Salamanca and Alcala in Spain. By the mid-
sixteenth century these institutions had assembled faculties, formed
academic divisions with full courses of study, and begun conferring
degrees.[5]

The African slave trade underwrote this invasion of ideas. Ferdinand and Isabella authorized the transport of enslaved Africans into
the Americas, a commerce that grew rapidly after the first slaves
were delivered in 1502. Catholic clergy traded, bought, and sold Africans in Atlantic markets, and forced them to labor on plantations,
in mines, and in towns. In 1530 a Dominican bishop begged King
Charles V to deregulate the Africa trade, which required a royal li-
cense, to allow colonists in Santo Domingo, Cuba, and Puerto Rico
greater access to labor. Santo Domingo and Cuba had active ports,
and both islands operated as distribution centers into the greater
Caribbean and into mainland settlements such as Yucatán and Vera
Cruz in Mexico. Traders also landed at Cartagena, Colombia, where

they shipped Africans to Portobello, Panama, marched them to the Pacific, and transported them south to Peru.[6]

At the College of San Pablo in Lima, Jesuits built their residence with enslaved African workers, and the order trafficked in adults and children for investment and labor. Africans toiled at the college and on its haciendas, elite Spanish colonists donated land and slaves to the school, and priests administered an extensive commercial enterprise. In Peru alone, Jesuits owned thousands of enslaved African people, whom they used to sustain a network of colleges and missions. "By the time of the expulsion of the Society of Jesus from Spanish America," writes historian Nicholas P. Cushner, "the colleges were ranked among the largest slaveholders in America."[7]

Forged during wars and conflicts that began with the Crusades and continued through the Counter-Reformation, the Catholic orders had the capacity to project and protect the faith at the boundaries of the empire. In 1608 Samuel de Champlain led the invasion of eastern Canada that established New France. Récollet and Jesuit priests soon initiated missions to the Wendat (Huron). The Compagnie de la Nouvelle France directed the governor "to bind the Huron nation to him . . . by subjecting it to the yoke of the gospel." Before his death in 1635, Champlain had dispatched priests to learn Native languages, settled missionaries among the Indians, pushed French villages closer to Native nations, encouraged intermarriage between Indians and French settlers, and invited Native people into the French colonies. The Jesuits began schools to catechize Indian children, and they opened an Indian academy in Quebec with a donation from the Marquis de Gamache. Clergy founded the Collège des Jésuites (1635) in Quebec to train Native men to evangelize the aboriginal nations. In 1663 Bishop François de Laval founded the Séminaire de Québec as the clerical headquarters of New France, and Louis XIV later ordered the addition of a dormitory for Indian boys.[8]

French colonists relied upon Portuguese and Dutch slave traders to provision the plantations in the Caribbean and at the mouth of the Mississippi. African slavery was also established in Canada. Jesuit superior general Paul Le Jeune had an enslaved boy who was

François de Laval
SOURCE: Séminaire de Québec

probably the first African in the colony. Olivier Le Jeune, as he was renamed, arrived during the Englishman David Kirke's 1629 conquest of French Canada. Father Le Jeune obtained him when the French retook that region under the Treaty of St. Germain. Following the restoration, King Louis acceded to the colonists' pleas for enslaved Africans in order to address labor shortages and maintain their competitiveness with New England and New Netherland.[9]

The colonists already had a thriving trade in Indians. "I am to baptize a little Hiroquois [Iroquois] child who is to be taken to France," Father Le Jeune wrote from North America in the early seventeenth century. The boy was "never to return to this country," he continued, as "he was given to a Frenchman." The four-year-old "cried all the time before his baptism, and ran away from us," the priest laughed; "I could not hold him." Le Jeune baptized the child, renamed him Louis in honor of the king, and shipped him off. French colonists created an extensive market in enslaved Indians whom they used in the Canadian settlements and the French West Indies. Bound Indians greatly outnumbered unfree Africans in Canada, and Catholic settlers in Montreal and Quebec formed a ready market for Native peoples taken in wars or raids throughout the Americas.[10]

Britain's rulers had also learned the strategic value of academies during their wars for territory, thrones, trade routes, and people. The medieval and early modern universities—Oxford (1096) and Cambridge (1209) in England; St. Andrews (1413), Glasgow (1451), Aberdeen (1495), and Edinburgh (1582) in Scotland; and Trinity College (1592) in Ireland—had been swept into the religious and political conflicts that gave birth to Great Britain. Hundreds of Oxford students dropped their books and began drilling with arms on campus during the English Civil Wars, 1642 to 1651. The crown and Parliament engaged in repeated purges of hostile students and faculty to bring the colleges into the service of their competing political causes. A clandestine Puritanism thrived at Cambridge despite monarchist efforts to make the faculty and scholars conform to the Church of England. Dissenting theology spread from Emmanuel and Sidney Sussex to other colleges in the university, including Trinity and Corpus Christi.[11]

Universities facilitated England's colonial campaigns in Scotland and Ireland, and they played a similar role in the Americas. The English sought to open a college during the formative years of Virginia. In February 1615 King James I directed his bishops to hold collections for "the founding & endowing of an ample Colledge" among "those Barbarians" of Virginia. Raising a college was part of a layered English strategy to maintain religious orthodoxy among the colonists and to check the power of the confederacy under Chief Powhatan, the father of Pocahontas. Thomas Dale, who brought Pocahontas's delegation to England the following year, and the Reverend Alexander Whitaker, minister to the colony, pleaded for the charter by reminding the crown of its obligation to evangelize and educate Indians. Dale had unsuccessfully tried to get the colonial government moved to Henrico, a James River outpost named for Henry, Prince of Wales. He courted the college to secure his investment, accelerate the conversion of the local Indians, and help turn Native people into tenants who could bolster commerce and security.[12]

After King James commanded "the College to be erected in Virginia for the conversion of Infidels," the Virginia Company apportioned ten thousand acres in Henrico to endow the Indian academy and a larger university. By 1619, when the first enslaved Africans

were traded into the colony, supporters had raised more than
£2,000 in Britain for the colonial school, collected donations for
a library and other necessities, and drawn up basic regulations.
The company dispatched carpenters, bricklayers, craftsmen, and
farmers to begin building the campus and cultivating the grants.
More than three hundred people under the direction of George
Thorpe settled the lands—some fifty of them missionaries tasked
with "the reclaiming of the Barbarous Natives." The Reverend
Patrick Copland, a Scot and an experienced East Indies missionary who had met Thomas Dale in Asia, agreed to be rector of the
college, receiving shares entitling him to three hundred acres of
Virginia land.[13]

Conflicts over territory and trade had already fractured relations between Christians and Indians. On April 18, 1622, Copland
delivered a thanksgiving prayer in London for Virginia, where he
was soon to resettle. A ship that returned to London that July carried reports that Chief Opechancanough, who came to power after the death of his brother Chief Powhatan, had attacked the
colony on March 22, massacred dozens of inhabitants, and destroyed the settlement. In 1624 Edward Palmer of London left
lands in New England and Virginia to support a college on a
Susquehanna River island, but his executors mismanaged the fund
and nothing came of his design. King James revoked the Virginia
Company charter that year and imposed royal government, an
upheaval that ended the first attempt to organize a Protestant college in America.[14]

Nonetheless, the seeds of the English universities were already
being planted. In its first quarter century New England received
more than a hundred Cambridge alumni and more than thirty
graduates of Oxford. Even young Trinity, in Dublin, was training
personnel for the colonies. John Winthrop Jr. graduated from
Trinity before his father—the first governor of Massachusetts
Bay—departed for North America. John Sherrard left Providence
Island in the West Indies to study in Dublin. The brothers Samuel and Increase Mather both earned advanced degrees from
Trinity.[15]

THE TRUE GOD AND CHURCH

In 1636 the Massachusetts General Court chartered a "colledge" in Newtown (Cambridge) and three years later named it in honor of John Harvard, a young minister at the First Church in Charlestown. In 1638 Rev. Harvard died of tuberculosis, leaving half his estate, about £780, and a library of more than two hundred books to further the training of the ministry. He was the son of two modest Puritans: Robert Harvard and Katherine Rogers of Southwark, London. Katherine Rogers was the daughter of a Stratford-on-Avon cattle merchant and alderman, and Robert Harvard was a butcher and tavern owner. In 1627 John Harvard had entered Emmanuel College, Cambridge, where he earned bachelor's and master's degrees before leaving with Ann Sadler, his wife, for Massachusetts. Several Emmanuel graduates, including Thomas Shepard and Richard Saltonstall, were founders of the colonial school.[16]

Shortly after the establishment of Harvard, Puritan ministers began sending missives to England that chronicled the spread of the Gospel in America. *New England's First Fruits*, the initial pamphlet, identified the nascent college as a symbol of Christianity's success. Readers learned that Puritan ministers were preaching to the Indians, Native people were embracing the true God, and the English were winning the Indians' affection and esteem by treating them "fairly and courteously, with loving termes, good looks and kind salutes." Known as "Eliot Tracts"—for the missionary John Eliot—these communications were written as the colonists achieved military dominance during the four decades between the Pequot Massacre in 1637 and King Philip's War in 1675. They included passionate vignettes of Indians accepting Christianity, coming to fear eternal damnation, seeking protection from disease and death by adopting the colonists' religion, and advertising their conversion by mimicking English customs and attire.[17]

British colonists did not blush over the strategic benefits of spreading their faith. Depopulation and political crises within the Indian nations emboldened the English. Mortality rates among the seaboard communities reached as high as 90 percent. "God and

Jesus Christ, God and Jesus Christ help me," Nishohkou's two-year-old child screamed before dying from the bloody flux (severe dysentery) that also had stricken his mother and siblings. "Father, I am going to God," Nishohkou's three-year-old said before expiring. Rev. Eliot reported that Nishohkou made a confession of faith. "That Winter the Pox came, and almost all our kindred died," Ponampam recalled of the events that caused his mother to take him at eight years of age and move closer to the colonists. The government of God "is now beginning to be set up where it never was before," the Reverend Richard Mather promised his British readers. "The greatest parte of them are swept awaye by the small poxe, which still continues among them," a grateful Governor John Winthrop wrote of the epidemics. "God hathe hereby cleared our title to this place." He estimated that fewer than fifty Indians remained in the immediate vicinity of the colony, and added that these remaining people had been penned and subjugated.[18]

Puritan expansion also benefited from a new institution: a missionary company vested with extraordinary privileges and authority. In 1649 Parliament created the Corporation for the Propagation of the Gospel in New England. The mission of the "New England Company" was to accelerate the Christianization of the North American Indians, and it served as a model for the later Society for the Propagation of the Gospel in Foreign Parts (1701) and the Society in Scotland for Propagating Christian Knowledge (1709).[19]

It was a momentous year for Protestants. In 1649 the defeated and dethroned King Charles I was tried and executed, and Parliament dispatched the warrior Puritan Oliver Cromwell to slaughter the Irish into submission. New England was a bastion of support for Cromwell, his army, and the short-lived English republic, and, as Lord Protector of the British Commonwealth, Cromwell hatched failed plans to seed Ireland and Jamaica with sympathetic and sturdy spiritual radicals from Massachusetts. The New England Company could hold and solicit funds, establish schools, and supply teachers and ministers. British subjects eagerly endowed the corporation through their wills, with rents from lands, and with yearly subscriptions. British colonists added to the company's treasury, which paid for everything from the tuition and board of Indian students to the printing presses that ran off thousands of copies of the Reverend John Eliot's Algonquian Bible, or "ye Indian Bible," the Algonquian catechism, and other primers and literature. Puritan divines sent testimonials on the advance of faith in America, and anyone in London could examine accounts of the corporation's revenues and expenditures.[20]

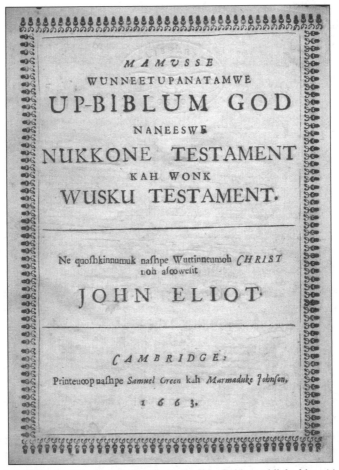

John Eliot's Algonquian translation of the Bible, published in 1663
SOURCE: Massachusetts Historical Society

A wave of Christian ministers, first from British universities and then from Harvard, evangelized Native communities. Harvard president Henry Dunster, an experienced missionary, encouraged Indian education, augmented the charter to include the evangelization of Native people, and broke ground for a new school. The mission included "the education of the English & Indian Youth of this Country in knowledge: and godliness." In 1655 his successor, Charles Chauncy, opened the Indian College, the first brick structure on Harvard Yard, at a cost of nearly £400. The two-story building sat next to Old College and across from Goffe College—each new building was designated "college"—which neighbored the president's house. It had study chambers, halls, and rooms for twenty students. Harvard offered free education to Indians and encouraged English students to learn Algonquian.[21]

In defense of the Indian College, Rev. Chauncy recalled the scholarly tradition of the church. He berated colonists who opposed schools and cultivated an ignorance that encouraged sin. Among the greatest failures of the New Englanders was the corruption of Native peoples, to whom Christians had traded guns and liquor with deadly consequences, he charged. A few years later the president reported the progress of two young Indian boys, Caleb Cheeshahteaumuck and Joel Iacoomis, who were attending the grammar school in Cambridge and whom Chauncy personally examined in Latin. In 1665 Cheeshahteaumuck graduated from Harvard, its first and only Indian graduate during the colonial period.[22]

In New England and Virginia, the English brought Indian children into schools to learn the ways of the Christian God and to swear loyalty to the English and their government. When the idea of removing children met cool receptions, they brought whole Native families into English villages. The Massachusetts General Court offered Indian parents a new coat every year that their child apprenticed in a Christian house. Rev. Eliot promoted these relocations to attack beliefs and break up traditions that acted as barriers to Christianization or offended English sensibilities. "Divers of the Indians Children, Boyes and Girles we have received into our houses," the 1643 report declared, "who are long since civilized, and in subjection to us." From 1651 to 1674, Eliot organized fourteen "praying towns"—communities of converted Indians, governed internally but under English supervision—where thousands of Native people lived apart from their unredeemed clans.[23]

The year that the Indian College opened, Harvard's governors revised the by-laws and regulations. Students had to wear their gowns or cloaks whenever they left their rooms, and their grooming and comportment had to be consistent with English custom for learned men. At Harvard and William and Mary, Native students also dressed in English clothes, marking their cultural submission. The English sought to correct Indians' appearance, speech, and beliefs. Master of the Latin school in Roxbury, Eliot prepared the most promising Indian youth in English, Latin, and Greek. Admission to Harvard required the ability to "make & speake or write

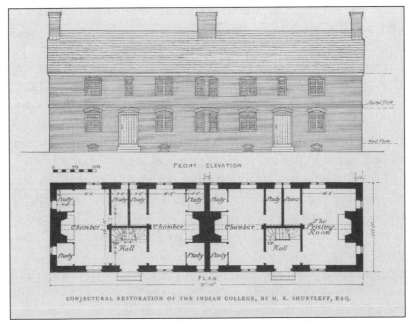

The vanished Indian College at Harvard, as drawn in 1936 for Samuel Eliot Morison's Harvard College in the Seventeenth Century
SOURCE: Harvard University Press

true Latin in prose" and proof that one was "Competently grounded
in the Greeke Language." The faculty forbade all Harvard boys
from speaking English even in casual exchanges, a regulation that
was freely and routinely violated. What was burdensome to English
students proved transformative to Native boys.[24]

Indians at the grammar level studied in English at both Harvard and the College of William and Mary. Those who entered the
advanced course were required to think and speak in the language
of imperial Europe. As the language of diplomacy, theology, philosophy, and law, Latin had served as a medium of power and authority in Europe. The hegemonic language of the Europeans
displaced Native languages and their attendant values and ideas.
Caleb Cheeshahteaumuck and Joel Iacoomis both forwarded Latin
addresses to the *honoratissimi benefactores* of the New England Company with independent confirmations of their proficiency in classical languages. An Indian named Eleazar in the class of 1679 left a
Latin poem eulogizing the Reverend Thomas Thacher, pastor of
Old South Church in Boston. Eleazar died before graduation. A
member of the class of 1716, Benjamin Larnel earned praise for his
Latin and Greek poetry. He too died before graduating. The English immersed Native students in Christian history, its literatures,
leaders, and governing values.[25] Trained in colonial schools and
colleges, Native youth returned to Indian villages as exemplars of
the benefits of English culture, or they separated themselves from
Indian communities to live among the colonists.

"The Lord delegated you to be our patrons . . . so that you may
perform the work of bringing blessings to us pagans," reads Caleb
Cheeshahteaumuck's Latin oration. "We were naked in our souls
as well as in our bodies, we were aliens from all humanity." Harvard's Indian students were, in Cheeshahteaumuck's words, "instruments to spread and propagate the gospel among our kin and
neighbours, so that they also may know the Lord and Christ." The
Puritans were, by this logic, mere media of providence—the un-
folding will of God. At the outbreak of King Philip's War, Harvard president Increase Mather took a moment to catalogue the
religious missions to indigenous peoples in the Americas to prove
the Puritans' faithful execution of God's directives.[26]

SERVUS COLLEGII

African slavery and the slave trade subsidized the college and the colony. In 1636, the year Harvard was founded, a group of merchants at nearby Marblehead (Naumkeag)—where residents had unsuccessfully maneuvered to house the college—built and outfitted a small ship and named it *Desire*. The following summer, *Desire* became the first slaver to depart from the British North American mainland. Under John Winthrop's instructions, Captain William Pierce sold seventeen Pequot War captives into bondage at Providence Island in the Caribbean in exchange for cotton, tobacco, salt, and enslaved Africans. The sale of prisoners from hostile nations became policy in Boston and Plymouth, a practice that also brought hundreds of enslaved black people into the colonies.[27]

The birth of slavery in New England was also the dawn of slavery at Harvard. *Desire* "returned from the West Indies after seven months," Winthrop noted in February 1638, and "brought some cotton, and tobacco, and negroes." It is not clear if the "Moor" who served Harvard's earliest students came to Massachusetts in the belly of *Desire*, but he remains the first enslaved black person documented in the colony, and his life more tightly braids the genesis of slavery in New England into the founding of the college. Nathaniel Eaton, the first instructor and schoolmaster, owned this man. Master Eaton had studied at Trinity, Cambridge University, and the Harvard trustees empowered him to design the curriculum and supervise the social lives of the students. Using £400 from the legislature and Rev. Harvard's bequest, Eaton erected a hall, began cultivating the grounds, and gathered the first class, which, Winthrop boasted, included "the sons of gentlemen and others of best note in the country." The boys took their meals from Mistress Eaton and paid the Eatons for room and board. A six-foot fence surrounded the college yard to help the Eatons control the movements of the students.[28]

The governors' faith in Master Easton was poorly repaid. Nathaniel Eaton was a volatile man who tussled with his own boarders and instructed the students by mixing whippings into lessons.

Students complained that they were regularly and severely beaten, their meals were either inedible or insufficient, the rooms were not cleaned, and the servants were recalcitrant and undisciplined. One student, Samuel Hough, returned to his room to find the Moor sleeping in his bed, and his classmates compared their plights to that of the slave. Some of the boys accused the Eatons of extorting money for services such as laundering. Rotting fish had been served, meat was scarce and foul when available, beer had been denied for extended periods, and on one occasion their "hasty pudding," or porridge, had been tainted with animal excrement. In 1639 the General Court tried Master Eaton and levied fines against him. The overseers fired him and closed the college for reorganization.[29]

When Harvard reopened, the colony had more numerous links to Atlantic slavery. After the destruction of the Henrico college Patrick Copland had settled in Bermuda, where he began trading with New England. In the aftermath of the Pequot War, Governor Winthrop documented the sale of hundreds of women and children, a dozen of whom were traded to Copland. The minister recruited British students from the West Indian plantations for Winthrop, making Harvard the first in a long line of North American schools to target wealthy planters as a source of enrollments and income.[30]

"Our pinnaces had very good receipts in the West Indies," the governor informed his son John. Merchants linked New England to the Caribbean and West Africa, where human beings were prime goods. After graduating in Harvard's first class, George Downing, Governor Winthrop's nephew, spent months preaching to the English in Barbados, Antigua, Santa Cruz, Nevis, and St. Christopher, where he measured demand for New England commodities and gathered advice on establishing slavery in the Puritan colonies. He explained that newcomers used English indentured servants until they could afford "to procure Negroes (the life of this place)." The plantations were so profitable that an enslaved African paid for himself or herself after only eighteen months. The Puritans quickly adopted slaveholding. In February 1641 "a negro maid" owned by Israel Stoughton—a founder and early benefactor of Harvard—received baptism and admission to the Dorchester church. "You may also own Negroes and Negresses," observed a Huguenot visitor in 1687; "there is not a House in Boston, however small may be its Means, that has not one or two. There are those that have five or six, and all make a good Living."[31]

New England and its college were producing scores of young men who coveted futures in the British Caribbean as planters and traders. "If you go to Barbados, you will see a flourishing Island, many able men," Downing enviously reported. "I believe they have bought this year no lesse than a thousand negroes." By the end of the century enslaved black people outnumbered white colonists almost three to one in Barbados and the island had become England's most valuable possession in the Americas. Winthrop's son Henry went to Barbados. His son Samuel relocated to Antigua. Stoughton's son died during a failed voyage to Barbados. Downing returned to England, where he counseled James, Duke of York, on the conquest of New Netherland, and was knighted for his service to the crown.[32]

George Downing informed his cousin John Winthrop Jr. that fish and meat were the "certainest commodityes" to sell in the Caribbean. Exactly a century later, Jeremiah Dummer, a Harvard graduate and patron of Yale College, credited New England for the profitability of West Indian sugar in Europe and for helping the British Caribbean hold off French and Dutch competitors. Wheat, corn, horses, timber, and staves flowed south from New England, which also supplied "Barrel Pork, Mack[e]rel, and refuse Cod-Fish for their Negroes." West Indian planters could reserve their laborers and lands for sugar production. Hundreds of ships left New England for the southern and Caribbean colonies, particularly Barbados, with virtually everything those colonies needed, an economic historian concludes, including low-quality fish for "the poor Guinea negroes whom the Royal African Company was pouring into the Spanish sugar Islands."[33]

As the population of enslaved black people grew, New Englanders crafted laws to regulate the unfree. Massachusetts required the whipping of slaves found on the streets at night or away from their owners' homes without consent, and moved to keep cash and arms out of the hands of black servants. No enslaved person could carry a stick or other potential weapon. The Boston selectmen maintained a census of free black men, who were required to maintain the roads and do other unpaid labor for the town. Curfews for enslaved people were imposed in Connecticut, New Hampshire, and Rhode Island; the last of these extended its law to include free black people. The punishment for violators was public flogging. Governments penalized manumissions to limit the growth of the free black population. The colonists burned enslaved people at the stake, hanged them, and sold them out of the region for actions deemed threatening. In a single term in 1681, a Massachusetts court sentenced Maria and Jack, two enslaved black people, to death for two separate cases of arson. Maria was burned—the first person punished in this manner—and Jack was hanged. The judges ordered that Jack's corpse be tossed into the fire with Maria. In 1704 John Campbell, a Scottish immigrant, began publishing the *Boston News-Letter*, which provides a record of the rise of slavery in the colony. Not only merchants but carpenters, midwives, booksellers, and butchers were buying and selling Africans.[34]

New Englanders were partners in the rise of Atlantic slavery. Puritan merchants carried food, timber, animals, and other supplies to the expanding markets of the English, French, Spanish, and Dutch colonies. Harvard historian Samuel Eliot Morison argued that the West Indies rescued New England. Puritans also supplied the Carolinas and Virginia and brought the products of slave labor and other materials back to New England, where they built new ships and launched new ventures. New Englanders entered the Atlantic slave economy as shippers, insurers, manufacturers, and investors. For two centuries the Caribbean and southern markets buoyed the New England economy, and ships from Massachusetts, Connecticut, Rhode Island, and New Hampshire filled West Indian ports.[35]

. . . AND OTHER WEAPONS

Colleges were imperial instruments akin to armories and forts, a part of the colonial garrison with the specific responsibilities to train ministers and missionaries, convert indigenous peoples and soften cultural resistance, and extend European rule over foreign nations. Christians launched their religious and educational missions to Native peoples from highly militarized spaces. The permanent French settlement in Canada began with a two-story wood building protected by raised cannons and a moat five yards wide and two yards deep. The ordered priests who evangelized the neighboring *sauvages* could measure their success as French colonists extended their commercial and military authority over the region.[36]

When they landed in Virginia in 1607, the well-armed English relied upon Powhatans for food and assistance, but in little time they began attacking Indians with impunity. Epidemics reduced the local Indian populations, and Christian expansionism and aggression pushed whole communities inland. Captain Samuel Argall, who arrived in 1609, was soon kidnapping, illegally trading, and waging private wars. He also forced the English claim upon Bermuda. The English fought the Appomattocs, Kecoughtans, and Paspaheghs, burning villages, taking hostages, stealing goods, and killing captives. In February 1611 Argall burned two Warraskoyak towns to punish a chief for violating a trade agreement. That same year Sir Thomas Dale, deputy governor and proprietor of the Henrico settlement, sent a hundred men in full armor against the Nansemonds. Long before the March 22, 1622, uprising, Indians were repelling the English invasion. The Henrico college was a symbol of subordination, a reminder of a decade of Christian triumph over Indians.[37]

In Jamestown and Plymouth, English colonists built palisades to protect their small makeshift settlements, hustled to supply themselves with food, and declared the governance of the Christian God by constructing churches. "One of the next things we longed for, and looked after was to advance Learning," reported New England's ministers. Establishing a colony required enormous and continuous outputs of labor, but still, in Virginia and

Massachusetts, the settlers began organizing colleges within a decade of their arrival. Defending these settlements meant taking
steps to hold off or defeat immediate and potential threats.[38]

Transatlantic travelers expected conflict, and weapons outnumbered Bibles on virtually every ship. The Pilgrims arrived at New
Plymouth aboard a floating arsenal and were prepared to fight
upon landing. Miles Standish stepped ashore with a small army to
fend off the Wampanoag if necessary. He then organized the male
settlers into companies and had them rehearsing for war before
they could feed themselves. They finished the fort and a palisade,
one mile in length and eleven feet high, to protect the buildings
and farms. "Furbish up your Swords, Rapiers, and all other pierc-
ing weapons," Edward Johnson instructed Puritan immigrants to
Massachusetts Bay. Johnson, who came on the *Arabella* with Governor Winthrop, warned that the devil plotted against the children of God. Ship horses and every thing that you might need to
defend this divine project, he continued. "Spare not to lay out your
coyne for Powder, Bullets, Match, Armes of all sorts, and all kinde
of Instruments for War." Supporters in England donated funds for
larger artillery pieces, bolstering the military capabilities of the
network of fortresses that was Christian New England.[39]

The distant threats to the English lay in New France, New Netherland, and New Spain, but Indians presented a more pressing concern. Colonists sought the best European military technologies
and adopted ruthless forms of warfare. They imported matchlock
and flintlock guns to terrorize their enemies. In May 1637, at the
culmination of Connecticut's Pequot War, the English surrounded
a village on the Mystic River, opened fire, set the buildings ablaze,
and then butchered five hundred people as they tried to escape the
flames. Captain John Underhill celebrated: "Downe fell men,
women, and children."[40]

The war left an inventory of Christian militarization. Captain
John Mason of Connecticut carried a thirty-two-inch double-edged
sword inscribed VENI VIDI VICI. Dazzled by the synchronization of
the guns, Captain Underhill had a spiritual moment in battle, feeling "as though the finger of God had touched both match and flint"
to destroy the Indians "without compassion." Sergeant William

Hayden, in Mason's force, brought a cutlass made for slashing in close combat and similar to those that many New England men used to train. John Thomson of Plymouth had a flintlock and a cutlass. "Having our swords in our right hand, our Carbin[e]s or Muskets in our left hand, we approached the Fort" to finish off the survivors, Underhill recalled. Cruder weapons could be made in the colonies, but Miles Standish brandished a rapier, a well-crafted European thrusting sword that required more training and skill to wield. The English burned the Pequot food supplies and took their blades to hundreds of young Indian men who put down their arms, attempted to surrender, or sought refuge with other tribes.[41]

The attack publicized the power of the Christian God to the benefit of New England and its college. Friends and leaders of the college participated in the war, and Harvard acquired about two thousand acres of land after the English divided up the Pequot holdings in southeastern Connecticut. Israel Stoughton led Massachusetts's forces against the Pequot and delivered about 250 captives for enslavement.[42]

Wondrous tales of red savages brought to Christ by the dauntless efforts of religious perfectionists found an eager audience in England, where metropolitan readers anticipated blood from such extraordinary encounters. The Puritans began the work of evangelizing Indians only after they achieved military supremacy—in the aftermath of the destruction of the Pequot and a long campaign to reduce the power of the Narragansett. Eliot established the praying towns along the coast and moved inland as disease, dispossession, and war made interior tribes more pliable.[43] The English sought the surrender of Indian peoples to the government of Christ and his earthly ambassadors, and there was no greater symbol of acquiescence than the neat arrangement of Native American men, women, and children in English churches and schools.

In 1662 John Winthrop Jr. sent the English chemist Robert Boyle a plan for turning Indians into wage laborers to ease the financial burdens on the New England Company and pull the most populous nations into commercial alliances with the English. Twelve years later Winthrop informed Boyle that the

Pequot, Narragansett, and Mohegan were "beginning to fall to worke & to be much civilized & . . . to embrace the Gospell." Boyle later bequeathed much of his estate to support the evangelization of Native Americans. His executors purchased Brafferton Manor in York, and distributed the rents in New England (to the New England Company and Harvard) and Virginia.[44]

THE EDUCATION OF KING PHILIP

In June 1675 Chief Metacomet, whom the English called King Philip, chose a definitive confrontation with the colonists over a slow reduction to vassalage. At least two Harvard-educated Indians served Metacomet, as translator and as strategist. The prominent presence of these Harvard Indians underscores the strategic deployment of academies in the Christian empires, the potential for Indians to use their education to resist colonialism, and Metacomet's predicament. The chief recounted a history of English abuses that rewarded the friendly posture of Native people upon the arrival of the first Christians with increasing aggression. He accused the English of using their might to displace Wampanoag leaders who defended their interests. Christians trespassed upon Indian lands to graze animals and hunt, cheated in trade, and stole land without repercussions. The courts and officials held Indians to account for minor violations of colonial law but the most respectable Indians could not gain justice against Englishmen, and no Englishman was subject to Wampanoag law. The Plymouth court empowered local selectmen to indenture any idle Indians, gave magistrates the authority to sell Native children out of the colony for property crimes, and assumed the right to regulate the movement and daily lives of all Indians in the neighborhood.[45]

The growth of the colonies, Indian population losses and military vulnerabilities, and the increasing economic dependence of indigenous communities on the English eroded Native sovereignty. Metacomet discovered that his translator, John Sassamon—who had attended Harvard under Eliot's largesse—had fraudulently

The Wampanoag chief Metacomet, known in English
as King Philip, in an image by Paul Revere
SOURCE: Yale University Art Gallery

transcribed a will to rob him of land. He accused Sassamon of betraying Wampanoag secrets. An Algonquian-speaking African captive who had escaped from the Wampanoag also alerted the English of Metacomet's plans. Sassamon had settled among the Wampanoag after expressing dissatisfaction with the English, acted as an interpreter and advisor, and served as a translator and witness for Metacomet's earlier land transactions. The English found the body of this "Christian that could read and write" in a lake. In retaliation, they tried three of Metacomet's lieutenants before a jury of twelve Englishman and six Indians. Earlier they humiliated Metacomet's brother Wamsutta, or King Alexander, who was ordered to the colony and berated. Wamsutta died upon returning from this meeting, and the Wampanoag suspected the

English of poisoning him. The English then hanged Metacomet's men.[46]

The last great contest for New England was cataclysmic. Despite the efforts of the colonial governments and the crown, Native
nations had acquired guns by trading with the French to the north,
the Dutch to the west, and in the black markets of the English
colonies. As early as 1630 a royal decree attempted to block the
trade in martial weapons. Plymouth banned selling, exchanging,
or loaning guns to Indians, forbade the repair of guns belonging to
Natives, and prohibited Indians from buying gunpowder. The
General Court tried to regulate access to everything from liquor to
horses, and routinely reminded colonists of the dangers of such
trade. Although Connecticut banned the sale of powder and arms
to Indians, the New Haven court called Richard Hubball to account in 1652 for selling gunpowder to hostile nations—a crime to
which Hubball casually confessed. The States General allowed
flintlocks only for Dutch residents of New Netherland and prescribed the death penalty to anyone who sold them to Indians. In
1639 the West India Company affirmed capital punishment for any
New Netherland settlers, regardless of social status, who armed
Indians, and it established rewards for informants. Those prohibitions failed utterly. Not only did Native nations trade for guns, but
they demanded the more expensive flintlocks, which could be used
in bad weather, and they often had them before Christian militia-
men. King Philip's forces had ample supplies of guns and had mastered their use and upkeep.[47]

For Harvard, it was an existential war. The college had been
struggling under the leadership of President Leonard Hoar, and
his successor, Urian Oakes, inherited an "afflicted and almost destroyed University." The colony was in armed struggle and the
school was suffering. While the students were exempt from fighting, most of them had deserted the campus. "I humbly beseech
Almighty God, the Father of Our Lord Jesus Christ, that He may
be pleased to shatter that very barbarity, whence ariseth our greatest peril of destruction," President Oakes prayed during his 1675
commencement address, "that from the barbarians who impend

and expend our lives, His boundless loving kindness will deliver us sound and whole."[48]

Decades later, Harvard president Benjamin Wadsworth went to the battlefield in Sudbury to place a stone at the site of his father's grave. In April 1676 Metacomet's allied forces had killed Captain Samuel Wadsworth and dozens of his men. Governor John Leverett guided Massachusetts Bay during King Philip's War, and in 1708 his grandson, of the same name, became the first lay president of Harvard, where he began the process of modernizing the curriculum. Another Harvard graduate, William Stoughton, whose father had participated in the massacre of the Pequot, assisted Governor Leverett. William Bradford, the son of the second Plymouth governor, was in the regiment that Metacomet outmaneuvered in Rhode Island. Major Simon Willard, a merchant, a fur trader, and a founder of Concord, had forty years experience in Indian wars when he joined the fight against Metacomet. His son, Samuel Willard, had graduated from Harvard in 1659 and later became a vice president of the college. Joseph Dudley, a 1665 graduate and the future royal governor of New England, battled the Narragansett. The Boston merchant and land speculator Captain Thomas Brattle had unsuccessfully negotiated with Metacomet before the war and led a company during the conflict. A son, of the same name, graduated from Harvard in 1676 and served twenty years as treasurer of the college. A second son, William, graduated in 1680.[49]

Several Harvard men fought King Philip's forces and died. One of Metacomet's earliest attacks resulted in the murder or imprisonment of more than a dozen relatives of the Reverend Joseph Rowlandson, class of 1652, including his wife, Mary Rowlandson, who authored a well-known captivity narrative. Gershom Bulkeley, a 1655 graduate, was surgeon to the English, Mohegan, and Pequot forces that pushed into Nipmuck territory, destroyed food supplies and forts, executed dozens of men, and took scores of hostages, mostly women and children. The Reverend Hope Atherton, who was in Bulkeley's Harvard class, accompanied Captain William Turner during his battle against the Indians at Montague. Atherton lost contact with his forces and suffered from hunger and exposure. His health never recovered and he died the following year. John Rayner, another Harvard-trained minister, died of exposure. Captain Joshua Scottow commanded forces from Black Point, Maine, and his son Thomas, Harvard class of 1677, later served in Indian campaigns.[50]

In August 1676 troops under Captain Benjamin Church cornered Metacomet near Mount Hope, Rhode Island, where he was shot dead by an English-allied Indian soldier. "His Head was brought into Plymouth in great triumph," reads the church record. The English dismembered Metacomet's body, mounted his head on a pole and paraded it around Plymouth, and sold his wife and son into slavery in Bermuda. Hundreds of Wampanoag, Narragansett, and their confederated peoples, particularly women and children, were traded to the Caribbean on ships that returned to the port towns of New England with enslaved Africans. Already decimated by disease and serial wars, the Indians suffered a defeat that erased thousands of years of history in New England. After the conflict, a French Protestant bragged that King Philip's War had ruined the Indians, "and consequently they are incapable of defending themselves."[51]

King Philip's War intensified Puritan demands for the complete domination of Native peoples, for which they had a ready blueprint in African slavery. The Boston merchant Nathaniel Saltonstall, Harvard class of 1659 and a prominent benefactor of the college, sent extensive updates on the war to a friend in England. In his second communication, Saltonstall attached an account of the concurrent discovery of a massive slave conspiracy in Barbados. The close economic ties between New England and Barbados gave rise to mutual sympathies. The report from Barbados also commented upon the northern Indian war. "Our Fellow-subjects in New-England have the 28th of the same Month, tasted of the same Cup, and was very hard put to it this last Summer by one King Philip an Indian King, who hath Revolted without Cause," one G. W. wrote from the island.[52]

In September 1680 the General Court transferred a portion of Metacomet's lands to the proprietors of a new township and Congregationalist church at Mount Hope Neck, which was renamed

Bristol for the English city. The town leveraged its future on its proximity to Newport and Providence, Rhode Island, the leading slaving ports in the northern colonies, and honored the city that was to be for decades the chief slaving port of England. Bristol's founding generation was filled with slave owners, including John Saffin, who soon became infamous when Judge Samuel Sewall exposed him for violating an agreement to free an enslaved black man. Following the war, New Englanders confined most of the remaining Indians to a string of reservations in Connecticut, Rhode Island, and Massachusetts. They also redefined unfree Indians, like Africans, to a category of property equivalent to livestock.[53]

King Philip's War also hastened the death of the Indian College. Morison argued that President Henry Dunster had promoted the Indian school to get the New England Company to pay for repairs to the Old College and subsidize English students. As soon as the building opened, President Charles Chauncy "began to hint that Harvard could find better use for it than to house Indians." The year before the war began, Daniel Gookin lamented that many Puritans took the deaths of Indian students as a sign that God was not yet ready to save them. A decade later, the New England Company "doth finde that there is only one Indian youth maintained and educated at the Colledge in New England." The board wanted ten Native students at Harvard, but most colonists saw few strategic benefits to enrolling additional Indian boys. President Mather was still including the "ancient Indian" preacher Hiacoomes in his new reports on the missions. Harvard's governors moved the printing press into the Indian College, where it was used to publish a Hebrew Bible and other material for English students. Supplies of the Algonquian Bible and catechism were destroyed during the war, and that inventory became a minor concern. The Labadists Jaspar Dankers and Peter Sluyter, who visited the colony after the war, found virtually no Indian-language publications when they called upon John Eliot to learn more about his mission. Mather sent some remaining copies of the Eliot Bible to the universities in Leiden and Utrecht in Holland.[54]

The Indian College came to a rather ignoble end. In November 1693 the corporation resolved that "the Indian Colledge be taken down, provided the charges of taking it down amount not to more than five pounds." The board then sought the New England Company's permission to reuse the bricks, which were eventually sold for £20.[55]

A COLLEGE FOR VIRGINIA

Reports of King Philip's success in New England heightened Virginians' fears of Native people. In 1675 the young, well-to-do English immigrant Nathaniel Bacon, to whom Governor William Berkeley had given a handsome plantation in the Virginia backcountry, gathered his own army. Bacon encouraged hostility toward Indians, including the Appomattox, the Occaneechee, and other friendly nations. He promised economic freedom to the colonists and physical freedom to any servants who joined his army. In 1676 his forces overthrew the governor, burned Jamestown, and brought Virginia under rebel rule for several months. Later that year Bacon died of dysentery. His death and the arrival of a royal fleet ended the uprising. The restored colonial government quickly executed two dozen of Bacon's lieutenants.[56]

Bacon's Rebellion did not lead to the establishment of the first college in Virginia, but the decision to organize a college responded to the lingering problems of defending the colony's expansive borders with Indian nations, regulating a large population of enslaved people, and governing a free population with a history of resisting political and religious authority. In 1693 King William III and Queen Mary II granted a charter. The trustees were primarily planters and merchants from the colony's leading landholding and slaveholding families. The Reverend James Blair, a graduate of Aberdeen and Edinburgh in Scotland, served as president for life, and governed the school for its first fifty years. The charter funded the College of William and Mary from the profits of slave labor, assigning a duty of a penny per pound on tobacco exported from Virginia and Maryland to support a president and professors. The crown also gave two 10,000-acre grants and the Virginia assembly allocated a duty on liquor, furs, and skins traded in the colony.[57]

The mission was to educate Christian youth, supply a trained ministry, and ensure that "the Christian faith may be propagated amongst the Western Indians, to the Glory of Almighty God." Rev. Blair and Governor Francis Nicholson promoted Indian evangelization. The trustees sent Blair on a fund-raising trip to England to publicize the progress of the colony. Well-placed friends such as John Locke, who had intellectual and financial interests in the Americas, proved useful as Blair sought donors. Indian missions were particularly marketable. Several Native boys attended William and Mary during its first years. In 1723 the trustees began the construction of a brick Indian college, Brafferton Hall.[58]

The Reverend Hugh Jones, the chaplain to the colonial assembly and a faculty member at William and Mary, argued the urgency of Indian conversion. He saw an intelligence and artistry in Indians that could be cultivated, but there was no similar divine light in black people, whom the minister viewed as "by Nature cut out for hard Labour and Fatigue." The trustees excitedly received "1000£ to buy Negroes for the College Use and Service." In 1718 alone the board purchased seventeen enslaved black people—hardly remarkable in a colony that paid its ministers in tobacco and where

Brafferton Hall, originally the Indian College, at the College of William and Mary
SOURCE: Library of Congress

the preachers were quick to fuss about exchange rates. Rev. Jones designed a course of instruction for Native students, but he relegated the education of black people to the whim of slave owners and even ignored the spiritual fate of the college's slaves.[59]

The strategic rewards of Indian missions were again paramount. Codified in August 1695, the Brafferton Fund, which paid for Indian education at Harvard and William and Mary, had regulations to ensure that a swift current of trained Indian ministers flowed back into their respective nations. The administrators encouraged the college officers to get as many Indian children as possible, from friendly or enemy nations, by invitation, purchase, or kidnapping. They placed Indian scholars under the direct supervision of the president and required regular censuses of Native students and reports on their progress. They set rates for boarding and educating Indian youth. The board then insisted that the governors "shall keep at the sd colledg soe many Indian children in sickness and healthe, in meat drink washing lodging clothes Medicines books and Education from the first begining of letters till they are ready to receive orders and be thought sufficient to preache be sent abroad to preach and convert the Indians."[60]

If the conquest and devastation of Indian peoples were mere expressions of providence, then attempts to hasten their fall could hardly be sinful. In 1711, when colonists in North Carolina were at war with the Tuscarora, Virginia governor William Spotswood demanded that the chiefs and leaders of the neighboring friendly nations surrender "Two Sons of the Chief Men in Each Town . . . to the Number of Twenty" to the College of William and Mary. President Lyon G. Tyler later admitted that the campus became a prison "where they served as so many hostages for the good behavior of the rest." Ultimately, about twenty Native children were being held on campus—including the sons and daughters of the chiefs of the Nottoway, Pamunkey, and Meherrin—and other Tuscarora were held for more than a year.[61]

GIFTS

Shortly after his graduation from Harvard, Jonathan Belcher, the son of a colonial slave trader, presented an Indian child as a gift in Europe, an act that symbolized the demographic devastation and violent conquest of the New England Indians and the ordinariness of unfreedom in the Christian empires of new Spain, New France, and British America. Academies and colleges, teachers and ministers, religion and science were as responsible for that ruin as forts, soldiers, armor, guns, and swords. Free and unfree, Indians were now relics of the English empire whom Belcher could treat as trophies, displaying them as the marvels of *his* country.

You negroes are treated here with great humanity and tenderness; ye have no hard task-masters, ye are not laden with too heavy burthens . . . ye grow cruel by too much indulgence: so much are ye degenerated and debased below the dignity of human species, that even the brute animals may upbraid you; for the ox knoweth his owner, and the ass his master's crib, even the very dogs also will, by their actions express their gratitude to the hand that feeds them, their thankfulness for kindness. . . . Such is the fidelity of these dumb beasts; but ye, *the beasts of the people*, though ye are clothed and fed, and provided with all necessaries of life, without care; in requital of your benefactors, in return for blessings ye give curses, and would scatter firebrands, death and destruction around them, destroy their estates and butcher their persons. Thus monstrous is your ingratitude!

—SENTENCING OF TOM (BRADT),
NEW YORK CITY, 1742

Oh Reader whoever thou art, it is impossible for you to conceive or me to describe the torture I sustain at the loss of these Slaves we have committed to a wat[e]ry grave[,] one of w'ch boys was to have been my own. . . . [I]n the afternoon got our slaves up and gave them an airing two more of which [I] imagine will die this night to my inexpressible grief, how unhappy is a person who undertakes the care of slaves.

—DR. WILLIAM CHANCELLOR, MAY 1750

CHAPTER 2

"Bonfires of the Negros"

The Bloody Journey from Slave Traders
to College Trustees

In 1771 a sixteen-year-old orphan assumed the day-to-day management of a St. Croix shipping house when his employer, Nicholas Cruger, returned to New York City. The wealthy St. Croix merchant Thomas Stevens had taken the boy in after the child's mother died. Apprenticing him in a merchant house was a predictable and somewhat generous act. Cruger supplied the Caribbean plantations with everything from fish and flour to mules. He also sold human beings. The teenager skillfully administered Cruger's ships and merchandise as they moved through a network of Caribbean ports, maximized profits by adjusting points of sale and seeking prime markets, and kept Cruger abreast of the performance of his captains and factors. His published poems and short essays brought him local fame. Two years earlier, he had written Stevens's son Edward to wish him well in his studies at King's College (Columbia) in New York City. He worried about his prospects in life and swore that he "would willingly risk my life tho' not my Character to exalt my Station." Now this precocious manager boarded one of Cruger's ships with funds from a subscription among the local merchants and set off for the

North American mainland. Nicholas Cruger's father and uncle were founding trustees of King's College, the Crugers and their in-laws served on the board through the American Revolution, and several of their sons attended the college. Hamilton's guardians placed him at the Presbyterian academy in Elizabeth, New Jersey. The following year Alexander Hamilton matriculated at King's. A job with a slave trader had rescued him from poverty. Donations from slave traders saved him from despair. His new life began with his arrival on a slave trader's ship. His New York and New Jersey sponsors included Crugers, Livingstons, Boudinots, and other elite families who enrolled him at a college funded and governed by merchants. His tuition and fees were paid from the sale of barrels of rum, manufactured on slave plantations, that Cruger's firm sent to New York.[1]

On the eve of the American Revolution, Alexander Hamilton entered college in a city transformed by the Africa and West Indies trades. Charitable gifts to fund the educations of poorer boys announced the social influence of the American slave traders, land speculators, planters, and financiers, who replaced British donors as the source of support for colonial churches, schools, libraries, and missions.

By the mid-eighteenth century, merchant wealth was reconfiguring the colonies. Impressive stores rose in the New England and mid-Atlantic ports, handsome townhouses stocked with European and Caribbean luxuries filled the old city streets, and country retreats sprung up in the outskirts of the big towns. During a six-month stay in Manhattan, the Boston artist John Singleton Copley painted thirty-seven portraits for upper-class families, including the Crugers, Livingstons, Verplancks, and Ludlows. The great landlords of colonial New York had transitioned into a more diverse range of investments, including shipping and insurance. These were the families that laid the foundations of the metropolis. They controlled the board of the New York Hospital. The majority of the eighty-three subscribers to the New York Society Library, the first public library in the city, were traders, and sixteen merchants served as trustees of King's College before the Revolution.[2]

American colleges had their genesis in this Atlantic economy. Colonial merchants were not for the most part scholars, but they

King's College, known today as Columbia University
SOURCE: Library of Congress

became the patrons of higher education. The wealthiest families had traditionally sent their sons to Britain to finish their studies and make connections. A fourth-generation Livingston, Robert, took his education at Cambridge, a distinction that he converted into a middle name—Robert Cambridge Livingston—to separate himself from his relatives and publicize his credentials. However, as their wealth increased and as their American identities evolved, merchant families became the sponsors and patrons of colonial colleges.[3]

Presbyterians and Reformed Dutch in New Jersey, Anglicans in New York, Anglicans and Presbyterians in Philadelphia, Baptists in Rhode Island, and Congregationalists in New Hampshire all benefited from the rise of the merchants. Between 1746 and 1769, a period of less than a quarter century, the number of colleges in the British mainland colonies tripled to nine. Ministers and merchants in the commercial centers of the Mid-Atlantic and New England organized the College of New Jersey (Princeton, 1746), the College of Philadelphia (University of Pennsylvania, 1749), King's (1754), the College of Rhode Island (Brown, 1764), and Queen's College (Rutgers, 1766). Not primarily intended to further Indian evangelization, these schools relied upon the generosity of the colonial elite. Even Dartmouth College (1769) in New Hampshire fits this pattern. Ostensibly founded for Indian education, Dartmouth had few Native American students, it soon became a training ground for white missionaries, and its president was experienced at soliciting colonial patrons.[4]

There was nothing all that remarkable in West Indian slave traders providing a scholarship to a gifted clerk. Far more noteworthy was the ascent of the merchants as the benefactors and guardians of colonial society.

THE RISE OF THE MERCHANTS

In 1672 the Royal African Company succeeded the Royal Adventurers to Africa, which was chartered in 1618 as the Governor and Company of Adventurers Trading to Gynney and Bynney. The Duke of York—who later ascended the throne as James II—was governor of the company and its largest individual shareholder. A list of prominent investors further raised the endeavor's profile. For example, John Locke owned at least £600 in Royal African stock and had earlier invested in the Royal Adventurers.[5]

Many of the great fortunes of New York were created while the monopoly was in effect. Frederick Philipse had arrived humbly. He came to New Amsterdam in the 1650s as a carpenter for the Dutch West India Company and labored in that capacity for years. As late as 1660 the company ordered him to renovate the Dutch Church at Midwout (Midwood, Brooklyn). A marriage to the wealthy widow Margaret Hardenbroeck de Vries, who had inherited a number of ships and a family business network, propelled Philipse into the merchant class. An astute and adventurous businesswoman, Margaret Philipse limited her second husband's access to her estate, managed the family businesses, and sailed with her own ships. She was one of a number of women merchants, landowners, and proprietors who came to power during the Dutch era.[6]

Frederick Philipse's instructions for a 1698 voyage to Madagascar survive. Piloting the barque *Margarit*, Captain Samuel Burgos was to trade for or purchase "two hundred good slaves or as many as the ship can carry." Philipse laid out the entire scheme: what route to follow; the names of his contacts, how to protect his ship; when to take on provisions for the crew and slaves, and what to buy; how to secure the slaves on board; directions for trading the supplies of liquor, guns, and money; cautions about piracy and other threats; where to register and clear the cargo; and the best seasonal periods for the return voyage. "Being arrived at that place . . . you are to trade with the Natives for Elephants Teeth, imploying the Brass Neck Collars, Arm Rings, Beeds, Looking glasses, boxes & such like things out of that cargoe to purchase them with," Philipse wrote. Barring the captain and crew from slave trading on their own, Philipse reminded Burgos that his share—to be paid upon his return to New York City in money, goods, and Africans— depended upon his success.[7]

That year Frederick Philipse was charged with piracy and evasion of the Navigation Acts for trading directly with non-English ports. The Madagascar slave trade itself married corruption, piracy, and kidnapping. To evade Royal African's monopoly, merchants had opened a trade from Madagascar. With vessels sailing into the South Atlantic, around the Cape of Good Hope, and into the Indian Ocean, these journeys could take two years to complete. Private traders from Britain and the colonies eroded Royal African's privileges. Merchants in New York joined in, trading illegally to West Africa and Madagascar. New York governor Cadwallader Colden later gossiped, "Several of the now principal families, I have been told, took their first rise to commerce with the Pirates." Philipse resigned from the governor's council, which enacted and executed laws and formed an appellate court for major cases. In an age of merchant adventurers, this was a modest scandal. All but one of his fellow councilors were accused of crimes. Nicholas Bayard, Thomas Willet, and William Nicholl were financing piracy, while William Pinhorne engaged in real estate fraud. Samuel Burgos had testified against William Nicholl and Governor Benjamin Fletcher, admitting that he had served under a captain who paid them £700 to unload goods pirated in the East Indies. Philipse remained the "wealthiest man" in the colony, he had an active merchant house, and he was the lord of Philipsburg Manor, comprising more than two hundred square miles of land.[8]

The great New York merchant houses were family networks that crossed the Atlantic world. Although their rights to hold property and make contracts were curtailed by English law, women traded actively and they were often at the center of these family enterprises. In July 1679 Robert Livingston married the wealthy heiress and widow Alida Schuyler Van Rensselaer. The couple acquired 160,000 acres of land near the village of Hudson and began investing in slaving voyages. Their first venture—the 1690 journey of the *Margriet*—traded slaves, sugar, and tobacco between Madagascar, Barbados, and Virginia. They bought interests in four additional ships, three with Peter Schuyler, Alida's brother. The Livingston children then married and maneuvered their way to greater wealth, consolidating about a million acres of land in two generations. The second generation's Philip Livingston and his wife, Catrina Van Brugh, sent their sons—Peter, John, Philip, and William—to Yale College to prepare them to manage the web of commercial sites and relationships in the Mid-Atlantic, New England, the West Indies, Europe, and Africa that formed Livingston Manor.[9]

In 1698 Parliament deregulated the slave trade while preserving a semblance of the African Company's privileges. With its merchants clearing fifty ships a year for Africa after the liberalization, Bristol overtook London as a slaving port in just a few decades, with more than two thousand total slaving ventures completed. Leading British banking and insurance houses such as Barclays and Lloyds rose from this commerce, and profits from the Africa trade were funding cultural and charitable institutions. By 1750 Bristol traders constituted a majority in the Company of Merchants Trading to Africa, which replaced the African Company.[10]

The end of the monopoly was no less significant in British North America. In 1698 John Cruger had emigrated from Bristol, England, to New York. A marriage to the heiress Maria Cuyler, of the powerful Albany and New York City family, made him a Hudson Valley landlord and a merchant. The John and Henry Cruger house launched its ships from Cruger's Wharf on the east side of the city and often registered its ships in Bristol. John Cruger held the New York City mayoralty from 1739 to 1744, and his son John was mayor from 1757 to 1766. Henry Cruger's sons administered businesses at key sites in the family's commercial complex. The younger Henry managed their business affairs in Bristol. John Harris went to Jamaica, Tileman to Curaçao, and Nicholas to St. Croix. Their sister Elizabeth married Peter Van Schaack of the prominent Albany clan.[11]

Young men from the mainland also went to the West Indies to find wealthy creole wives with whom they could increase their property and enlarge their commercial networks. Philip Livingston, son of the first lord of the manor, dispatched his sons, William and Henry, to Antigua and Jamaica. Peter and Philip Livingston both worked in Jamaica. The younger Philip Livingston met his wife in Jamaica, as did Henry Cruger Sr. His sons Tileman and Nicholas Cruger married women from Curaçao and St. Croix, respectively. Armed with family wealth and often college educations, these young traders headed south to expand their fortunes. Other merchant sons were also in the Caribbean. Gedney Clarke Jr. was in Barbados, William Lloyd operated in Jamaica, DePeyster and Duyckinck houses opened in Curaçao, and David Beekman kept a plantation and merchant house in St. Croix.[12]

THE BLOODY JOURNEY TO PROSPERITY

In the late summer of 1730 John Walter of New York and Arnot Schuyler of New Jersey contracted with Captain Jasper Farmar for a slaving mission. They had just finished building *Catherine*, and they registered it within weeks of its maiden voyage. Farmar piloted the ship to the Angola coast, where European and American traders were partnering with the dominant kingships, supplying them with arms and keeping up with their demands for and tastes in foreign goods. Trade shifted these coastal economies from fishing and agriculture to slaving. New York merchants were regular clients who made Angola the most important trading center in West Africa by the latter part of the eighteenth century. Atlantic merchants carried more than two and a half million people from this region, about 40 percent of all the enslaved Africans traded that century. Farmar returned on September 27, 1731, paying dues on one hundred and thirty people at Perth Amboy, New Jersey, and New York

City, but *Catherine* could hold almost twice as many captives as he reported. The captain logged the deaths of thirty African people.[13]

Even the statistics from well-documented journeys are imperfect. Deaths that occurred before ships departed Africa often went unrecorded, transatlantic mortality rates were high and the causes of death frequently unnoted, and merchants routinely underreported their human cargoes to avoid duties in the Americas. Enslaved people were physically and emotionally compromised by the time they were loaded into ships, having survived violent acquisitions from kidnappings and raids. Long marches to the coast and confinement while local dealers waited for slave ships left captives malnourished and ill.[14]

Lengthy imprisonments in narrow, cramped, and filthy holds accelerated the spread of diseases during return voyages that lasted several weeks. The poor diet provided the captives delivered few nutrients. A year before *Catherine*'s first voyage, a ship's surgeon had complained that mashed beans or peas mixed with salted, rotting fish and fed, sometimes forcibly, to the Africans on his ships further undermined their health. Dehydration was a primary cause of death. A pint of water, a standard daily ration, and water from meals failed to compensate for the loss of water from perspiration, vomiting, and diarrhea. Physical exhaustion and dehydration could bring changes in mental health ranging from depression to delirium. Medical technologies enhanced these threats to life. Common treatments such as bleeding, purging, and administering enemas compounded dehydration, sapped nutrients, and further weakened victims. Those who survived transport found themselves in British plantations where they confronted frequent epidemics and innumerable other risks.[15]

Farmar's notes suggest a combination of problems during his journeys. In August 1732 John Walter partnered with John, Peter, and Adoniah Schuyler to send *Catherine* on a second slaving expedition, again under Captain Farmar's command. Skilled captains were prized, and Farmar had proved himself worthy. Patrolling the coast of Angola, Farmar and the crew bought 257 children, women, and men, although he paid duties on only half that number when he returned to New Jersey in July 1733. His log also contains the death record for the last five months of the mission. It begins, "Died One Woman Slave" and continues: "a man slave . . . a woman . . . a Boy . . . a fine Manboy . . . a fine young man . . . a man . . . a man . . . a man . . . a man . . . a girl . . . a man . . . a man . . . a Large Boy . . . a Boy . . . a Boy . . . a girl . . . a young man . . . a young woman . . . 2 boys . . . a Boy . . . 2 Boys . . . 3 Men [and] 1 Boy . . . a Girl . . . a Boy." Farmar, Walter, and the Schuylers' enterprise killed thirty people, including several people who died after the ship reached Perth Amboy.[16]

MERCHANT METROPOLIS

The unfree population of the Mid-Atlantic and New England grew with this trade. The number of black people in New York City had doubled to more than fifteen hundred between the end of Royal African's monopoly and the launch of Captain Farmar's first slaving voyage. In April 1712, thirty enslaved Africans and a few Spanish Indians revolted in New York City and killed nine white people. The rebels included people recently imported from Africa and a larger number of slaves born in the American colonies. The "Spanish Indians" were captives from Native nations allied to Spain during the colonial wars in Florida and the Caribbean. The government responded to the uprising with punishments designed to terrorize unfree people and laws to protect against future rebellions. The Common Council set curfews on enslaved adults. It imposed penalties on masters and mistresses who failed to properly govern their slaves. The colony sought to keep cash and weapons out of the hands of slaves. Colonists were prohibited from privately trading or contracting with enslaved people. Africans were forbidden from gathering in groups greater than three. Legislators also displayed a growing mistrust of free black people, whom they described as a constant source of danger. The black population continued to grow. A decade after Jasper Farmar's first Africa voyage there were more than two thousand people of African descent in Manhattan, a fifth of the city's population.[17]

On a Sunday early in February 1741, several enslaved black men pitched pennies in Captain Jasper Farmar's yard. Jack (Farmar) organized the game, but, according to later testimony, it was a ruse that Kingston (unknown), Peter (Tudor), York (Debrosse), Tom (Bradt), Oronoko (Marston), and their partners used to coordinate one branch of a conspiracy that shocked New York City. Philip (Duyckink) admitted to being there but swore that he had heard no talk of revolt or of "the Long-Island negroes coming over to assist the New-York negroes in killing the white people." Tom testified that Jack had forced him into the plot. Jack confessed to gambling but denied the conspiracy. Jasper Farmar undoubtedly was surprised to discover that his slave and his house were at the center of a massive intrigue. A decade after his first Africa voyage, Captain Farmar lived comfortably on Manhattan island. He had brought hundreds of enslaved Africans into the New York market in less than three years, and he owned several human beings.[18]

On March 18 a fire burned the roof of the governor's residence in Fort George. Exactly one week later, the roof of a house in the southwest district of the city burned. On April 1, another week later, a fire destroyed Winant Van Zant's warehouse on the east side of the city. On Saturday, April 4, townspeople rushed to a fire in a cow stable on the west side of town. Just as they brought it under control, they were called to a blaze in the loft of Ben Thomas's house. The following morning someone found coals under a haystack near Joseph Murray's coach house on Broadway. On Monday morning a fire erupted in the chimney of a house at Fort Garden. At noon residents saved a house near the Fly Market from burning. That afternoon flames shot up the side of one of Adolph Philipse's storehouses.[19]

Scholars have vigorously debated the existence of this plot. Rivalries and lingering grievances among the elite influenced the events. Justice Daniel Horsmanden, who published the only complete account of the trials, seized upon the alleged conspiracy to raise his political profile. White people's insecurities and vulnerabilities predisposed them to fear and see a conspiracy in the events of March and April. Residents of the city had suffered food shortages following a severe winter, depressed commerce, and a drain on manpower and resources due to the Anglo-Spanish War in the Caribbean. A succession of revolts and conspiracies heightened their fears. Many New Yorkers remembered the uprising of

1712, and authorities investigated another plot less than a decade later. In the 1730s slaves rebelled in St. John's and Jamaica. In 1734 enslaved people in Somerset County, New Jersey, plotted to rise up against their owners. They planned to cut the throats of the white men and take horses and supplies for an escape to Indian country. New Yorkers also followed the deadly revolts in Antigua in 1736 and South Carolina in 1739.[20]

"There yet continues a great Suspicion of the Negroes, as well as of other bad People lurking about this Town, which causes the Military Watch to be continued here," warned Lieutenant Governor George Clarke, who was convinced that "the late Fires in this City were kindled by wicked People." Rumors of a slave uprising swept the city, fueled by allegations that black people had been overheard cursing the white inhabitants. "The chief talk now in Town is about the Negroes conspiracy," Elizabeth DeLancey reported to her father, Cadwallader Colden. The lord of Coldengham also received a letter from an anonymous source in Massachusetts warning that New York was repeating the New England tragedy of 1692 when Puritans hustled innocent women to their deaths during a wave of hysteria over witchcraft. "I intreat you not to go on to Massacre & destroy your own Estates by making Bonfires of the Negros," the author pleaded, "& perhaps thereby loading yourselves with greater Guilt than theirs."[21]

As white residents' anxieties about a general slave uprising peaked, the city's traders were completing several slaving ventures. As the Africans were allegedly conspiring, John Walter and Arnot Schuyler—who had hired Captain Farmar—brought the *Arent* into port. Peter Van Brugh Livingston's sloop *Sea Nymph* approached Manhattan, having already stopped in South Carolina, just as New York's white population was beginning to panic. On Saturday, April 11, Mayor John Cruger summoned the Common Council to investigate the fires and rumors, approve rewards for any white persons providing evidence of arson or conspiracy, grant freedom and cash to any slaves who brought such evidence (a provision that also compensated their owners), and pay any free black person, mulatto, or Indian coming forward with information. The following week, a ship from St. Christopher came into port with slaves for the merchants Edward Little, William Craft, and Nathaniel Marston.[22]

On April 21 the New York Supreme Court of Judicature summoned a grand jury, comprising seventeen merchants—including several men who soon became founders, trustees, and patrons of the colleges in New York and New Jersey—to examine evidence and testimony taken during the past weeks. Officials interrogated and arrested Africans belonging to the colony's most prominent families: Jay, Van Horne, Philipse, Gomez, Cruger, Clarkson, Rutgers, Schuyler, Duane, DePeyster, Bayard, Roosevelt, Van Cortlandt, and Livingston. Elizabeth DeLancey later alerted her father of the conviction of Philipse and Roosevelt slaves. Othello (DeLancey) was hanged on July 18 for enlisting others in the plot and acting as captain of one branch of the scheme. That same week, newspapers excoriated the boldness of several black men and an Indian at their executions: "On Saturday last five lusty jolly Negros and one Spanish Indian were hang'd on account of the said Plot, and one pretended Negro Doctor was burnt. One of those that were hang'd behaved with such unparalel'd Impenitence and Impudence as greatly to amaze the Spectators."[23]

In the backdrop of the furor, vessels carrying enslaved Africans streamed into New York's harbor. Between the jury's April 21 impaneling and the end of the trials on August 29, at least twenty slaving vessels docked in New York. Philip Livingston, Philip Van Cortlandt, Stephen Bayard, David Gomez, Peter Van Brugh Livingston, and Mordecai Nunez dominated that summer's commerce. Merchants also testified during the trials, but the threats to the colony did little to reshape their decisions. Peter Van Brugh Livingston even used a technicality to avoid service.[24]

White New Yorkers gained some solace from the sight of slaves being tried before a jury of masters. The people had been subjected to "many frights and terrors," Justice Frederick Philipse reminded the jury. Justice Philipse tried dozens of enslaved people, including Cuffee (Philipse), who was accused of setting fire to a storehouse belonging to the judge's uncle and boasting that he was going to free the family of its fortune. Cuffee was also part of a group of black men who held cockfights on Adolph Philipse's land, where they planned parts of the rebellion.[25]

A revolt would not be likely to spare the Philipses. The grandson of the first lord of Philipsburg, the chief justice had inherited an empire. He was born in Barbados, where his father, Philip Philipse, died while managing the family's business. To secure his grandson's future, the elder Frederick Philipse gave his namesake his "Joncker's" (Yonkers) plantation:

> I give grant devise and bequeath to Fredrick Filipse my grandson born in Barbados . . . all those lands and meadows called the Joncker's plantation, together with all and singular houses, mills, mill dams, Orchards, gardens, *Negroes, Negroes children, cattle, horses, swine, and whatever else belongs to me* within that patent.[26]

He also received the family seat in Manhattan, a string of properties and estates stretching north to Putnam County, and the King's Bridge, a toll bridge that his grandfather had built in 1693 to span Spuyten Duyvil Creek and link Manhattan island to the mainland at the Bronx. Besides the Yonkers slaves, he inherited several of his grandfather's personal servants: "a Negroe man called Harry with his wife and child, a Negroe man called Peter, [and] a Negro man called Wan [perhaps Juan]." He got the boat *Joncker* and a quarter of his family's commercial ships. Adolph Philipse acquired a full share of the shipping enterprise and houses, lots, lands, meadows, warehouses, and mills along the Hudson River, including much of Putnam County. His father had also left him numerous enslaved people: "the Negroe man called Symon, Charles, Towerhill, Samson, Claes, Billy, Mingo, Hendrik, Bahynne, and Hector, the Negroe boy Peter, the Indian woman called Hannah and her child, the Negroe woman Susan the younger and the Negroe woman Mary." Adolph's sisters, Eva Van Cortlandt and Anne French, took parts of the shipping business, warehouses, Manhattan houses, and lands.[27]

Slave traders controlled the bench and the jury during the 1741 trials, proceedings that they used to calm public outrage and reassert merchant rule. The traders responsible for the colony's insecurities vetted the danger and credibility of those threats. The families who exposed the colony to conspiracies and rebellions directed the legal proceedings. Thirteen enslaved black people were burned and eighteen were hanged. Officials also hanged two white women and two white men. The court exiled a small group of white people and sold dozens of enslaved black men and women out of the colony.[28]

ORDINARY HORRIFIC AFFAIRS OF TRADE

In the aftermath of the proceedings, slaving in the colony receded briefly. The following summer, six slave ships docked in Manhattan, a fraction of the number that arrived before the conspiracy. The trepidation soon eased. On June 18 the brigantine *Ancram* entered New York harbor from St. Kitts, completing a voyage for Robert Livingston Jr. The Cuylers and Crugers had also capitalized on their investments, adding their slave ships to the numerous arrivals of the other merchants. The Cuylers' *Happy* returned to New York City from Jamaica with a cargo of enslaved people, while the Crugers received a shipment of Africans out of St. Christopher on the *Mary*. Henry Cuyler partnered with Philip and Robert Livingston, whose *Oswego* carried fourteen bound people from Jamaica. King George II compensated Governor Clarke for his services and losses with a £4,000 payment drawn from duties on Barbados and the Leeward Islands. In the following decade New York's leading Atlantic merchants put more ships to sea and fully reestablished the Africa trade. This was more than a normalization of commerce. It reflected the activity of the family networks that undergirded the Atlantic system and the city's integration into and dependence upon a dangerous and brutal trade.[29]

One of the younger Philip Livingston's investments is instructive. On May 13, 1751, the *New-York Gazette* announced that children, women, and men were to be sold from the *Wolf* at the Meal Market at 10:00 A.M. the following Friday. The sloop's arrival, the advertisement, and the customs records obscure frightful events. The *Wolf* left New York City in September 1749 and reached the African coast in mid-November. Competition between Dutch,

English, Portuguese, French, and American slavers and shortages of healthy captives prolonged the journey. Captain Gurnay Wall patrolled the shore for fourteen months, hopping from port to port, trading rum and other goods for small numbers of people. Dozens of human beings were imprisoned belowdecks as Wall tried to fill every space. "We know we are destined to stay till we do purchase a full complement," sighed Dr. William Chancellor, the ship's surgeon.[30]

A ship was a moving jurisdiction. Besides setting terms with owners and investors, captains had the administrative tasks of hiring sailors, fixing wages, taking on provisions, establishing daily routines, and maintaining order. Piloting ships into waters patrolled by pirates and filled with other risks tested technical skill and nautical knowledge, employee management, and personal courage. Captains established regulations, judged infractions, and imposed punishments. In the first week of his 1709 voyage to Barbados, the captain of the *Thomas and Elizabeth* instructed the young Harvard graduate and historian Thomas Prince to write a code of conduct for the ship. Prince assigned corporal punishments for infractions that included missing religious services, drunkenness, dereliction, and profanity. Disease could destroy a journey, and captains either needed the services of skilled surgeons or acquainted themselves with the medical arts. At times they presided at the funerals of their crewmen or officers. In the summer of 1733 a Captain Moore lost his Harvard-trained surgeon to a fever during a return from Guinea. On the African coast, slave ships became jails with hundreds of people incarcerated on board. A successful voyage required guarding against innumerable external threats to the endeavor while constantly taking the pulse of the crew and the slaves to protect against mutinies and insurrections.[31]

As the *Wolf* approached the Gold Coast, Dr. Chancellor's fears overwhelmed him. "I am now got into a most shocking part of the world," he entered in his diary upon seeing Africa. "Merciless wretches" were hiding on shore, and the sailors were certain that if they left the ship they would "be immediately cut up, broil'd on the coals, and devour'd." The Africans, the surgeon added, "often eat their own children," and all disputes on shore ended in one person digesting another. Members of the crew took turns hiding with arms belowdecks to protect against an attack.[32]

Merchants increased cargoes by laying enslaved people on their sides, chest to back, with little more than a couple of feet of vertical space. Makeshift platforms were built between the floor and deck to expand capacity. Stripped nude to make them easier to wash down and secure, shackled in pairs, and often branded for identification, these prisoners spent long periods in rat- and insect-infested bowels of ships, interrupted only by a regimen of feedings, airings, and exercise under threat of whips, blades, and guns. A ship's surgeon protested that the intolerable stench and heat during one voyage limited his visits belowdecks, where the floor was so covered in blood and excrement that "it resembled a slaughter-house." While in Britain training to fill a chemistry professorship at Yale, Benjamin Silliman observed conditions that "equally disgust decency and shock humanity" when a friend took him on a tour of a Guinea ship docked in Liverpool. "It was just finished,

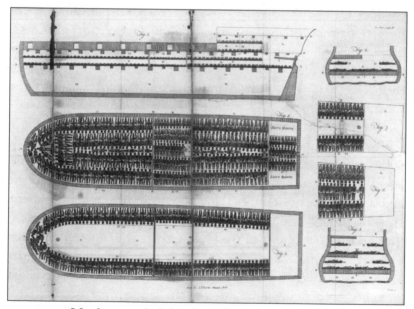

Merchants packed their human cargoes tightly into the
holds of slave ships. Diagram from 1808
SOURCE: The Granger Collection

and had not then been employed," he recalled, "the narrow cells and the chains, which were as yet unstained with blood . . . were all ready for the victims." Even that brief glimpse into a new ship horrified this son of a slave-owning family. "There will be a day when these things shall be told in heaven!" he predicted.[33]

Dr. Chancellor complained bitterly about the *Wolf*. Water flowed freely into the ship during storms, forcing the crew to stand ankle deep belowdecks or risk being swept into the ocean. "These sorts of vessels are terrible things to have slaves in, especially so great a number sick & none but myself to look after them," Chancellor complained. By May 1750 the three dozen people chained belowdecks, many of them small children, were ill. The holds for the Africans were so cramped and their detention so prolonged that several could not walk without assistance. Chancellor recorded their suffering and his anxieties as the enterprise crumbled. "I am in the very height of my miserys," he admitted during the summer, "not only from the deaths of the slaves, but the reflection, that by the Capt[ain] is cast on me on that acc[oun]t."[34]

Lingering doubts about their ability to control enslaved people had led white northerners to demand children, whom they believed to be less rebellious and more susceptible to Christian instruction. "For this market they must be young[,] the younger the better if not quite Children, those advanced in years will never do," the merchant and King's College trustee John Watts advised Gedney Clarke in 1762. "I should imagine a Cargo of them not exceeding thirty [in total] might turn out at fifty pounds a head gross Sales." A year earlier John and Susanna Wheatley had gone aboard *Phillis* at the Long Wharf in Boston and purchased a sickly girl who was covering herself with a piece of old carpet. Owning several older black people, the Wheatleys were shopping for a child to serve them as they aged. They named her Phillis (Wheatley) in honor of the ship.[35]

Before they became the presidents of the College of New Jersey and Yale, respectively, the Connecticut evangelist Jonathan Edwards and the Rhode Island minister Ezra Stiles both purchased African children through the captains of slave ships in Newport. In 1738 the Boston merchant Peter Faneuil empowered Captain Peter Buckley to sell several hogsheads and barrels of fish in Antigua, and use the proceeds to buy a "strait limbed Negro lad . . . from 12 to fiveteen years" with a docile temperament. "I have lost one of my Negroe boys, who died of a Consumption [tuberculosis]," William Vassall, a Harvard graduate and Boston resident, informed his plantation manager, James Wedderburn, in Jamaica, "& want another in his room very much." Vassall instructed his overseer to find, purchase, and ship a "sprightly lively healthy young Negroe lad about 14 years old," who could act as a personal servant and butler, spoke English, and had no bad habits. Governor James Bowdoin, who established the Bowdoin Prize at Harvard and whose namesake endowed Bowdoin College in Maine, authorized a family member to buy a "light-timber'd Negro boy" for his home.[36]

On Tuesday evening, May 29, a five-year-old girl succumbed to the conditions on the *Wolf.* Wednesday morning the surgeon went below and "found a boy dead[,] at noon another, and in the afternoon another." The doctor believed that his medicines were too potent; he had not expected Captain Wall to take on small children. "This morning early found another of the boys dead," he recorded the following day, "the sight was shocking and to see likely boys floating over board is a misery to all on board." On Tuesday, June 5, Dr. Chancellor brought up the corpse of a three-year-old girl. He conducted an autopsy, and "found in her Intestines 7 worms some of them 12 & 13 Inches, roll'd up together in a bundle." On Saturday a third little girl expired. The new week began with the doctor carrying up a dead girl. Two days later, on June 13, he autopsied a baby and witnessed her "stomach chock'd full" of worms. Two enslaved people were dying each week, most of them children. The fourteenth brought the passing of two small boys, including another child "whom I might call my own," lamented Chancellor. This boy had ulcerated lungs. On Thursday, June 21, a boy and a girl died. Deaths continued to mount.[37]

Little children were primary casualties of Livingston's investment. "At noon threw over a boy slave who died," the surgeon casually noted on July 13. This was the second child discarded that month. "I forgot to mention that yesterday to add to many misfortunes we threw over board a child of 3 years," Chancellor jotted a week later. This little girl had suffered with green flux, white flux, and bloody flux—manifestations of severe dysentery—and measles during her long imprisonment. Dr. Chancellor became more comfortable handling dead children, but the escalating casualties had his emotions swinging between compassion and rage. He twice accused the Africans of murdering each other, and even blamed them for dying—the journey being at "the mercy of vile slaves"— since every lost life prolonged the voyage. August began with Chancellor removing "12 large worms" from the corpse of a baby girl. Three little girls and two other captives died that month. The crew tossed scores of human bodies into the water as the *Wolf* cruised along the African coast for more than a year.[38]

Despite a revolt before they departed for America and the deaths of two imprisoned Africans at sea, Captain Wall piloted the *Wolf* into New York harbor in May 1751, completing a horrific, but ordinary, slaving voyage. The Livingston network, tying interests in New York, Great Britain, the West Indies, and the African coast, again paid off. According to Dr. Chancellor's diary, Captain Wall purchased 147 people on the African coast, but Philip Livingston reported only 66 at New York City. Wall claimed seven people as part of his contract. Livingston had killed almost as many people as he traded. He and Wall then quickly put the survivors up for sale.[39]

FROM TRADERS TO TRUSTEES

By 1753 William Livingston, the youngest brother of Philip, was unquestionably the most vocal opponent of the Anglican college that was being planned in New York City. His father, the elder Philip, had sent him to Yale and then to study law. William Livingston had little interest in the bar or the merchant house. He was more of a literary man. He became a prominent advocate of the arts and sciences in New York City and a strident opponent of corruption in the colonial government. He was a founder of the New York Society Library and the Society for the Promotion of Useful Knowledge. Beginning in 1746 he threw his energies into a plan for a college in New York City. However, the Anglican minority soon began maneuvering for an Episcopal seminary under

the leadership of Samuel Johnson, an Anglican priest from Connecticut, who would also be installed at Trinity Church. The successful founding of the Presbyterian College of New Jersey had
touched a nerve among New York's Anglicans. Eighteenth-century
New Yorkers were as likely to see conspiracies from above as they
were to see plots from below. The Anglican grab on the college
aggravated deeply rooted fears of the Church of England and the
crown's desire to crush dissent in the colonies. William Livingston
led the backlash. He accused the Anglicans of religious tyranny,
and they charged that Livingston was manipulating public opinion to protect the Presbyterian college.[40]

In 1753 William Smith, a Scottish Anglican educated at King's
College in Aberdeen, saw his proposal for a New York academy
wither during this conflict. Benjamin Franklin recruited Smith to
help raise the status of his Philadelphia academy. "I am sorry it
meets so great opposition," Elizabeth DeLancey, daughter of Cadwallader Colden, later wrote of the factionalism that continued to
jeopardize her husband Peter DeLancey's hopes for a college.[41]

William Livingston's three-year war against the college dimin-
ished the Anglican victory, took a heavy toll on advocates such as
Governor James DeLancey, and tarnished the public image of the
school before it ever received a student. However, he had been less
successful at drawing his merchant brothers to the cause. Philip,
John, and Peter Livingston became trustees, sponsors, or benefactors.[42]

The division within Livingston Manor is suggestive of a greater
social and economic transformation in New York. There was a tension between the sectarian origins of the colonies and the development of an Atlantic commerce, particularly the slave trade,
dependent upon intercolonial economic and social relationships.
Merchants were, in fact, a visible presence and important faction
in the governance of the new school.

In the charter of King's College, George II appointed his clerics
and public administrators as ex officio trustees: the archbishop of
Canterbury, the governor, secretary, and treasurer of New York,
the justices of the supreme court, the mayor, and the senior
Episcopal, Dutch Reformed, Lutheran, French Protestant, and

Presbyterian ministers. The public trustees included slaveholders and slave traders such as Mayor David Holland and Abraham De-Peyster. Perhaps to calm the public, Governor DeLancey, recruited the rest of the board from the city's commercial leaders: Frederick Philipse, John and Henry Cruger, Paul Richard, Joseph Robinson, John Lawrence, John Watts, Leonard Lispenard, Joseph Reade, Nathaniel Marston, Oliver DeLancey, Henry Beekman, Joseph Haynes, John Livingston, Philip Verplanck, Philip Livingston, and David Clarkson. In the following decades the trustees continued to come from this stratum, including Ludlows, Duanes, Provoosts, and Morrises. William Alexander, a Livingston in-law, and Beverly Robinson, the husband of the merchant princess Susannah Philipse, joined the board along with Charles Ward Apthorpe, whose Elmwood estate in upper Manhattan drew comparisons to the grandeur of ancient Rome.[43]

King's was a merchants' college. In its first two decades it enrolled nearly ninety sons of the commercial class, more children of Atlantic traders than any other college in British North America. Although a fire destroyed many of the treasurer's reports for colonial New York, the slaving activities of the trustees show through even

Philip Livingston, a founding benefactor of King's College
(Columbia) and Queen's (Rutgers)
SOURCE: Brooklyn Historical Society

this damaged and incomplete record. In the month before the execution of the charter, several governors or patrons traded slaves. In
September 1754 the sloop *Polly* docked in Manhattan holding seven
enslaved Africans with its other cargo. Two people died during the
Polly's return. This was just a few weeks before Nathaniel Marston,
a partial owner of the venture, became a trustee. That same month
Philip Livingston's sloop returned from the African coast, and the
following month John Livingston's ship completed a voyage to Jamaica. In the years before he became a trustee, David Clarkson had
partnered in several slaving voyages. Matthew Clarkson, a future
trustee, was active in the trade long after the opening of King's. The
number of trustees trading in slaves increased through the 1750s.[44]

In May 1755 Governor DeLancey brought the charter—which
Attorney General William Kempe, a trustee, had prepared—to
Edward Willett's house to swear in the new board. Trinity donated
two square blocks north and south of Robinson Street between
Church and Chapel. In exchange the Reformed Dutch and Presbyterians accepted Anglican affiliation, which meant an Anglican
president and the use of that church's prayers. Samuel Johnson accepted the presidency and Anglicans dominated the original trustee
board. Justice Daniel Horsmanden, a trustee who donated at least
£500 to the college, administered the board members' oaths.[45]

The influence of the merchants rested in large part on their willingness to leverage the slave economy. "I Do give and bequeath
unto my said Nine grandchildren after the Decease of my said
Wife Sarah Each and every one of them a Negro slave such as my
said son in Law & Daughter or the survivor of them shall think
proper," wrote Peter Van Brugh. He left his grandson Peter Van
Brugh Livingston a portion of a family house, lot, and furnishings,
and he gave his granddaughter Sarah Livingston ownership of his
"Negro Bett," or a surviving black woman, upon his wife's death.
His wife, Sarah, took possession of a collection of properties in
Albany and New York City along with "all my Negro slaves, Horses,
Cattle, households of furniture, utensills, and all my moveable and
personall estate." His daughter Catrina Van Brugh and son-in-law
Philip Livingston took a half share in a house, lot, and furnishings,

> Philadelphia, June 25. 1747.
> *Just Imported,*
> In the Brigantine G E O R G E;
> from *G U I N E A*;
> And to be fold by CHARLES WILLING;
> SEveral likely Negro Men and Boys;
> alfo to be fold by faid Willing, Barbados Rum and
> Sugar; and a Variety of Dry Goods, lately imported
> from England.

Advertisement from Charles Willing, trustee of the College of
Philadelphia, today's University of Pennsylvania
SOURCE: Pennsylvania Gazette

and a piece of the larger estate upon Sarah Van Brugh's death. Philip Livingston received slaves and commercial slaving interests from his parents and his in-laws, and he left both to his own children, including Peter Van Brugh and Philip, as did their in-laws. For example, James Alexander added to this fortune after his son William married Philip and Catrina's daughter Sarah.[46]

A landless Scottish noble who had trained as an attorney in Glasgow and London, James Alexander became a wealthy lawyer and land speculator in East Jersey. He married Mary Sprat, a Provoost widow and daughter of the DePeyster family, whose considerable business experience as a merchant trader aided his rise. By the time of his death, Alexander held large estates in New York and owned as much as sixty thousand acres of land in New Jersey.[47]

Preserved in the records of Peter Van Brugh Livingston, James Alexander's 1745 will included a grant to support the new enthusiasm of the merchants: "I do give to the use of a colledge for the education of youth to be erected in the Province of New York the Sum of one hundred Pounds New york money." Alexander increased his gift to the planned "colledge" with payments that the colony

owed him for his service in the assembly. Public money for the new
school came directly and indirectly from slavery and the slave trade.
"The Dutys on Rum Wine & Negroes have heretofore supported our
Civil List" is how the trustee John Watts described that dependence.
For two decades the colonial treasurer Abraham DePeyster collected
taxes on the human merchandise moved through the port. Ship's
captains entering New York vouched to DePeyster for the accuracy
of their manifests for "Slaves, Wine, Rum, or other distilled
Liquors, Shrub, Cocoa, or dutiable Dry-Goods." James Alexander
also donated £50 "to the use of a colledge for the Education of
youth to be erected in the Province of New Jersey."[48]

The traders could afford to be magnanimous. Churches, hospitals, libraries, and colleges were the rewards of a broad social investment in Atlantic slavery. The *New-York Post-Boy and Weekly Gazette*
broadside that announced the trustees' swearing-in ceremony carried a single advertisement: "*two likely Negro Boys, and a Girl, to be
Sold. Inquire of* William Griffith, *opposite* Beekman's Slip." The sym-
bolism of that sheet being paid for by a notice for the sale of black
children is appropriate, for the participation of the founders in slave
trading was one of their more distinguishing characteristics.[49]

Throughout the Mid-Atlantic and New England, higher education had its greatest period of expansion as the African slave trade
peaked. In September 1742 the merchants of Philadelphia set exchange rates in response to a shortage of hard currency. Those endorsing that published agreement included most of the men who
later served as the governors of the College of Philadelphia.
Quaker Philadelphia was a hub in the transatlantic commercial
network. The founders of the new school included the Quakers
James Logan and Lloyd Zachary. By the mid-eighteenth century
there were more than eighty Quaker slave traders in London. David and John Barclay, who freed their Jamaican slaves shortly after
inheriting a plantation, donated to the Philadelphia college and
served as its London agents. Philadelphia traders carried provisions and enslaved people to Barbados and the rest of the British
Caribbean. Several of the trustees were West Indies merchants,
and the board actively sought donors and students from those

islands. Provost William Smith had come to mainland North America with Josiah Martin, a royal councilor and planter from Antigua, whose slaves had participated in the rebellion of 1736. Martin was a founding trustee of King's, and he enrolled two of his sons at Philadelphia.[50]

The board included a number of men who traded in indentured British and German servants and enslaved Africans. The bifurcation of the Pennsylvania economy between agriculture and a rising system of manufactories brought calls for laborers with different skills and backgrounds. Meeting these demands had lasting political and social consequences. It sparked cyclical struggles between the Quaker minority and a growing population of European immigrants, who demanded political representation and sought the freedom to war against Indians for control over lands at the western border of the colony. Those who arrived as indentured servants often carried an even greater sense of entitlement upon their emancipation.[51]

Commerce strained the Quaker ethic. In 1684 a British firm had brought 150 enslaved Africans to Philadelphia. "It were better they were blacks," William Penn, the founding proprietor, decided the following year while addressing the colony's labor needs, "for then a man has them while they live." In the eighteenth century the number of Pennsylvania merchants in the Africa trade jumped significantly. William Allen and Joseph Turner, both founding trustees of the College of Philadelphia, formed a partnership that brought slaves from the British Caribbean and servants from Europe. David Barclay represented Allen and Turner in London. The two investors advertised for runaways, including people fleeing their New Jersey iron foundry; used their firm to facilitate slave catching; and sold people from their offices. Aging Philadelphia merchants often drifted into manufacturing to limit their exposure in the riskier Atlantic trade. Prominent families such as the Allens, Turners, and Whartons shaped the iron industry, which used enslaved black and indentured white labor. Allen and Turner invested more than £20,000 in a single foundry. One of Pennsylvania's wealthiest men, William Allen, sent three sons to the college, two of whom also became trustees.[52]

PRESIDENT JOHNSON TEACHING HIS FIRST CLASS.

Samuel Johnson teaching his first class at King's College,
in a nineteenth-century illustration
SOURCE: New York Public Library

Philadelphia mayor Charles Willing, a charter trustee of the
academy, owned three ships and organized at least six slaving expeditions. A 1747 advertisement he took out announced that "several likely Negro Men and Boys" were to be sold from "the
Brigantine *George* from Guinea." He was also offering rum and
sugar from Barbados and a variety of goods from England. Thomas
Willing, the mayor's son, partnered with Robert Morris in one of
the colony's largest slaving outfits, Willing and Morris, which sold
hundreds of Africans into the Pennsylvania and Delaware markets. Later the president of the Bank of the United States in Philadelphia, Thomas Willing also spent more than thirty years on the
board of the college.[53]

The Philadelphia college was a beneficiary of these trades in
unfree people. A Scot who first settled the Caribbean, John Inglis

relocated to Philadelphia, where he sent four slavers to the Carolinas and West Indies in less than a decade. His father-in-law, George McCall, and brother-in-law, Samuel McCall, also a founding trustee, invested in more than fifteen slaving voyages. William Plumsted, another charter trustee and also a son-in-law of George McCall, sent two slaving vessels to sea while serving on the board; one, in partnership with David Franks, brought a hundred enslaved people from Guinea to Philadelphia. John Searle, the son of a slaver and an experienced Madeira trader, was part of a second generation of merchants who became trustees as slave importations into Pennsylvania and Delaware peaked.[54]

The merchants pulled the school into the unfree economy. "A Likely young Negro Woman, who can Wash, Iron, and cook well; also a young Negro Girl, about 14 Years of Age," began John Inglis's 1739 announcement for two slaves whom he advertised as smallpox survivors. Inglis also sold British indentured servants—primarily tradesman and farmers—and Caribbean and English wares from his Front Street store. After advertising the wide variety of dry goods at his merchant house, he noted that he "had to sell two likely young Negro Men fit for Town or Country Service." Thomas Lawrence moved black people in the local markets, including a Barbadian woman named Hannah who ran away in 1739, and Elizabeth Gregory, born on Long Island, who escaped in 1749.[55]

In 1759 the firm of Tench Francis, a founder of the Philadelphia college, sent Obadiah Brown and Company of Providence an update of the insurance rates for *Wheel of Fortune*, a schooner being configured for a voyage to the African coast. William Coxe, Francis's son-in-law and a graduate of Philadelphia, partnered in a 1762 slaving voyage that brought seventy-five people from Gambia to Pennsylvania on the schooner *Sally*. The Browns became benefactors and governors of the College of Rhode Island, which the trustees renamed in 1804 to recognize a gift from Nicholas Brown.[56]

Merchants in Providence and Newport dominated the American arm of the African slave trade. In 1764, the charter year of the College of Rhode Island, the brigantine *Sally*—belonging to Nicholas, John, Joseph, and Moses Brown of Providence, known collectively as Nicholas Brown and Company—left on an African voyage that proved disastrous. The Brown brothers provided Captain Esek Hopkins—younger brother of College of Rhode Island chancellor Stephen Hopkins, later a signer of the Declaration of Independence—with careful instructions: where and how to trade on the African coast, money and materials for purchasing people, directions for unloading the captives into the Caribbean markets, and a specific request to return to Providence with four teenage boys for the family's use. The competition for slaves and the scarce supply of captives on the African coast prolonged Hopkins's work. From November 1764 through August 1765 Captain Hopkins trolled for human beings, paying off kidnappers and trading rum, guns, knives, powder, cloth and clothing, beads, tobacco, onions, and other goods for children, women, and men. When the ship finally set sail for the West Indies, nineteen people, many of them children, had already died, including a woman who hung herself between the decks. The captives rose up during the journey across the Atlantic, and the crew killed eight people and seriously wounded several others. Death and suicide marked the remainder of the voyage—only 88 of 196 Africans survived.[57]

A product of a middling family in New Jersey, Jasper Farmar's work as a slave ship's captain gave him entry to the merchant class. He withdrew from the dangerous Africa trade and increased his wealth by captaining ships between New York and London. Farmar used his earnings to invest in his own ships, open a merchant house with his brother Samuel, and partner in the Africa trade. By midcentury he was involved in slaving ventures with the merchant and King's College trustee John Watts. Some measure of his success came when his heir, Jasper, enrolled at Queen's College in New Brunswick. The charter trustees of Queen's came from the most prominent slaveholding and slave trading families in the region, and they included Philip Livingston, Robert Livingston, Theodorus Van Wyck, Peter Schenck, and Abraham Hasbrouck. The college sat in the Dutch slaveholding belt that stretched from Elizabethtown to Trenton, and its founding president, Jacob Hardenbergh, and first tutor, Frederick Frelinghuysen, were slave owners. Its earliest graduates were from slaveholding Dutch families, among them the Schencks, Van Cortlandts, and Van Hornes.[58]

THE ERA OF MERCHANT BENEVOLENCE

As slave traders and planters came to power in colonial society, they took guardianship over education. The Boston merchant Nicholas Boylston willed £1,500 for the Boylston Professorship of Rhetoric and Oratory, one of Harvard's first endowed chairs. He made large sums bringing luxury goods into the colony during the French and Indian War, after Thomas Boylston—his brother, business partner, and executor—had enhanced their rather comfortable inheritance through the slave trade. In their 1765 will, the Maryland slaveholders Peter and Susannah Bayard created a scholarship at the College of New Jersey for worthy but impoverished students. The gift was made in memory of their son John—"a youth of an Extraordinary Genius Carefully Improv'd by a Liberall Education"—who had died a decade earlier. In his 1775 will, Cornelius Van Schaack instructed his executors to set aside a fund for the education of his grandchildren. His son Peter, a lawyer, attended King's College, from which his grandson Henry Cruger Van Schaack also graduated.[59] Such generosity had costs.

"You do me great Honour, Sir, in presuming such favourable Things of my Administration," President Samuel Davies of New Jersey told the head of the Livingston clan in 1760. Such families built and maintained colonial academies. "If my future Management Should be so happy as to deserve the Continuance of your Charity, I shall esteem it the greatest Blessing I can enjoy in Life," Rev. Davies continued. A founder of the college, Peter Van Brugh Livingston served on the board for more than a decade, cementing a family connection to Princeton that lasted for generations.[60]

The Dutch Reformed and Presbyterian Livingston family generally sent their children to the colleges of the dissenting churches in New England and New Jersey. Before the American Revolution, two Livingston men governed New Jersey and a half dozen Livingston boys enrolled in the school. Six members of the family finished King's in the same period. After increasing his fortune in the Africa trade, Philip—whose ascendance at Livingston Manor was marked by the horrendous voyage of the *Wolf*—became an elder and deacon in the Dutch Reformed Church of New York City

He donated liberally to King's College, and in 1766 he became a founding trustee of the Dutch Reformed Queen's College. The high point of his public life came when he represented New York in the Continental Congress and signed the Declaration of Independence.[61]

A slave trading and slaveholding family with branches across the Northeast, the Ogdens fit the profile of the dynasties that came to rule colonial education. They descended from a patentee of Elizabeth, the first permanent European settlement in New Jersey. Originally Elizabethtown, this was the area where a small number of black people who fled Manhattan during the hysteria of 1741 were quickly rounded up and burned. It was also the birthplace of the College of New Jersey. Slave ownership in East Jersey was "common," and the area housed a number of active traders. In 1730 Captains John and David Ogden commissioned the schooner *Union* in New Jersey and launched their new ship on its first African voyage during Christmas week. Slave owners and dealers, the Ogdens were also generous patrons of the northeastern colleges. By the time Robert Ogden stepped down as a trustee of New Jersey, seven of his children and relatives had graduated. Despite the closing of King's College during the Revolution, the Ogdens established a family tradition there too, with at least three Ogden men taking degrees before the outbreak of the war. Two Ogden boys enrolled at Philadelphia within a few years of its founding.[62]

The American college was an extension of merchant wealth. In 1746 Philip Livingston, from the second generation of the family, donated the money for the Livingston Professorship in Divinity at Yale, the first such chair in the history of the struggling New Haven college, in gratitude for his sons' educations. Peter Van Brugh Livingston, his son, and Peter Schuyler also gave to Yale, where President Thomas Clap, who created the chair, kept close account of such patronage. It did not take long for the merchant families to become academic officers. For example, College of New Jersey treasurer David Ogden graduated from Yale in 1728, shortly before his uncles sent the *Union* on its first Africa voyage.[63]

Donations from Britain were also frequently linked to the slave economy. Samuel Holden, the director of the Bank of England, gave Yale a small library. His bank catered to the wealthy planters of the British West Indies. The officers of Harvard appointed John Lloyd Jr., the London financier and insurer, as their agent to collect on their behalf, a decision that likely responded to the benefactions pouring into British universities from West Indian planters and merchants. The College of William and Mary chose the London firm Perry, Lane, and Company, which had an extensive business with the slave colonies, as its representatives in Britain.[64]

In the decades before the American Revolution, merchants and planters became not just the benefactors of colonial society but its new masters. Slaveholders became college presidents. The wealth of the traders determined the locations and decided the fates of colonial schools. Profits from the sale and purchase of human beings paid for campuses and swelled college trusts. And the politics of the campus conformed to the presence and demands of slaveholding students as colleges aggressively cultivated a social environment attractive to the sons of wealthy families.

If you made me your wife, Sir, in time you may fill a
Whole town with our children, and likewise your villa.
I, famous for breeding, you, famous for knowledge,
I'll found a whole nation, you'll found a whole college.

—A POEM TO GEORGE BERKELEY, CA. 1725

Yesterday morning between three and four o'clock, I
was awakened by the cry of fire. . . . The [Princeton]
College fire engine and buckets being brought, all
possible means were used to extinguish the flames, but
to no purpose; the fire burnt till seven o'clock, when
the whole house laid in ashes. . . . The students upon
this occasion behaved with a becoming boldness which
does them honour. . . . The fire is supposed to have
been occasioned by the carelessness of a negro wench,
who left a candle burning when she went to bed.

—*PENNSYLVANIA PACKET*, (FEBRUARY 1, 1773)

I suppose you have heard before this that Princetown
College is burnt to the ground, tis supposed by some
of the students.

—ADRIANA BOUDINOT

CHAPTER 3

"The Very
Name of a West-Indian"

Atlantic Slavery and the Rise
of the American College

A seventeenth-century ship's surgeon who rises to captain his own commercial adventures to unknown and exotic lands could easily be spotted for a slave trader. Lemuel Gulliver studies at Cambridge University before apprenticing as a surgeon and completing his education at Leiden, Holland. He sails to the West Indies and the African coast. He is captured and has chances to kidnap, passes judgment upon alien cultures, and interferes in the domestic and foreign affairs of other nations in a world in which the qualities of ruthlessness and immorality, justice and generosity are distributed in counterintuitive ways. Britain is on trial in *Gulliver's Travels* (1726). Through Gulliver, Jonathan Swift exposes the appalling realities of the empire's unseemly commercial relationships. Gulliver discovers the humane and admirable traits of different beings. The inhabitants of these strange lands with their varied virtues and vices, strengths and weaknesses, triumphs and failures, expose the ugliness of the real world. When Gulliver returns to England, he declares his loyalty to the crown but pleads against sending the king's forces to these far-off places. England's colonial endeavors mocked its religion and its claims to civilization. "As those countries which I have described do not appear to have any desire of being conquered and enslaved, murdered or driven out by colonies; nor abound either in gold, silver, sugar, or tobacco," Gulliver counsels, "I did humbly conceive, they were by no means proper objects of our zeal, our valour, or our interest." Eighteenth-century English literature, including Daniel Defoe's *Robinson Crusoe* (1719) and *New Voyage Round the World* (1725), mimicked popular travel and exploration accounts and exposed how fully the British mind had turned toward the Atlantic.[1]

In 1765 the Reverend John Witherspoon published his own fantasy novel about a community of servants who form themselves into a corporation, or union, for their protection and to benefit their masters. Another of Swift's productions, a humorous advisory for servants, may have influenced Witherspoon, although there were other contenders. Located in the interior of Brazil, Witherspoon's servants are not and never were slaves. They use their union to acquire and seize greater control over the society. This combination had but two major goals, Witherspoon narrates: "the increase of their wages, and the diminution of their labour." In the end, these leveling impulses plunge them into despotism and generate the novel's few ironies. The laborers bestow fancy titles upon themselves for trifling accomplishments, invent wonderfully silly excuses for growing their salaries and dishonoring work, and bully or abuse each other into a social stagnation that opens them to an inevitable conquest from some foreign power. Witherspoon's novel lacks the humor of Jonathan Swift and the drama of Daniel Defoe, but the difference is not simply a matter of talent. The satire of Witherspoon's *History of a Corporation of Servants* is undermined by the author's ambivalence about colonialism and servitude.[2]

John Witherspoon spent virtually all of his first forty-five years in a narrow corridor, roughly seventy miles of the Scottish Lowlands, stretching from Fife on the east coast to Paisley on the west, where he acquired his education and ministerial experience. He watched as the Atlantic merchants gilded cities such as Glasgow and Edinburgh, transforming their universities, their populations, and their prospects. He took account of Scottish and Scots-Irish emigrants, including his own relatives, pouring from Britain into the Americas. The political philosopher Adam Smith was born the same year as Witherspoon, also in the Lowlands. Smith attended the University of Glasgow while Witherspoon enrolled at St. Andrews. Witherspoon then headed to Edinburgh and Smith to distant Oxford. Smith became professor of moral philosophy at Glasgow. Witherspoon took the pulpit of the church in neighboring Paisley. Atlantic slavery and the British imperial system framed their intellectual and professional lives. "Fortune never exerted more cruelly her empire over mankind, than when she subjected those nations of heroes to the refuse of the jails of Europe, to wretches who possess the virtues neither of the countries which they come from, nor of those which they go to," Smith protested against the enslavement of Africans by the "sordid master(s)" of Europe. He treated the subject again when he argued the economic irrationality of slavery in his *Wealth of Nations*. By that time, Witherspoon had chosen a radically different course: he had emigrated to the Americas to become a college president, a minor colonial proprietor, a slave owner, and a supplicant of the planter class.[3]

Nassau Hall at the College of New Jersey, now Princeton University
SOURCE: Library of Congress

In 1768 Benjamin Rush visited the home of Elizabeth Mont-gomery Witherspoon to convince her to let her husband take charge of the struggling College of New Jersey (Princeton). The young Pennsylvanian was in Scotland finishing his medical degree at the University of Edinburgh when the passing of President Samuel Finley left his alma mater in turmoil. Rush was a frequent dinner guest at the Witherspoons'. He believed the minister predisposed to moving to the Americas, but Elizabeth Witherspoon was not excited about the colonies. Rev. Witherspoon declined the offer more than once and even nominated other clergy for the presi-dency. "I think the College of New-Jersey would flourish, as much under him as ever it has done under any of his Predecessors," Rush assured a fellow graduate, praising the Scottish minister's fine man-ners, nimble mind, and broad intellectual interests. He compared Witherspoon to the two prior presidents: "He appears to be Mr. [Samuel] Davies and Dr. [Samuel] Finley united in one man." Rush was delighted that Rev. Witherspoon commanded the pulpit and preached without resorting to a written text for his sermons. The student's enthusiasm helped sway the Witherspoons. John Witherspoon resigned his church in Paisley, began raising money for their journey and for the college, sold his home, and prepared to depart. Several local families accompanied him. "I believe you must look out for an Island to settle a Colony[,] 4 or 5 families seem determined to go," the incoming president jested.[4]

That was no fantasy. An extended family that reached across Britain's colonial empire prepared the way for Witherspoon's jour-ney to North America and inspired new strategies for rescuing the College of New Jersey.

AN INQUIRY INTO THE NATURE AND CAUSES
OF THE WEALTH OF COLLEGES

Catholics dominated higher education in the first two centuries of the European invasion of the America, but Harvard enjoyed a vir-tual monopoly on the wealthy inhabitants of the Protestant colonies. Even the founding of academies in Virginia and Connecticut did little to break the Cambridge college's grip on the American elite. William and Mary operated as a regional college, and Yale lacked the facilities, staff, and connections to seriously rival Harvard.

The first potential challenge came from the West Indies. In 1710 General Christopher Codrington's bequest for a West Indian college was transferred to the Society for the Propagation of the Gospel in Foreign Parts (SPG)—a London-based missionary corporation chartered by William III in 1701—to supply the British colonies with orthodox ministers. Queen Anne's governor general in the Leeward Islands, Codrington had arranged for the SPG to receive perpetual funding from the labor of hundreds of enslaved black people.

> I give and bequeath my two Plantations in the Island of Barbados to the Society for the propagation of the Christian Religion in Foreign parts erected and established by my late Good master King William the third, and my Desire is to have the Plantations Continued Entire and three hundred negroes at Least always Kept thereon, and a Convenient Number of Professors and Scholars maintain'd.

The SPG held title to the plantations, people, and money. Christopher Codrington had designated funds to establish a college in Barbados. That endowment included more than three hundred enslaved black people on two estates totaling eight hundred acres. The general also left large gifts to Oxford University, his alma mater, to support its faculty, students, and religious missions.[5]

The Codrington experiment drew attention in New England and Britain. George Berkeley, the Anglican dean of Derry, Ireland, doubted that such a plan could work. An advisor to and supporter of several American schools, including Harvard, Yale, and, later, King's (Columbia), Berkeley had visions of establishing his own colonial academy. Burdened by "so much wealth and luxury," Barbados, he predicted, would ruin a college. Just provisioning faculty and scholars would be prohibitively expensive on an island where virtually every inch of soil had been turned to commercial agriculture under slave labor and where food and other necessities were generally imported. Money and privilege had corroded the

morals of the island Christians, who would be unsuitable neighbors for students. Rev. Berkeley warned that such proximity to
crass commercialism "might tempt the readers or fellows of the college to become merchants, to the neglect of their proper business."[6]

Hugh Hall Jr., a Barbadian who attended Harvard, confirmed
many of Berkeley's suspicions. He returned to the island to discover
that there was little for a Renaissance man to do. The son of a judge
and councilor, Hall was sent at age seven to live with his grandmother in Boston. In 1713 he graduated from Harvard and took a
master's degree three years later. His father then called on him to
apprentice in the family's merchant house. In 1718 the younger Hall
wrote his British factors confirming his successful entrance into the
slave trade: "We have sold ye Number of Seventy one Negroes, of
which Forty three are Men, seven Woemen, Fifteen Boys, & Six
Girls; whose whole Amount is Nineteen Hundred & thirty five
Pounds." Smallpox and dysentery reduced the number of survivors
and lessened their value, he confessed, although the investment still
proved profitable. Hall soon returned to Boston, where he built a
thriving merchant house, continued slave trading, and administered
his Barbadian plantations. "Several very likely Young Negro's of each
Sex just Arrived to be Sold by Mr. Hugh Hall[,] Merchant, on
Credit, with Good Security," reads a May 1728 advertisement in the
New-England Weekly Journal. Customers who came to his warehouse
could also buy West Indian rum, sugar, and goods from Europe.[7]

Several Harvard alumni and officers purchased slaves from other
graduates of the college in a fairly cozy commercial network. Hall
moved slaves into New England, the Mid-Atlantic, and the South.
For more than twenty years Thomas Hubbard of Boston served as
treasurer of Harvard. A 1721 graduate, Hubbard invested routinely
in slaving voyages and sold "fine young Negro Boys and Girls; also
Cotton Wool and Old West India Rum" from his Summer Street
home. "Sale of Three Negroes, Eight barrels of Sugar & one h[ogs]
h[ea]d of Rum," Hall recorded in one journal entry during a year in
which he sold scores of black people from Barbados alone. The
Reverand Benjamin Colman bought Frank, an enslaved man from
Barbados, through Hugh Hall. Rev. Colman served nearly fifty
years as an overseer of Harvard. He was also minister of the Brattle

Hugh Hall, Barbadian native, Harvard alumnus, and
prosperous slave trader
SOURCE: Metropolitan Museum of Art

Street Church and a governor of the New England Company. The fellows chose Colman to succeed John Leverett as president of Harvard, but the legislature declined to ratify his appointment over concerns about his religious orthodoxy.[8]

Although half of the graduates of the earliest colleges became ministers, that fact had little impact upon the pattern of alumni slaveholding. Northeastern parishes routinely gave black people to ministers, and divines bought and sold human beings, distributed slaves in their wills, advertised for runaways, and sold people at auction. A 1698 graduate, the Reverend Thomas Symmes, recorded the births of four enslaved people in his house. In the decade beginning in 1701, Harvard graduated at least twenty young men who became ministers and masters, virtually all of whom took pulpits in New England. Slaveholding clergy occupied some of the most influential churches in the colonies, including several in Boston, Charlestown, and Cambridge.[9]

Harvard-trained divines often dabbled in mastery. "His kindliness took such forms as the spending of hours in teaching his negro slaves, some of them raw from the Guinea Coast," a biographer noted of Benjamin Colman; however, that benevolence "did not prevent his advertizing them for sale 'on reasonable terms.'" In 1709, two years after his graduation, Thomas Prince boarded the *Thomas and Elizabeth* for a journey to Barbados. Prince was horrified by his first glimpse of Caribbean slavery. The Africans were "all absolute slaves, till kind Death . . . [wrenched the]m out of ye hands of Tyrannick masters" who had brazenly deprived black people of any chance at salvation or thoughts of a future independent of their owners'. Minister of South Church in Boston and a historian of New England, Prince possessed a thorough understanding of the intimate economic connections between New England and the British West Indies. Still, on August 9, 1729, Rev. Prince bought Ocraqua, an enslaved African carried to Boston on one of Hall's ships. The York minister Samuel Moody, a 1697 graduate, received a black woman as a gift from his congregation. The parishioners rethought the propriety of that gesture a year later and sold her for a male slave who could serve in the minister's house without raising suspicions. Rev. Moody also owned Dinah, an enslaved Indian woman.[10]

Harvard's West Indian ties paralleled New England's commercial and social connections to the British Caribbean. Dorothy Saltonstall and her husband, John Frizell, gave Harvard hundreds of pounds from a fortune built in the Barbados trade. Born in Windsor, Connecticut, Dudley Woodbridge finished his life as a Barbados planter. In 1717 Woodbridge, class of 1696, traveled to London, where he presented a grand scheme to the directors of the Royal African Company for restructuring the slave trade in the Caribbean. By regulating the quality of the slaves and licensing traders, the company could make commerce safer and more efficient, extend plantation slavery into the less developed islands, and increase profits. West Indian traders, including Hugh Hall, regularly complained that business in the islands was chaotic and poorly governed. The African Company accepted Woodbridge's plan and appointed him director general and attorney in Barbados with authority in the Windward Islands and Cuba.[11]

Cultivating this West Indian elite became an important task for any successful college administrator. Harvard's officers had earlier missed an opportunity with Woodbridge. "I formerly had intentions of sending my Eldest Son, Dudley, for New England," he wrote to Rev. Colman, "but now resolve him for London in a few days." Losing the tuition of an island official and slave trader was a major blow, worse still because Woodbridge was a native son and an alumnus. Woodbridge tried to mellow the impact by promising his two-year-old to Harvard. However, his uncle, the Reverend Timothy Woodbridge, had recently founded Yale College, where Timothy and Abigail Woodbridge sent their sons, and where the family redirected its giving.[12]

Administrators cherished the West Indians. Hall informed Colman that Barbados's ministers and planters had "miserably Neglected & Disregarded" General Christopher Codrington's bequest and instructions. Colman saw the philanthropic and missionary aims of the gift as a model for work in New England. Hall warned that there was little chance of raising a college in Barbados, and, he added, "I am Afraid the Pious Legacy of General Codrington's for the Propagation of the Gospel among our Poor Negroes here will be Imprudently Thrown away if not wickedly Murthered." Unfortunately, General Codrington had never visited "our Cambridge," Hall continued, since Harvard would have put the gift to better use. It was not until 1745 that the SPG and the governors founded Codrington College, thirty-five years after the bequest, as a small seminary.[13]

The general dedicated a fraction of his estate to educate a fraction of the enslaved population, but even that gesture was received poorly among the planters. Many leading white Barbadians had lived through the 1675 conspiracy, which involved slaves on the majority of the plantations. One of the chief conspirators came from the Halls' estate. In 1693, the year Hugh Hall Jr. was born, the enslaved population rose up again. The colonial government responded with a campaign of terror that included castrating dozens of black men. It is little wonder that his Barbados neighbors were gutting the Codrington grant. White Barbadians believed that Africans "had no

Codrington College in Barbados
SOURCE: New York Public Library

more Souls than Brutes, & were really a Species below Us," Hall
responded in disgust. Such scorn, coming from a slave trader and
slaveholder, was a telling measure of how rapidly racial ideas were
coalescing in the minds of Christian colonists throughout the
Americas. In the aftermath of the 1712 revolt in Manhattan, white
New Yorkers also stridently rejected the religious training of Africans, cursed the men who instructed them, and, as the Reverend
John Sharpe of the New York garrison lamented, developed "a vile
conceit that the Negroes have no immortal Souls but are a sort of
speaking brute destined by God to a State of Servitude."[14]

The southern plantations captured the imagination of Harvard's
students. An alumnus and the college librarian, John Gore abandoned the academic life to become a ship's captain. In the summer
of 1711, Gore was almost killed when a French privateer attacked his
ship off Antigua. Hugh Hall confided to President Leverett that he
was somewhat torn at having "strangely Metamorphosed from a
Student to a Merchant." Many alumni were making that choice. "If
you have a good Trade for Negroes [you] may purchase forty or
Fifty Negroes," William Ellery, a 1722 graduate, instructed Captain
Pollipus Hammond, "get most of them mere Boys and Girl[s], some
Men, let them be Young, [but] No very small Children." Ellery built

his merchant house in Newport, Rhode Island, where he launched multiple slaving ventures. During his final year at Harvard, Cotton Tufts "meditated on what I've learnt that's worth the knowing," and concluded that he had gained little. When Tufts graduated from Harvard in 1749, his ambition was to use "this small [college] Degree" to open "a Rich lasting & large store."[15]

Tufts had innumerable role models. In 1729 the Jamaican planter Leonard Vassall donated land in Boston for Trinity Church at about the same time that his son William enrolled at Harvard. In 1743 William inherited his family's plantations, which he governed from New England. Vassall sought a more genteel and learned life than he could lead in Jamaica, and the revenue from his Jamaican plantations and manufactories afforded him that leisure. In a single month he sent letters instructing his overseer to purchase thirty "choice new Negroes" and asking his retailers to find the best available translations of *The Iliad* and *The Odyssey*, a rare volume on rhetoric, and a complete leather-bound edition of Cicero's works in Latin: "If you cannot get the best Latin Paris edition do not send any." Vassall was unusual in his concern about the conditions on his Jamaican estates, routinely reminding his overseer and manager to avoid the excesses of violence that were so common on the islands and which he had seen during his childhood.

> I am glad ye have got the promise of the first Choice of 10 Ten Gold coast Negroes at £60 p[er] head, & hope by the time of this reaches you you'll have purchase the whole of the 80 new Negroes I desired ye would buy for my Estate. I greatly approve of your Method of managing my Estate particularly my Negroes, and am greatly Obliged to ye for your attention and earnestly beg the continuance of it. I am more & more persuaded of the propriety of having sufficient strength on my estate to do all the Work on it without hiring and without pushing or overworking the Negroes so as to hurt & discourage them.[16]

Many Harvard men built their careers on the Caribbean and Africa trades. By the end of the eighteenth century, Peter Chardon

Brooks was on his way to becoming the wealthiest man in New England, having amassed a fortune by insuring ships in the West Indies, Africa, Europe, and Asia trades. Brooks was named by his father, the Reverend Edward Brooks, after Peter Chardon, a friend and Harvard classmate who was the son of a successful Boston merchant and who died in the West Indies in October 1766, a few months before young Brooks's birth. Hugh Hall of Barbados and Boston and Peter Chardon Brooks of Medford and Boston typified a generation of planters, merchants, investors, and underwriters who rationalized and integrated the financial and commercial economies of the Atlantic world.[17]

PLANTING PREACHERS

Founded in 1670, South Carolina was, in Peter Wood's description, "the colony of a colony"—a beneficiary of the success, agricultural overdevelopment, and rigid hierarchy of Barbados, which caused many experienced islanders to move to the mainland. Not just the lower orders but wealthy planters relocated in hopes of expanding their holdings for future generations. About half of the early colonists came from the British West Indies, and Barbadians dominated that migration, bringing administrative skills, slaves, and money. More than half of the slaves came from Barbados and, as on the island, enslaved people soon were the majority of the population. The northward migration of the Barbadians helped to make Harvard the most influential college in the colonial South. The islanders and New England's Puritans had long been kindred colonial adventurers. William Sayle, the first governor of South Carolina, had earlier recruited Puritans to come to the Caribbean and now brought experienced island settlers to the new colony. In 1696 the South Carolina legislature codified the links between the colonies when it copied the Barbados slave code.[18]

From 1670 through 1715, English and Scottish immigrants sold as many as fifty thousand enslaved Indians to the British West Indies. In fact, they exported more enslaved people than they imported. The immigrants lacked capital. By trading with neighboring nations for furs and enemies captured during wars and raids, the Carolinians created the wealth to purchase enslaved Africans. "The four Indian Women with their two Children, put to sale on Satturday the 9th Instant, were sold together for seventy-five Pounds," notes a February 1717 entry in the journal of the Indian trade commissioners. The commissioners licensed agents with the authority "to trade, deal and barter within the English Settlements of this Government, with any Indians in Amity with the same, for Skins, Furs and Indian Slaves" and authorized outposts where friendly Indians could bring in goods, rest, and wait for other traders. One of the most important factories was in Cherokee country, where Indian captives were held before being marched into Charleston. The Indians-for-Africans trade reduced the risk of enslaved Indians fleeing to their own lands or inciting conflicts and brought a population of African slaves who lacked knowledge of the local geography and languages but possessed important agricultural skills, particularly in rice production.[19]

The Scottish immigrants at Stuarts Town were poor but formed commercial relationships with the Yamasee, who supplied them with Indian slaves from raids into Florida. The Yamasee acquired a range of goods, including arms and powder, that shifted the balance of power with their rivals. By the early eighteenth century, Yamasee and Creek raiding in Florida had destroyed the Apalachee and dealt a serious blow to Spain's Indian allies. Carolina's Indian slave trade reached Florida and the Mississippi Valley. The English armed the Chickasaw and conducted joint campaigns against the Arkansas and the Choctaw. West Indian planters could avoid taxes on servants since Indians were "duty free" in this intercolonial trade and such exchanges operated outside the monopoly of the Royal African Company. Two slave economies, one Indian and one African, built Carolina, and both escalated violence in the region, provoked an arms race between Native nations, and left innumerable communities destroyed and depopulated.[20]

Colonial officials had great difficulty controlling this volatile marketplace. The arming of allied nations adjusted relations between Native powers and between Europeans and Indians. The incentive among the British settlers to view all Native people as hostile added to the tensions. The commissioners struggled to keep settlers from enslaving friendly and free Indians living near the colonies. The Cherokee were particularly vulnerable. A large and well-armed nation, the Cherokee lodged numerous complaints about the capture and sale of their citizens. In 1713 Thomas Welch, who was authorized to trade with the Chickasaw, threatened a commissioner with a gun when he came "to sett free two free Indian Women and their Brother detained . . . as Slaves." The commissioners also had trouble regulating their factors and colonists, who routinely demanded that Indians deliver slaves as compensation for injuries, real and imagined, or as payment for debts.[21]

As the proprietors turned to the Caribbean to shape the political economy of Carolina, they gazed north to secure its spiritual well-being. In 1695 William Norman went to New England in search of ministers and missionaries. Joseph Lord, who graduated from Harvard in 1691, accepted the challenge. Lord joined a band of young men who headed south in December 1695. They formed Dorchester, along the Ashley River and about twenty miles from Charleston, with a grant of several thousand acres. Rev. Lord returned to New England to encourage other migrations, securing Hugh Adams, a fresh Harvard product, who assisted the Charleston church after the untimely death of Harvard's Benjamin Pierpont. Abigail Hinckley, the daughter of the governor of Plymouth, married Lord and joined him in the endeavor. The younger John Cotton, Harvard class of 1657, became the new pastor at Charleston. William Grosvenor, a 1693 graduate, left for Carolina after failing to raise a church in Brookfield, Massachusetts. Daniel Henchman, class of 1696, joined the original Ashley River settlement. Would-be Harvard president Benjamin Colman had planned to go to Carolina after his graduation but changed his mind when he got a chance to travel to London. Rev. Lord ministered in the colony for twenty years, eventually returning to New England when the Yamasee War—a two-year conflict beginning in 1715 between the English and several Indian nations—threatened the area and the consolidation of Anglican power in the colony made life increasingly uncomfortable for dissenters.[22]

Wherever the Barbadians traveled, Harvard followed. The

college showered South Carolina with its graduates, who served as ministers, doctors, lawyers, teachers, and tutors. After graduating in 1710—as the Carolina colonies were separating, north and south—William Little began a career as a merchant and lawyer in North Carolina, where he later became chief justice of the colony's supreme court. Jonathan Belcher, a 1699 alumnus, pleaded in England for the governorship of the young colony. When the Reverend Josiah Smith, class of 1725, suffered a stroke that limited his ministry at the Presbyterian Church in Charleston—one of innumerable slaveholding churches in the Americas—the congregation hired Samuel Fayerweather, class of 1743, as an assistant pastor.[23]

On the eve of the American Revolution, Josiah Quincy Jr. took a spring journey to South Carolina to recoup his health. "His plantations, negroes, gardens, & c. are in the best order I have seen," Quincy observed while relaxing at Joseph Allston's Oaks estate. In a letter to his brother Samuel, he complained that liquor outpaced stories and jokes at every table and any worthy topic was always vulnerable to being displaced by a discussion of "rice, indigo, Negroes, & horses." During his three-month stay, the father of a future Harvard president documented the "mischief" of slavery and the undemocratic realities of planter rule, but he also vacationed with the plantation aristocracy by following the commercial and religious ties between Harvard and Atlantic slavery.[24]

"YOU'LL FOUND A WHOLE COLLEGE"

At a time when colonial colleges were actively courting merchants and planters for survival, George Berkeley insisted that academies had to avoid the influences of that crude economic gentry. Britain had financed colonial schools, churches, and missions in the seventeenth century, but the rise of the North American merchants freed colonists to fund their own projects without metropolitan interference. The minister unfolded an ambitious plan to open a seminary independent of the commercial centers at the exact moment when merchants were coming to dominate the British colonies.

In the 1720s Rev. Berkeley won Parliament's support for his

proposal to build an Anglican college on the island of Bermuda to advance the Christian faith in the plantations and increase religious orthodoxy. He sought a large enough supply of Native children to allow him, in little time, to graduate about a dozen Indian ministers with master's degrees each year. Rev. Berkeley planned to attract youngsters from the friendly communities near the English settlements and kidnap children from hostile nations. He warned that these young "savages" should be no older than ten—mature enough to have mastered their native languages, and immature enough to have not fully embraced the "evil habits" of their nations. Snatched as children and educated at St. Paul's College in Bermuda, these Indians would return home as "men of their own blood and language" to stamp out the vestiges of indigenous civilization and cultural resistance. In 1729 George Berkeley arrived in Newport, Rhode Island, to wait for the Royal Treasury to release £20,000 that had been appropriated for his project. He bought a farm, renamed it Whitehall, and began buying enslaved black people.[25]

The deployment of academies to subdue Indians repeats in colonial history. Just a few years before he became provost of the College of Philadelphia (University of Pennsylvania), the Reverend William Smith urged Protestants to adopt Jesuitical—that is, mischievously cunning—tactics against the Indians. The plan was similar to Berkeley's: settle a few scholars among the Native nations of New York, where they could master the Indian languages and then build "one good School for Education." However, Rev. Smith was far more comfortable relying upon the wealth of the commercial elite. Rev. Smith believed that educating Native children would catalyze cultural transformations in Indian country, permanently tilting the sympathies of these nations toward the English.

> In these Schools, some of the most Ingenious and Docile of the young Indians might be instructed in our Faith and Morals, and Language, and in our Methods of Life and Industry, and in some of those Arts which are most useful. . . . To civilize our Friends and Neighbours;—to strengthen our Allies and our Alliance;—to adorn and dignify Human Nature;—to save Souls from Death; to

promote the Christian Faith, and the Divine Glory, are the Motives.

Before he became the president of the College of New Jersey, the Reverend Samuel Davies used his success evangelizing black Virginians to show the practicality of a new "scheme" to send missionaries and teachers to the Cherokee and the Catawba. "This little harvest among the Africans," Davies prayed, "is but a Presage of one more extensive among the Indian Natives of America."[26]

Berkeley objected only to the location of such schools. Harvard and Yale, the seminaries of the dissenting churches, had disappointing results and "have so long subsisted to little or no purpose," he bluntly concluded. Poorly trained American preachers and the castoffs of the English clerical community preyed upon the colonists, to the detriment of the faith. Samuel Johnson of Connecticut and Stephen Hopkins of Providence traveled to Newport to attend meetings with Berkeley, decades before they became founding officers of King's College and the College of Rhode Island (Brown), respectively. Berkeley planned St. Paul's as an Anglican seminary removed from the corrupting influences of avaricious settlers. Traders and planters did not dominate Bermuda as they did Barbados, Jamaica, and the other British possessions. Berkeley particularly doubted Barbados with its "high trade" and "dissolute morals." Bermuda had ample supplies of food and other necessities, and it was independent of but still accessible to the more populous colonies.[27]

In 1732 Berkeley's Bermuda college plan unraveled after political transitions in England eliminated his funding. The defeated priest gave Whitehall, which totaled about ninety-six acres and was valued at £3,000, to Yale. The rents from this small slave plantation funded Yale's first scholarship, for the best students in Greek and Latin, and its first graduate-level courses. A member of the Yale class of 1733, Eleazar Wheelock—later an Indian missionary and founder of Dartmouth College—was the first recipient of the Berkeley grant. The faculty awarded the Berkeley scholarship to several young men who became college presidents, including Aaron Burr, later of New Jersey, and Thomas Clap of Yale.[28]

Berkeley also distributed his supplies. He gave Harvard

a selection of literary, philosophical, and theological texts. Yale received a large library, which Thomas Clap praised as the best single collection to cross the Atlantic. Yale also got portraits from Berkeley's holdings, and a share of the subscriptions for St. Paul's. (The trustees later named a section of the campus and one of the residential colleges for Bishop Berkeley.) "The daily increase of learning and religion in your seminary of Yale College give me very sensible pleasure, and an ample recompense for my poor endeavors to further those good ends," Berkeley wrote to Rev. Clap.[29]

The idea of separating the religious and commercial cultures of the colonies effectively died with Berkeley's project. In 1738 Chauncey Whittelsey won the Berkeley scholarship at Yale, which he used to finish his education and acquire a tutorship. A few years later, he declined invitations to pastor churches, resigned his academic post, and became a merchant.[30]

"THE VERY NAME OF A WEST-INDIAN"

In 1759 the trustees of King's College sent solicitations to select "gentlemen in the several Islands in the West Indies." Likely influenced by George Berkeley, the governors promoted the New York school as a royalist institution—unflinchingly loyal to the crown, a tool for bolstering Anglican authority in the British colonies, and a check on the power of the dissenting churches. A few years after their initial plea, the trustees were recruiting West Indian agents: Richard and William Moore in Barbados; Henry Livingston, Tileman Cruger, and Daniel Moore in Jamaica; Josiah Martin and David Williams in Antigua; and William Coventry and John Willett in St. Christopher. The board authorized multiple West Indies campaigns, using paid and volunteer lobbyists, during the following years.[31]

"The stupidity of many of our Gov[ernor]s is such that it looks as if they would let their Coll[ege] come to nothing," President Samuel Johnson complained to his son in 1762. Rev. Johnson accused the trustees of injuring the college by neglecting meetings and privileging fund-raising. The board cared little about academic matters. The prior graduating class had had only three students, all from elite local families. "But what need for so many Tutors for so few scholars?" the president challenged. In 1762 the trustees solicited the archbishop of Canterbury, the boards of the universities in Oxford and Cambridge, the Royal Society, the Antiquary Society, the Lord of Trade and Plantations, the Society for the Propagation of the Gospel in Foreign Parts, and the Society for the Encouragement of Arts, Manufactures, and Commerce, while also approving another Caribbean campaign and authorizing James Jay to seek donations in Europe. A year later they accepted Rev. Johnson's resignation and installed a new president: the Reverend Myles Cooper, a twenty-five-year-old Anglican priest who had recently arrived as professor of moral philosophy, earned the moniker "Rambling Cooper" for his eagerness to travel for fund-raising or any other purpose, and lacked Johnson's intellectual gravity and academic myopia. Cooper and the governors significantly expanded the college, added a medical school, and, on

President Myles Cooper of King's College
SOURCE: Columbia University

the eve of the American Revolution, initiated a plan to draw all the
colleges in New England and the Mid-Atlantic into a single Anglican university governed from New York.[32]

Such fantastic designs reflected an unbounded confidence in the
power of the slave economy. John and Isaac Lawrence were successful New York merchants, the former a trustee of King's and the latter a graduate of New Jersey. Their family business had connections
to the Caribbean and South America, and included a brother, William, a planter in Demerara, Guyana. That trade funded their social
lives: public offices, college and hospital trusteeships, and serving,
under Philip Livingston's presidency, as board members and officers
of the New York arm of the First Bank of the United States.[33]

In the second half of the eighteenth century, American colleges
faced south. The board of Rhode Island sent Hezekiah Smith, himself a trustee, to canvass the large Baptist communion in South
Carolina and the congregations in the neighboring colonies. In 1770
the Reverend Eleazar Wheelock settled in Hanover, New Hampshire, to build Dartmouth. For decades he had kept an Indian school
in Connecticut to supply Native nations with trained ministers,
improve the security of the colonies, and extend his political and
social influence. His marriages—to Sarah Maltby, the daughter of
the famed Connecticut minister John Davenport and the widow of
a ship's captain, and Mary Brinsmead—increased his social status
and property. He used his social ties to solicit donors in the colonies
and in Europe. In 1765 he sent the Mohegan minister Samson Occom, his first Indian student, on a two-year fund-raising tour of
Britain. Within months of his arrival in Hanover, Rev. Wheelock
accepted his first black student, Caleb Watts, whom he began
privately preparing for a mission to the West Indies.[34]

College officers sought slave traders and slaveholders as governors, competed for the fees of young men from slave-owning families, and sent emissaries to the plantations in search of gifts and
students. Struggling to meet their debts, the board of the College
of Philadelphia directed Provost William Smith to appeal to the
wealthier residents of South Carolina, where the school, particularly through its medical program, had social connections. Smith
was an Anglican priest and, because of the Barbados migration,

Anglicans had come to power in South Carolina. The provost returned early in 1772 with more than £1,000 in subscriptions. Solicitations to the prosperous families of Jamaica and the other British West Indian islands quickly followed. This time the trustees dispatched Professor John Morgan, a member of the first undergraduate class and a founder of the medical school. Morgan secured £6,000 in one trip.[35]

Rev. Smith's prayers for students naturalized these transactions. Instructing his students to pray for all colleges, seminaries, and academies that advanced the faith, he noted that each person, no matter how rich or mean, had to excel at his or her station for Christian institutions to blossom. Campuses revealed the divine plan beneath even the most basic social hierarchies. "Bless all Orders of Men amongst us, from the highest to the lowest," he told his boys. "Lord give them all Grace in their several Stations to be instrumental to the Spreading abroad of thy holy Christian Religion, and promoting the publick Good."[36]

More than one Philadelphian was canvassing the British Caribbean. "The Brig[.] *Nancy*, Capt. Hanse, sailed last Saturday for Jamaica, in whom went Passenger Dr. Hugh Williamson, of this City. His Business, we hear, is to collect Benefactions for the Academy at Newark," reported the *Pennsylvania Chronicle*. A member of the first graduating class of Philadelphia, Williamson studied for the Presbyterian ministry and then became professor of mathematics at the college. He left in 1764 to study medicine under William Cullen at Edinburgh, finishing his medical degree at Utrecht, Holland. Now a charter trustee of the New Ark Academy (University of Delaware), he sailed for the Caribbean in search of donors and scholars. The board had also taken subscriptions in Maryland and South Carolina, but there was diminishing value to vying for patrons who had repeatedly been petitioned by other colleges. To lay the ground for his tour, Dr. Williamson penned an address to the people of Jamaica that celebrated the New Ark mission and the advantages of an education in Delaware. Besides lower tuition, the academy offered a comfortable and safe environment for training young minds. "The noise and tumult of such places are unfriendly to study, they are dangerous to the morals of youth," he wrote of the urban centers of Europe and North America while lauding the serenity of Delaware.[37]

By the early eighteenth century, North Carolinians were using slavery to fund education, and leaving money, rents, and whole plantations to endow schools. In the 1750s Presbyterian settlers established advanced academies, and in 1767 the Reverend David Caldwell opened a "log college"—a Presbyterian frontier school—in Greensboro. Presbyterian slaveholders and missionaries combined to charter the University of North Carolina (1789), the nation's first public university. William Richardson Davie led the drive for a charter in the state legislature, and he enjoyed the support of prominent planters and politicians like Benjamin Smith, who donated twenty thousand acres of land. Joseph Caldwell, a 1791 graduate of New Jersey, became a professor at and later the president of the new university. In 1795 David Ker, a Scots-Irish Presbyterian who graduated from Trinity College in Dublin, became the first professor at North Carolina. The following year, Ker left with his wife, Mary Boggs, who was born in Ireland, to become a Mississippi cotton planter.[38]

By midcentury Harvard's monopoly over West Indian students and donors crumbled as Atlantic commerce multiplied the economic and social links between the mainland and the Caribbean. Judah Monis, the first instructor of Hebrew at Harvard, had been a merchant and rabbi in Jamaica, where a number of the undergraduates originated. Yale's trustees began raking the Caribbean for donors. There were other attractions. George Whitefield Kirkland, twin brother of Harvard president John Thornton Kirkland, became a Caribbean merchant and worked as a mercenary in South America to dig himself and his father—Samuel Kirkland, the founder of Hamilton College—out of debt. Both twins had attended Dartmouth.[39]

West Indian and southern plantation families were among the founders of the midcentury colleges and well represented in their governments, faculties, and student bodies. The officers of New Jersey tried to escape the competition for pupils in New England and the Mid-Atlantic by wooing the children of the southern and Caribbean gentry. Before he turned to the planters, the Reverend John Witherspoon had unsuccessfully tried to use friendships forged during his visit to Holland, prior to emigrating to the

Americas, to convince the leaders of the Dutch Reformed Church to abandon the new Queen's College (Rutgers) in New Brunswick and partner in the College of New Jersey.[40]

"The very name of a West-Indian has come to imply in it great opulence," wrote Rev. Witherspoon in a rhetorical bow before the white inhabitants of the British Caribbean. In 1772 the trustees approved a Caribbean campaign and appointed Witherspoon's son, James, who had graduated two years earlier, and the Reverend Charles Beatty as their West Indies agents. President Witherspoon's missive to the plantations laid out the appeal: It was safer for planters to send their children to New Jersey than to England, he cautioned, where unscrupulous men preyed upon privileged youngsters from the Americas. An education at Nassau Hall had other advantages. Princeton had all the comforts of urban life without "the many temptations in every great city, both to the neglect of study and the practice of vice." The latter comment was aimed especially at New York and Philadelphia, but also at New Haven and Cambridge. And if colonial colleges were dangerous, then British universities were damned. In the colonies, teachers lived on campus and supervised the students, he explained, while English universities were too large and too decentralized for instructors to properly guide the scholars. New Jersey was close enough to the Caribbean to allow parents to visit and expect regular communication, but distant enough to keep students from running home and becoming idle. Rev. Beatty died shortly after he arrived in Barbados, and the trustees quickly formed a new committee to plan another West Indies campaign. How much income they raised in the Caribbean is unclear, but Witherspoon drafted forms for donating money and property, and the number of West Indian students at the college increased in the following years.[41]

Rev. Witherspoon had his own colonial investments. He authored his appeal to the British Caribbean at the same time that he was using his name to recruit displaced Highlanders to take up tenancies through his Nova Scotia land partnership. In league with John Pagan, a Glasgow merchant, Witherspoon lured Scottish tenants to North America with free passage. A historian of the Scottish clearances highlighted this particular investment as evidence of the "real abuses" suffered by people forcibly displaced and pushed to emigrate during the systematic transformations of tenancy and landholding in the Highlands. Such forced émigrés were vulnerable to exploitation, and Witherspoon's project was rife with it. In the summer of 1773, the passengers of the *Hector* departed for Nova Scotia too late to clear ground for farming and only to discover on arrival that their allotted territories were inland and unsuitable. Tradition holds that they physically took supplies from Witherspoon's agents, left a receipt for these materials, and suffered through a string of desperate seasons. President Witherspoon later invested his Nova Scotia profits in new lands in New Hampshire.[42]

THE WITHERSPOON LEGACY IN AMERICA

"Killed, people say, by family troubles—contentions, wrangling, ill blood, among those nearest and dearest to her," Mary Chesnut gossiped in September 1861 after learning of the death of Betsey Witherspoon, a prominent widow of Society Hill, South Carolina. "Cousin Betsey" became a greater topic of discussion than the Civil War during the following days. The local elite, some relatives, shed tears over the loss, but suspicions that Betsey Witherspoon had been killed soon transformed their mourning into rage. "Murdered by her own people. Her negroes," Chesnut cried. Witherspoon's son hired a detective, and other relatives demanded that the slaves be hanged or burned. Confessions revealed a new version of the events: John Witherspoon had learned that his mother's servants had taken her china, silver, and linens to a party in a neighboring town while she was away from the estate. He came to the house to accuse them and threatened to return the next day to deliver whippings. That night the servants took action, according to the son, smothering the elderly woman in her sleep and arranging the scene to suggest a natural death, but an examination of the corpse and the scene found bruising and some blood. "These are horrid brutes—savages, monsters," Chesnut wrote in shock as memories of other uprisings and plots among enslaved people filled her mind and her diary. She cursed New England for its slaving past, northerners for their anti-slavery righteousness, and "those pernicious Africans," upon whom she wished a fate that most white people reserved for Indians: "free them or kill them, improve them out of the world."[43]

The Witherspoons of Society Hill were part of President John Witherspoon's family web. In 1732 a large group of Witherspoons, including a second cousin named Gavin, had left the Scottish colonies in Ireland for the Americas. They decided upon South Carolina, where the proprietors were recruiting white settlers with offers of large land grants. Branches of the Witherspoon family were already there and, in the following year, more Witherspoons arrived from Ireland and Scotland. It was the Witherspoons who helped bring Presbyterianism to Carolina even as Harvard divines were rushing into the colony. Gavin Witherspoon's sons became legislators and his grandsons matriculated at South Carolina College (University of South Carolina). There were more than a hundred thousand enslaved people in the Tidewater region. The Witherspoons acquired numerous plantations and significant wealth, and some later fought and died for the Confederacy. Grandson John Dick Witherspoon and his wife, Elizabeth "Betsey" Boykin Witherspoon, had owned as many as five hundred black people by the time her body was discovered in September 1861.[44]

The long, broad shadow of the great Scottish minister John Witherspoon has obscured the prominent role of his relatives, including his sons, daughter, and grandchildren, in the story of American slavery. Rev. Witherspoon used the family networks of the Scottish diaspora to revolutionize higher education in America. By the era of the Civil War, his Presbyterian communion had brought the American college to the banks of the Mississippi River by carrying it on the backs of enslaved black people.[45]

Witherspoons were immigrating to the Americas before the divine agreed to leave Paisley, Scotland, for Princeton, New Jersey. President Witherspoon helped reconstitute this kin network while traveling and raising funds for the college. His near and distant relations included planters, merchants, and statesmen in Virginia, the Carolinas, Alabama, Tennessee, Florida, Kentucky, Texas, and the Caribbean. By the time the diarist Mary Chesnut recorded her Civil War experiences, at least four generations of the president's family were wound into many of the wealthiest families of the South.[46]

Witherspoons had spread throughout the colonies. Rev. Witherspoon named his youngest surviving son after David, his favorite brother and a West Indies merchant. Dr. Witherspoon's boys attended New Jersey during his presidency. David became a lawyer and then married the wealthy widow Mary Jones Nash of North Carolina, daughter of Governor Abner Nash. With that union David Witherspoon acquired the largest holding of slaves, 113 people, in New Bern, and set himself on the path to becoming chief justice of the North Carolina Supreme Court. A founding trustee of the college, the merchant Peter Van Brugh Livingston and his brother-in-law William Alexander helped make New Bern the center of a trade in furs and naval stores with New York. David Witherspoon's will distributed slaves and land to his children, and directed that three slaves be hired out and the income from a plantation with slaves be designated to pay for his son, John, to attend college in Princeton. (The grandson of the president ultimately chose the University of North Carolina.) Rev. Witherspoon's estranged son John junior, a medical doctor, settled in South Carolina with a distant cousin. Daughter Frances married the Charleston, South Carolina, physician, historian, and legislator Dr. David Ramsey, a graduate of New Jersey.[47]

Outnumbered only by enslaved Africans, more than one hundred thousand Scots-Irish immigrants—Scottish Presbyterians who left the Ulster Plantation in Ireland—had made the journey to North America in the sixty years before the Revolution. They clustered along the westernmost British settlements, particularly in Pennsylvania, and then migrated south and west to the Carolinas, Georgia, Tennessee, and Kentucky. Samuel Finley, Witherspoon's predecessor at the College of New Jersey, arrived in this wave. In his two-decade reign as governor of North Carolina, Gabriel Johnston, a Scot and a former professor at St. Andrews University in Scotland, pushed the legislature to accept a common school system and began the first movement for a university in the colony. Turmoil in the heavily Presbyterian Scottish Lowlands pushed rural tenants into the migrations. The transformation of landholding, tenancy and land use, the imposition of a cash economy, and escalating rents broke up Highlands clans, creating, by the 1760s, new migrations to eastern Canada and North Carolina. About ten thousand Highlanders left for North America in the decade after the Seven Years' War, and such outmigrations continued into the nineteenth century.[48]

John Witherspoon decided that the real competition between colleges would be determined not in New England or the Mid-Atlantic but in the southern and Caribbean plantations. When he had arrived in Princeton on August 12, 1768, John Witherspoon found "the low state of the College" and chastised his Presbyterian communion: "What a shame it was that while Episcopalians & Dutch and all others had endowed their colleges . . . only [we] should be in a desperate State." He brought three hundred new library volumes from Holland and London. Other books were on order, and the range of topics reflected the new president's liberal intellectual leanings. He established a feeder program—a grammar school under his authority and styled on an academy in Glasgow. Rev. Witherspoon began a comprehensive restructuring of the college, with an enhanced curriculum and frequent, lengthy fund-raising trips. He had the Rev. John Rodgers of New York introduce him to prominent New Englanders. Witherspoon then presided at his first commencement, and swiftly departed for the South to raise money and find students.[49]

Princeton was a useful marketing tool. Founded to defend religious freedom, the College of New Jersey under Witherspoon forged intimate ties to human slavery. With high proportions of slaveholding families, Princeton was among the most welcoming places in the northern colonies to the sons of planters. A biographer boasted of the minister's striking success at attracting the children of the colonial elite: Virginia's Washington, Randolph, Lee, and Madison lines; the Macon and Hawkins families of North Carolina; Reeds from Delaware; Livingstons, Stocktons, and Patersons from New Jersey; and the Morris and Van Rensselaer families of New York. The pattern of recruitment and enrollment at New Jersey conformed to the geography of American slavery. The percentage of young men from the South more than doubled during Witherspoon's tenure, while the proportion of students from elite backgrounds more than tripled. The population of students from

New Jersey fell as the president engineered classes with slaveholding majorities, including prominent Virginians such as Henry Lee Jr., future United States president James Madison, and Caleb Baker Wallace, later a minister and college founder. "I learn from Messrs Madison & Wallace how much I am indebted to you for your favourable Opinions & Friendship," Witherspoon wrote to Henry Lee Sr., "the Continuance of which I will do best to deserve."[50]

When the American Revolution began, William and Mary was the only college in the South, but seventeen colleges were founded in that region by the end of the eighteenth century. A Scot, James Blair, was the key figure in the establishment of William and Mary, an Anglican college, and Scottish Presbyterians were overrepresented among the founders and governors of southern colleges between the Revolution and the end of the century. The third-largest Christian church—but considerably smaller than the Baptists and Methodists—the Presbyterians built more colleges than any other denomination in pre–Civil War America.[51]

Scottish migrations informed Witherspoon's vision; ultimately, the Scottish influx and the Presbyterian ascendance helped the Princeton college supplant Harvard as the most influential institution in the South. Witherspoon turned his students into an army of preachers and educators who pursued the Scottish and Scots-Irish pioneers. These graduates bound the Presbyterian communion across regions and became Witherspoon's ambassadors. Affirming a commitment to education that defined the Scottish Enlightenment, the Presbyterians imposed themselves upon the intellectual and political cultures of the colonies. Presbyterians, for example, were overrepresented among tutors in the South. Well-to-do planters and merchants routinely turned to college presidents to find "suitable" scholars, and President Witherspoon used these requests as opportunities to solidify ties to the southern elite.[52]

In 1773 Colonel Henry Lee—the grandfather of General Robert E. Lee—asked his son to help locate a tutor for the children of their family friend Robert Carter, of the Nomini Hall plantation. Henry junior recommended Philip Vickers Fithian, a Connecticut native who had just graduated from New Jersey. "Dr. Witherspoon is very fond of getting a person to send to him," a friend wrote. The young man met with the president on the morning of August 9 to hear about the job: teaching English to Colonel Carter's five daughters, and English, Latin, and Greek to two of his sons and a nephew. It was a generous offer: £35 sterling per year, room, board, and the use of a handsomely equipped library, a horse, and a slave. With Witherspoon's blessing, Fithian accepted and prepared to leave for Westmoreland County, Virginia, in the fall.[53]

Young Fithian recoiled from the cruelty inflicted on enslaved people and the bravado of southern male culture. In one particularly poignant moment, he returned to his room to record the gruesome boasts of a dinner guest:

> For Sulleness, Obstinancy, or Idleness, says he, Take a Negro, strip him, tie him fast to a post; take then a sharp Curry-Comb, & curry him severely til he is well scrap'd; & call a Boy with some dry Hay, and make the Boy rub him down for several Minutes, then salt him, & unlose him. He will attend to his Business, (said the inhuman Infidel) afterwards!—But savage Cruelty does not exceed His next diabolical Invention—To get a Secret from a Negro, says he, take the following Method—Lay upon your Floor a large thick plank, having a peg about eighteen Inches long, of hard wood, & very Sharp, on the upper end, fixed fast in the plank—then strip the Negro, tie the Cord to a staple in the Ceiling, so that his foot may just rest on the sharpened Peg, then turn him briskly round, and you would laugh (said our informer) at the Dexterity of the Negro, while he was relieving his Feet on the sharpen'd Peg!

Fithian lasted only a year. John Peck, another of Witherspoon's students, replaced him. Born in Deerfield, New Jersey, Peck had little trouble adjusting to plantation society. He easily adapted to living off black people's labor and fully embraced southern civilization, eventually marrying Anne Tasker Carter and settling in Richmond County, Virginia, with a gift of land and slaves from the colonel.[54]

New Jersey alumni were key architects of the academic

revolution in the South. They organized Transylvania College
(1783) in Lexington, Kentucky, the first college west of the Alleghenies. Governor Thomas Jefferson and the Virginia legislature provided the charter, a small band of proprietors negotiated with the
Cherokee to secure the territory, and the Reverends John Todd
and Caleb Baker Wallace, both graduates of New Jersey, joined
the board. Princeton men were the most conspicuous delegation
promoting the University of Georgia (1785). New Jersey graduates
also established the University of Tennessee (1794). Before the Revolution Presbyterians had supported the ill-fated Queen's College
in Charlotte, North Carolina. In 1771 Governor William Tryon
and the legislature chartered the college—funded by a levy on liquor in Mecklenburg County—but their act was rejected in London. Princeton men were the decisive lobby behind the chartering
of the University of North Carolina, and one of them, David Witherspoon, was serving in the North Carolina legislature during the
debates about the university. In 1794 New Jersey graduates chartered Greeneville College (Tusculum) in Tennessee.[55]

Products of a northern academy funded by Atlantic slave traders,
New Jersey alumni were ready for the task of planting colleges
among slaveholders. Bondage subsidized these labors. Born in Ireland and raised in Pennsylvania, John Todd entered the second
class at New Jersey. After graduation, the presbytery assigned him
to an underserved district outside Richmond, Virginia. The "frontier minister" helped found Hampden-Sydney College (1783) and
Transylvania. Todd also acquired more than fourteen enslaved
black people and twenty thousand acres of land. Alexander Martin,
class of 1756, served as the first president of the board of trustees for
the University of North Carolina. A native of New Jersey, Martin
had taken a well-worn professional path. He had a long business and
public career, served three terms as the governor of North Carolina,
and owned a plantation with nearly fifty slaves. Samuel Spencer, a
member of the 1759 New Jersey class, was also on the board of the
new University of North Carolina. Born in Connecticut, he went
south after college and amassed a personal estate that included five
thousand acres of land and about twenty slaves.[56]

Reproducing New Jersey's educational and theological style by recruiting its graduates as trustees, faculty, and tutors, the new Presbyterian colleges maintained close executive and organizational subservience to Princeton. Samuel Stanhope Smith, born and raised in Chester County, Pennsylvania, gained his administrative and teaching experience at Hampden-Sydney. President Witherspoon sent his son David to assist. In 1775 Rev. Smith married Ann Witherspoon, daughter of the president, and later earned a professorship at the College of New Jersey. In 1795 Smith succeeded his father-in-law as president. Similarly, in 1812 the trustees of Princeton Theological Seminary elected the Reverend Archibald Alexander, a past president of Hampden-Sydney, as their first president. Rev. Alexander was educated at Liberty Hall Academy (Washington and Lee), and he began his career as a plantation tutor.[57]

A moral comfort with bondage and a willingness to use the slave economy to spread the denomination facilitated the southern and westward march of New Jersey's alumni. In 1782 Witherspoon's students founded Liberty Hall in Lexington, Virginia, as the first southern franchise of the Princeton college. The board comprised New Jersey alumni, including Caleb Baker Wallace, the primary fund-raiser. The trustees bought and sold black people as part of their endowment, and leased their surplus black workers to raise additional cash. A surviving advertisement records this relationship. Liberty Hall's trustees posted bills announcing that they were hiring out "twenty likely Negroes belonging to Washington College: consisting of Men, Women, Boys and Girls, many of them very valuable," for the following year from the front of the courthouse in Lexington.[58]

President Witherspoon made the College of New Jersey the intellectual headquarters of the Scottish and Scots-Irish communities in America, turning a young northern school into a southern and West Indian intellectual and cultural force. The contest was not won, but the competition was changed forever. Harvard, William and Mary, Yale, Philadelphia, King's, Queen's, Rhode Island, and Dartmouth launched new campaigns for the loyalty of wealthy planters and traders.

Given their access to these colleges, white colonists in the West Indies and the South had little need for local schools. The wealthy

Sea Captains Carousing in Surinam by John Greenwood. Chancellor Stephen Hopkins, College of Rhode Island (Brown), is sleeping at the table next to his brother, the slave ship's captain Esek Hopkins.

SOURCE: Saint Louis Art Museum

planters of South Carolina sent their sons north, which allowed them to delay establishing advanced academies until the nineteenth century. In 1774 Edward Long accused Jamaica's planters and officials of failing to fund academies, thereby causing the racial declension of white people. Elite white women were sent abroad for education and, therefore, had some culture, Long continued, but the majority of the white women spoke "drawling, dissonant gibberish" and acquired the "aukward carriage and vulgar manners" of enslaved black women. Despite its wealth, by the late eighteenth century Barbados had but a few dozen teachers on the whole island. The historian Eric Williams found that the entire educational infrastructure of the British Caribbean colonies comprised little more than Codrington College and a single secondary school in Jamaica.[59]

It was the stark and rigid stratification of colonial society that John Witherspoon exploited to stabilize the College of New Jersey. It was the security that human slavery provided free men, the wealth that slave traders and slaveholders could generate, and the social networks of plantation economies that brought Witherspoon to the American academy and that carried the American academy into modernity.

In a quarter century at the helm of the College of New Jersey, Rev. Witherspoon instructed hundreds of young men who became leaders of Revolutionary America. His protégés included President James Madison, twenty United States senators, three justices of the Supreme Court, thirteen governors, twenty-three congressmen, and scores of ministers, college presidents and professors, and military officers. One scholar summed up his influence: "Dr. Witherspoon not only led his students, but all the Scotch and Scotch-Irish Presbyterians of the country, bodily into the Revolutionary movement."[60]

In 1776 the Reverend John Witherspoon signed the Declaration of Independence, marshaling the dissenting tradition of his own Presbyterian faith in support of the cause of rebellion and calling upon his antityrannical and anti-English roots in defense of American freedom. He and his contemporaries had established their own intellectual freedom upon human bondage. They had also bound the nation's intellectual culture to the future of American slavery and the slave trade.

To answer for their Master's Blood,
which they've unjustly spilt;
And if not Pardon'd, sure they must,
Remain with all their Guilt.

—"A FEW LINES ON OCCASION OF THE UNTIMELY
END OF MARK AND PHILLIS" (1755)

For Sale. A fine MULATTO WENCH, about eighteen
years of age, plain cook, and extraordinary good
washer, warranted sober, honest and no runaway; she is
of a mild temper, easily managed, and would be an
acquisition to any person, being remarkably honest and
trusty. To prevent trouble her price Four Hundred and
Fifty Dollars, notes with good indorsers; or she will be
changed for an elderly Wench with one or two
children, or field slave; the difference of value on either
side paid in cash.

—S. BEVENS, MASTER, COLLEGE OF CHARLESTON,
CITY GAZETTE, MARCH 22, 1805

Attending servants come,
The carriage wheels like thunders roar,
To bear the pensive seniors home,
Here to be seen no more.

—GEORGE M. HORTON, "THE GRADUATE LEAVES
COLLEGE" (1845)

CHAPTER 4

Ebony and Ivy

Enslaved People on Campus

Approached more easily by canoe than by land, Dartmouth College depended upon enslaved labor. New Hampshire governor John Wentworth had lured the Reverend Eleazar Wheelock from Connecticut with a generous charter and control of a section of the Connecticut River. In 1770 the freeholders of Hanover ceded three square miles of land and jurisdiction to the college. Rev. Wheelock set out for Hanover with a small group of students, his family, and eight enslaved black people: Brister, Exeter, Chloe, Caesar, Lavinia, Archelaus, Peggy, and a child. While preparing to leave his wife and children to campaign in Britain for Wheelock's academy, the Reverend Samson Occom had pleaded with his mentor for the use of a slave and a team of oxen to get his home and farm in order. Recognizing Wheelock's reliance upon enslaved labor, Occom conceded, "Let me have a yoke of Oxen if you can't spare a Negroe." In 1770 Wheelock sat down in "My Hutt in Hanover Woods" to update the aging British evangelist George Whitefield on the college's progress. He owed much of his success to the slaves whom he continued acquiring. Governor Wentworth donated at least two

people, including London Dow. There were more slaves than faculty, administrators, or active trustees; in fact, there were arguably
as many enslaved black people at Dartmouth as there were students in the college course, and Wheelock's slaves outnumbered
his Native American students.[1]

The decline of Rev. Wheelock's Indian mission is significant.
Wheelock was using the relationships that the Mohegan minister
had made in England, including a friendship with William Legge,
Earl of Dartmouth, to advance this new project. Most of his Native students were now children, studying in his grammar school.
At least two of Wheelock's slaves, Chloe and Exeter, studied at
the Indian school. Moreover, the president was occasionally curing the "bad habits" of these Indians by putting them to work with
his black slaves. In November 1777 Rev. Wheelock complained to
the Abenaki sachem Joseph Gill that his children, Anthony, Joseph, and Montuit, were only interested in play. The boys delighted in being delighted. They lacked discipline, he continued,
and when given chores and tasks, they protested that they were
only there for school. Wheelock's solution was to "send them into
the field with my laborers to learn every branch of labor, if it be for
only a few days." In its first two centuries, Dartmouth graduated
fewer than twenty Native Americans; it had produced that many
white alumni within five years of its founding—or its first three
graduating classes.[2]

African slavery was thriving in the new college towns. A trustee
of Queen's College (Rutgers) reminded himself of a scheduled
report from President Jacob Hardenberg by scribbling a note on a
strip of newspaper carrying an advertisement for the capture of the
college trustee John Lawrence's black teenager and her baby.[3] The
ubiquity and persistence of servitude on both sides of the college
wall was not a mere consequence of the colonial academy's location
in the greater Atlantic economy. Human slavery was the precondition for the rise of higher education in the Americas.

Enslaved Africans came to campus through a violent remapping
of the continent. By the mid-eighteenth century, nearly three hundred thousand black people constituted a fifth of the population in
the British mainland colonies and dwarfed the Native populations

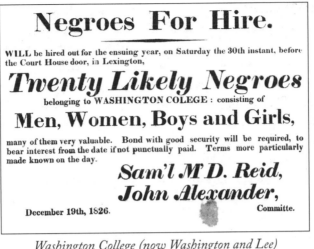

*Washington College (now Washington and Lee)
advertised slaves for hire in 1826.*
SOURCE: Library of Congress

east of the Appalachians. In little more than a half century, there were more people of African descent in the new nation than indigenous peoples in all the areas of North America that now form the continental United States.[4]

The slave trade and enslaved labor sustained thriving economies that closed the gaps between the European outposts, constricted the boundaries of Indian country, and ultimately toppled sovereign Native nations. Africans had been in New Spain and New France almost from their founding. The Pilgrims and Puritans had made peace with human slavery soon after their migrations began. The smallpox epidemic that ravaged the Northeast in 1702 took the lives of dozens of enslaved Africans. In 1715 the Connecticut government had attempted to ban the importation of enslaved Indians to reduce hostilities; nonetheless, the African slave trade caused the unfree population to boom. By 1730 there were about seven hundred slaves in Connecticut. By midcentury, black people outnumbered unconverted and "praying" Indians in Massachusetts, Connecticut, and Rhode Island. Several hundred black people were laboring in Boston, and enslaved Africans were ordinary in the seaboard towns of New England and on the western frontier.[5]

At the borders of Iroquoia, the Dutch and the English used enslaved black people to raise forts, clear and cultivate farms, and
maintain towns. European expansion throughout the Hudson Valley required unfree labor. By the 1740s, the African population in
the New York colony surpassed the population of the Iroquois Confederacy, which comprised six nations located between the Hudson
River and the Great Lakes: Mohawk, Oneida, Onondaga, Cayuga,
Seneca, and Tuscarora. One of every six people in Manhattan was
an African, and the black population of Kings County (today's
Brooklyn) was nearing a third of the total. There were large con-
centrations of enslaved Africans in the outlying farming districts of
Long Island and New Jersey. Black people accounted for 20 percent
of the population of Bergen County and about 10 percent of the
population in the rest of eastern New Jersey. More than ten thousand Africans were toiling in Pennsylvania at midcentury, as depopulation reduced the Lenape and Susquehannock to dependency.
There were a thousand enslaved people in Philadelphia, and their
numbers were swelling in all the backcountry counties.[6]

The growth of the black population had even greater effect on
Native nations in the South. Africans were about a third of the
population in Maryland, and 40 percent, more than a hundred
thousand people, in Virginia. By the 1750s, twenty thousand black
people were enslaved in North Carolina, and their numbers doubled in the next decade. There were more African people, nearly
fifty thousand, than Indians or white settlers in South Carolina.
The black population of the Carolinas was greater than the combined Cherokee, Choctaw, Chickasaw, and Creek populations. The
entire Cherokee nation comprised ten thousand people, there were
fifteen thousand Choctaws and Chickasaws, and fewer than fifteen
thousand Creeks. By 1750 Georgia's founding prohibition against
slavery fell to expediency and profiteering; white settlers had smug-
gled thousands of slaves into the region, and, within a few decades,
black people were nearly half the total population. At midcentury,
Virginia governor William Gooch could boast that "we have no
Indian nations of any strength" within striking distance of the
colony, and only the Cherokee and the Six Nations exercised any
real power.[7]

Wars and depopulation in Native nations, the rapid growth of the enslaved black population, and European immigration opened new lands to settlement. For two centuries, college officers had insinuated themselves into these territories by using land grants and leases to tap into the wealth being generated in the unfree agricultural economies. In 1662, a year before he chartered the Séminaire de Québec, Bishop François de Laval purchased the seigneurie de Beaupré, one of the royal fiefdoms of New France. Christian colonists in Canada already had an active market in Native people, and they were petitioning Paris for greater access to enslaved Africans. The bishop later bought the Île d'Orléans in the St. Lawrence River and a number of manors. In 1680 Laval transferred his colonial seigneuries, the Méobec abbey and several priories in France, gifts from King Louis XIV, and most of his personal possessions to the seminary.[8]

At the other end of Harvard's bonds and mortgages—the interest-bearing instruments that trustees used to secure their cash assets—were men such as Edmund Quincy of Braintree, Massachusetts, who owned Africans and Native Americans, and Nathaniel Byfield, a founder of Bristol, Rhode Island. Byfield had formed the partnership that established the new town on lands confiscated at the end of King Philip's War. He also owned Bristol's first merchant ship, which carried supplies to the West Indian and South American plantations. Elias Parkman opened his home to sell "a parcel of likely Negro boys and one girl" from the Guinea coast. Parkman rented one of Harvard's Boston properties. In the fall of 1706 John Campbell, another tenant of the college, gave away "a Negro Infant Girl about Six Weeks Old" without reference to her parents. A slave owner, Campbell used his position as Boston postmaster and his paper, the *Boston News-Letter*, to facilitate the purchase and sale of enslaved people, the capture of unfree people who absconded, and the shipment of bound Africans and Indians throughout the colonies.[9]

Yale and William and Mary also acquired tens of thousands of acres in the British colonies. In a single 1732 act, the General Assembly of Connecticut gave Yale parcels in Canaan, Goshen, Norfolk, Cornwall, and Kent totaling fifteen hundred acres. Yale's board negotiated leases, hired managers and agents, collected rents, inspected the properties, and bid on neighboring parcels to expand their holdings. The governors of William and Mary held vast estates throughout the colony and regularly leased the college slaves to earn income and reduce costs. In 1742 they sent a committee of two to investigate a report that slaves had escaped from their Nottaway plantations and "to endeavor to put things to right."[10]

In 1732, when George Berkeley donated Whitehall, his Rhode Island plantation, to Yale, he increased the college's real estate holdings and its ties to slavery. Yale's board rented Whitehall to a sequence of slaveholding tenants. Captain Silas Cooke, a long-term Whitehall lessee, had lost nine enslaved Africans and three enslaved Indians when he was captured privateering in the West Indies during the French and Indian War. In August 1776 Cooke wrote to the merchant Aaron Lopez, a personal friend, for help finding Sharpe Cooke, an enslaved man who worked as the distiller at Whitehall. He suspected that his servant was hiding among Lopez's slaves in Newport. Angered at the loss of this skilled slave, Captain Cooke begged Lopez to have him arrested. "If any Body in Providence wants such a fellow, [I] will sell him cheap," he added in frustration.[11]

Lands, leases, and laborers were the bases of an American feudalism. "The Universities in Britain and Ireland were liberally endowed with lands, by your Maj[es]ty's Illustrious Predecessors," James Jay respectfully reminded King George III before requesting a twenty-thousand-acre bounty for King's College (Columbia) in New York. The trustees craved real estate. In just a couple of decades, royal governors helped them amass more than fifty thousand acres.[12]

College overseers regularly appealed to local officials, colonial governors, and the crown for land. The trustees of the College of New Jersey (Princeton) delayed building a campus while they essentially auctioned their school to competing towns. They eventually decided upon Princeton after its boosters offered about two hundred acres and Governor Jonathan Belcher promised "to adopt it as a child." The board sought and acquired little land thereafter— the campus hardly grew during the first century—but it successfully attached the school to the powerful Morris, Penn, Livingston, and Alexander families, who were replicating Scotland's lord-tenant relations in the colony. "I suppose you have heard that Dr. Wheelock has obtained a Charter for a College . . . and has about 20 Thousand Acres of Land as an Endowment, from the Governor & other gentlemen who are largely concerned in lands," President James Manning of the College of Rhode Island (Brown) jealously informed a London patron.[13]

Governor Thomas Penn gave the College of Philadelphia (University of Pennsylvania) his twenty-five-hundred-acre Perkasie estate in Bucks County. Enslaved Africans had worked these holdings for decades. William and Hannah Penn had kept slaves as personal servants and laborers, and they had even punished one of their enslaved women by selling her to Barbados. Thomas Penn's gift sat in a region where German and Scottish immigrants and their slaves were pushing into Indian country, and where the trustees were extending bonds and mortgages to settlers. Governor Penn donated an additional £500 and promised annual contributions of £50. He prohibited the sale of the estate, and instructed the board to invest his money in real estate to ensure a steady annual income for the college.[14]

THE PEOPLE IN THE PRESIDENT'S HOUSE

In his biographical portraits of the graduates of Harvard, the librarian John Langdon Sibley took mastery as a measure of wealth, and explained the frequency of slaveholding officers and alumni by reminding readers that owning black people was a habit of "most prosperous men." President Increase Mather, class of 1656, used "his negro"—a gift from his son Cotton Mather, class of 1678—to run errands for the college. "This Day, a surprising Thing befell me," Cotton Mather noted around Christmas 1706, "it seems to be a mighty Smile of Heaven upon my Family." The congregation at the Old North Church presented Rev. Mather with a young black man. "I putt upon him the Name of *Onesimus*," Mather continued, estimating his value at nearly £50.[15]

Incoming presidents often brought enslaved people to campus

or secured servants after their arrival. Harvard president Benjamin Wadsworth owned an enslaved black man named Titus, who lived with the president's family. "I bought a Negro Wench," Wadsworth wrote in October 1726, just two days before he moved into the president's quarters. "She came to our house at Cambridge this day, I paid no money down for her," he added, but owed £85 on credit. Wadsworth later hired two free women servants, including Desire Simon, a Native American.[16]

As Harvard's chronicler had done, a Yale historian asserted that "it was a common custom of the times to own Negro or Indian slaves" to explain the conspicuous presence of bound people at the founding of the college. In October 1701 the Reverend James Pierpont of New Haven and a group of Connecticut ministers secured a colonial charter for the new "Collegiate School." On November 11, seven of the ten trustees traveled by horseback to a meeting at the home of Thomas Buckingham in Saybrook. Timothy Woodbridge arrived from Hartford. Noadiah Russell came alone from Middletown. Israel Chauncy of Stratford and Joseph Webb of Fairfield met Samuel Andrew in Milford. James Pierpont joined them at New Haven, and they rode to meet Abraham Pierson in Kenilworth. This procession was "followed on horseback by their men-servants or slaves."[17]

Abraham Pierson served as the college's first rector. His father had trained at Cambridge University and then migrated to the colonies to serve with John Eliot as an Indian missionary; he authored an early Algonquian guide to Christian scripture. Dissenters from New Haven organized a number of settlements. Pierson followed Robert Treat, who raised a Puritan outpost in Newark, New Jersey. The colony attracted freemen by offering grants of 150 acres and equal plots for each able male servant or half parcels for lesser servants. Rev. Pierson brought most of his congregation to the new town, which was named for his ancestral home in England, and he left his children large farms that they used to become a substantial slaveholding family. After graduating from Harvard in 1668, Abraham Pierson joined his father at First Church in Newark. The younger Pierson presided at the Newark church until about 1692, when he resettled in Connecticut.[18]

Two slaves—Tom and Pung—passed between the three Pierpont brothers, Benjamin, John, and James. They were by no means the only links to the slave economy in the Pierpont inventory. Benjamin Pierpont, a 1689 graduate of Harvard, took the pulpit of a congregation in Charleston, South Carolina, where he acquired slaves, a plantation, and several parcels of land. In 1685 James, Harvard class of 1681, was called to pastor First Congregational Church in New Haven, Connecticut. He eventually inherited Benjamin's "plantation in South Carolina . . . [along] the Ashley river" and two lots in Charleston. To provide for the spiritual health of the Palmetto City, Benjamin Pierpont gave two additional lots to support a Presbyterian minister. If unclaimed after five years, these lots would go to James.[19]

Slaveholding was common among Yale's early faculty and governors. Elisha Williams, Harvard class of 1711, acquired a significant estate, including land and slaves, from his marriage to Eunice Chester. Williams ran a preparatory school in Wethersfield, Connecticut. In September 1725 the Yale board appointed Williams rector of the college. With only a rector and a single tutor, Yale was a modest institution, and Williams spent the next fifteen years teaching, managing students, and stabilizing the college's finances. The Reverend Eliphalet Adams, who prepared boys for Yale and Harvard in his New London home, owned several slaves, including one person donated by his parish. He once baptized five of his servants in a single year. Fluent in Mohegan, Rev. Adams also served under the Society for the Propagation of the Gospel as an Indian missionary. The Reverend Thomas Clap, a 1722 graduate of Harvard, was a lifelong slaveholder. Clap became rector in 1740, and five years later the board named him president, the first in Yale's history. Rev. Clap and his wife made a personal pact to free their slaves; however, Clap's administration wedded Yale's fortunes to those of New England's Atlantic merchants.[20]

In 1756 the Reverend Ezra Stiles, a former tutor and a future president of Yale, placed a hogshead of rum aboard a ship leaving Rhode Island and instructed Captain William Pinnegar to trade it for a black child on the Guinea coast. The minister later named the boy Newport after his point of entry. As legend has it, Stiles confronted the moral problem of his actions after the transaction was completed. Finding the ten-year-old child in his kitchen crying, "the whole truth flashed upon the master's mind, and he saw the evil he had done," a fellow college president confessed. Stiles had separated Newport forever from his family and home, condemning him to a life of service in a foreign land. The minister promised to educate and train the boy in an attempt to partially repair that damage. On March 12, 1775, Rev. Stiles "baptized my Negro Man Newport . . . and admitted him into full Communion with the Church." Three years later, Ezra Stiles assumed the presidency of Yale. "At noon arrived here two Carriages from New Haven a Caravan & Wagon sent by the Corporation of Yale College to remove my Family," the new president noted. That week Rev. Stiles "freed or liberated my Negro Man Newport."[21]

Such moments of moral reckoning were rare. When he organized the College of Philadelphia, Benjamin Franklin was a slave owner. He had purchased his first "negro boy" while he was in his twenties, and he later used several slaves in his shop and his home. He brought two enslaved people, including his personal servant, Peter, on his travels to England. "We conclude to sell them both the first good opportunity, for we do not like negro servants," Franklin once protested to his mother. In fact, he did not manumit any of his servants. Although he later led the Pennsylvania Abolition Society, Franklin's career as a master ended as his slaves died or fled. The Quaker communion expelled Stephen Hopkins, the founding chancellor of the College of Rhode Island, for continuing to hold slaves after the Friends had condemned the institution. Hopkins's slaves included St. Jago, who was named for the Caribbean port. The Reverend James Manning, a graduate of New Jersey, brought his slave with him when he assumed the presidency of the new college in Rhode Island. Hopkins and Manning eventually came to oppose slavery.[22]

A succession of eight slave owners presided over the College of New Jersey during its first seventy-five years. In 1733 Jonathan Dickinson, the charter president, purchased a black girl from a neighbor in Elizabethtown. The Newark minister Aaron Burr, who replaced Dickinson, bought a black man from the New York merchant John

Livingston. Jonathan Edwards, who took control in 1758, grew up in a slaveholding house in East Windsor, Connecticut, and he later used enslaved labor in his mission to the Stockbridge Indians. In June 1731 he had traveled to Newport, Rhode Island, to buy Venus, a fourteen-year-old black girl, for £80. During his years in Delaware and Virginia, the Reverend Samuel Davies taught enslaved people to read, welcomed them into his church and home, and baptized hundreds of black people. "A number of them," Davies wrote while reflecting upon his own slaves and the larger black community, "are the genuine Children of Abraham." When the Reverend Samuel Finley died, his estate, including six black people, was auctioned from the president's house in Princeton. John Witherspoon began buying slaves within a few years of his arrival from Scotland. By 1784 two enslaved black people were listed among the taxable property of President Witherspoon. Samuel Stanhope Smith, Witherspoon's son-in-law and successor, made observations about a house slave to inform his famous thesis on human complexion. Ashbel Green acquired an enslaved girl from his marriage to Elizabeth Stockton. The Greens later brought the child from Philadelphia to Princeton, where she worked in the president's house.[23]

Despite the dire financial situation of his school, President Jacob Hardenbergh of Queen's College in New Brunswick acquired a slave in 1793, just two years before the trustees were forced to close the college for more than a decade. In 1795 the board suspended classes, released the faculty, sent the students home, and vacated the campus; still, Father Hardenbergh managed to acquire a second slave that year. More than a decade passed before the governors could reopen the college.[24]

Although the Reverend Eleazar Wheelock had taken in his first Indian students in the 1740s to supplement his income, he did not formalize the Indian school until 1754, about the same time that he began buying and selling human beings. Early in 1757 the minister paid William Clark of Plymouth £50 for a "Negro man named Ishmael, being a servant for life." In the spring of 1760 he bought Sippy (perhaps Scipio) from Timothy Kimball in Coventry. A few days later, the reverend paid Peter Spencer of East

Jonathan Dickinson by
Edward Ludlow Mooney

Aaron Burr Sr. by
Edward Ludlow Mooney

Jonathan Edwards by
Henry Augustus Loop

Samuel Davies by
James Massalon

The first eight presidents of the College of New Jersey
SOURCE: Princeton University

Samuel Finley by
Charles Walker Lind

John Witherspoon after
Charles Willson Peale

Samuel Stanhope Smith by
Charles B. Lawrence

Ashbel Green by
an unknown artist

Haddam £65 for his "Negro man servant named Brister aged about twenty one years."[25]

Slavery subsidized Wheelock's mission. In 1762 he gave Ann Morrison £75 for "a negro man named Exeter of the age of forty ought years[,] a negro woman named Chloe of the age of thirty five years[,] and a negro male child named Hercules of the age of about three years[,] all slaves for life." Worried that Chloe might be afflicted with rheumatism, the minister secured a guarantee from Morrison, who promised in writing to give him a £5 rebate in case "that difficulty should return upon her by means whereof she be disabled from business." Wheelock also made deals to protect the spiritual and physical health of enslaved people. "Nando [perhaps Fernando] will not hear anything of coming to Dartmouth," Gideon Buckingham responded in February 1772. A year earlier, Wheelock had requested that the Buckinghams transfer ownership of Nando and his wife, Hagar, to erase a £100 debt and to end what Wheelock saw as Nando's abusive behavior toward Hagar. "I believe the situation here would be very agreeable to Nando as it is to my negroes who have agreeable company enough and live well," Wheelock surmised. "I have a great variety of business I can employ Nando in." Apparently Nando had already been promised his freedom. Wheelock offered to liberate him and provide a twenty-acre farm if he accepted Christ and changed his behavior.[26]

Of course, the minister's primary concern was accessing labor. In the spring of 1773 Rev. Wheelock found himself in competition for Caesar, an enslaved man whom he was renting. Wheelock wrote to Caesar's owner, Captain Moses Little, confused over two different messages that arrived about the fate of the enslaved man. One instructed him to return Caesar by canoe, while a neighbor claimed to have permission to employ Caesar at his house. Dartmouth's president had his own designs. "I have concluded to buy the Negro if he proves to be the slave which you take him to be," Wheelock began, provided the price remained £20. The minister promised payment as soon as a title was secured. As the American Revolution approached, Rev. Wheelock found himself short of cash but in need of supplies and labor. "I understand the money must be paid down for the cheese, I have expectation of getting

Dartmouth College in an 1834 engraving
SOURCE: Library of Congress

the hard money & I am not quite certain of paper," he begged Asa Foot. "As to the Negro, I don't know when I shall be able to pay for him." Nonetheless, Wheelock alerted Foot that he would likely want another man and a woman the following summer.[27]

Such transactions fill the historical records of American colleges. In 1770 Domine Johannes Ritzema accepted "a young Negro, valued at £45," from John Van Zandt to satisfy rents owed to the Dutch Reformed Church of New York City. That exchange cleared Van Zandt's obligations, and the church agreed to a new fifteen-year lease on the property. Father Ritzema was both a founder of Queen's College and, as the senior Dutch Reformed minister in Manhattan, a charter trustee of King's College. Ritzema had also been a delegate and signatory to a 1765 New Jersey convention that endorsed Eleazar Wheelock's British fund-raising campaign. As William R. Davie was organizing the groundbreaking for the University of North Carolina, he stopped his work to sell a "negroe girl slave [named] Dinah," whose age he estimated to be thirteen, to Elijah Crockett to compensate him for his "negroe man called Joe," who had died while under Davie's supervision.[28]

College governors were quite comfortable negotiating the slave economy. Wheelock's last will and testament reveals no great anxiety about mastery. Brister was to remain enslaved, although he had served the Indian mission for two decades and had been a trusted personal attendant to the president. Wheelock's will freed only a single person. "To my servant Boy Archelaus[,] I give his freedom from slavery when he shall arrive at the age of twenty five years," the president promised, while giving the boy a fifty-acre plot in Landaff, New Hampshire. Emancipation was conditioned upon Archelaus proving to the satisfaction of the county presbytery that he could support himself and be "trusted with his freedom."[29] Wheelock's son and successor, John, increased the family's slaveholdings.

VIOLENCE AS AN ACADEMIC MATTER

Shortly after his graduation from Harvard, Benjamin Wadsworth served as chaplain for a Massachusetts delegation to negotiations in Albany, New York, between the English and the Iroquois. The Bay Colony committee, led by Samuel Sewall and Penn Townsend, was made up of Harvard graduates. New York governor Benjamin Fletcher and the wealthy landholders Stephen Van Cortlandt and Peter Schuyler hosted the August 1694 meeting. John Allen and Caleb Stanley came from Connecticut. Governor Andrew Hamilton of New Jersey arrived with his aid John Pinchon. Twenty-five Iroquois sachems from the Five Nations attended the negotiations. On the third night of their journey from Boston, the Massachusetts delegates saw "a negro coming from Albany," which led them to become "very suspicious." Concluding he was a runaway slave, they seized him. Wadsworth and his companions tied the man up and then camped for the evening, intending to bring their prisoner to the Albany authorities. The captive managed to get free while they slept, take a gun and possibly a sword, and escape. "We thought of him," Wadsworth noted in disappointment.[30] When Rev. Wadsworth acquired his first slave is not certain, but the future president of Harvard seemed quite displeased with the results of his early foray into slave catching.

Masters regulated their slaves with violence. In 1698 the Reverend Samuel Gray, a founding trustee of the College of William and Mary, murdered an enslaved child for running away. Rev. Gray struck the boy on the head, drawing blood, and then put a hot iron to the child's flesh. The minister had the boy tied to a tree, and then ordered another slave to whip him. The boy later died. Gray argued that "such accidents" were inevitable, a position that seems to have succeeded, as a court declined to convict him. The congregation at Christ Church in Middlesex County gave him a considerable quantity of tobacco to resign. The following year, Gray settled at a parish in Westmoreland. He later became the pastor of St. Peter's Church in New Kent.[31]

When Benjamin Wadsworth ministered the First Church in Boston, he gave his parishioners a series of sermons on household order, including a lecture on slavery. Wadsworth warned his congregation not to "pinch" their servants by denying them the food, drink, clothing, medical attention, and periods of rest necessary to their health. They should give their slaves time for prayer and private contemplation, give them to God and pray for them, and let them read the Bible and other books that would enhance their faith. Householders should protect their slaves, he continued, and keep them busy enough to avoid sin, but not so exhausted as to impair their well-being. Leaning on biblical references, the future Harvard president also instructed his congregants to beat their slaves. Corporal punishments were needed to chastise and deter wrong, for "a servant will not be corrected by words." Preferring the biblical term "correction," the pastor warned his audience to avoid "rage and passion" and "cruel and unmerciful" acts, instead always choosing the mildest penalty that would effectively cure the fault, remembering that a good master needed neither tyranny nor terror. Rev. Wadsworth instructed the slaves sitting in his church to willfully submit to every godly action and demand made by their masters, including physical punishments. A servant's life should be consumed in work and prayer, interrupted by brief moments of rest for sustenance.[32]

Perhaps Wadsworth's call for Christian mastery and thoughtful violence responded to the long history of brutality in the colony.

Neither church nor academy moderated the horrors of slavery. A "negro woman was burned to death," the Reverend Increase Mather had written in his diary in September 1681, adding that this was the first "such death in New England."[33]

It was not the last. On Thursday afternoon, September 18, 1755, Phillis and Mark (Codman) were dragged on a sled through Cambridge to the commons just outside the gates of Harvard College. Drs. William Kneeland and William Foster, both Harvard graduates, testified against them during their trial for the murder of Captain John Codman of Charlestown. Before they decided to kill their owner, the two slaves had set fire to his workhouse. Enslaved people in Boston apparently knew of a successful poisoning, which they used as a model. It was a conspiracy of several slaves. Robin (Vassall), owned by Dr. William Clark of Boston, stole arsenic from his master's apothecary for the Codman slaves. Some accused black people were sold out of the colony, but the court sentenced Phillis and Mark to death. "A terrible spectacle in Cambridge," Professor John Winthrop exclaimed after watching the executions with students and other faculty. "Mark, a fellow about 30, was hanged; & Phillis, an old creature, *was burnt to death*." Winthrop was Hollis Professor of Mathematics and twice declined the presidency of the college. The authorities suspended Mark's corpse in chains at the Charlestown commons, where it remained for decades, long enough to serve as a landmark for Paul Revere during his midnight ride. This was not the first execution that the sophomore Edward Brooks—the father of Peter Chardon Brooks—had witnessed. During his freshman year, he saw William Welsh hanged for killing Darby O'Brien in a fight on the Boston wharfs. Westborough minister and Harvard graduate Ebenezer Parkman scornfully recorded the events in his diary: "Another barbarous Murder is Committed, and by another Irishman."[34]

While Africans and African Americans were the vast majority of the bound laborers at colleges in New England, the Mid-Atlantic, and the South, they were not the only unfree people. In 1764 Patrick Field, a twenty-three-year-old Irish indentured servant, escaped from Manhattan in uniform: light brown livery with green fronting and a dark wig with a single curl. Before he departed, he compensated himself, breaking into a desk and taking $50 in silver and gold coins, rings, shirts, cravats, stockings, two silver buckles, and his letter of indenture, which he allegedly forged to pass as a free man. The clothing had the initials "M.C.," and Myles Cooper, the president of King's College, promised a £10 reward to anyone who captured and returned his servant. He described Field's height, alerted readers to his "ruddy" complexion, and warned that he was often intoxicated and had a remarkable gaze when drunk.[35]

If servitude was ubiquitous on campus, then violence was also routine. "As we all know[,] Negroes will not perform their Duties without the Mistress's constant Eye especially in so large a Family as the College," President William Yates and the governors of William and Mary reminded their housekeeper. Enslaved people lived in the kitchens of the main hall and president's house, and in slave quarters scattered around the campus. The governors also took it upon themselves to field complaints from students and to determine how slaves should be "corrected" in response. Students often violated such rules. In 1769 John Byrd, an undergraduate, picked up a horsewhip and ran after a slave when the servant, who was working for the housekeeper, failed to respond to his call. On February 6, 1773, Eleazar Wheelock ordered the sheriff to go to the kitchen and arrest his slave Caesar, the Dartmouth College cook. Accused of making defamatory remarks about Mary Sleeper, a white woman staying at the president's house, Caesar was brought before Rev. Wheelock. The minister heard testimony from Caesar and the guest. Wheelock used his judicial authority to declare Caesar guilty, and he sentenced him to a £10 fine plus court costs. The president instructed the constable to take Caesar into town and deliver seven stripes with a whip if he failed to pay the fines.[36]

Not all the violence was physical—governors and officers also broke up families to acquire and sell enslaved labor. "This day my brother Augustus & myself have made a Division of all the moveables belonging to the Estate of our mother Judith," wrote Cornelius Van Horne, "such as furniture, plate, linen, wearing apparel, Negroes & c." Augustus Van Horne later served as treasurer of King's College, and his family had close ties to other regional colleges. A month before the property division, James Van Horne put five prime family farms on sale. The set included his Perth Amboy seat, which was so large that it could be divided into four working farms with meadows, woods, a wharf, orchards, and other amenities. The rest of the farms were near Princeton and included such fixtures as barns, meadows, timberlands, orchards, mills, and a "Negro House." These property divisions and sales included people. Their father and mother, Cornelius G. Van Horne and Judith Jay, had left their sons a sizable bequest, one enhanced by Cornelius's first wife, Joanna Livingston of Livingston Manor. Cornelius Van Horne had invested in a slaving journey every year for more than a decade beginning in 1717. His sons split the family holdings, selling off many of the properties and collecting debts. In 1764 Augustus married Ann Marston, of the prominent slave-trading family. Ann and Augustus's eight children then pulled the family even closer to the commercial elite through marriage.[37]

Belinda (Watts) was put on sale during the winter of 1762 despite her owner's judgment that she was "a simple innocent Creature & a very good Cook" who had become "a most necessary Servant." The King's College trustee John Watts took the unusual step of contracting with a slave dealer to sell her in Virginia because his family disapproved of her religious practices. Frustrated with the low offers, Watts turned to business acquaintances to intervene. Increasingly, he blamed Belinda for the soft market:

> She is not as the New England Men say dreadfull hand-some, nor very young, yet I would be content to give for just such another harmless, stupid Being, that possessed only the quality she does of Cooking, a hundred pounds, with great readiness, that however can be no Government to you in the sale of her.[38]

President John Maclean Jr. of the College of New Jersey lived in slave households and on campuses with slaves for most of his formative years. His father had studied medicine and science at Glasgow, Edinburgh, London, and Paris, and came to the United

States in 1795. Benjamin Rush arranged for Maclean to give a series of lectures in Princeton, and the trustees appointed Maclean,
barely twenty-five years old, to one of the first chemistry professorships in North America. Maclean also became a slave owner. In
January 1809 Maclean sold "a Negroe boy named Tom between
twenty and twenty one years of age" from his home in Princeton.
Professor Maclean later taught at William and Mary.[39]

"I regret to record that there were slaves,—some slaves by purchase, others by descent, or slaves born under our roof," recalled
Benjamin Silliman of his childhood in eighteenth-century Connecticut. Yale president Timothy Dwight had convinced Silliman—a 1796 graduate and a tutor—to drop his legal training and
pursue chemistry. Silliman went to Philadelphia and Edinburgh
to study science, then returned to New Haven to begin one of the
most influential careers of the antebellum academy. "Our northern
country was not then as fully enlightened as now regarding human
freedom; there were house slaves in the most respectable families,
even in those of the clergymen in the now free states." Silliman's
mother and father had numerous enslaved black people on lands
outfitted with separate slave quarters.[40]

Reflecting on his family history, Professor Silliman insisted that
northerners had crafted "a mild form [of slavery] indeed." In what
became something of a custom for his generation, he portrayed
himself as a victim of foreign decisions rather than familial ones,
arguing that England "forced slavery and the slave-trade upon the
colonies." Whippings were uncommon and women servants were
always spared that punishment, he argued. New England slaves
rarely ran away, they were well fed, and their tasks were light.
Northerners did not track human beings "by the gun and the blood-
hound," nor did they dress them in the "ball and chain" or "iron
collar." His own family history disproves many of those claims.
With more slaves than any other household in Fairfield County,
Mary Silliman was able to pay her sons' tuition and fees at Yale by
selling two enslaved people from her declining Holland Hills farm.
By the time her boys graduated, she still owned about a dozen
people, eight of them children less than twelve years old.

Benjamin returned to be overseer of Holland Hills, to rebuild their estate, and to help his mother maximize her profits under Connecticut's gradual emancipation law, which the Sillimans freely violated.[41]

Even on college campuses, slaveholders could not maintain the fiction of gentle or humane servitude. Violence undergirded bondage. "The record of slaves who were branded by their owners, had their ears nailed, fled, committed suicide, suffered the dissolution of their families, or were sold secretly to new owners in Barbados in the last days of the Revolutionary War before they became worthless never seems sufficient to refute the myth of kindly masters," Catherine Adams and Elizabeth H. Pleck conclude.[42]

SLAVERY ON CAMPUS

In the daily routine of a college there was a lot of work to be done, and enslaved people often performed the most labor-intensive tasks. In the mornings, the professors and scholars needed wood for fires, water for washing, and breakfast after morning prayers in the chapel. As students ate, their rooms were cleaned, chamber pots emptied, and beds made. Multiple meals had to be produced every day in the kitchens. Ashes needed to be cleared from fireplaces and stoves, and floors needed sweeping. Clothes and shoes were cleaned and mended. Fires were lighted and maintained. Buildings wanted for repairs, and servants were impressed into small- and large-scale projects. There were countless errands for governors, professors, and students. "Titus my serv[a]nt, brought from mr. Treasurer [James] Allen (to whom I sent a Rect) Ninety Pounds Bills of Credit, being for the third Quarter, ending 17 Mar. last," President Wadsworth recorded in the spring of 1728. Workers on more remote campuses cultivated farmlands, purchased and traded at markets, kept animals and butchered meat, and manufactured other goods on-site. In Princeton, President John Witherspoon consolidated a five-hundred-acre estate, a mile from the college and with an uninterrupted view of the campus. At least one slave remained at Tusculum, where the president maintained a working farm to pursue his agricultural interests while renting the remaining lands to tenants.[43]

Faculty and officers often testified to the difficult lives of enslaved people, but not always sympathetically. Professor Hugh
Jones of William and Mary bitterly demanded that the slaves be
segregated, "for these not only take up a great deal of Room and are
noisy and nasty, but also have often made me and others apprehen-
sive of the Danger of being burnt with the College thro' their Carelessness and Drowsiness." The Reverend Samuel Kirkland, founder
of Hamilton College, encountered numerous enslaved and free
black people during his early missions among the Iroquois. The
Indian commissioner Sir William Johnson had slaves at his Mount
Johnson estate along the Mohawk River in New York. There were
also numerous black people living as residents and adoptees in Iroquoia. "I should not come here and live so much like a negro as I
do," Rev. Kirkland complained to his mentor Eleazar Wheelock;
"I have lived more like a dog than a Christian minister." Kirkland
believed that his miserable living conditions were hurting the prestige of the faith among the Indians.[44]

Access to enslaved people could be the difference between success and failure for colonial schools. Eleazar Wheelock spent his
early years in Hanover supervising the building of a sawmill, gristmill, and two barns to supply the campus and to generate income.
By the 1773 printing of his *Narrative of the Indian Charity School*—
itself a fund-raising tool—he had overseen the raising of several
outbuildings and was in the process of finishing a malt house. The
college had eighty acres of cleared land, twenty planted with English grain and eighteen with Indian corn. Nearly fifteen tons of
hay had been stacked to lessen the cost of keeping cows and oxen.
His pamphlet promised additional progress: "My labourers are preparing more lands for improvement." Nathaniel Hovey, who settled in a neighboring town in 1773, confirmed the progress over the
next decade. Captain Hovey estimated that "there have been cleared
upwards of three hundred acres of land at the expence of Dartmouth College and of Moors [Indian Charity] School, that there
has been a gristmill & a sawmill built and not less than two miles
of road laid out and made."[45]

After the 1764 chartering of the College of Rhode Island, the
trustees began soliciting money to prepare the grounds and build

an academic hall. The active slaving towns of Providence and Newport housed a number of wealthy merchant families and high proportions of slaveholders. The prosperous slave trader Jacob Rodriguez de Rivera donated ten thousand linear feet of wood during the subscriptions for the first college building. Henry Laurens, another prominent slaver, also contributed supplies. Other residents donated the labor of their slaves. Henry Paget promised Pero, his sixty-two-year-old slave, for about a month. Another local master offered Job, an Indian slave, for more than a week.[46]

A small army of slaves maintained the College of William and Mary. "I promise you the College is very large & well built, with gardens and outhouses proportioned," the proud parent William Gooch wrote to his brother. "The more wealthy scholars had negro boys to wait on them," adds a historian of the college. In 1754 alone, eight students, including the brothers Charles and Edward Carter, paid fees to house their personal slaves on campus. The college also owned dozens of people.[47]

In 1773 George Washington escorted his stepson, John "Jacky" Custis, and Jacky's slave, Joe, to New York City. The general had vetoed the idea of placing the young man at William and Mary, fearing that the combination of planter wealth and loose discipline would only aggravate his son's personal faults. Washington hoped that living in the North would tame Jacky's penchant for gambling and expensive luxuries. He also wanted to control Jacky's indecent behavior—womanizing, secret engagements, and having sex with slaves. But King's College was not a place to learn self-discipline. Rev. Cooper outfitted Jacky with a suite of rooms, catered to his every desire, and sent misleading reports on his progress to Mount Vernon. The teenager informed his mother that he was being treated "in a particular Light" because of his status, and that he appreciated the "distinction made between me & the other students." On his way to New York, Washington had a string of dinners and celebrations with governors, generals, leading merchants, and the members of elite social clubs—the strata of society that administrators needed to access. Although he had plenty of privileged boys under his charge, Cooper seized this chance to cultivate the southern aristocracy. "I dine with them (a liberty that is not

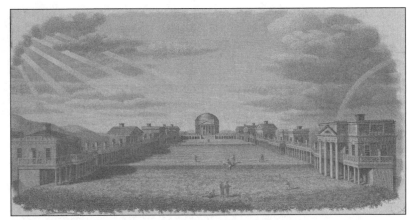

*Jefferson's University of Virginia. Detail from an 1827 map by
Henry Schenck Tanner after a drawing by Benjamin Tanner*
SOURCE: University of Virginia Library

allow'd any but myself)," Jacky boasted of his relationship to the
faculty, and "associate & pertake of all their recreations." An unre-
formed Custis left college after two years. He wasted much of his
fortune, died within a decade, and left his children to be raised by
his mother and stepfather.[48]

The American campus stood as a silent monument to slavery. In
September 1793 William Richardson Davie presided at the laying
of the cornerstone for the new campus of the University of North
Carolina. The ceremony employed the rituals and symbols of Free-
masonry. Davie described the "great doings of the Masonic brethren, with your correspondent wielding a silver trowel and setting
a stone in mortar." Once the ceremonies were concluded, black
laborers filled the area to begin constructing the university. When
the founders of South Carolina College (University of South Carolina), began planning the architectural style of their campus,
they looked not to their southern peers but to the colleges in New
Jersey, Rhode Island, and New Hampshire for inspiration and
advice.[49]

Enslaved black people built Thomas Jefferson's intellectual monument: the University of Virginia. Construction materials came
in large loads along the James River and were hauled up to

Charlottesville. Black workers, including youth, were used to bring supplies to the campus and raise the buildings. As construction began, expenditures for the dozens of enslaved people "hired" by the university totaled more than $1,000 per year. The individual cost was determined by age and perceived physical ability, and the college calculated the expense of feeding and maintaining each slave through the contracted period. At the end of their terms of service, enslaved workers were outfitted with fresh outer- and undergarments and shoes before being returned to their masters.[50]

BOYS WILL BE MASTERS

Governors and faculties used slave labor to raise and maintain their schools, and they made their campuses the intellectual and cultural playgrounds of the plantation and merchant elite. They sought the loyalty of wealthy colonists such as the Newport merchants Christopher and George Champlin, who sent ships to Africa, Asia, and the West Indies. "After being detained two days at Providence and having an agreeable Journey to Boston, I arrived at Cambridge the Saturday after the Vacation was up," Christopher Grant Champlin informed his father. "I have been in [Harvard] College about a week." After painting and papering his room, young Christopher was satisfied with his accommodations.[51]

Officers catered to these children. One doting father sent President Samuel Johnson of King's College "schemes" for turning his son into a responsible man. "This child of mine is I find already . . . adept in the little arts of shifting," he cautioned. The board of the College of Philadelphia promised to "look on the Students as, in some measure, their own Children, treat them with Familiarity and Affection." That attention continued after graduation. The governors vowed to "establish them in Business Offices, Marriages, or any other Thing for their Advantage." There were rewards for such devotion. Godfrey Malbone, a Virginian who settled in Newport, Rhode Island, after his graduation from Harvard, entered the slave trade, created one of the region's largest fortunes, and became a benefactor of colonial schools.[52]

The combination of wealthy patrons, privileged students, and ambitious regional promoters brought colleges into the service of the colonial elite and brought large numbers of enslaved people into college towns. By the mid-eighteenth century there were nearly nine hundred enslaved black men and women in Boston and fifty-five in Cambridge. Professor Winthrop of Harvard estimated that 15 percent of Boston's residents were black, while official figures put the black population at 10 percent. Several dozen black people lived in New Haven during that time, and the African American population climbed to nearly three hundred by the eve of the Revolution. Most white families in Princeton and New Brunswick owned at least one black person. By the 1780s enslaved people were more than a fifth of the population of New Brunswick, while one of every six residents of Princeton was enslaved.[53]

First Church in Cambridge—an extension of Harvard—reflected the racial order of elite colonial society. In 1757 the college paid a seventh of the cost to replace the old church. The trustees decided the location and orientation of the new meetinghouse. They selected a pew for the president, reserved the entire front section for the students, and dictated the size and configuration of the scholars' seats. In a later exchange, the Harvard Corporation agreed to a modest reduction in the size of the students' gallery, "provided, that the part we thus cede to the Parish shall not be occupied by the negroes." First Church baptized, buried, or administered other rites to scores of black people owned by prominent Harvard families, including Philip (Danforth), Zillah (Brattle), Cuffy (Phipps), Jack (Tufts), and Cuba (Vassall). "Titus, Presid[en]t Wadsworth's Man Servant . . . was also admitted to full Communion," reads an entry on October 13, 1729. In 1741 Edward Wigglesworth, the first Hollis Professor of Divinity, watched his slave Hannibal receive communion, and twelve years later Gerald, Hannibal's son, was baptized. Edward Wigglesworth and his son of the same name held the Hollis Professorship as a family entitlement for most of the eighteenth century. Even after slavery was outlawed in Massachusetts, college officials continued to rely upon black labor. In October 1789, a decade after the state courts had erased the legal foundations for servitude, Harvard president Joseph Willard had his "negro man Servant" Cesar baptized.[54]

Students often used enslaved people for amusements ranging from boxing to singing, dancing, and fiddling—diversions that were common at colonial colleges. Samuel Curwen, a student during Wadsworth's administration, carried a small notebook in which he had transcribed the college laws in Latin, but such reminders did little to calm the campus. In the spring of 1737, the Harvard faculty barred Titus, "a Molatto slave of the late Rev[eren]d Pres[iden]t Wadsworth," from entering the students' rooms or even coming to campus after he was found drinking with the undergraduates. Three years later, the professors had to repeat their prohibition on students associating with the Wadsworths' slave. In September 1751 they punished several undergraduates for "making drunk a Negro-man-servant belonging [to] Mr. Sprague, & that to Such Degree as greatly indanger'd his Life." Included among the culprits were four members of Harvard's class of 1754: Samuel Foxcroft, the future minister of the First Congregational Church in New Gloucester, Maine, and the son of the pastor of Boston's First Church; Samuel Quincy, later a loyalist solicitor who prosecuted British soldiers after the Boston Massacre; John Hancock, the shipping heir, future governor, and signer of the Declaration of Independence; and Samuel Marshall, who went on to study medicine in London and then established a practice in Boston.[55]

Harvard's supposedly pious young students proved especially unruly. The faculty had to suppress everything from "foolish talking" to fornicating. Garishly dressed boys bedeviled the seventeenth-century governors, who responded with strict prohibitions on "strange ruffinalike or New-fangled fashions," including gold and silver adornments and long, curled, parted, or powdered hair. President John Leverett dealt with John Nutting, who forged money to pay his tuition, and Benjamin Shattuck, who engaged in sexual misconduct. On election day in 1711 a student named Hussey walked through town in women's clothing, accompanying "scandalous p[eo]ple." President Wadsworth would have his own stories to tell. In the middle of the night, Nathaniel Hubbard Jr. and John Winthrop Jr. stole ropes that they used to hang the dog of a local resident. In June 1726 Eliza Bacheldor's father was searching the yard for Jonathan Hayward, who had had sex with his daughter. In 1733 the Jamaican planter Leonard Vassall sued a tutor who slapped William Vassall in the face for failing to remove his hat. Students disturbed the peace with fireworks and bonfires, and their undergraduate years could be measured in busted fences and broken windows. "The Glass [was] broken in the Chamber next over the Kitchen & the Hebrew School," the governors complained during their March 1753 meeting. Several months later they were investigating the students' "abusive & insolent" behavior toward the Hebrew instructor. The faculty imposed fines and punishments for this "great Disorder." The overseers warned Edward Brooks's freshman class of heavy penalties for using the valedictory address or their status as head of class to make threats.[56]

Yale's officers also policed vandalism, violence, and other disorders. Citizens began complaining about intoxicated undergraduates as soon as the college moved to New Haven. Things got worse with time. Jesse Denison, of the class of 1756, was keeping a pistol in his room. In February 1753 he carried the loaded gun into town and used it to threaten a local resident during a disagreement. Denison then fired his pistol in public, "tho, as he says, not with any Design to do them any Mischief." Several years later the freshmen celebrated commencement by patrolling the yard with clubs, making menacing gestures and frightening sounds. One student even "brandished a naked sword." The trustees had to lock the college to keep the boys from dancing and carousing at night. They punished "extravagant" dress and barred local taverns from selling students "any rum, brandy or distilled spirits, or any liquor mixed of either of them on any occasion whatsoever." Nonetheless, by 1765 the officers were asking the New Haven authorities to police the commencement.[57]

Perhaps taking a lesson from the older schools, the trustees of New Jersey and King's prepared lengthy lists of infractions and punishments for their first classes. The New Jersey officers threatened to expel any student found guilty of "Drunkenness, Fornication, Lying, Theft or any other Scandalous Crime." They prohibited the scholars from bringing wine or liquor into their rooms, playing dice or cards, frequenting taverns, or associating with disreputable people. King's governors also forbade cockfighting, dice, and other gaming, and warned the students to pass by houses of vice and prostitution and avoid "any persons of known scandalous behaviour." The governors set fines for slandering and maiming other people. Several years later they banned all women from residing at the college—except for the cook—and then had the campus fenced and hired a porter to watch the gate. Despite these precautions the Manhattan campus remained volatile. John Jauncey, a senior, challenged President Myles Cooper "to fight with pistols, before ye whole Class, whilst they were engaged in their Recitation." He was expelled.[58]

College boys felt particularly entitled to terrorize slaves and servants. In April 1772, while President Cooper and the faculty examined the senior class in the chapel, Beverly Robinson, an upperclassman, attacked one of the servants. "Robinson spit in the Cook's Face, kicked, & otherwise abused him," reads the record. Despite his violent temper and consistently poor academic performance, Robinson received a mild punishment: confinement to campus for two weeks and additional academic assignments from Cooper. The son of a trustee and the heir to an elite slave trading line, Robinson graduated in 1773. He later became a trustee.[59]

At Williams College, the students paid a black man, whom they nicknamed "Abe Bunter," to see him smash his head with wooden boards and barrels. "Probably no more formidable battering-ram of this species could be found anywhere," joked a historian of the college. The author was decidedly unconcerned with the real name of "Abe Bunter"—a moniker that mocked this unfortunate career—or the grotesqueness of the transactions. Instead, he insisted that "Bunter" had a "phenomenally thick skull" and described him as a "barbaric figure" who "haunted the campus" with "his one tremendous 'talent.' "[60]

The students at the University of North Carolina enjoyed "pranking" slaves in Chapel Hill. George M. Horton, an enslaved man who sold fruit in town, learned to read and write by manipulating these exchanges, and he became known in town for his poetry. Such encounters could easily turn violent. In September 1811 dozens of students began rioting, destroying property, ransacking the rooms and halls, and attacking the college servants. The undergraduates accused the faculty of imposing harsh and unfair punishments and disregarding student opinions. The teachers and officers remained in the buildings into the evening to restore order. Culprits were brought in for questioning, but explosions of gunpowder interrupted the meetings. When the faculty went to locate the new disturbances, they reported, "a little Negro was found in a corner of the room of one of these young men" hiding because one of the students had just fired a gun at him. Just a few years later, three students got drunk and broke into a local house, where they threatened the residents and assaulted a slave.[61]

FROM COLLEGE GREEN TO "NIGGER HILL"

Little places named for forgotten black people dot the northern states. Many of these secluded communities have ties to American colleges. Jonathan Jackson, class of 1761—a third-generation Harvard student, preceded by his father and his maternal grandfather—used his education and an inheritance to establish himself as a merchant, selling rum and other goods to Africa traders and dealing to the West Indies. The Harvard network brought repeated public appointments that rescued him from serial business failures and allowed him to maintain his household: "one discrete Woman and a Negro Fellow." On the eve of the Revolution, Jackson emancipated Pomp Jackson, who then fought with the colonists. Pomp Jackson removed to Pomps Pond, near Phillips Academy in Andover, Massachusetts, at about the same time that future Harvard presidents John Thornton Kirkland, the son of the Indian missionary Samuel Kirkland, and Josiah Quincy, the nephew of the headmaster, were there preparing for college. The pond was named not for the black veteran but rather for Pomp Lovejoy, a black man who retreated to this remote spot after gaining his freedom from Captain William Lovejoy.[62]

Once enslaved on the Princeton campus, Betsey Stockton finished her life a free woman, a teacher, and a missionary to Hawaii. Her death in 1865 brought numerous tributes. Leading citizens of Cooperstown, New York, raised a fund for a bronze tablet recognizing her mission but could not find a site that would accept it.

Pomps Pond, Andover, Massachusetts
SOURCE: Andover Historical Society

"She is one of the most remarkable women I ever conversed with," remembered President James Marshall of Cedar Rapids College (Coe College). Late in 1822 Stockton had left New Haven on the *Thames* to teach and evangelize in Hawaii, where her facility with languages proved invaluable to the Lahaina and Maui missions. After her return in 1825 she taught at colored schools in Cooperstown and Princeton. An intellectual elite attended her Princeton funeral. President John Maclean officiated, assisted by the mathematician John Thomas Duffield and the theologian Charles Hodge. Stockton was buried in Cooperstown, in the family plot of the Reverend Charles Samuel Stewart, with whom she had worked in Hawaii.[63]

Phebe Ann Jacobs was born in Beverwijck, New Jersey, in the British and Dutch farming belt that stretched from Elizabeth to Trenton. Maria Malleville Wheelock—the daughter of Dartmouth president John Wheelock and Maria Suhm, who hailed from a slaveholding family with ties to New Jersey and St. Croix—had received Phebe as a gift from her mother. Malleville, as she was known, married Dartmouth professor William Allen. In 1820 they all went to Brunswick, Maine, after Allen accepted the presidency of Bowdoin. As slavery ended in Maine, black families

Betsey Stockton, from a photograph c. 1863
SOURCE: New York State Historical Association Library.

began relocating to several of the ungoverned coastal islands—
commonly called the "Negro Islands"—including Malaga, not far
from the college. There was also a "Negro Island," originally named
Gilman, just south of Dartmouth, near the falls in the Connecticut
River from which the campus drew power. Enslaved people had
been building Brunswick long before there was a college. Andrew
Dunning, a signer of the petition for incorporation, brought slaves
to settle the area. More than a dozen black people were living there
a half century later, and the greater region had an active slaving
history. When Maria Malleville Wheelock died, Phebe Jacobs
moved off campus, supporting herself by washing and ironing for
the students. Jacobs died alone in her "little habitation."[64]

Campus folklore and place names record the story of slavery in
college towns. These local legends and landscapes are a diary of
the long, intimate association between the academy and slavery.
Dartmouth president John Wheelock had inherited "Brister, Archelaus, Lavinia or Anna and the infant child," his father's oxen, tools,
"horses and as many swine as he shall have occasion for." Under
the second Wheelock administration, the number of enslaved
people in Hanover doubled. Unfree people continued to toil at the
college and in the Wheelock household until legislative decisions

and a changing international market eroded mastery in New Hampshire. Many of these free African Americans worked for the college and the students. Professor John King Lord recalled Jenny Wentworth as a "good nigger," his term for a pious, hardworking black person. The black community clustered just south of the campus and apart from white residents, who now cast them as a nuisance and a problem. Evidence of the tension was written into the very geography of the place, which included the college, the town, and a modest elevation that was popularly derided as "Nigger Hill."[65]

PART II

Race and the
Rise of the American
College

The number of purely white people in the world is
proportionably very small. All Africa is black or tawny;
Asia chiefly is tawny; America (exclusive of the new
comers) wholly so. . . . And while we are, as I may call
it, scouring our planet, by clearing America of woods,
and so making this side of our globe reflect a brighter
light to the eyes of inhabitants in Mars or Venus, why
should we, in the sight of superior beings, darken its
people? Why increase the sons of Africa, by planting
them in America, where we have so fair an opportunity, by excluding all blacks and tawnys, of increasing
the lovely white and red?

—BENJAMIN FRANKLIN, "OBSERVATIONS
CONCERNING THE INCREASE OF MANKIND
AND THE PEOPLING OF COUNTRIES" (1751)

Look round you! behold a country, vast in extent,
merciful in its climate, exuberant in its soil, the seat
of Plenty, the garden of the Lord! behold it given to
us and to our posterity, to propagate Virtue, to cultivate
the useful Arts, and to spread abroad the pure evangelical Religion of Jesus! behold Colonies founded in
it! Protestant Colonies! free Colonies! British Colonies!
behold them exulting in their Liberty; flourishing in
Commerce; the Arts and Sciences planted in them.

—PROVOST WILLIAM SMITH, *THE CHRISTIAN
SOLDIER'S DUTY* (1757)

I am very sorry to hear by the publick Papers that the
Indian War is not at an End. I can not conceive what
it is these People are aiming at, but I am afraid, we
ourselves are not intirely blameless.

—SAMUEL BARD, EDINBURGH UNIVERSITY,
TO DR. JOHN BARD, NEW YORK, 1764

CHAPTER 5

Whitening the Promised Land

Colleges and the Racial Destiny of
North America

On December 14, 1763, Edward Shippen rushed a letter to Pennsylvania lieutenant governor John Penn alerting him that "a Company of People from the Frontiers had killed and scalped most of the Indians at the Conestogoe Town early this morning." Getting their name from the Paxtung Presbyterian Church in the backcountry, fifty well-armed "Paxton Boys"—a gang of Scots-Irish immigrants—rode into Conestoga and murdered several Susquehannocks: an elderly woman, three elderly men, a young woman, and a small boy. They butchered the corpses and torched the cabins. Before the attack, several residents had left for a local foundry to sell homemade baskets, bowls, and brooms, and thereby escaped the slaughter. Governor Penn delivered a message to the legislature condemning the cold-blooded murders and requesting funds to secure the remaining Indians, and Shippen, who was the Penns' agent in the backcountry, announced warrants for the perpetrators.[1]

"I am to acquaint your Honour that between two and three of the clock this afternoon, upwards of a hundred armed men . . . rode very fast into town . . . stove open the door and killed all the

Indians," Shippen wrote apologetically on December 27, less than two weeks after the first massacre. That afternoon men armed with rifles, tomahawks, and other weapons stormed into town, invaded the workhouse where the Indians had been moved for safety, and murdered the three surviving families: three men, three women, three girls, and five boys. For decades before the massacres, European immigrants had pressed into Indian country, raising the values of lands held by the eastern elite and generating new social tensions and political disputes. In December 1763, however, the Paxtons shattered the founding covenant of Pennsylvania—peaceful coexistence with Native peoples—by destroying the Susquehannock in a surge of racial violence. On January 2, 1764, Governor Penn authorized a £200 reward for the leaders, having already ordered his justices and sheriffs to hunt them. A month later the Paxton Boys, rumored to be two hundred strong, headed toward Philadelphia to wipe out the Lenape people and display their power at the door of the proprietary regime. They made it to about Germantown before a gathering military response forced them to turn back.[2]

Edward Shippen was at least a passive conspirator in the destruction of the Susquehannock. He had, by his own account, at least two days' notice of the raiders' plans to attack Lancaster, where the Indians were being secured. He took no additional defensive actions. The Paxton Boys rode into town in the middle of the day, went directly to the workhouse, and, in a matter of minutes, entered the building and executed the remaining Susquehannock families. The sheriff and coroner tried to reason with the raiders but offered no physical resistance. Shippen did not even reach the scene until after the Paxtons were back on their horses and parading out of town.[3]

The fate of the American college had been intertwined from its beginning with the social project of dispossessing Indian people. For nearly fifty years Shippen sat on the board of the College of Philadelphia (University of Pennsylvania); in fact, several officers and trustees had personal or professional interests in the backcountry. The Penn family held sizable backcountry estates, and John Penn joined the board just months after the massacres.

Provost William Smith and trustee Richard Peters both owned property in Paxton. The most experienced land agent in the colony and the provincial secretary, Peters helped perpetrate the infamous Walking Purchase of 1737, in which William Penn's sons, John and Thomas, took more than a thousand square miles of Lenape land. James Logan, also a trustee, completed the swindle by forcing the arrangement on the Lenape and securing the support of the Six Nations of the Iroquois, who also helped remove the Lenape from eastern Pennsylvania. William Allen, chief justice of the colony and a charter trustee of the Philadelphia college, got ten thousand acres of disputed lands in a single grant and eventually established Allentown in the Walking Purchase territory. Peters also helped execute the Treaty of Fort Stanwix (1768), which resulted in the removal of the Lenape, Shawnee, and Ohio Iroquoian peoples in the rich Ohio Valley and the advance of white settlements across the Alleghenies.[4]

William Penn's colony was an enterprise. Individual colonists could purchase land directly from Penn, who also collected taxes. Colonists received incentives for importing servants. Penn sold tens of thousands of acres to land companies in Germany, Wales, London, and Ireland. Throughout the Mid-Atlantic, colonial authorities and land speculators recruited non-English Protestants to take up farms by purchase or tenancy. Scots-Irish immigrants poured into the Pennsylvania backcountry in the decades before the massacres. Tens of thousands of Germans—Palatines, Amish, Moravians, and Lutherans—went there too, carried to America on hundreds of vessels dedicated to that trade. In the 1740s the governor estimated that more than sixty thousand Pennsylvanians, three-fifths of the inhabitants, were German, a population that grew to more than a hundred thousand in the next decade. Swiss Mennonites settled as did Swedish Lutherans. Jews found acceptance as merchants and traders in Philadelphia and in the backcountry. Nathan Levy and David Franks, for example, held land claims in Upper Paxton a decade before the massacres.[5]

Men in the immigrant trade were overrepresented on the board of the Philadelphia college. Founding trustees John Inglis, Robert

Strettel, Edward Shippen, and George McCall brought German
and British immigrants and indentures into Pennsylvania. The
Philadelphia glassmaker Caspar Wistar, an early benefactor of the
college, built an Atlantic trading network and an impressive fortune on this German migration. Charles Willing, Philadelphia's
mayor and a trustee, owned a firm that used twenty-two ships to
transport more than four thousand Germans to the colony before the American Revolution. His son, Thomas, later partnered
with the financier and land speculator Robert Morris—who made
his money trading tobacco grown by slaves in Maryland—in a
firm that aggressively looked to exploit the war economy during
the American Revolution.[6]

Philadelphia rose on the interdependent trades in enslaved Africans, European immigrants, and lands from Indian clearances,
and men engaged in all three enterprises dominated the college.
They drew settlers into the backcountry by maintaining a thriving
slave market, which also provided bound labor for an expanding
manufacturing sector. Slaves augmented the workforce at the Berkshire Furnace iron works and at Charming Forge. In 1743 the
evangelist George Whitefield invited the United Brethren—a denomination that rose from the Mennonite and German Reformed
churches—to settle upon lands north of Philadelphia that he had
purchased from the Lenape with the intent of opening a school for
black children. Whitefield abandoned that project, and the Brethren established one of their many North American missions.[7]

In the wake of George Whitefield's 1740 American tour, a new
evangelical furor had awakened the colonies, where plans for new
schools began taking shape in the synods of New York and Philadelphia. In 1740 Whitefield opened an ephemeral charity school in
Philadelphia. When David Brainerd fell under the evangelical
sway, Yale president Thomas Clap expelled him. Protests from the
Reverend Jonathan Edwards and other leading New Lights, those
who embraced evangelicalism, failed to soften Yale's governors.
The alignment of Harvard and Yale against evangelicalism, which
culminated in the Harvard faculty's 1744 public condemnation
of Whitefield for appealing to what they saw as the emotional

stupidity of the people, further radicalized the evangelicals. In 1746, as has been previously discussed, the revivalists organized the College of New Jersey (Princeton). Among its founders were men who studied under the evangelical preacher William Tennent in Neshaminy, Pennsylvania. Brainerd headed to Elizabethtown, New Jersey, where he became a student of Jonathan Dickinson, the founding president of the new college. In 1749 leading Philadelphians drew up a constitution for an academy, chose Benjamin Franklin as the president, purchased the "New Building" that had housed Whitefield's school, and reserved free meeting space for Whitefield and the evangelist Gilbert Tennent.[8]

Evangelicalism generated social experiences that recast the denominational boundaries of the British colonies as immigrants changed the landscape of American religion.[9] There were other ideological, economic, and military pressures transforming the colonies. The Atlantic market—particularly the trades in enslaved Africans and European immigrants—drew merchants and farmers into continuous intercolonial exchanges and created new dependencies. A revolution in the arts and sciences spread a secular language for describing the connections between Euro-Americans, for understanding and legitimating their social privileges, and for crafting a shared history. European wars of succession and empire, culminating with the French and Indian War from 1754 to 1763, raised common threats and rationalized military and administrative bureaucracies throughout British America.

The General Assembly of Massachusetts sent Colonel Ephraim Williams and a few other English families to Stockbridge, Massachusetts, where the Reverend John Sergeant, a Yale alumnus, maintained a mission to the Housatonic and Mahican. Rev. Sergeant married Abigail Williams, the colonel's daughter, and they created a training ground for a generation of Connecticut missionaries. Before taking the presidency of the College of New Jersey, Jonathan Edwards preached at the Indian mission in Stockbridge, where he also gathered intelligence on Native nations. In 1743 the Society for the Propagation of the Gospel dispatched David Brainerd to preach to the Mahican east of Albany and west of Stockbridge.

Brainerd regularly traveled to Stockbridge to study the Indian languages. Gideon Hawley, a Yale graduate, and Timothy Woodbridge, also a Yale alumnus, began their careers in Stockbridge.
Brainerd, Hawley, and Woodbridge later organized missions in
New Jersey and Pennsylvania. Colonel Williams used the Stockbridge settlement to acquire tracts of Indian land in western Massachusetts, much of it taken through theft, rigged town votes, and
manipulations of law. At the outbreak of the French and Indian
War, Williams redrew his will to provide for his mother and siblings. His peace of mind was purchased by his land and slaveholdings. He gave £100 to each of his three sisters, and he instructed his
brothers to provide their mother an annual stipend from their inheritance: "my homestead at Stockbridge, with all the Buildings and
Appertenances thereunto belonging, with all the Stocks of Cattle
and Negro Servants now upon the place." The slaves included Moni,
an adult woman, a boy named London, and a girl called Cloe.[10]

Frenzied land speculation set the context for these missions and
reshaped white-Indian relations in New England, the Mid-Atlantic,
and the South. The College of New Jersey supported Brainerd's Lenape ministry. Hawley raised a church on disputed land across the
Pennsylvania border. Woodbridge took a share in the Susquehannah Land Company—a private stock company that purchased
western tracts to relocate Connecticut residents—in exchange for
representing its interests with the Six Nations, the Lenape, and the
Ohio Indians. A broad segment of Connecticut residents became,
almost overnight, committed to defending and asserting ancient
charter rights to territory in Pennsylvania. Certainly some of this
obsession was driven by land speculation in Connecticut that created a false scarcity, but it was also part of a greater colonial
phenomenon.[11]

In 1746 Peter Jefferson, a surveyor and minor planter from Virginia, had been part of a party that mapped one portion of Thomas
Lord Fairfax's five-million-acre Virginia holding. Jefferson later
invested in the Loyal Land Company, a private partnership active
in the territory that became Kentucky. He taught his eldest son,
Thomas, to survey, which Thomas then taught to his friend Meriwether Lewis. Upon his father's death, Thomas Jefferson inherited

stock in the land company, and he received the plantation where he later built his Monticello estate. White settlers gained that territory in the Piedmont and Shenandoah Valley of Virginia in a 1722 negotiation with the Iroquois at Albany, New York, in which the colonial government conveniently accepted the Iroquois's authority over the Indians of Virginia. In 1769, after he left William and Mary to finish his training in a law office, Thomas Jefferson began purchasing western lands with Virginia colleagues including Patrick Henry, an active speculator.[12]

In 1748 George Washington, only sixteen years old, had left Virginia to help survey Lord Fairfax's lands on the Pennsylvania border. That same year his brothers joined Thomas Lee in the Ohio Company, a partnership that sought to break the French hold on the frontier by colonizing a half-million-acre tract along the Ohio River. Virginia's elite dominated the new corporation. In 1753 Governor Robert Dinwiddie sent George Washington, now a Virginia militia colonel, and his troops to western Pennsylvania to send back intelligence on the French operations and movements. Colonel Washington strung forts along Virginia's northernmost boundaries to protect the Fairfax lands and the new British settlements. His aggressive defense of the Ohio Company outposts helped to spark the French and Indian War. Throughout his career Washington casually pursued his interests in western lands during his military assignments and engagements, and for good reason: Virginia governor Lord Dunmore compensated soldiers during the French and Indian War, in part, with promises of land. Washington received twenty thousand acres on the Ohio and Kanawha Rivers and purchased other claims. By the time of his death, his largest real estate holdings lay beyond Virginia. The activities of land-speculating Virginians, Anthony F. C. Wallace argues, caused a series of colonial and international conflicts that began with the French and Indian War and ended with the War of 1812.[13]

"PURELY WHITE PEOPLE"

Awakened Christianity provided a spiritual complement to an emerging economic and political entitlement. Midcentury white colonists claimed a divine right to North America. "We are become a great and growing people," declared Provost William Smith of this manifesting destiny, "extending, and likely to extend, our empire far over this continent." He pointed to "seminaries of Learning and the advancement of useful Science" as the instruments of this enlargement. The growth of the colonies was now a greater moral good than the conversion of Indians, since the advance of white civilization would best advertise the triumph of Protestantism. He offered a peculiar proof: Britain sat west of continental Europe because God wanted its people to claim America. The vicar of Newcastle, Delaware, John Brown, confirmed that it was in the strategic interests of the colonies to continue the culture wars upon Indians, and he even fantasized about a future in which Native Americans and Africans would thank white Christians for their efforts.[14]

Colleges, although church-based, intensified this vision. No longer instruments for civilizing "savages" and "heathens," eighteenth-century colleges became mechanisms for unifying the colonies. The first Jewish students on the American campus matriculated about 1750, a century after the first Native American scholars; and, paradoxically, Jews gained access at the very moment when Christians were doubting the value of educating Native people.

Founder of the College of Philadelphia, Benjamin Franklin began his published condemnation of the Conestoga bloodshed by casually accepting that Indian populations "diminish continually" whenever "settled in the Neighbourhood of White people." While Franklin rejected the vulgar theology of the backcountry presbyters who claimed divine authority to shed the blood of anyone with "a reddish brown Skin, and black Hair," he shared the basic tenets of their beliefs. A dozen years before the massacres, Franklin had expressed his concern that "the number of purely white people in the world is proportionably very small." His antislavery sentiments were conceived from a fear that Africans would darken the complexion of America. "Excluding all blacks and tawnys" could reverse this fate. Franklin praised the "lovely" red complexion of the Indians, a compliment made easier by his belief that they were doomed. President Ezra Stiles of Yale also anticipated the continued passive reduction of Native Americans. He had even invested in it: in the decade before the Conestoga massacres, Stiles, who graduated from Yale and was working there as a tutor, had become a stockholder and active supporter of the Susquehannah Company.[15]

Despite his rejection of homicidal violence, Benjamin Franklin was taken with the possibility of purifying North America. His "tawnys" were the German and Scottish immigrants crowding into the Pennsylvania backcountry. A longtime slaveholder, businessman, and land speculator, Franklin worried over the demographic consequences of his own economic actions. He made significant investments in legal and illegal schemes to grab western lands, combining with prominent Pennsylvanians including Samuel Wharton to outmaneuver their southern and northeastern rivals for control of the fertile regions across the Appalachian Mountain range. In 1766 he partnered in the Vandalia Company, later the Walpole Company, with the British banker Thomas Walpole to lobby for millions of acres in Ohio. George Washington's firm, the Mississippi Company, which included aristocratic Virginians such as Francis Lightfoot, Richard Henry Lee, and Arthur Lee, was also speculating in this region. Later, Franklin and his son united with Sir William Johnson, the Indian commissioner in New York, in a failed attempt to gain sixty million acres for the ephemeral Illinois Company.[16]

The American college eased the tensions between Franklin's financial and social concerns. Large settlements of foreign people in the backcountry threatened to "Germanize" the colony, and Franklin feared that they could no more be assimilated than they could "acquire our Complexion." But Provost Smith and several of his trustees were urging the colony to open backcountry schools to protect the immigrants from the corruptions of their "savage neighbors" and "Jesuitical enemies." The Anglican priest also sought to drive a wedge between the backcountry Germans and the seaboard Quakers.[17] American colonists no longer trusted that colleges could civilize Indians, but they were confident that they could civilize Germans.

It is a fair measure of the velocity of racial thought in colonial North America that Franklin's "tawnys" did whiten, and rapidly. They even whitened in Franklin's mind. The belief in the biological supremacy of white nations allowed him to flatten the cultural barriers between European peoples and bridge the religious or denominational divisions that had been the organizing bases of the colonies. In 1787 Franklin became the largest single donor—giving an initial £200—and the namesake of Franklin College (Franklin and Marshall) in the backcountry. Benjamin Rush, the scientist and signer of the Declaration of Independence, was a charter trustee of the new "German College." Rush predicted that "our children will be bound together by the ties of marriage, as we shall be by the ties of friendship, and in the course of a few years by means of this College the names of German—Irishman & Englishman will be lost in the general name of Pennsylvanian." Four years earlier, Dr. Rush had organized Dickinson College in nearby Carlisle, Pennsylvania. Leading Virginians were speculating west of the Appalachian boundary, in Kentucky, where they raised Transylvania College, a Presbyterian frontier school.[18]

The whitening of colonial society and the secularism of the Enlightenment created some space for Jews. In 1762 the Manhattan merchant and King's College (Columbia) trustee John Watts wrote to Moses Franks—the son of the New York slave traders Jacob Franks and Abigail Levy—recommending Dr. James Jay, who "has undertaken to serve our College & I hope may succeed." Franks was a foreign agent for King's at the time of Jay's British fund-raising trip. Watts's business partner Oliver DeLancey, a trustee, was married to Phila Franks, Moses's sister. Franks had joined the Watts and DeLancey firm in numerous West Indies investments, and he had served as Watts's London representative. The contributions of Jewish merchants as privateers in the Atlantic colonial wars encouraged greater religious tolerance. Judah Hays, a prominent West Indies trader, was among the New York merchants whose ships attacked French interests. Moses Michael Hays, his son, was a founder of the Massachusetts Bank and a benefactor of Harvard College. Rabbi Gershom Mendes Seixas later served three decades as a trustee of King's College. Jacob Rodriguez de Rivera and Aaron Lopez of Newport gave generously to the College of Rhode Island (Brown), where such gifts, large and small, moved the trustees to open the college to Jews. Rodriguez de Rivera also donated to Yale.[19]

By midcentury, colonial campuses were changing remarkably. In 1750 Isaac Isaacs graduated from Yale. Seven years later, a Jewish student enrolled at the College of Philadelphia. In 1772 Moses Levy finished Philadelphia, the least restrictive colonial school. A dozen Jewish students graduated from Philadelphia before the Revolution. In that same era, Isaac Abrahams completed the undergraduate course at King's. A woman, Richea Gratz, was one of four Jews—Hyman Gratz, and Jacob and William Franks, were the others—in the first graduating class of Franklin College.[20]

Many Americans saw this new strategic and social potential of colleges. As colonial and British troops were mustering in Albany, New York, during the summer of 1755, Colonel Ephraim Williams had looked to the future by designating funds in his will for a college. He was killed at the Battle of Lake George. In the following decades, hundreds of white families moved into western Massachusetts, where Williams had considerable property, and where the government was actively eliminating Indian claims. In 1793 the residents of West Township (Williamstown), Massachusetts, requested that endowment for Williams College.[21]

Although he never attended college, George Washington crafted a philosophy of education that emphasized the need for schools and the benefits of making higher education more accessible. He saw a danger in sending American youth to study abroad, where they were exposed to antirepublican ideas. The president bequeathed $4,000 in local bank stock to Alexandria Academy (1785), a school for poor and orphaned children; a hundred James River Company shares to Liberty Hall Academy (Washington and Lee); fifty shares of the Potomac Company for a proposed university in the District of Columbia; and stock from both land companies to fund "the establishment of a University in the central part of the United States." Washington prayed that the latter institution would help Americans overcome "local prejudices and habitual jealousies" by "spread[ing] systematic ideas through all parts of this rising empire."[22]

THE RACIAL DESTINY OF AMERICA

Old and New Light, Anglican and dissenter, Tory and rebel, British and continental, the people of the North American colonies embraced a new future. Evangelized by their pastor, John Elder, the Paxton Boys believed that it was the racial destiny of white Christians to possess the earth. Enlightened humanism could easily be hijacked by racialism; it required only that the individual and natural value of human beings be assigned as a group characteristic rather than a universal one. For white Americans, racial beliefs intermingled with the spiritual promises of evangelicalism and the economic benefits of territorial expansion to affirm their future. Those who condemned the Paxton Boys objected to the means that the mob employed but not to the society that its members imagined. During the French and Indian War, William Smith urged greater militarization of the backcountry, and he mentored Thomas Barton, a backcountry apologist for the destruction of the Susquehannocks. A product of Trinity College in Dublin, Rev. Barton served as one of the first tutors at Philadelphia and took an honorary master's degree there a few years before the bloodshed.[23] Even the most rhetorically affectionate pleas for Native people conceded a dreadful fate for Indian nations. These were not friends but eulogists.

The French and Indian War was a global conflict that American colonists also saw as a struggle between the races. The Reverend Samuel Davies prepared a company of his Virginia neighbors for battle with gory images of the torments that awaited them if they fell to "the savage Tyranny of a mungrel Race of French and Indian Conquerors." Evangelical ministers on both sides of the Atlantic accepted the war as a punishment from God. Samuel Finley, who like Davies later served as president of New Jersey, instructed his Pennsylvania and Delaware parishioners that it was their spiritual duty to defend the Protestant God. Davies coordinated missions to the

Cherokee and other Indian nations in the Carolinas and Virginia, where the growth of the white population had sparked recent violence. He also urged his Scots Presbyterian neighbors to evangelize their slaves, but it would take more than vibrant preaching to convince southern slaveholders that "those stupid despised black Creatures, that many treat as if they were Brutes, are in this important Respect, upon an Equality with their haughty Masters."[24]

Provost Smith told a Philadelphia battalion that they were defending their communities against the combined threat of "popish Perfidy, French Tyranny[,] and savage Barbarity." Professor Paul Jackson, the Latin instructor at the college, assumed a captaincy. Rev. Davies warned a Virginia militia company that they were saving children from being "torn from the Arms of their murdered Parents," educated by savages, and "formed upon the Model of a ferocious Indian Soul." Smith even wrote a song to teach Indians' their social status:

> *Indian* Nations! Now repeat,—
> "Heav'n preserve the *British* State!
> "And the *British* Chief, and Race,
> "And these Lands,—and bless the Peace."[25]

As the conflict raged, the Reverend John Witherspoon addressed the annual meeting of the Society in Scotland for Propagating Christian Knowledge (SSPCK) at Edinburgh. Witherspoon cautioned that Britain was suffering God's wrath for its failure to evangelize the Native peoples of America. There was a divine warning in France's allegiance with the "Indians, a great part of whose territory we possess, and whom, with a contempt equally impolitic and unchristian, we suffer to continue in ignorance of the only living and true God." Catholic missions were the foundation of the French-Indian union, and Protestants needed to counter the designs of that "politic, but fraudulent nation." Military strategy and religious duty were one. The North American conflict proved the need for the British missionary companies' efforts among Indians, a strategically necessary "exercise of Christian charity."[26]

American campuses became militarized spaces during the
eighteenth-century imperial wars; they also became increasingly
hostile to Indians. A commencement at the College of New Jersey
included the singing of an ode that wedded the fate of the school,
familiarly known as Nassau Hall, to the outcome of the French
and Indian War:

> Unmov'd at War's tremendous Roar,
> That Consternation spreads from Shore to Shore,
> O'er solid Continents, and tossing Waves,
>
> From Haughty Monarchs down to Slaves . . .
> Peaceful Nassau! In thee we sing—
> We sing great George upon the Throne,
> And Amherst brave in Arms,
> Amherst brave in Arms.

This was no hollow tribute. The graduates and audience specifically sang praises to General Jeffrey Amherst, the commander of
King George III's North American forces, for pursuing the Indians to avenge "sacred British Blood." A decade later, Rev. Witherspoon accepted the presidency of the Princeton college. His
commitment to Native education largely evaporated. He tutored
three Lenape students and a few other "Indian boys," but no Native students graduated under his tenure and indigenous students
were soon gone from the campus.[27]

WHITENING THE PROMISED LAND

On August 6, 1760, the merchant Abraham DePeyster, treasurer
of the New York province and a founding trustee of King's College,
collected duties on eighty-three enslaved people brought from Africa to Manhattan on the sloop *Sally*. Colonel Henry Bouquet, a
Swede fighting in the British army and stationed in North America during the French and Indian War, purchased York, one of the
Africans being held on board.[28] Enslaved black people routinely

accompanied the British and colonial forces as cooks, laborers, and servants. Young black boys were often used as drummers. It is significant that Bouquet bought a slave during a prolonged and vicious military campaign.

The century of the Enlightenment brought the high point of the African slave trade and the rise of systematic racial extermination. At the end of the French and Indian War, Lord Amherst informed Colonel Bouquet of his continuing doubts about even friendly and allied Native peoples. "I never will put the least trust in any of the Indian race," the general warned. That statement followed an intense summer of strategizing, during which Bouquet and Amherst had cursed Indians, conspired for revenge, made plans to kill any who had taken up arms, and plotted to eliminate the Native presence from all the territory between Fort Pitt and Lake Erie. The subject of racial cleansing bound these communications. "I will try to inoculate the [Indians] with some blankets that may fall into their Hands, and take care not to get the disease myself," Bouquet replied. By distributing smallpox-infected blankets as gifts, the colonel promised to destroy Indian resistance and then hunt the survivors "with English dogs, supported by rangers and some light horse." In just a few casual sentences, Amherst and Bouquet designed a campaign to "effectually extirpate or remove that vermin."[29]

As Jeffrey Amherst and Henry Bouquet plotted, Councilor John Watts of New York, a trustee of King's College, fumed over the western forts and towns sacked by the Indians. A confederacy from more than a dozen nations, including the Ojibwa, Shawnee, Wyandot, Miami, and Lenape, had risen against the British forces and white settlers in the Great Lakes region in response to Amherst's violations of their sovereignty in the aftermath of the French and Indian War. Named Pontiac's Rebellion, after an Ottawa chief who exhorted pan-Indian resistance, the uprising shocked war-weary English colonists. In a letter to his occasional business partner Moses Franks, Watts concluded that "our formerly stupid Savages are become great Proficients in Warr." In other exchanges, Watts estimated the size of the English forces being gathered to wipe out the Lenape and Shawnee, whom he dismissed as "human Beasts." John Bard, a King's alumnus who was studying medicine in Edinburgh, sent regrets to his father over the continued violence on the frontier but added his suspicion that the colonists might be responsible.[30]

Under the pseudonym "A Lover of This Country," Rev. Smith published a laudatory history of Henry Bouquet's campaign against the Ohio Indians. The frontier remained tense. Edward Shippen was demanding that Bouquet compensate the backcountry settlers for their services. William Trent was representing Pennsylvania farmers who had lost crops, homes, cattle, and slaves to Indian war parties. Trent, Samuel Wharton, and other Pennsylvania lawyers and merchants pursued these claims against various, even random, Native nations and communities for years.[31]

The French defeat made even more tangible the colonists' sense that the continent was theirs, and Pontiac's Rebellion provided an immediate justification to pursue that claim. Several years later, a member of the first class of the College of Philadelphia, which graduated during the war, began a Caribbean fund-raising appeal for New Ark Academy in Delaware by rhetorically making indigenous people disappear to underscore the power of Christian education and English civilization: "A vast tract of land, which had been inhabited by a few small tribes of barbarous savages, in a short time is become the happy residence of *three millions of British subjects*."[32]

The fates of the colleges were again fused with the hostilities. Among the odd pieces of business that appeared on General Amherst's desk were numerous petitions from schools. Eleazar Wheelock asked Amherst for a grant in New York, where the Mohegan minister Samson Occom's work in the Oneida nation had prepared the ground, and where Wheelock had been courting the Onondaga and the Mohawk. The remnants of several Indian nations from New England found refuge among the Iroquois, increasing Occom's and Wheelock's influence in the region. President Samuel Johnson accused the governors of King's College of failing to seek aid from the victorious general, but on May 10, 1763, after they installed a new president, the trustees formed a committee "to wait upon Jeffrey Amherst and Governor [Robert] Monckton with Subscription paper and request their Bounty." Lord Amherst responded to Wheelock: "The Design is a very Commendable One, and I

President Eleazar Wheelock of Dartmouth College
SOURCE: Hood Museum, Dartmouth College

should be Extremely happy in having it in my power to be any ways Instrumental in Civilizing the Indians; and in promoting Seminaries of Learning in this Country." He declined to grant the minister's request, however, insisting that he lacked the power to dispense confiscated lands and forwarding Wheelock's appeal to England.[33]

An early supporter of the Susquehannah Land Company, Dr. Wheelock also considered relocating his school to Pennsylvania despite the resistance of Commissioner William Johnson, who privately labeled this one "of the Schemes that had their birth in N[ew] England" and were "calculated with a View of forming Settlements so obnoxious to the Indians." Johnson was concerned about the New Englanders' territorial ambitions in New York and Pennsylvania, having already sided with the Penn family in the controversies over Connecticut's western claims. The Susquehannah Company offered Wheelock a sixty-square-mile grant for his Indian academy.[34]

Nonetheless, even as the enmity between the colonists and Native peoples peaked, college officers were promoting Indian education to raise money in Britain. In 1753 the Presbyterian Synod of New York sent Samuel Davies and Gilbert Tennent to England on behalf of New Jersey, the school's second tour in fewer than five years. "And oh! how transporting the Tho't, that these Barbarians may be cultivated by divine Grace in the use of the proper Means, and polished into genuine Disciples of the Blessed Jesus!" Rev. Davies prayed before his departure. They raised £3,000 during a two-year tour.[35]

By the time Samson Occom arrived in England on behalf of Rev. Wheelock's school, these American agents were bumping into one another as they rushed to meet potential donors. In 1762, during the war, Provost William Smith took the dangerous trip to England, only to find James Jay appealing to the same patrons for King's College in New York. The Archbishop of Canterbury combined the campaigns and divided the proceeds between the two schools; altogether the Pennsylvanians took away nearly £7,000, while the New Yorkers claimed £10,000. In letters to the English clergy and the crown, Smith and Jay stressed that their colleges were struggling to recover from "the Ravages of a destructive War, which laid waste a considerable part of both Provinces." Occom's tour had modest results in Ireland because the Reverend Morgan Edwards had just finished scouring the Protestant settlements for the College of Rhode Island. In London, Rev. Occom ran into Jay in the midst of an appeal. Jay was emphasizing the religious and strategic benefits of converting Native peoples, countering popish missions from Canada, and unifying what had always been an especially diverse colony. He was knighted for his efforts.[36]

Although he still promoted himself as an Indian teacher, Rev. Wheelock was shifting his energies to the college and its white students. He confronted an Anglican hierarchy suspicious of Congregationalist expansion, eroding support for Indian instruction in New England, and power brokers such as William Johnson who controlled access to more promising western missionary fields. A special SSPCK committee held a portion of the £12,000 collected by Samson Occom, and forwarded the interest to the college at a time when the Indian academy was a minor concern.[37]

The Mohegan minister Samson Occom

There was, in fact, little Native education at Dartmouth. On June 15, 1774, Dr. Wheelock penned a letter introducing and recommending Levi Frisbie to Arent DePeyster, the commander of Fort Michilimackinac, at the nexus of Lakes Huron and Michigan. A year earlier he had sent Captain DePeyster a copy of his history of the Indian mission, and now he was calling on their acquaintance to help Frisbie gain access to the northwestern nations. Three days later Rev. Frisbie pushed a well-stocked canoe into the Connecticut River and paddled toward Canada to settle some of Wheelock's students among the northern nations, where they planned to learn the northern and western languages and recruit Indian children. The four-month expedition, much of it by water, was disappointing. The delegation never reached the western territories. Where they did go, they found it difficult to evangelize under the gaze of Catholic priests. Frisbie returned with several boys for the charity school: "the oldest is not above fifteen years old; and they all have a good deal of English blood in their veins."[38]

Wheelock had developed a preference for "white Indians" from lower Canada—many of whose ancestors were English captives—whom he believed were better suited to Christian education and Anglo culture. He seems to have acquired a similar preference for "white Negroes." In 1770 Caleb Watts began privately studying geography, rhetoric, theology, and philosophy under Wheelock. Watts was the son of an English woman and a black man. Wheelock had initially intended to use Watts for a West Indies mission. At the outbreak of the Revolution, Wheelock sent Watts to the South in hopes that the black preacher could help the colonists prevent slave revolts during the upheaval of the English invasion. Not only were there few Indians at Dartmouth, but Indian students were increasingly unwelcome. Colonel Samuel Stevens warned Wheelock that he would remove his brother from the college if the young man was required to live in quarters with Indians rather than boarding in town with a white family.[39]

"From what I can gather it is to be a grand Presbyterian College, instead of a School for the poor Indians," President James Manning of Rhode Island commented upon Wheelock's New Hampshire initiative. Manning feared that Dartmouth was a hundred miles from any sizable Indian community, and it had but a few highly assimilated Native students "who are brought up like us." The Rhode Island president predicted that the money that Nathaniel Whitaker and Samson Occom raised in Britain would be "greatly prostituted." Two years later Ezra Stiles confirmed Manning's doubts: "Dr. Wheelock[']s Indian College . . . has already almost lost sight of its original Design." The task of finding Native students became less attractive as tensions between England and the colonies extinguished British funding. The same shifting fortunes soon led the trustees of William and Mary to close their Indian College and convert the building, Brafferton Hall, into a dormitory for white students. "Doc[to]r Wheelock's Indian Academy or Schools are become altogether unprofitable to the poor Indians," proclaimed an outraged Rev. Occom, who complained that his mentor had done "little or no good to the Indians with all that money we collected in England."[40]

In the aftermath of the French and Indian War, the new strategic and economic interests of the colonists reoriented religious outreach. The Reverend Samuel Johnson endorsed William Johnson's "plan for civilizing and converting the Indians by first a school for the six nations at Fort Hunter." The Anglican hierarchy saw the techniques that the dissenting churches had used against the Indian nations in New England as a model for New York. A Connecticut native, Rev. Johnson examined Wheelock's Indian school and concluded that "he has certainly fallen upon the right method for converting the Heathen, by civilizing their children, & teaching them Husbandry, & the arts & manufactures, while he teaches them Christianity."[41]

The colonists' desire to reduce the commercial and military power of the Iroquois excited an interdenominational competition to establish a college within the Six Nations. As soon as he was installed as the rector of Trinity Church in New York City, Samuel Auchmuty began lobbying for a greater Anglican commitment in Iroquoia. Wheelock had long advertised his academy as the Protestant response to Catholic intrusions from Canada into New York and New England. He recruited Iroquois students to his schools and sent several ministers, including Samson Occom and Samuel Kirkland, to the Iroquois Confederacy. "Religious principles are debauched by the stupid Bigots that Wheelock is continually turning too go among them," Rev. Auchmuty complained to Commissioner Johnson. He charged that poorly trained missionaries, "Wheelock[']s Cubs," were in Iroquoia advancing not religion but the political and economic interests of the dissenters. "Such Wretches ought not to be suffered to go among the Indians."[42]

Differing plans for a Six Nations College were advocated by

William Smith of Philadelphia; Myles Cooper, who succeeded Samuel Johnson at King's; Eleazar Wheelock; Samuel Kirkland, the SSPCK's missionary to the Oneida and Seneca; and John Brainerd, who replaced his brother in the Lenape ministry in New Jersey. William Johnson blocked many of the dissenters' efforts. He pointed Wheelock to the Carolinas, where, he suggested, an academy could help to subdue the Cherokee, Choctaw, and Creek. Meanwhile, Anglicans in New York City were designing a school on the Reverend Henry Barclay's estate in Mohawk territory, which they planned to link to King's. Commissioner Johnson was quietly exploring building his own academy at Mount Johnson on the Mohawk River, which neighbored a major Mohawk town and Fort Hunter.[43]

The emerging political crisis between Britain and its mainland American colonies preempted this final culture war. The Iroquois and the colonists were rapidly approaching a more decisive conflict. Enraged settlers had exterminated an entire community on the southern border of Iroquoia, and British forces had attempted genocide to the west. Massive commercial partnerships were targeting Indians' lands in western Pennsylvania, Ohio, Illinois, Kentucky, and Mississippi. During a 1765 funeral in Iroquoia, the Seneca Onoonghwandekha implored the delegates to remember the "ruined" Indian nations to the east. These people had been defeated and disarmed, and made into peasants and servants. The fiercest men now labored like "mere women." Samuel Kirkland was there and recorded the speech. Onoonghwandekha warned that if the Six Nations failed to unite and fight against the colonists, "we shall be sunk so low as to hoe corn & squashes in the fields, chop wood, stoop down & milk cows like *negroes* among the Dutch people."[44]

RAZING IROQUOIA

"Civilization or death to all American Savages" was an odd chant for an army fighting England. On July 4, 1779, General Enoch Poor's men remained in camp at Wyoming, Pennsylvania, feasting and singing in celebration of the third anniversary of the Declaration of Independence. The officers worked to build hatred toward Indians among men who likely needed little encouragement to despise Native peoples. In the presence of friendly Indians, the white soldiers drew liquor rations and entertained themselves by watching and mocking Indian dances. "A sufficient number of large boats are to be designed for the conveyance of all liquors belonging to the several state stores," an officer in the Eleventh Pennsylvania Regiment reported. The quartermaster general also bought liquor from the local residents and threatened to punish anyone who attempted to evade the military's liquor monopoly. General George Washington ordered wildness. He instructed General John Sullivan to do his business "with as much impetuosity, shouting, and noise, as possible," and to "make the troops act in as loose and dispersed a way" as was consistent with maintaining minimal military discipline. Washington also wanted "as many prisoners of every age and sex as possible" to be used as hostages and demanded "that the country may not be merely overrun, but destroyed." Have the men "rush on with the war-whoop and fixed bayonet. Nothing will disconcert and terrify the Indians more than this."[45]

The troops mustered in a region where German and Scots-Irish immigrants had been settling for most of the century. Land companies based in several colonies were active in this territory. George Washington had surveyed the area in 1753 while a Virginia militia officer. Two years before the Revolution began, Virginia governor John Murray, Earl of Dunmore, had tussled with Governor Thomas Penn of Pennsylvania over western lands. Murray had investments in the Ohio Valley and his government was under pressure to make good on the land warrants for veterans of the French and Indian War. When fighting began in spring 1775 between British and colonial troops, Dunmore had forced terms upon the Shawnee and Ohio Iroquois, requiring that they abandon claims south of the Ohio River and surrender all the black people living in their villages.[46]

Numerous Native nations were already involved in the colonial insurgency. The Reverend Samuel Kirkland had put himself in the service of the new government. In the spring of 1777 Kirkland brought an Oneida sachem to New Jersey to treat with General Washington; at this meeting the Six Nations were informed that the colonists now had French support. Indian nations generally attempted neutrality in this civil war, but British and American policy aimed to force them into the conflict. "If we are conquered our Lands go with yours," Chief Solomon of the Stockbridge assured the revolutionaries, "but if we are victorious we hope you will help us recover our just Rights." The predicament of the Stockbridge left little room for diplomacy: their remaining lands were encircled by the colonists, they housed one of the oldest and most successful Christian missions, and the British had proven to be unreliable partners in the past. The Six Nations divided. The Oneida fought with the colonists. Joseph Brant (Thayendanegea) led a large Mohawk faction to the British, and the Seneca eventually joined the English. The war posed an existential threat to the sovereignties of numerous nations. General Nathanael Greene advised Washington to make a summer attack on Iroquoia from three directions in order to inflict maximum damage on the food supplies and ease the burden of moving armies, equipment, and provisions.[47]

Washington imposed strict secrecy on his officers and repeatedly instructed them to hide the target of the expedition from their Native allies, particularly the Ohio Indians and the Oneida. He intended to force the western Indians to decide between Iroquoia and their own lands, and to make the Oneida choose between their own families and houses and those of their Iroquois brothers and sisters. He left Colonel Daniel Brodhead specific instructions on what to do when the plan could no longer be hidden: "Contrive ways to inform them, that you are going to meet a large force, to fall upon and destroy the whole country of the Six Nations," and tell them that if they "give the least disturbance . . . the whole force will be turned against them; and that we will never rest, till we have cut them off from the face of the earth."[48]

Washington intended to shatter the Six Nations. "Our army here is very respectable notwithstanding so many & so great detachments are made from it to Rhode Island against the Indians, to Fort Arnold, & c.," Dr. William Shippen wrote from his military camp at White Plains, New York. William Livingston had his troops stationed on the eastern border of Iroquoia, cutting off any escape and providing reconnaissance on British forces, Tories, and hostile Indians. Lieutenant Colonel Philip Van Cortlandt, an heir of the founder of the New York manor, served in General Poor's army. General Philip Schuyler, who led the later Montreal campaign, headed a family that spent a century encouraging conflicts that advanced their land claims in New York. After the Revolution, Schuyler was among the most aggressive usurpers of state and federal authority over the Iroquois lands. There were Stocktons, Ogdens, Hardenberghs, and other elite colonial families in the officer corps, and the rank and file of the New Jersey and Pennsylvania regiments included numerous backcountry settlers.[49]

Several prominent Christian clerics dressed for war, including John Rodgers of New York City; Andrew Hunter, later a trustee and professor at the College of New Jersey; Israel Evans, a graduate of the same school; and William Rogers, who became a professor at Philadelphia after the war. The Reverend Thomas Barton enlisted as a chaplain. Already a paid agent and advisor to the new government, Kirkland took a commission as a chaplain and interpreter in Sullivan's armies. Ministers offered Sunday services for the regiments and blessed their enterprise. Rev. Rogers opened the Fourth of July holiday with a celebration of the Declaration of Independence and a sermon that expounded on the biblical call to "remember Jehovah, who is great and terrible, and fight for your brethren, sons and your daughters, your wives and your houses." The men could choose a Dutch Reformed, Baptist, Presbyterian, or Congregational service, and they could also select ministers from their own colonies.[50]

The campaign sought to end Indian raids on the western frontier and reduce any long-term barriers to settler expansion. "While the Six Nations were under this rod of correction," Washington boasted to the Marquis de Lafayette from his post on the Hudson River, Colonel Brodhead led six hundred troops to destroy the towns and food supplies of the Ohio Indians. Washington had threatened the Ohio nations to keep them still during the Iroquois campaign, but he also wanted to open the Ohio and Mississippi river valleys. "Correction" was the euphemism that Master Washington used to order the whipping of his black slaves, and its application to Indians was more than rhetorical. "These unexpected and severe strokes have disconcerted, humbled, and distressed the Indians exceedingly," he assured the French general. Sullivan's troops imposed their common racial vision upon the landscape. They responded with severity to the significant African American and Afro-Indian presence in Iroquoia. The Mohawk leader Joseph Brant alone had dozens of free and enslaved black people—many of the latter taken during colonial raids—on his estate. In April 1779 Colonel Goose Van Schaick's men attacked an Onondaga town, taking three dozen prisoners and executing fifteen others, "particularly a Negro who was their D[octo]r." In fact, Sullivan's forces reported killing every black person they captured.[51]

His men also grasped the greater design of the campaign. "I should not think it an affront to the Divine will, to lay some effectual plan, either to civilize, or totally extirpate the race," Major Jeremiah Fogg, Harvard class of 1768, wrote of the Native population. Fogg found the idea of befriending Indians offensive, and he doubted that any lasting peace could be maintained in the absence of a military threat. That suspicion reflected the popular digestion of academic discourses about race. "To starve them is equally impracticable for they feed on air and drink the morning dew," he concluded in support of more violent measures.[52]

Sullivan had five thousand soldiers at his command. By the time they completed their mission at the end of September 1779, the troops had razed forty Iroquois towns and demolished several hundred buildings, including longhouses, storage houses, and churches and schools. On August 14, Lieutenant Erkuries Beatty's regiment burned the Susquehanna River town where Gideon Hawley had built his mission a generation earlier with the encouragement of the Susquehannah Land Company directors. Beatty's father was the Rev. Charles Beatty, an evangelical Presbyterian who succeeded William Tennent in the Scots-Irish stronghold of Neshaminy. This town was filled with "good Log houses with

Stone Chimneys and glass windows[,] it likewise had a Church."
The army destroyed a Christian town in the name of the Christian
God. A month later Dr. Jabez Campfield's New Jersey regiment
arrived at Shannondaque, which was "the best built Indian Town
I have yet seen, the houses mostly new, & mostly log houses." In
early September, Lieutenant Charles Nukerck, a New Yorker,
marveled at "an Old Inhabited Town—their Houses large and
Elegant [and] b[ea]utifully painted"—off the shores of Cayuga
Lake.[53] That too they burned.

The troops were often genuinely shocked at the refinement of
their allegedly savage enemies. They commented repeatedly upon
the advanced construction of Iroquois houses, longhouses, public
buildings, barns, and shops. "The situation of this village is beautiful," admitted Lieutenant Colonel Adam Hubley after entering
Chemung. A couple of weeks later, he saw "the finest village we
have yet come to." This town "contains about forty well-finished
houses, and every thing about it seems neat and well improved."
Hubley was breathless when his forces invaded the heart of the
Seneca nation, the most populous and powerful branch of the confederacy. "Oh! Britain, behold and blush," he gasped upon seeing
Genesee, a town of more than a hundred handsome buildings. A
carpenter from New Hampshire, Captain Daniel Livermore,
agreed: it is "the best town I have seen." Lieutenant John Jenkins
was born and raised in New England and worked for the Susquehannah Company in various capacities, including as a land surveyor. After the war, he settled in the Pennsylvania backcountry.
Jenkins entered the capital of the Seneca in early September and
carefully noted the features of this "very beautiful town" and territory in his journal. Gazing upon the ruins of one town, William
McKendry counted about sixty houses that had cellars and wells.
"It was a fine settlement before it was destroyed," he reluctantly
conceded, "considering that they were Indians."[54]

In the name of white civilization, the army eradicated Indian
civilization. As his troops torched Iroquoia, General Washington
sent encouragement. Tearing down villages was but part of the
task. "The nests are destroyed," Major Fogg quipped, "but the birds
are still on the wing." Throughout the march, the men admired and

envied the abundance, quality, and range of food. The invasion was timed to leave the Iroquois with neither shelter nor food as winter approached.[55] It required more than a million man-hours to raze the structures, food stores, plantations, orchards, and livestock.

The colonial army burned millions of pounds of vegetables and fruits that had been stored for the winter or had not yet been harvested. Soldiers poisoned water supplies with animal carcasses. Lieutenant Beatty helped torch "about 150 acres of the best corn that Ever I saw (some of the Stalks grew 16 feet high) besides great Quantities of Beans, Potatoes, Pumpkins, Cucumbers, Squashes, & Watermellons." Sergeant Thomas Roberts of New Jersey saw "no End hardley" to one plantation. Lieutenant William Barton's "whole army has subsisted for days" off a single Seneca farm. "This morning we had a dainty repast on the fruits of the savages," Major Fogg gleefully reported. Some soldiers became bitter when officers prohibited them from grazing in the orchards. When General Sullivan proposed reducing the troops' meat, flour, and salt rations by half in exchange for the freedom to eat from the Iroquois supplies, the men responded "by unanimously holding up their hands and giving three cheers." The soldiers stayed up late into the evening "feasting on these rarities," including cobs of corn more than a foot long, and then burned what they could not eat or carry. A New Jersey regiment marched through a cornfield plucking snacks. In a single Cayuga village Sergeant Major George Grant's men destroyed a vast orchard, "about 1500 Peach Trees, besides Apple Trees and other Fruit Trees." Sullivan's forces girdled or burned thousands upon thousands of trees. During a late September feast, the men prayed to extend the campaign against the western Indians rather than to go home.[56]

Colonel Van Cortlandt had led an especially comfortable life but nonetheless marveled at "the finest Fields of Corn I Ever saw." As they destroyed Chemung and ripped through Seneca country, his troops fed freely. "We have Lived like princes untill this time and shall for 5 or 6 weeks longer," the colonel wrote to his brother in August 1779. Toward the end of the campaign several regiments camped near the Hudson. "This day Genl. Washington rode through this camp," William McKendry excitedly recorded in early

November when the commander came to consult with General Sullivan.

Washington achieved his aim of breaking the military power of the Six Nations. The campaign left thousands of Iroquois desperate. "I very much apprehend that these Indians will join the enemy," General Schuyler warned James Duane a couple of years later. The tragedy needed to be abated. Schuyler even requested discarded clothing to help his "distressed Oneida Friends."[57]

"GOD'S GOOD PROVIDENCE"

It was a violent transfer of sovereignty. In a 1783 sermon celebrating the American Revolution, Yale president Ezra Stiles lauded the rise of the "Whites" whose numerical growth alone proved divine favoritism toward the children of Europe. God intended the Americas for "a new enlargement of Japhet," the minister began, invoking the curse of Ham, and Europe's children were quickly filling the continents. Not a single Indian nation, including those allied to the Americans, was represented at the negotiations in Paris, which established a new sovereignty over an enormous slice of North America. Stiles defensively insisted that Protestants had faithfully purchased Indian land to erase any sense of historical wrong. He also crafted a bizarre defense of conquest: the surviving Indians benefited from colonialism since the value of their remaining territories had increased thousands of times. Projecting the growth of the white population to three hundred million, Rev. Stiles predicted "a constant increasing revenue to the Sachems and original Lords of the Soil" from whatever lands the survivors could hold.[58]

This odd rationalization of a human tragedy was made worse by President Stiles's belief that any remaining social injustices would disappear with Native Americans and Africans, whose decline seemed inevitable. It was "God's good providence," the president continued, that the vanishing of nonwhite people would also erase the moral problem of dispossession and enslavement. Breaking with a long theological tradition, Stiles applied the curse of Ham to Indians too: "I rather consider the American Indians as Canaanites."

These were Noah's least fortunate descendants, and their destruction proved God's benevolence toward white people. Stiles fathered a new metaphor: the United States was "God's American
Israel." Filled with allusions to superior blood and other suggestions of European supremacy, President Stiles's sermon exposed
the tight braiding of eighteenth-century natural rights philosophy,
science, and theology. "Can we contemplate their present, and an-
ticipate their future increase, and not be struck with astonishment
to find ourselves in the midst of the fulfillment of the prophecy of
Noah?"[59]

White Christians had used their experiences and histories with
Native Americans and Africans to assert their own divine privilege, and they were weaving these same ideas into universal and
dangerous "truths" about the nature of human populations. In
the decades after the war, hundreds of thousands of white people
moved into Iroquoia and western Pennsylvania.[60] They surrounded
and segregated the last of the Indian nations as they laid claim to
new entitlements.

Samuel Kirkland also returned. In 1791 he authored a "Plan for
Education for the Indians," in which he proposed a college in
Oneida to bring several youth from the Six Nations each year for
instruction and then return them to their communities as teachers.
The original design included Indian trustees and white and Indian
resident students. In a letter to Joseph Brant, Kirkland detailed the
benefits of the school for the Iroquois. However, after it was chartered in 1793, Hamilton Oneida Academy—named for Treasury
secretary Alexander Hamilton, a trustee and a veteran of Washington's army—enrolled "only one eight-year-old Indian boy." The
Indian grammar school floundered and went several years without
a teacher, which Kirkland blamed on a lack of funds. The secretary
of the Society in Scotland for Propagating Christian Knowledge
later begged Rev. Kirkland to explain the failure of Indian education at Dartmouth and Hamilton. "Indeed we are still left very
much in doubt whether any efforts however ably or zealously conducted will have effect in any considerable degree to change the
character of the Indian Tribes," the Reverend John Kemp regret-
fully admitted from Edinburgh. His questions were less an attack

on Kirkland and Wheelock than a reflection of the SSPCK's frustration with Indian missions. Perhaps, Kemp queried, the attempt to civilize indigenous peoples was itself destroying them. Perhaps, he probed in even more dire terms, "it is true as has been strongly asserted to us, that they decline so fast in number that there is reason to apprehend a speedy extinction of the race." By 1799 Hamilton had fifty students—but not one Indian.[61]

Joseph Brant by Gilbert Stuart
SOURCE: Fenimore Art Museum

My work being done and my mind at ease, I lay hold of the first opportunity of spending an hour with you, & communicating to you, a little of the satisfaction I feel myself. The Day before yesterday I was dub'd a Doct[o]r. with all the form & ceremony necessary upon the occasion. Doct[o]rs Monro senior & junior, with Doct[o]r Cullen were in all my private Tryals.

—DR. SAMUEL BARD, 1765

Once a stable for horses,
Now a College for asses.

—GRAFFITI, COLLEGE OF PHYSICIANS
AND SURGEONS, CA. 1820

Have they not, after having reduced us to the deplorable condition of slaves under their feet, held us up as descending originally from the tribes of *Monkeys* or *Orang-Outangs?* . . . Has Mr. Jefferson declared to the world, that we are inferior to the whites, both in the endowments of our bodies and our minds?

—DAVID WALKER, 1829

CHAPTER 6

"All Students & All Americans"

The Colonial Roots of
Racial Science

Decades before he became president of the United States, Thomas Jefferson contemplated the future of the lands beyond the western boundary of white settlement. After his inauguration, President Jefferson hired his Virginia neighbor Meriwether Lewis as his private secretary, and the two men secretly got to work on a plan to map the West. Jefferson had earlier turned to the American Philosophical Society (APS) in Philadelphia, where his interest in a continental expedition bore no fruit. Having personally taught Lewis to survey, President Jefferson now dispatched his emissary to the APS for a crash course in natural history, botany, geography, and medicine. There was certainly no better site in the United States to prepare for the expedition. Benjamin Smith Barton, the younger Caspar Wistar, and Benjamin Rush trained Lewis and set the scientific and medical agenda for the expedition. Lewis also took guidance from practical experts on Indian affairs, navigation, and cartography, including Andrew Ellicott of Lancaster, an experienced surveyor who had traversed the Mississippi. In Indiana he joined up with Captain William Clark and, predictably, his enslaved black man York. Lewis and Clark added other people along the way, including Sacagawea, an enslaved Shoshone woman. At roughly the same time, Jefferson authorized his minister to France, Robert Livingston, to negotiate the purchase of New Orleans. By the spring of 1803, Napoleon Bonaparte's desperation for money and his inability to recapture Haiti after its revolution allowed the United States to secure the whole of the Louisiana Territory for $15 million, pennies per acre. Lewis officiated at the transfer ceremonies in St. Louis the following year.[1]

THE AMERICAN INVASION OF EUROPE

The academy refined and legitimated the social ideas that supported territorial expansion, a process that transformed the people of the new nation from revolutionaries to imperialists. It advanced the project through which the United States extended its borders across the North American mainland. Jefferson had access to researchers who were a recent addition to American society. Colonial students had been crowding the medical and science programs of Europe for two generations, carrying the political and social beliefs and desires of their communities to the intellectual centers of the Atlantic world. Students from North America crafted a science that justified expansionism and slavery—a science that generated broad claims to expertise over colored people and thrived upon unlimited access to nonwhite bodies. They did not abandon the search for truth; they redefined truth. Atlantic intellectuals had deployed science to prove the prophecies of the Bible, and now, with similar vigor, they pursued the visible and manifest truths of the material world.

Race did not come *from* science and theology; it came *to* science and theology. Racial ideas were born in the colonial world, in the brutal and deadly processes of empire building. Science and theology deferred to race, twisting and warping under the weight of an increasingly popular and sweeping understanding of human affairs that tied the social fates of different populations to perceived natural capacities. Atlantic intellectuals operated under social and economic constraints that limited and distorted the knowable. The greatest accomplishments of the Enlightenment occurred within the inhumane and destructive realities of colonialism.

Students from New England and the Mid-Atlantic, Virginia, the Carolinas, Maryland, and the Caribbean were common at Oxford and Cambridge in England, Trinity in Dublin, and Edinburgh and Glasgow in Scotland. In 1695 the Barbadians Allan Lyde and Richard Carter, the son of James Carter, arrived at Cambridge, and six years later Richard Salter sent his son Timothy from Barbados to Cambridge. The second-generation Richard Henry Lee of Virginia—"Richard the Scholar"—studied at Oxford. A biographer adds that he afterward made a habit of keeping "his notes in Hebrew, Greek, and Latin." Fewer colonial students went farther north, to Aberdeen University in Scotland, but, as with Edinburgh and Glasgow, many of its graduates left for the British colonies. In 1729 Andrew Rosse took his degree from the University of Glasgow, where his father taught and his brother became dean of faculty, and set up in Virginia as a merchant.[2]

There were enough Americans at the University of Edinburgh to found a Virginia Club. Before the American Revolution, fifty colonial doctors belonged to the Royal Medical Society and colonists had even served in the presidency. In 1754 William Shippen Jr. of Pennsylvania graduated from the College of New Jersey (Princeton); he then left to study medicine in Edinburgh and London. He was part of a remarkable North American migration to Scotland. The political and institutional cultures of Scotland were decidedly antimonarchical, which attracted American students as the conflict between the colonies and England intensified. Scottish migrations to North America had familiarized the colonies with Scotland's intellectual and religious cultures. Classes at Scottish universities were usually in English, and the colleges had shifted instruction from the tutorial system to a more liberal arrangement of fee-based lectures and demonstrations. Students could select the most popular professors and subjects, repeat courses, and pay for tutors when needed. A single diary entry reveals quite a bit about Shippen's education: "Rose at 6 operated till 8, breakfasted till 9, dissected until 2, dined till 3, dissected till 5. Lecture till 7, operated till 9, supped till 10 then bed."[3]

Benjamin Rush of Philadelphia was smitten with the science course at Edinburgh, which he viewed as the intellectual gateway to countless fields of knowledge. "I have now ye Honour of being a member of the Medical Society," he boasted to Jonathan Smith, a schoolmate in the New Jersey class of 1760, "an institution which was founded in ye Year 1737 by some students of Physic [physiology and pathology], and is now so reputable that most of ye Professors in ye College are members of it." Rush studied with the famed anatomist Alexander Monro, listened to debates on innovations in medical science, and gloried in the faculty decision to make the examinations and graduation requirements more numerous and rigorous, which "will tend to keep up the Reputation of the College. It[']s now in ye Zenith of its Glory, the whole world I believe does not afford a Sett of greater men than are at present united in ye College of Edinburgh." Hugh Williamson, a member of the first class of the College of Philadelphia (University of Pennsylvania), also studied at Edinburgh. He took a range of offerings, including anatomy and surgery, theoretical medicine, and materia medica, or pharmacology. Like other young men of means, he sought additional training in England and finished his education at the University of Utrecht, Holland.[4]

Samuel Bard braved the dangers of the Seven Years' War to cross the ocean and pursue medical training. When he finally reached Scotland, he informed his parents—the New York City surgeon John Bard and Suzanne Valleau—that he was safe, had rented a small comfortable room, and was taking meals "with several agre[e]able young Gentlemen, all students & all Americans." He later reported that he was spending his evenings revising notes from a chemistry course with the renowned William Cullen and diagramming the medical and scientific equipment being employed and refined at the university. A graduate of Edinburgh and a physician, Cadwallader Colden had brought John Bard to New York on the recommendation of Benjamin Franklin. Colden later hosted Samuel for a summer at Coldengham, his grant in Ulster County, New York, where Jane Colden, the daughter of the councilor, tutored the boy in botany. In 1765 Bard completed his thesis

Cadwallader Colden, acting governor of New York, by Matthew Pratt
SOURCE: New York State Museum

on the medical uses of opium—volunteering with his friends for his own experiments. His father then sent him to polish his skills in London and Paris.[5]

This was not a passive transfer of information from European intellectuals to colonial students. American scholars were expanding knowledge in ways that transformed Atlantic academies. Benjamin Smith Barton of Lancaster, Pennsylvania, was raised in his father's Anglican mission among the Lenape. During his term at Edinburgh, Benjamin Barton offered lectures on the indigenous peoples of North America and albinism in the colonies. He later became a member of the Royal Medical Society. Samuel Bard proudly forwarded "a Copy of the Papers which I read before the Medical Society this Winter" to his father with apologies for any errors in "the first Fruits of my medical labours."[6]

The colonies contained valuable information. Cadwallader Colden's interests in science and Native American cultures combined in his studies of botany. Native communities cultivated medicinal herbs and plants, and by the eighteenth century white colonists were actively cataloguing Indian remedies. Descriptions of the colonies and travel accounts regularly included natural history and Indian pharmacology. John Wesley, founder of Methodism, encountered Creek and Cherokee medicine during his brief mission in Savannah, Georgia, and then published *Primitive Physic*, a discourse on natural medicine and healing, upon his return to England. Dr. Colden's extensive political experience with the Iroquois Confederacy had given him opportunities to study the treatment of disease and injury in Native communities, Indian materia medica, and regional natural history. In February 1764 the Edinburgh botany faculty awarded Samuel Bard their gold medal.[7]

Colonial intellectuals shared ideas and data acquired in Africa and the Americas. European academies were synthesizing much of this material. William Byrd II of Virginia went to England when he was seven years old. The son of a wealthy Virginia planter, Byrd was there to acquire a classical education: Latin, Greek, Hebrew, French, music, logic, history, and mathematics. After a short return to North America in 1696, the young man gave a presentation before the Royal Society in London on an eleven-year-old black boy from Virginia who had been brought to England. Born with a pigmentation disorder, the boy developed irregular patches of discolored skin on his neck and chest. The affected areas increased as he aged. Byrd determined that the "wonderfully White" spots, at least as pale as "the Skin of the fairest Lady," were not the same as the skin of white people, as "the Skin of a Negro is much thicker." White skin appeared more alive, he concluded, while noting that the boy was otherwise healthy and would likely lose all of his color in time. The Royal Society later selected Byrd as a fellow; he was the first Virginian to receive that honor. In 1716 Cotton Mather informed the Royal Society that his slave Onesimus had taught him inoculation as practiced in Africa. Mather convinced

Dr. Zabdiel Boylston of Boston to test the procedure, which Boylston did using his teenage son and his two slaves.[8]

The rise of scientific racism—the attempt to discover the social destinies and identify the assumed divisions of human populations—required Americans. Alexander Monro, Alexander Monro Jr., William Cullen, and Andrew Duncan made few references to complexion and race in their science lectures at Edinburgh. Early medical and science faculties generally taught under the assumption that their research would verify Christian monogenism—the belief that all human beings descended from a single pair. It was frequently colonial students taking degrees in Scotland and England—as in France and Holland—who searched for other answers to the demographic puzzles of their world. Americans produced essays, dissertations, lectures, and letters that mark the triumph of race over science. "The present era will be famous for a Revolution in Physic [medicine]," Rush predicted, and American colonists were catalysts.[9]

The collected experiences and testimonies of colonists and European travelers accelerated investigations into the history of human beings, and raised new questions about the range of physical diversity between populations, the influences upon culture and character, the origins and ancestry of language, and the determinants of longevity. Americans struggled to discover the spiritual and material causes of intelligence, culture, character, and social fate. Colonial students were complicating, multiplying, and offering answers to these questions.

SHADE-SHIFTING JEWS AND INDIAN CURIOS

The spectrum of skin color corresponds to climatic variation, explained the Reverend Samuel Stanhope Smith in 1787, and the logic of God's creation manifests in human adaptations to nature. His influential treatise on complexion, delivered before the American Philosophical Society, defended monogenism against emergent theological and scientific arguments about the separate origins of varied populations of people. Not just the color of our skin but our carriage, manners, appearance, and intellect demonstrate our environmental destiny, Rev. Smith expounded. His belief that color was a reaction to environment affirmed his faith in the shared creation of mankind. Meaningless, brute work deepens color, distorts human features, and dulls the senses, he continued. In savage society, people lack the knowledge and freedom to protect themselves from the punishments of nature, intensifying their complexions. The living conditions, diet, and habits of poor and heathen peoples add to their swarthiness. In civilized society, color relents as one ascends the social ladder. Beauty too is biased toward the higher orders of society, since leisure encourages a concern for the aesthetic; thus, physical attractiveness is more frequently expressed in fair skin.[10]

The laboring classes are invariably darker and more primitive in their features and gait than the upper classes. Black skin differs from white, Smith allowed, but only in that it announced the failure to realize natural and social potential. Each station of life, everywhere, carries corresponding degrees of exposure to natural and climatic conditions, the cumulative effects of which color the social geography of human history. Africans, Asians, and Americans are darker than Europeans; however, the most civilized nations in Europe are fairer than its less advanced nations, and within the most progressive nations the elite are whiter than the commoners.[11] The gaps between the palest and the most sable peoples, the brightest and the dullest, the most civilized and the most savage are real, but they are neither eternal nor impassable.

Such environmental arguments, particularly the assertion that complexion was unstable, bolstered religious liberalism. Rev. Smith was certain that "no example can carry with greater force on this subject than that of the Jews," whose religion kept their family lines braided and largely unfrayed although they were scattered across the globe. Jews were "marked with the colours" of every nation despite being descended from a single people and intermarrying over centuries. Their complexions conformed to the climatic realities of their locations in Europe, the Middle East, Asia, and Africa. A generation later, Hugh Williamson invoked the black and white Jews of Asia to explain the skin color of Native

Americans. These works rested upon a century of research. In the early 1700s Cotton Mather had treated color as an environmental reaction to dismiss the idea that it should operate as a barrier to the Christianization of enslaved Africans. By midcentury Georges-Louis Leclerc, Comte de Buffon, examined the Jews and Jewish history to understand how environment influenced complexion for his encyclopedic compilation, *Histoire Naturelle*.[12]

"There is an obvious difference between him and his fellow-students in the largeness of the mouth, and thickness of the lips, in the elevation of the cheek, in the darkness of the complexion, and the contour of the face," Rev. Smith wrote of Quequedegatha (George Morgan White Eyes), a fifteen-year-old Lenape scholar who matriculated in 1779. Professor of moral philosophy and vice president at New Jersey, Smith succeeded to the presidency upon the death of his father-in-law, John Witherspoon. Professor Smith estimated that the Indian student "is much lighter than the complexion of the native savage," as he had been losing color since his arrival on campus. The boy remained darker than his classmates primarily because his entrance into Christian society came after the age of seven, when his physical characteristics had already begun to set. "But these differences are sensibly diminishing," the minister said, and one could observe Quequedegatha's color and features seeking the standard of his peers.[13]

By animating human complexion, Smith sought to reconcile volatile ideas about the human family. Mounting information about human populations, the spectrum of language and culture, and phenotypic variation destabilized knowledge about color forged in the prior two centuries. The expansion of the African slave trade and African slavery, along with the devastation of Amerindian nations, seemed to reveal the group meanings and social consequences of such dissimilarities. Edward Long's influential *History of Jamaica* concluded that "the White and the Negroe are two distinct species" and specifically rejected the idea that skin color was primarily a consequence of environment. By correlating complexion and climate, Rev. Smith accommodated data on the increasingly complicated human family while respecting the Judeo-Christian belief in single origin. He also made the marker of civility achievable for nonwhite people, although his argument did nothing to decouple the association between Europe and civilization.[14]

A leading theologian embracing science to rescue Christian monogenism provides an enlightening peek into the social processes through which knowledge gets produced. Eighteenth-century colleges were the primary sites for processing growing and discordant bodies of information about human beings, an occupation that marshaled the expertise of theologians and scientists. Scholars struggled—and at times competed—to craft coherent explanations for the diversity of the world's peoples. Professor Smith both generated new ideas and refined existing theories about Indian peoples and human color in his APS address.

The rise of scientific racism, like theological racism, required interventions in the academic and intellectual realms, from the passive distortions of unreliable and biased sources to the active invasions of slave traders and slave owners seeking intellectual proofs for their suspicions and assertions about the nature of color. Lamenting the lack of trustworthy conclusions about race after two centuries of conquest and enslavement, Thomas Jefferson turned to science, praying that "the subject may be submitted to the Anatomical knife, to the Optical glasses, to analysis by fire, or by solvents."[15]

Rev. Smith had a terrible task in a world adorned with Indian skeletons. Collecting and cataloguing aboriginal peoples had become an Atlantic industry. At the end of the seventeenth century, Cotton Mather cracked the jaw off the skull of Metacomet, or King Philip, the Wampanoag sachem who nearly conquered the New England settlements in the seventeenth century. Mather's neighbor, the jurist Samuel Sewall, better known for authoring an early antislavery tract, sent Native American scalps to the London doctor and researcher Charles Morton. Jefferson also collected and exchanged human remains. When he attended William and Mary, Brafferton Hall still housed the Indian College, and Native Americans were about 10 percent of the student body. To satisfy his own interests about the nature of indigenous peoples, Jefferson ventured off his plantation to neighboring Indian mounds, where he ordered his slaves to break into graves. Long-buried skulls crumbled in his hands as he searched for evidence for his speculations. In 1779 he established a professorship in anatomy and medicine at William and Mary, beginning its medical program. He later personally designed the anatomy theater for the University of Virginia.[16]

Throughout the Atlantic world, planters, slave traders, soldiers, explorers, merchants, and missionaries were producing, by accident and by design, the material for an emerging science. "They are the best temper'd People, and make better Slaves than any of the Rest," ship's surgeon T. Aubrey concluded of one of four subgroups of Africans. He described these people as being "a natural Black" color and "lusty, strong, vigorous, chearful, merry, affable, amorous, kind, docile, faithful, and easily diverted from Wrath." In contrast were the groups with thin, short black hair and "dark russet" skin who made for terrible slaves because they were "naturally sad, sluggish, sullen, peevish, forward, spiteful, fantastical, envious, self-conceited, proper at nothing, naturally Cowards, very indecent, and nasty in all their Transactions." Merchants, officers, and crewmen often wrote and spoke of Africans with such authority and certainty. Those of a more "yellow" complexion were also to be avoided, a natural tendency to laziness and stupidity unfitting them for any useful service. "Chocolate Colour[ed]" peoples with short brown hair possessed an enviable blend of independence and bravery but were prone to certain chronic ailments.[17]

When the Scottish philosopher David Hume contemplated human variety, he was using these kinds of sources. Historically people had managed to rise from the lowest orders of society, but "there are Negroe slaves dispersed all over Europe, of which none ever discovered any symptoms of ingenuity." Dismissing rumors of a learned black Jamaican, Hume countered that this man was likely receiving exaggerated praise for modest achievements, "like a parrot, who speaks a few words plainly." Race required the creation of a new global intellectual authority. Edward Long cited Hume in his 1774 history of Jamaica, concluding that science had shown an absence of intelligence in Africans.[18]

Thomas Jefferson agreed, adding that the most celebrated black people in his lifetime—including the young poet Phillis Wheatley—had only managed a poor aping of the genius of the white race. "Religion, indeed, has produced Phyllis Whately; but it could not produce a poet," he derisively commented. "The compositions published under her name are below the dignity of criticism." Nature, not slavery, explained the intellectual inferiority of the Negro, Jefferson continued, borrowing directly from Hume and Long. Slavery in antiquity was harsher, but the most oppressed classes of ancient Rome and Greece authored great prose and verse. His condemnation of the enslavement of Indians as "an inhuman practice" was rooted in his sense of their potential for civilization. Even their rude carvings and rough drawings showed innate understandings of design and artistry. They possessed brilliance, "which only wants cultivation." Jefferson argued that the 1774 speech of Logan, a Mingo (Ohio Iroquois), rivaled the speeches of Cicero in its eloquence, and Indians "astonish you with strokes of the most sublime oratory." In contrast, he continued, "never yet could I find that a black had uttered a thought above the level of plain narration; never seen even an elementary trait of painting or sculpture."[19]

The Virginian judged black people ugly and artless. Beauty and passion manifested in red and white skin, but blackness was an "eternal monotony," an "immovable veil" that covered the senses and expressions of African peoples. Jefferson's extended analysis of the bodily functions and secretions, odors, emotions and natural reactions, physicality, intelligence, and social relations of black people was borrowed from Edward Long, who had used similar arguments in deciding that black people constituted a separate species from white people, one more akin to nonhuman primates. Jefferson advanced his allegations of African brutishness with a base assertion of "the preference of the Oran-ootan for the black women over those of his own species." Long had contended that orangutans displayed basic emotions and a rudimentary intelligence, which, he added, approximated the capacities of Africans. Male orangutans "conceive a passion for the Negroe women," the doctor elaborated, "such as inclines one animal towards another of the same species."[20]

Long and Jefferson used anatomical metaphors throughout their respective works. Eighteenth-century theorists refined evidence and arguments from a broad range of sources, often importing medical and biological jargon to form and address cultural and social questions. The Comte de Buffon's *Histoire Naturelle*, a primary source for later researchers, assumed expertise over everything from the appearance, intelligence, and odors of varied African populations to their moral and cultural proximity to the European norm.[21] The hunt to find race catalyzed a social science that could discover facts in even the casual observations of travelers.

Atlantic colleges took these myriad pieces of social information and forged "truths" about human difference. The merits of a college could be reasonably measured by its collection of human remains, a good catalogue of skulls, skeletons, and skins being a considerable advantage in a competitive academic market. The January 1764 fire that destroyed Harvard Hall took with it one of the earliest academic museums:

> The entire library of five thousand volumes, excepting some two hundred that were lent out at the time, was consumed; the whole philosophical apparatus, the portraits of presidents, benefactors . . . were burnt up; the stuffed animals and birds, model of the *Boston* man-of-war, piece of tanned negro's hide, "Skull of a Famous Indian Warrior," and in fact the entire "Repositerry of Curiosities," were seen no more.

New Hampshire governor Benning Wentworth—a Harvard graduate, who later endowed Dartmouth College—and the New Hampshire legislature helped to rebuild the collection.[22] The profession and hobby of collecting and exhibiting Indians spread alongside the perception of Native Americans as defeated and extinct peoples. If Dartmouth ever was an Indian college, it ceased being that when the administration began warehousing Indian remains and taking in donations to enhance its human collections. In 1797 the trustees established a medical school, and the following year Dr. Nathan Smith began lectures in Dartmouth Hall. (Smith later left to help establish the medical school at Yale College, where Bishop George Berkeley's earlier gift included a supply of texts on anatomy, surgery, and medicine.) He built a modern medical program at Dartmouth and instituted instructional dissections. "Doct[or Alexander] Ramsay is now engaged in making an

Anatomical museum for Mr. Professor Smith," Lyman Spalding, a medical student, reported in November 1808. "We are all obliged to labour with our own hands at these preparations; in fact the rooms are an immense workshop, you see every kind of anatomical manufacturing going on." Trained at Edinburgh, Ramsay had already produced a hundred anatomical preparations and instituted a course of anatomical demonstrations. "He is all fire and animation while speaking, chaining down your attention and carrying you along with him convincing you of the truth of his doctrines by demonstrative facts," continued Spalding, who was excited to use his hands rather than "hearing dismal psalm tune lectures." Amherst and other nineteenth-century colleges also established Indian museums. In Philadelphia, the scientist Samuel Morton gathered the largest assemblage of skulls on the continent.[23]

Colonial scholars returned from Europe and laid the foundations of American science. Samuel Bard began advocating an American academy of science similar to the royal societies of Britain and France. It was not an attempt to mirror Europe; in fact, Bard was motivated by a concern that Americans had too reflexively deferred to European science and too uncritically accepted the conclusions of European researchers. Besides the danger of learning through "hearsay," Bard cautioned, the Americans needed a science and philosophy that addressed their "peculiar" natural and environmental realities. He predicted that scientific independence would improve the intellectual products of Europe by testing them against the realities of the Americas, give rise to new knowledge, and result in "new truths [being] discovered." Bard's generation created this continental science. William George Nice, a Virginian who later studied under Benjamin Smith Barton at Philadelphia, heard lectures that encompassed the history of European medicine, the medical theories of and personal anecdotes about leading European scientists such as the Monros and Cullen, and correctives on this science from American researchers who had practiced in the West Indies and mainland North America and now constituted the primary authorities on color.[24]

By that time, Atlantic intellectuals had transformed nonwhite peoples into human curios, whose very bodies held answers to the puzzles of society. Anatomy had generated an intellectual revolution, and the coldly intimate act of dissecting colored corpses demonstrated the social power of the academy and the temporal reach of science.

DISSECTING EIGHTEENTH-CENTURY THOUGHT

"For this purpose any healthy penis will do," instructed Andrew Fyfe, "but large ones are generally preferred." His primer sought to improve instruction by locating specimens that lent themselves to dissection and exhibition. "Select the hand of an aged female . . . that has died of a lingering disease," reads one preparation. "The liver of a child is to be preferred to that of an adult," goes another, "it occupying much less room." He offered twenty-one different preparations for a fetus. Old alcoholics had the best kidneys for laboratory and classroom study, the Edinburgh anatomist continued. "Still-born children . . . afford a number of beautiful preparations," he noted, while assuring students that a variety of kidneys also guaranteed a compelling public display.[25]

The American invasion corresponded to the ascendance of anatomical studies in the European academy. In the early fourteenth century, Mondino de Luzzi introduced instructional dissection at the University of Bologna (established 1088), where he held the chair in anatomy and surgery. By 1407 Parisian students could attend dissections, and the connections between anatomy, surgery, and medical science were firming. In Leiden and Amsterdam, Dutch surgeons raised the profile of their profession in part by establishing the value of medical dissection. In 1632 the young Rembrandt van Rijn painted *The Anatomy Lesson of Dr. Nicolaes Tulp*, which was commissioned by the Amsterdam surgeons guild. By the early eighteenth century, anatomy was fully entrenched in the British universities.[26] Anatomy transformed surgery into an art, and dissection became the foundation of medical instruction and research in Europe.

As early as 1648 the Reverend John Eliot had observed that plantations needed anatomists to advance religious work among Indians by countering the powwows with science. The Puritan missionary recognized the strategic benefits of spreading European science and the social rewards of allowing colonial doctors to improve their skills. Eliot did not believe that dissection would discover eternal differences or racial divisions between Indians and Christians; rather, he may have been encouraged by a contemporaneous event. Giles Firmin, a graduate of Cambridge University who became a gentleman farmer and physician in Ipswich, Massachusetts, performed a dissection for students interested in medicine. Firmin's anatomy lesson came just prior to Eliot's call for instructional dissections. In the following century, the governors of Harvard took up the task of promoting anatomy. In the summer of 1712 the trustees resolved to give the students the opportunity to dissect "once in four years Some Malefact[o]r" that the court could provide.[27]

A half century later, Samuel Bard jealously informed his father that two Americans, William Shippen Jr. and John Morgan, were planning a Philadelphia medical school on the Scottish model. Shippen presented the trustees of the College of Philadelphia with recommendations from the Edinburgh faculty and an endorsement from Thomas Penn. Opened in 1765, it was the first medical school in the British colonies. The faculty consisted of Shippen's contemporaries. Morgan, a graduate of Philadelphia, had apprenticed in a doctor's office and completed a four-year term as a military doctor. Benjamin Smith Barton returned to Pennsylvania to become professor of natural history. Benjamin Rush, a native of the city, joined the Philadelphia faculty after he finished Edinburgh. Rush also enhanced his wealth through a marriage to Julia Stockton, daughter of the New Jersey jurist, landowner, and slaveholder Richard Stockton, later a signer of the Declaration of Independence. Stockton gave the couple the Mount Lucas estate and mansion near Princeton. Caspar Wistar, son of the affluent German immigrant and glassmaker, attended Philadelphia and then studied medicine at Edinburgh. Wistar returned to teach anatomy, chemistry, and surgery in the medical college, where he later served as a trustee.[28]

But the success of medical colleges depended in part on their access to corpses, which raised the possibility of new uses for the bodies of subjugated peoples. The Philadelphia medical program began with Shippen's lectures on anatomy in 1762. On November 16

Shippen commenced his anatomy course at the Pennsylvania State House. That year the Pennsylvania Hospital gave Shippen "the body of a negro, who had committed suicide." Five years earlier, on April 9, 1757, Tom, a black man enslaved to Joseph Wharton, became the first patient to die at the hospital. The doctors drew up policies for handling corpses and expanding opportunities for dissection. Bodies from suicides and the corpses of criminals were soon being transferred directly to Shippen's anatomical museum. The hospital also served large numbers of black patients, who became the material of its research program. Darius Sessions, a West Indies merchant and deputy governor, favored moving the College of Rhode Island (Brown) to Providence, a large town, to access the public library, excellent private collections, ample supplies and uninterrupted communications, and an abundance of physicians and anatomical authors who could enhance the students' educations.[29]

"In studying the art of healing we commonly begin with Anatomy," Morgan declared in his 1765 manifesto, ranking anatomy with surgery and physic as the three pillars of medical science. In Philadelphia's medical school anatomy was a required course. Undergraduates at Harvard organized their own Anatomical Society, which procured a skeleton, hosted lectures and discussions, and performed animal dissections before the college had a medical school. Professor John Winthrop donated medical texts and specimens.[30]

Medical colleges proliferated in the colonies in the decades after the French and Indian War. Samuel Bard had feared that the power struggle between Anglicans and Presbyterians in New York and the advanced efforts of the Philadelphians were possibly insuperable barriers to opening a medical school in the city.

I wish with all my heart they were at New York, that I might have a share amongst them, and assist in founding the first ~~Physical~~ Med[ical] Colledge in America; I do not want ambition to prompt me to an undertaking of this kind at New York; and I have had some conversation, with my friend Mr. Martin about it, but I am afraid that being so near the Philadelphians, who will have the start of us by several years, will be a great obsticle, and another allmost

insurmountable one is the parties which exist in New York;
for if such a thing was to be undertaken it ought to be in
conjunction with the [King's] colledge which alone would
be sufficient, to make the Presbeterian partie our Enimys.

In 1767 Dr. Samuel Bard became a founder of the medical course
at King's College (Columbia) in New York City, where he served
as professor of the theory and practice of physic and later as a dean
and trustee. One of the city's most distinguished doctors, Bard
was President George Washington's personal physician while the
national government was in New York City. In 1814 he guided the
merger of the new College of Physicians and Surgeons (1807) with
Columbia's medical school.[31]

The genesis of American medical science corresponded to the
rise of anatomy and the ascent of race. "The Study of Anatomy, as
the foundation of Medicine, is a truth so well established, and so
universally acknowledged, as to leave no room for observation,"
William Nisbet wrote in his compilation of the Edinburgh medical curriculum. Race governed the intellectual cultures of the Atlantic world. Nisbet's exploration of anatomy started by asserting
that racial difference, like sex, was certain:

> Nor is the difference between the species, or between the
> white and negro, less remarkable than the difference be-
> tween the sexes. Thus, in examining the skeleton of a negro,
> the cranium is distinguished by its figure by the narrow and
> retracting forehead and hindhead; by the flat bone of the
> nose, by the great distance betwixt the nose and mouth, by
> the small retracting chin, by the great distance betwixt the
> ear and fore part of the mouth; by the small distance be-
> tween the foramen magnum and back part of the head, by
> the large bony sockets which contain the eyes, by the wide
> meatus auditorius, and by the long and strong under jaw.[32]

Anatomical dissection, in particular, promised answers to questions about the nature of humankind that had lingered in science
and theology. On his return journey from a 1773 trip to South

Carolina, Josiah Quincy Jr. attended a lecture from "young Dr. [William] Shippen" at the Philadelphia medical college. Quincy was highly impressed with Shippen's knowledge but even more taken with the facilities: "The curiosities of this hospital are far beyond any thing of the kind in North America."[33]

BODIES ACADEMIC

Shortly after the founding of Dartmouth, Dr. Joseph Lewis, a personal physician to President Eleazar Wheelock, peeled the skin from the body of a deceased black man named Cato and boiled the corpse in a kettle to free the skeleton for study. He took Cato's skin to be tanned at the shop that served the college, then used it to dress his instrument case. Physicians, surgeons, and students on numerous campuses conducted anatomical dissections and created anatomical specimens decades before their institutions opened medical schools. Human bodies were even more of a commodity once medical programs were organized. Dartmouth's faculty struggled with the legislature to access corpses, an issue that drove one of its founding faculty, Nathan Smith, to Yale. There were other ways to acquire bodies. In 1811 Dartmouth's medical school moved into its own building, where the basement was soon piled with human and non-human bones. The medical students entertained themselves with this collection by using it to terrorize the campus and the town at night. A number of those skeletons were likely those of enslaved and free black people who had worked for Dartmouth. Although slavery was declining in New Hampshire, the college had been one of the largest slaveholders in the colony and the state, and its officers buried enslaved and free black laborers in the college cemetery.[34]

The medical profession and medical schools in colonial North America were founded on the bodies of the poor and subjected. Harvard's governors expected that the corpses of criminals could be transferred to the school just as John Eliot had assumed that Indians could be dismembered. However, Christians generally judged the value of science apart from the appropriateness or morality of scientific techniques. The introduction of anatomy to

North American colleges was disquieting since there was little consensus about whose bodies could be breached.

Colonial students who studied in Europe had already experienced the social tensions caused by instructional dissection. The elder Alexander Monro moved his anatomy classes out of Surgeons' Hall to the Edinburgh campus to hide from the public. In April 1725 a mob attacked his students for stealing corpses from the nearby Greyfriars Kirkyard. The administration paid soldiers to protect the University of Glasgow from mobs seeking to retaliate against the medical faculty. When the governors proposed relocating the anatomy labs to the new Hunterian Museum, the staff protested that such a move would make them the targets of violence. William Hunter studied and researched at Glasgow and Edinburgh before moving to London, where he took advantage of new regulations that allowed for instructional dissection in medical courses. John Hunter began his career helping his brother secure bodies for his popular anatomical lectures, which used Parisian-style interactive learning. Glasgow's faculty and students ultimately began exploiting their proximity to Ireland to meet their needs without disturbing their city. In the 1830s a scandal involving murders to supply corpses shook Edinburgh and claimed the career of the leading anatomist Robert Knox.[35]

Americans had a different solution. Located on Broadway at Duane Street, the New York Hospital—where the King's College medical faculty rented dissection laboratories—had an ample source of cadavers at its southeast corner: the "Negros Burial Ground." The faculty and students harvested colored corpses from the African cemetery for years, dragging cadavers across Broadway to the dissecting table. "We went from the city, following the Broadway, over the valley, or fresh water. Upon both sides of this way were many habitations of negroes, mulattoes and whites," reads an October 1679 entry in Jasper Dankers's travel journal. "These negroes were formerly the proper slaves of the [West India] company," it continues, but were now laying out farms and raising houses north of the city "on this road, where they have ground enough to live on with their families." More than a century later, African Americans' ambitions left them easy prey for medical students. In 1807 the regents chartered the College of Physicians and Surgeons in New York City. It was the same year that white residents began complaining about the odor from hundreds of corpses in the vault of the African Methodist Episcopal Church, or Mother Zion, which suffered from a lack of land and security. There remained few if any protections on the bodies of black people living in the city, be they enslaved or free, and white New Yorkers had even less concern about the fate of dead black people.[36]

On April 20, 1773, Daniel Hewes published a notice for an anatomy class for midwives and practitioners in Providence, Rhode Island. He claimed a lengthy career in surgery and medicine, familiarity with a wealth of medical texts, and a reputation among leading physicians. For a nominal fee, Hewes offered medical instruction or consultations on medical cases. As evidence of his professional standing and accomplishment, he added that the government of Massachusetts had awarded him the body of a "Negro Malefactor," which he wired into a skeleton for use as a teaching tool and a guide for setting bones and joints.[37]

White people still had ample reason to worry about their fate after death. In 1764 the King's College trustee John Watts promised Governor Robert Monckton that he would recommend the addition of an anatomist to the faculty, but warned that there was little hope of success given a lack of funds and a shortage of students. Popular disdain for doctors and medical training contributed to his doubts. "We have so many of the Faculty allready destroying his Majesty[']s good Subjects," Watts joked, that the public "had rather One half were hanged that are allready practicing, than breed up a New Swarm." Such fears affected every level of society. Later in the century, President George Washington's deathbed instructions to his family, friends, and personal slave, William Lee, included a reminder to "have me decently buried; and do not let my body be put into the vault in less than three days after I am dead."[38]

Money and status provided some comfort in death, such as the security of being placed in church tombs and vaults or in fenced churchyards—practices that acquired new social meaning in the age of anatomy. Captain Jasper Farmar, the slave trader and merchant whose servant helped organize the 1741 conspiracy in Manhattan,

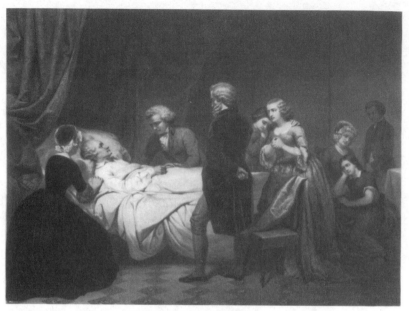

George Washington's deathbed scene as painted
by Junius Brutus Stearns
SOURCE: Library of Congress

was shot aboard the ship *Charming Jenny* by sailors whom he was trying to impress into service during the French and Indian War. His militia company escorted his body to Trinity Church, where it was interred next to the altar. In 1788 his wife, Maria Farmar, died. Her funeral followed "the ancient Dutch custom." Mourners enjoyed spiced wine and tobacco pipes before accompanying her body from her home at Hanover Square to the church. The coffin was draped in black cloth with a Dutch epigraph on a copper plaque. She was entombed next to her husband at Trinity in a service presided over by Anglican and Dutch clergy.[39] Slave trading had purchased the Farmars some eternal comfort.

Most corpses had no such protections. By 1769 Joseph Warren, a student at Harvard, had organized an underground anatomy club. His younger brother John Warren later transformed this group into a secret society, the "Spunkers," to procure human bodies for instruction. Their adventures included sneaking about in the evening in boats, in carts, and on foot looking for new graves. John Warren did most of the demonstrations with the assistance of several Harvard students who went on to successful medical careers: Jonathan Norwood, William Eustis, David Townsend, and Samuel Adams, the son of the patriot. The American Revolution advanced the medical arts in Cambridge by generating a reliable supply of British and Hessian dead. In 1782, the year before the British surrender, Harvard's trustees established a medical college and appointed John Warren to the first professorship in anatomy and surgery. The war had also accelerated the professionalization of medicine in New Haven, where a medical society emerged immediately after the peace.[40]

Human tissue was the currency of medical science. An advertisement for an anatomy course in Philadelphia promised real human body parts. The medical faculty at Columbia organized an association to encourage the study of surgery and anatomy. Doctors at Rutgers Medical College on Duane Street in New York City lured students with assurances that its anatomy professor "teaches with THE KNIFE," dissecting in front of the class, displaying and describing the pieces, and offering opportunities for student interaction and private instruction. In 1789 New York began formally supplying medical colleges and doctors with the cadavers of executed felons—a controversial "postmortem punishment" and extension of the power of the state. The legislature also assigned penalties for grave robbing.[41]

Aristocratic notions that accepted the violability of the lower classes failed to resonate in a society inching toward republicanism. In 1765, the year that Shippen became professor of anatomy at Philadelphia, a mob of sailors violently interrupted his class, destroyed his lab, confiscated severed human limbs, attacked his carriage, and vandalized his house. The tensions were not limited to the City of Brotherly Love. Wealthier people who lived near a hospital or medical college sat graveside after the burials of relatives or friends, hired watchmen to look after the deceased, and even exhumed caskets to confirm that bodies had not been resurrected.[42]

In October 1787 the *New-York Morning Post* announced that the young surgeon Wright Post would be offering lectures on anatomy and surgery at New York Hospital. Months earlier the founders and faculty of the medical school had become trustees of the college when the New York State legislature revised and reaffirmed Columbia's charter, appointing at least eight physicians to a board that had had only two doctors in the prior thirty years.[43]

Despite that acknowledgment of the growing prestige of medicine and science, Chief Justice Richard Morris—grandson of Lewis Morris, the first lord of the Morrisania Manor in the Bronx—sympathized with the rioters who sacked the hospital the following year. The trouble began on April 13 when a group of children were frightened by a human arm that had been left in a window to dry. Three hundred people surrounded the building, roughed up doctors, held students hostage, confiscated cadavers, and took or destroyed dissection equipment. To calm the crowd and protect the hospital, city officials jailed at least four of the students. The following day the rioters returned to inspect the hospital. Then they went looking for corpses at Columbia and later conducted house-by-house searches of every physician practicing in the city. The authorities acquiesced to each of these demands. Appeals from John Jay, Governor George Clinton, Mayor James Duane, Alexander Hamilton, Chancellor Robert Livingston, and Baron Friedrich Von Steuben failed to reassure the crowd, which now numbered in the thousands. The rioters hit or beat Von Steuben, Jay, and other officials. They murdered a "Negro Boy Slave" belonging to William Livingston at the jail. Unable to defend the hospital or the medical students, the governor ordered the militia with muskets and horse. The troops killed three rioters.[44]

The New York Journal complained that Manhattan had been terrorized unnecessarily because the practitioners had access to the bodies of executed felons and the unclaimed corpses of drifters and the poor. Students supplemented this allotment by "ripping open the graves of strangers and negroes, about whom there was little feeling," Joel Tyler Headley found, but went too far when they "dug up respectable people, even young women, of whom they made an indecent exposure."[45] Grave robbers who deferred to the economic hierarchy still offended antiaristocratic beliefs about the individual value and equality of human beings, unalienable dignities that supposedly continued into death.

Academics struggled against these moral and political limitations. "You have doubtless been informed of the great disturbance lately excited at this Institution by the base and unjustifiable conduct of some individuals who in a secret and clandestine manner opened a recess of the dead, and taking there from a body, exposed the same (instead of a subject regularly and lawfully procured without wounding the feelings of humanity) in the medical department for anatomical dissection," President John Wheelock of Dartmouth confessed to the Hanover attorney and official Benjamin Gilbert on December 18, 1809. That day, Wheelock's administration promised to prevent the repetition of this "criminal act" and assured Gilbert of the full cooperation of the faculty and governors in any investigations of any member of the college participating in body snatching or illegal dissections. They unilaterally selected officials from all the surrounding towns to form a visiting committee with the right to examine the medical department's labs and lecture rooms and the rooms of the medical or science students to pursue any rumors or reports of grave robbing. The medical students elected a committee of five who made a formal admission and apology to President Wheelock and the faculty. Their actions were "nothing short of sacrilege" and had unfairly damaged Professor Smith's reputation.[46]

"Whereas rumors of an unpleasant nature are circulated purporting that Bodies from the Cemeteries of the City have been brought to this College for dissection," the trustees of Physicians and Surgeons began apologetically in 1814, before condemning such extralegal practices. It was the year of their union with Columbia College. The board mandated that the anatomy professor inspect all corpses to guarantee that they had been obtained legally and were treated "in a decorous and proper manner." Such declarations were typically made with a wink. Just a few years later, the trustees aggressively bargained for a lot neighboring the medical school to enhance "safety and convenience" and "answer for the purposes of a stable." The anatomist Wright Post put up the money. The new lot provided a more private and secure way to receive corpses stolen during the students' "nocturnal expeditions." A contemporary Columbia medical student, Moses Champion, assured his brother, Dr. Reuben Champion Jr., that the school's "anatomical museum is very extensive" and that the medical classes were already dissecting in rotation: six classes to a cycle, with four students in each class. In 1819 Governor DeWitt Clinton ordered a watch for Potter's Field and placed a $100 bounty on grave robbers—"no doubt to appease the people," Champion complained, while admitting that the college had received more than thirty corpses that term.[47]

Professors, administrators, and students used bribery and collusion to create body-snatching networks that included local grave-diggers and mayors. "I heard that they would there give fifty dollars for a [human] subject," Charles Knowlton recalled with delight. He became a skilled grave robber while apprenticing under Dr. Charles Wilder in Templeton, Massachusetts. Knowlton sold corpses to Dartmouth Medical School to pay his tuition, support himself, and fund private study in physicians' offices to supplement his courses. In 1823 he passed his exam for the doctor of medicine degree. He was jailed the following year for body snatching in Royalston. Dixi Crosby, an 1824 graduate of Dartmouth's medical program, disgraced himself and his family by grave robbing in his hometown of Gilmanton, New Hampshire; nonetheless, in 1838, Dartmouth extended Crosby a professorship in anatomy and surgery. Manhattan's medical colleges dispatched body snatchers to upstate New York during the winter to exploit a cold climate that preserved corpses in the ground and during transportation. Philadelphia's medical schools had a secret pact not to compete for corpses, to reduce the risks of public or professional scandals.[48]

"Civilization seems not to have removed the prejudice of the popular mind against the dissection of the human body," complained Edward Dixon, an 1830 graduate of Rutgers Medical College. The union of Columbia's medical school with Physicians and Surgeons created a powerful lobby that weakened Rutgers's medical program—once second only to Philadelphia's. The rivalries also intensified the quest for cadavers. Dixon viewed this sport, however tasteless, as a logical consequence of an ill-conceived public policy. As editor of the *Scalpel*, a professional journal for surgeons, Dr. Dixon later vilified the hypocrisy of a government that held surgeons liable for "the most trivial blunder" while jailing those who exhumed bodies in order to practice their craft. After he was released from jail, Dr. Charles Knowlton gave two lectures on the battle between science and superstition. In the decade before the Civil War, the professors of medicine at the University of the City of New York (New York University) were still lobbying the state legislature to deregulate dissection.[49]

Between the Revolution and the Civil War, seventeen separate mobs attempted to stop dissections and resurrections. In 1824 citizens from New Haven and West Haven raided the medical college at Yale after they discovered that the body of Bathsheba Smith, the teenage daughter of a local farmer, had been stolen from its grave. The residents found her corpse in the cellar of the school and carried it in a wagon through the city. Yale's students rushed to the medical school with guns and clubs, and officials eventually called out the militia. The Connecticut legislature responded by toughening the laws against body snatching and providing deceased criminals to medical programs. In 1830 a mob invaded Castleton Medical College in Vermont. The residents of Lexington, Kentucky, repeatedly vandalized Transylvania Medical College. Body snatchers trespassed upon the spiritual dignity of their most vulnerable neighbors in their most vulnerable state and disturbed the psychic comforts of the living. Doctors and students reached into the graves of those who could not protect themselves in death and practiced upon their bodies, rendering their corpses little more than "meat." Those most vulnerable to exhumation and dissection were from the lowest social orders: African Americans, Irish, and Indians.[50]

Experimentation on colored corpses had fewer ethical, legal, and political constraints. The American printers who kept European anatomy texts and dissection manuals in constant circulation often sold these primers on newspaper pages that carried advertisements for slaves. The announcement for the anatomy course at New York Hospital, which appeared just months before the riots, ran alongside a plea for the capture and return of Isaac Allen, a twenty-three-year-old black baker enslaved to Ann Payne, and an alert that Bartholomew Andrew was looking to purchase a black boy through his dry goods store on William Street. White people's unlimited access to the bodies of slaves could hardly be thought to cease at death. Free black people and poorer white residents had

The dissecting room at Jefferson Medical College, Philadelphia
SOURCE: Library of Congress

greater, but not full, self-determination. Researchers routinely accessed the corpses of poor and subjected people. In Philadelphia they took cadavers directly from the poorhouse, a practice that was certainly repeated in Manhattan, where the leading professors at the medical colleges were attending physicians at the almshouse.[51]

A PENIS OF A DIFFERENT COLOR

Atlantic slave traders, planters, and land speculators funded the rise of colonial science, incentivized a competition to prove the natural bases of social relations, and exposed colored peoples to invasive and involuntary research. The rampant violations of nonwhite bodies in daily life repeated in the social order of the human sciences. American and European medical students used anatomies that read like primers on the proper preparation and exhibition of Negroes and Indians. American medicine exploited colored bodies precisely because the racial civilization placed them—free or enslaved, alive or dead—beyond the protection of the law or of moral civilization. By the end of the eighteenth century Indians and Negroes stood as universal objects of anatomical inquiry, science had generated a world of myths about their bodies, and the dissection of their corpses was a cornerstone of research.

Influenced by the work of colonial theorists such as Edward Long and Thomas Jefferson, the English physician Charles White was certain that science had established racial difference to an extraordinary degree of specificity. Anatomists, he celebrated in 1799, had even proved black men's penises to be larger than those of white men. "I have examined several living negroes, and found it invariably to be the case," White reported of his research upon black people confined to the asylum in Liverpool. There were real-world consequences to such observations. They reinforced notions of African primitivism and encouraged scientists to take black people to the cutting table. On both sides of the Atlantic, colored people in public institutions became prey for race researchers. Claims about the size of black men's penises led White and his contemporaries to hypothesize about corresponding peculiarities in the genitalia of black women, and a search for clitoral elongation, peculiar vaginal folds, extraordinary buttocks, and outsized breasts and nipples began anew. Johann Friedrich Blumenbach, for example, dismissed the suggestion that African women had larger than normal breasts based upon his own research but affirmed the "cloud of witnesses" who testified that black women's breasts were "long and pendulous." He was also compiling data on black penises. Andrew Fyfe's anatomy text, published in the United States through Philadelphia, instructed students to seek large penises for dissection.[52]

White's assignment of this particular characteristic fit neatly with Fyfe's directions for choosing specimens to point students toward Africans. Social and scientific racism demanded such desecrations. Black penises, for example, were on view in natural history museums and academies across Europe and North America. Charles White and Johann Friedrich Blumenbach even kept such trophies in their offices.

Science, at their benign Command,
Holds out her guiding Ray;
Nor Suffers Error's treach'rous Hand
To lead our Steps astray.

—HYMN SUNG BY CHARITY SCHOLARS,
ST. GEORGE'S CHAPEL, NEW YORK, 1783

A new era is arising in which the powerful and wealthy are with generous ardor responding to the claims of science and humanity. Thrice honored be New England, that the jubilee of that inauguration has been already heard within her boundaries and that her liberal sons while providing for the intellectual and moral wants of the community, through their rich endowments in behalf of knowledge, are by the generous training thus diffused, preparing the way for that time when power and riches will be everywhere blessed as the customary ministers of philanthropy.

—WILLIAM BARTON ROGERS, ADDRESS
AT WILLIAMS COLLEGE, 1855

I may as well note that this College [of Physicians and Surgeons], established by an act of the Legislature of the State in 1791, has had among its trustees, since it commenced operations in 1807, some of the best merchants in New York.

—WALTER BARRETT, *THE OLD MERCHANTS OF
NEW YORK CITY* (1863)

CHAPTER 7

"On the Bodily and Mental Inferiority of the Negro"

Institutionalizing Race in the American Academy

A bastardy case in New York City, *Commissioners of the Almshouse v. Alexander Whistelo, a Black Man* (1808), reveals the broad influence of the popular science of race—the social consumption of academic theories about human variation—and the political vulnerability of scientific research. Ultimately, the *Whistelo* trial was about much more than paternity. The court heard from an impressive number of experts, and it engaged profound questions, including the morality of slavery. The judges required answers to the complex issue of the operation of race: how color and its perceived qualities transferred across generations, when and why racial characteristics manifested, and how race shaped the individual and how it behaved in larger populations. They relied upon science to access the explanatory power of race, despite the fact that the testimony and deliberations exposed doubts about the reliability of this knowledge. The witnesses belonged to royal academies in Britain. They had founded medical programs, scientific societies, and professional associations in the United States. They held professorships at a cluster of American universities and had earned undergraduate and advanced degrees from the best universities in Europe and the United States. Those credentials and affiliations signaled the institutionalization of medicine and science in the American academy. The process of establishing medical and science programs at American universities brought scientific research under the financial control of the commercial elite and ultimately domesticated science. *Whistelo* was a modern trial. The trial uncovered a scientific academy building a new intellectual order upon divisive, unequal, and brutal social relations. The medical witnesses used the proceedings to advance the social and intellectual authority of science. The judges deferred to their expertise. But the paths that the experts took to show the value and power of science were also the paths through which science got deployed in politics. The expansion of the northern and southern academies in the decades before the Civil War accelerated the politicization of science and the institutionalization of race.

Whistelo's spectacle came largely from the hubris of science, law, and modernity, but the evidence explained more about the life of Lucy Williams, described as a "mulattress" and a "yellow woman," than about her child's paternity. In April 1806 Alexander Whistelo propositioned Williams, telling her that he was divorced and never intended to return to his wife. "I refused," she recalled, "for I did not choose to have him—I did not love him." Cast by the defense as a whore, a woman of low character, questionable morals, and a liar, Williams provided a reluctant and poignant account of the violent events that led to her pregnancy. Under the guise of going to visit his female cousin, Whistelo took Lucy Williams to a "bad house," where he locked her in and forced himself upon her. Under cross-examination, Williams also admitted that a white man later "turned the black man out [of bed] with a pistol" and took his place. She fought this attacker too, but was overpowered and again raped. Later that spring, when Whistelo returned to New York City from a tour at sea, Williams told him that she was pregnant. She was certain that he was the father because she believed the sexual connection with the white attacker insufficient for conception. On January 23, 1807, Lucy Williams gave birth to a girl.[1]

Troubled by the baby's complexion—lighter than those of Lucy

Williams and Alexander Whistelo—the commissioners of the almshouse, where Williams and the child were being supported, turned to the magistrate's court to rule on paternity under a new state bastardy law. Reproduction and fertility within and between the varied branches of humankind, however categorized, were a core fascination of race research. The court could access more than a century of compiled knowledge on this subject. European encounters with and observations of the colored world quickly worked their way into the academy. Such exchanges—both scientific and those that amounted to little more than global gossip—fed a historic intellectual engagement with the anthropology of the Americas, Africa, and Asia.

During June and July 1808 the judges took sworn statements from the region's leading physicians and researchers. Dr. Joshua Secor, who delivered the child, testified to the infant's appearance at birth. George Anthon, a professor and trustee at Columbia College, was the first outside expert to address the court. Dr. Anthon pointed to Williams's and Whistelo's "woolly" hair as proof the defendant could not have fathered the child, whose hair "has every appearance of its being the offspring of a white person." David Hosack, who had employed Whistelo as a coachman, also determined that the father had to be a white man or light mulatto man. Dr. Hosack had attended the College of New Jersey (Princeton), earned a medical degree in 1791 from the University of Pennsylvania, and then finished his training at the University of Edinburgh. At the time of the trial he taught surgery, clinical medicine, physic, obstetrics, and midwifery at Columbia and at Queen's College (Rutgers). Wright Post, professor of surgery at Columbia, explained the science behind the seeming consensus that Whistelo was not the father: "When persons of different colors have connection together," he instructed, "their offspring is generally of a color approaching to a mixture of both the father and the mother."[2]

The case might have ended there if not for the court's predisposition to hold Alexander Whistelo accountable and for the statements of two nonconforming doctors: Samuel L. Mitchill and Edward Miller. Professor of physic and clinical medicine at the College of Physicians and Surgeons in New York City, Miller

offered something of a compromise. The child's hair and complexion suggested that Whistelo was not the father, he stated, but her
"thick lips and flat nose are the indication of the father's being an
African." Samuel Mitchill was more adamant, insisting that it was
not only possible but probable that Whistelo was the father. A
professor at Columbia and a professor of natural history and botany at Physicians and Surgeons, Mitchill argued that the earlier
testimony treated skin color as too stable and predictable a characteristic. Miller and Mitchill were colleagues. A 1789 graduate of
the medical program at Pennsylvania, Miller had even coauthored
an address to physicians with Mitchill.[3] Now the pair united to
provide enough doubt to continue the proceedings.

Confused by the child's complexion and the contradictory expert testimony, the magistrates and the attorneys agreed to have the
case heard anew before a panel comprising Mayor DeWitt Clinton,
the city recorder, and three aldermen. Beginning August 18, 1808,
the mayor's court took direct testimony from Lucy Williams. The
prominent physician Benjamin Kissam, who had studied medicine
at Edinburgh and founded the New York Academy of Sciences,
informed the judges that, after "examining those parts of the child
which particularly indicate the color of the race," he did not believe this to be the child of a black man. Dr. Kissam was sure that
the child's father had to be white.[4]

The court combed the mid-Atlantic colleges for race experts. David Hosack returned. He assured the judges that the laws of nature
negated the possibility of Whistelo being the father of the child.
Despite his broad training in Atlantic science, Hosack had his conclusions rigorously challenged as the almshouse's lawyer tried to
limit the damage of his testimony. Asked if "irritation, terror, or
surprise" at the moment of conception could have altered the appearance of the child, the professor dismissed this possibility. Asked
if albinism might explain the child's light appearance, Hosack rejected this suggestion. The surgeon Wright Post defended Hosack's
position. "There were instances of black men with black women
producing children as fair as this," he allowed, "but they were excep-
tions to the general laws of nature." The court then heard from the
doctor credited with introducing vaccination to New York City.

Valentine Seaman graduated from Pennsylvania's medical school and was an expert on childbirth and midwifery. He was a particularly strong defense witness. A surgeon at New York Hospital, he also served as the visiting physician for pregnant women confined at the almshouse. Dr. Seaman concurred with the majority, concluding that Whistelo could not be the father of Williams's child.[5]

Five of the *Whistelo* witnesses had studied at Edinburgh, and most were corresponding members of British medical and science societies, which circulated much of the available literature on race and forensic medicine. Andrew Duncan had used his chair in the institutions of medicine at Edinburgh to enact a series of lectures on forensics, provide medical testimony in criminal and civil cases, and conduct medical investigations for courts. As Duncan explained:

> Many questions come before courts of justice, where the opinion of medical practitioners is necessary either for the exculpation of innocence, or the detection of guilt. In many cases, on their judgment, questions respecting the liberty and property of individuals must be determined by the civil magistrate.

In 1792 Duncan published his lectures on medicine and law, which included lessons on pregnancy and childbirth. Additionally, the Edinburgh medical curriculum had been published years before the trial. The series had comprehensive volumes on dissection and anatomy, including material on human genitalia and the reproductive process.[6]

Dominated by Edinburgh graduates and affiliates, the second round of testimony again appeared of a single mind. A president of the Medical Society of New York County and a founder of Physicians and Surgeons, James Tillary testified that there were "no principles of physiology nor philosophical data" to support the idea that this was the child of a black man. Born in Scotland, Dr. Tillary studied at "the great medical school of Edinburgh," a colleague later noted, but left and finished his surgical training in the British army. He came to New York during the American Revolution and

stayed after the British surrender. William Moore, a professor at
Columbia and Queen's, also exonerated Whistelo. He had done
his medical training in London and Edinburgh, and, in 1793, received an honorary doctor of medicine degree from Queen's. Moore
served as president of the local medical society and, like Post and
Kissam, had worked as a doctor for the almshouse. Dr. Anthon
again testified and further strengthened the defense.[7]

A Pennsylvania alumnus, Matthias Williamson, dramatically
called the question: "If this was the child of that woman by that
man, it is a prodigy," he declared, and "he did not believe that
prodigies happened, though daily experience unfortunately proved
that perjuries did." Williamson enjoyed close ties to the families
who funded and governed the colleges in Princeton and New
Brunswick. Brought in because of his long residence in the South,
John C. Osborn was equally vehement that Whistelo could not be
the father of the child and that the child's complexion was not the
consequence of albinism or any other extraordinary condition.
The prior year Osborn had moved to New York City from North
Carolina and joined the faculty of Columbia, teaching obstetrics
and the diseases of women and children. Benjamin DeWitt, professor of chemistry at Physicians and Surgeons, closed this cycle of
testimony with an assurance that the child's father was likely white
and certainly not black.[8]

The almshouse's case now rested upon the testimony of Dr.
Samuel Mitchill. The Columbia professor held to his opinion. After defining the racial categories of mulatto, quadroon, and sambo,
Mitchill informed the court that there were reliable rules of race
but these operated with greater complexity than the majority opinion permitted. For instance, changes to skin color, hair color or
texture, and the presence or absence of hair were all possible during conception. The doctor added that he had little reason to doubt
Lucy Williams's sworn testimony that Alexander Whistelo was
the father of her child. Under direct and cross-examination, Mitchill
provided a spirited rehearsal of cases in which skin color changed
at various periods in the life cycle. Aside from albinism, which
he argued rarely presented in New York, changes in complexion
were common. He offered examples of the malleability of color

documented in his own research, historical accounts, biblical texts, and classical literature. He even revived the idea that shocks during conception or irritations to the minds of women could influence the appearance of babies: A pregnant woman who discovered the slaughter of a favored domestic animal later gave birth to a deformed infant. Mitchill swore that he had seen the child, armless with disfigured legs, playing in the street, and he personally interviewed the parents to learn the cause.[9]

The defense could not easily dismiss Dr. Mitchill. He had so excelled in the medical program at Edinburgh, during the high point of its scientific influence, that Columbia awarded him an honorary master's degree upon his return to the United States. A professor at Columbia, Physicians and Surgeons, and Queen's, he later became the founding vice president of Rutgers Medical College after it reopened, under the equally famous David Hosack. Mitchill wrote on subjects ranging from medicine to mineralogy and published the nation's first medical journal. Within a decade of the trial, DeWitt Clinton dedicated a public lecture on New York history to the "Honourable Samuel L. Mitchill." At the time of his testimony, Samuel Mitchill was a United States senator from New York.[10]

Tested repeatedly by the defense, Senator Mitchill was certain that science, history, and religion supported his position. A midwife in New Brunswick, New Jersey, had told a woman in labor about the circumcision of a Jewish infant, he recounted, and the agitated woman then brought forth a boy child with a diseased penile foreskin. A Scottish case involved a man who repeatedly put off the demands of his amorous wife; after he accidentally spilled ink in her shoes, the spurned woman produced a black child. However, by the end of his testimony, the longest examination of the trial, Mitchill's conclusions hinged on the testimony of Lucy Williams rather than his braiding of literary and historical proofs.[11]

The expert testimony confirmed Whistelo's innocence. But the court still suspected him, and therefore called two additional experts. The noted Philadelphia physician Felix Pascalis Ouvriere assured the judges that science could solve the riddle of paternity. In 1795 Pascalis had won a prize from the Hartford Medical Society for the best essay on the causes of the yellow fever outbreak in

Dr. Samuel Latham Mitchill, United States Senator,
who testified in the Whistelo *trial*

New York, and he also investigated the Philadelphia outbreak of
1797. One aspect of his research was examining the course of
disease in black people by exploring the relevant medical and plantation literatures. Africans, he told the judges, had definite characteristics, the three most obvious being their curly hair, dark hue,
and elongated heels. In his compendium of the Edinburgh curriculum, William Nesbit identified the latter as a specific skeletal
feature of Africans. Pascalis added that at least one of these characteristics was evident even in perfect mulattos and other mixtures. Under cross-examination, Pascalis argued that an emotional
or other shock would more likely produce abortion or deformity
than a change in complexion. Dr. Pascalis concluded that Whistelo was not the father of the child. Sir James Jay was the last
physician to testify. A Columbia graduate and a founder of Physicians and Surgeons, Jay had once served as Columbia's European

fund-raising agent. He definitively informed the court that the child was not Alexander Whistelo's.[12]

The defense's summation stressed that the great majority of the expert witnesses had scientifically concluded that Alexander Whistelo did not father the child in question. It also attempted to dismantle and ridicule the testimony of Professor Mitchill—the only scientist to openly support the almshouse's case—accusing him of attacking "the doctors en masse" to defend Lucy Williams's virtue. A sarcastic assault on her character followed:

> Soon after the vernal equinox, in the year of the vulgar era one thousand eight hundred and six, an Adam-colored damsel submitted to the lewd embraces of a lascivious Moor, and from that mixture sprang three miracles.
> 1st. In the course of one month's time she quickened and conceived.
> 2d. She bare a child, not of her *primitive* and *proper* color, nor yet of the African—but strange to tell, of the most degenerate white.
> 3d. And the greatest of all these wonders, she remained, as the counsel for the Almshouse charitably testifies, a lady of virtue and unblemished credit![13]

The almshouse's attorney had earlier argued that if Williams intended to commit perjury, then she had more incentive to accuse the white man. Whistelo's lawyer reversed that logic. The defense cautioned that the court risked establishing a dangerous precedent that would make black men forever vulnerable to supporting the bastard children of white men. It urged the judges not to allow women to keep white men to sleep with and black men to pay for the pleasure. Using the scientific testimony, the defense now attacked the almshouse's entire case:

> Ten or twelve of the most experienced physicians declare this thing next to impossible. . . . Some of the professional witnesses have resided long in those countries where, if such facts were natural they must have fallen within their

notice; but they never saw one such as would warrant their belief in this case—others have practised in that particular and useful branch which enables them to judge with certainty in matters of this nature; and envy cannot deny of them that they have brought more into the world than they have sent out of it. The very gentlemen who ushered into life the babe, whose name will be bright in the annals of zoology, physiology, pathology, and all the *ologies*, (Dr. Secor,) agrees that it is the child of a white man.[14]

The impact of this lampooning became clear when the judges ruled on the evidence. Their decision respected the prestige of science in Atlantic thought, and it exposed their confidence in the capacity of science to find truth. The court maintained an unshaken belief in the provable existence and logical operation of race despite the conflicting arguments, wildly speculative claims, and inconsistent testimony that it had heard.

The mayor began by restating the conundrum: "The defendant is a negro—the mother a mulattress—and the child has the hair and most of the features of a white, the color, indeed, somewhat darker, but lighter than most of the generality of mulattoes." The virtually unanimous testimony of the medical experts vindicated Whistelo, Clinton continued. Sir Jay and Dr. Pascalis agreed on this matter and enjoyed the support of "the president of the Medical Society, and several professors and other distinguished physicians." Mayor Clinton then noted that the court "obviously" had less confidence in the testimony of Lucy Williams than in the statements and conclusions of the experts. Supported only by Senator Mitchill, who had merely shown the improbable to be possible, the almshouse failed to sway the judges, who absolved Alexander Whistelo.[15]

THE TRIUMPH OF SCIENCE

Ecclesiastical courts had routinely handled fornication and adultery cases in the early years of the colonies. Over the next century, civil authorities began determining questions of paternity, while church officials adjudicated sexual morality. Civil courts approached these matters as investigations into paternity rather than sin—the purpose being to establish financial responsibility, not necessarily moral culpability. The mid-eighteenth-century scandal that enveloped the Reverend Wilhelm Christoph Berkenmeyer, accused of fathering a child with his enslaved woman, Margareta Christiaan, was largely resolved within the Lutheran Church of Athens, New York. In that same period, Job Comecho, a Native man from Natick, Massachusetts, was sitting in prison "charged with the maintenance of a Bastard child." To raise money, Comecho sold five acres of Natick land to Prince Vitto, a black man who formerly had been enslaved to the Reverend Oliver Peabody, Harvard's missionary to the Natick Indians. The selectmen of Lebanon, Connecticut, seized "two male bastard negro children" from Debb, a Pequot woman, and bound them out until age twenty-five to spare the town the cost of their upkeep. As late as 1803, the church in Groton, Massachusetts, required parents who had children within seven months of their marriage to make public confessions.[16]

One of the *Whistelo* trial's most modern features was the judicial assumption that questions of generation, or paternity, were beyond the reach of the church and theologians. Questions of faith and morality were not absent at the trial, but research into race had spurred an intellectual revolution in British and American academies that encouraged a new legal deference to science. Judges and lawyers validated the power of science, and scientists certified the precision of the law. *Whistelo* was a product of two extraordinary social and intellectual developments: the ascent of science, particularly race science, as a secular corrective on religion, and the consequent dissociation of the academy and the church.

The morality of slavery was quietly debated in *Whistelo*; in fact, it had to be. "It seems to be the destiny of mankind to arrive at perfection in the sciences," wrote a student of Joseph Hawkins, adding that the current generation had to push the limits of knowledge. Friends were publishing Hawkins's account of his travels to Africa to support him after he lost his vision. Dr. Felix Pascalis Ouvriere, who testified in *Whistelo*, contributed a letter recommending the book, which, he argued, confirmed his impressions from his encounters with enslaved people in the Caribbean. Pascalis added that the travel diary proved the immorality of "trafficking with slaves and prisoners of Africa, and keeping, consequently, those nations in the customary ignorance, barbarity and warfare."[17]

The sociologist Nancy Stepan finds that the majority of early race scientists opposed slavery. Many researchers believed that the scientific study of race would confirm the egalitarian presuppositions of Judeo-Christian faith. In 1752 the Reverend Thomas Church invoked this religious tradition in science during the Lady Sadleir Lecture at the Royal College of Physicians, London. "*The* Lord *hath created the physician*," Church said of the divine origins of science. God endowed human beings with the intellectual capacity to understand and cure illness, blessed mankind with the compassion to serve those in need, and provided the physical materials to remedy the sick. He reminded the new physicians of the miraculous workings of the human body and the other wonders of nature that reflected divine inspiration.[18]

The Judeo-Christian belief in the common origin of all mankind had extraordinary influence on early science, and it was affirmed during the *Whistelo* trial. The expert testimony synthesized a generation of research that used linguistics, physiology, history, and geography to establish not the equality but the unity of humankind. Articulated in religious and scientific language, monogenism had the potential to deliver a serious blow against those who used distinctions of color to justify enslavement.

Whistelo occurred at a formative moment in the history of Euro-American science. The experts were students of physical and abstract science, society, and nature. About 1802 Dr. Hosack purchased land outside the city boundaries to establish the Elgin Botanical Garden, the first of its kind in the United States. It served as a laboratory for students training in medicine, the natural sciences, and pharmacology. When the New York Horticultural Society was incorporated in 1822, David Hosack was its president and Wright Post and Samuel Mitchill served on the executive committee.[19]

The trial doctors were researchers in fields as diverse as botany, horticulture, history, natural history, philosophy, chemistry, anthropology, physiology, anatomy, and geology, and they belonged to medical faculties that were self-consciously reproducing the learned societies and research structures of the best European universities. Three of the witnesses—Hosack, Moore, and Post—led the local dispensary, which had both charitable and academic functions. An interest in the history of man and nature placed Hosack and Mitchill among the founders of the New-York Historical Society (1804). Several of the doctors were students of religion. The scientific fascination with the natural world reflected, in part, the allure of creation. Religion drew many scientists to fields such as botany, zoology, and geology, which eventually incubated evolutionist thought. Inheriting their perception of science from the Enlightenment, these scholars pursued a science that constantly interacted with faith. Born the same year as the *Whistelo* trial, Charles Darwin later abandoned the medical course at Edinburgh to pursue divinity at Cambridge University.[20]

Whistelo offers a detailed cross section of the state of science and intellectual society in the early national academy. The witnesses focused obsessively on the physicality of Alexander Whistelo, Lucy Williams, and the little girl because most were convinced that black and white people differed by development but not by design. Johann Friedrich Blumenbach's research into the physical and natural history of human beings, including his seminal categorization of the human races by region and color, was circulating in the major science centers during the period when the *Whistelo* experts trained. His work on human anatomy was also widely available in the years before the trial. Assuming the common origin of mankind, Blumenbach sought answers to human diversity in the geography, environment, and history of its various branches. An edition of his *Elements of Physiology* had also been published in Philadelphia, where four of the *Whistelo* doctors had studied.[21]

Early race researchers were secure in their belief that, however derived, the scientific answer to human origins would confirm a single genesis. The research of the French scientist Georges Cuvier was also available to the *Whistelo* experts. The field of comparative anatomy, argues Stepan, which Cuvier and his Parisian contemporaries pioneered, laid the foundations of race science. It allowed researchers such as James Cowles Prichard to address the questions of racial differentiation using modern scientific tools.[22]

The Edinburgh connection is significant. In 1681 Charles II had chartered the Royal College of Physicians in Edinburgh and, before the close of the century, its Surgeons' Hall hosted courses in chemistry and materia medica. In 1705 the university established a professorship in anatomy and soon funded professorships in chemistry and medicine. By 1726 the medical department was organized into a separate college, the first and best in Britain and, within decades, a rival of the faculty at Leiden, Holland.[23]

Philadelphia was especially receptive to the medical and scientific culture of Scotland. Edinburgh alumni established the colonies' first medical school through the College of Philadelphia (University of Pennsylvania), and by the end of the eighteenth century Philadelphia graduates dominated the medical faculties in the mid-Atlantic schools. In 1769 Dr. Benjamin Rush, a graduate of New Jersey who earned a medical degree at Edinburgh, became professor of chemistry and, later, professor of the institutes and practice of medicine at Philadelphia. Upon Rush's arrival, the college expanded its medical curriculum into a full medical school on the Scottish model.[24]

At least four of the *Whistelo* witnesses studied under Rush as the Pennsylvania medical program was experiencing remarkable growth. Valentine Seaman, a health commissioner during the 1795 yellow fever outbreak in New York City, admitted that influence. His report on the epidemic paid tribute to Rush's "innovations" in treating the fever in Philadelphia two years earlier. The New York surgeon also used his dedication to acknowledge the excellent medical education he received under Dr. Rush.[25]

During his testimony at the *Whistelo* trial, Dr. Samuel Mitchill, who likely had prolonged the case with his wildly speculative but forceful counterarguments, made repeated reference to an emerging literature on complexion. His investigation of a black man who had turned white concluded that the case undermined the logic of slavery and racism: "Such an alteration of color as this militates powerfully against the opinion adopted by some modern philosophers, that the negroes are a different *species* of the human race from the whites, and tend strongly to corroborate the probability of the derivation of all the *varieties* of mankind from a single pair." The ability to treat color as a fluid variable triggered by climate and nature incited a direct attack on racial slavery. "How additionally singular would it be, if instances of the spontaneous disappearance of this sable mark of distinction between slaves and their masters were to become frequent?" Senator Mitchill wondered.[26]

Raised in a large Quaker family in Hempstead, Long Island, Mitchill reached his scientific conclusions in part through the pacifist and egalitarian impulses of his faith. Several months after the *Whistelo* verdict, Senator Mitchill emancipated Jenny Jiggins, a twenty-eight-year-old black woman. In 1811 he freed a black man, Ned. In June 1816 he released another black woman, Betsy, through the New York Manumission Society. The senator was not the only slaveholder at the trial. Mayor DeWitt Clinton, who sat in judgment, was born into a slaveholding family. Drs. Obsorn and Pascalis had extensive medical experience in the South and the Caribbean, and David Hosack and William Moore, both faculty at Columbia and Queens, and James Jay of Columbia all owned slaves.[27]

If European intellectuals—particularly British and French researchers—dominated the study of race in the emerging fields of anatomy, natural history, and anthropology, much of their evidence came from the observations and other productions of the individuals at the frontiers of Europe's contact with Africa, the Americas, and Asia, including slave owners and slave traders. "New World" students carried a wealth of knowledge. While Scotland exercised broad influence over the rise of American science, Scots were a minority of the student body at Edinburgh, where one of every six students was from the Americas. Colonial students abounded in the science and medicine courses, and Americans were generating much of the new scholarship on medicine, pharmacology, and disease in the colonial world.[28]

RACE AND THE LIBERATION OF THE ACADEMY

There was a political incentive emboldening this science: to the extent that science supplanted theology, it eroded the remnants of ecclesiastical control over the academy. But if science could be used to displace theology by claiming a superior position for understanding human history and social relations, then it could also be impressed into the service of slavery. In fact, the politics of slavery hastened the ascent of the academy in public affairs. Even at the height of the scientific challenge to slavery, that opening was well lighted. Judeo-Christian theologians used the curse of Ham to evade the conflict between their inescapable belief in the common origins of mankind and their support for, or acquiescence to, the social tyranny of modern slavery. The journey for scientists was never that complicated.

Scientists generally believed that the social hierarchies of the world would prove as natural as the common origins of all peoples. They assumed the inferiority of colored bodies while closely guarding their commitment to the basic humanity of all people. During the *Whistelo* proceedings, Felix Pascalis argued that all racial mixtures tended toward equilibrium—meaning either a complexion between those of the mother and father or the balancing of complexion with other features. As an example, Dr. Pascalis proudly claimed a relative, the Haitian general André Rigaud, a dark-skinned mulatto, who also "had the features and form of a white man—was very handsome and well made." The physician's belief in the existence and superiority of white features did not require an abandonment of his faith in a shared genesis. He sat in elite intellectual company. Georges Cuvier isolated three races—Caucasian, Mongolian, and Negro—with the first of these dominating the cultural and intellectual history of humankind, and producing the "handsomest [people] on earth."[29]

This construction of the sciences allowed humankind to have a single origin but varied progress; thus a contemporary racial hierarchy was consistent with a single genesis. The first graduate of the College of Physicians and Surgeons, John Wakefield Francis, received the honor of being invited to immediately partner in practice with his mentor, David Hosack. A key witness in *Whistelo*, Hosack was among the most accomplished physicians and scientists in the nation. Francis had excelled as a student at Columbia, where he graduated in 1809. Two years later he earned his medical degree at

Dr. John Wakefield Francis
SOURCE: Library of Congress

Physicians and Surgeons, and the following year he added a master's degree from Columbia. In 1813, just before the city's two medical faculties united, Francis was appointed professor of the institutes of medicine and materia medica. He later served as professor of obstetrics and forensic medicine at Rutgers.[30]

One of the most instructive moments in his career came while he was an undergraduate at Columbia. Just months before the *Whistelo* trial, John Francis had presented the findings from his undergraduate research in a paper titled "On the Bodily and Mental Inferiority of the Negro." Francis read his thesis at the inaugural meeting of the Medical and Surgical Society of the University of the State of New York, which comprised the medical faculties of Columbia College and Physicians and Surgeons and was charged with regulating and governing medical education. The medical society included at least half of the *Whistelo* witnesses.[31]

TRADING SCIENCE

The transition to a more focused scientific racism required not a leap but a casual step. The institutionalization of medicine—the organization of science faculties and medical colleges in the colonies—happened as slave owners, planters, land speculators, and Atlantic merchants began sponsoring scientific research. The families who paid for the establishment of medical schools and science faculties also oversaw those developments. The founding of medical colleges on American campuses brought science, particularly the human sciences, under the political and financial dominion of slave traders, slave owners, and their surrogates. The class influences upon science were apparent during the *Whistelo* trial. The court invited experts whose educational credentials, professional titles and appointments, and institutional affiliations mapped the half-century rise of academic science in North America. That deference was, in fact, a fair reflection of how fully science had been tamed. As slaveholders and slave traders paid for medical colleges and science faculties, they also imposed subtle and severe controls on science.

As Atlantic slavery underwrote the production of knowledge, it distorted the knowable. "When a governing board sat down to consider the affairs of the colonial college," the historian Richard Hofstadter observed, "there was usually assembled at the table a group of men who were accustomed to seeing each other frequently at the counting houses, in each other's homes, and in the vestries of churches." As noted earlier, John Morgan, a founder of the medical school at Philadelphia, traveled to the West Indies to make connections and raise money. The cofounder of the medical college, William Shippen Jr., had extensive land interests in Pennsylvania, and was tied through marriage to regional dynasties including the Livingstons of New York and New Jersey. On April 3, 1762, Shippen had wed Alice Lee of the prominent Virginia plantation family.[32]

The New York surgeon John Bard, president of the local medical society, secured his family's economic position by investing in land and slaves. His son Samuel's education at King's College (Columbia) and Edinburgh was a departure from his career path. Surgeons traditionally received their training as apprentices, while physicians studied the arts and sciences at universities. The two professions were also divided by specialty: surgeons performing external and mechanical treatments, such as bleedings and amputations, and physicians focusing on internal medicine. Dr. Bard fully supported his son's professionalization, offering suggestions for scientific and medical reading, and lovingly supervising Samuel's study habits, dress and manners, social activities, and courses. He gave Samuel detailed advice on courting a wife. He sent money for his expenses, encouraged him to seize every educational opportunity while abroad, and, self-conscious about their colonial status, reminded him of the importance of "appearing like a Gentleman."[33]

While Samuel Bard was studying in Scotland, his father invested in Hyde Park, a 3,600-acre plantation along more than three miles of the Hudson River in Dutchess County, New York, with a resident overseer "to support his the said John Bard[']s slaves in good and sufficient Cloathing and Bedding." When Samuel Bard returned to New York City to establish its first medical college, he turned to merchants for support. His son William eventually married Catherine Cruger, the daughter of the St. Croix slave trader Nicholas Cruger, and his daughter Eliza married John McVickar, professor of political economy at Columbia and heir of a West Indies and China trader whose ships carried the products of slavery and opium. William Bard became a founder of the New York Life Insurance and Trust Company. In 1860 William and Catherine's son John Bard founded St. Stephen's College (Bard) as a preparatory school for General Theological Seminary in New York City. Bard donated a chapel and land for the campus. Columbia eventually honored John McVickar and Samuel Bard with the memorial McVickar Professorship of Political Economy and the Bard Professorship of the Practice of Medicine.[34]

The son of a humble Maine family, Isaac Royall used his early maritime experience to launch serial slave trading ventures. He bought an Antiguan sugar plantation and entered elite society. In 1737 the Royalls returned to New England with twenty-seven enslaved black people and built an estate in Medford—on the site of the original grant of Governor John Winthrop—just a few miles north of Cambridge. Ten Hills Farm (a portion of which is now the campus of Tufts University) included a grand main house and slave quarters. In 1739 Isaac junior inherited the estate and increased the holdings; more than sixty enslaved black people worked Ten Hills during his tenure. In his 1781 will, Royall bequeathed two thousand acres to Harvard College to provide a perpetual fund for a professor of law and a professor of anatomy and physic. The following year the trustees used that gift to establish Harvard Medical College under John Warren, anatomy and surgery; Benjamin Waterhouse, physic; and Aaron Dexter, chemistry and materia medica. In 1817 the governors belatedly established Harvard Law School.[35]

American science evolved with American slavery. Beginning in 1780, just before the establishment of Harvard Medical School, businessmen and bankers began dislodging academics and clergy on the Harvard Corporation. That change came as the officers tried to stabilize revenues during the American Revolution. A growing ideological struggle between Unitarians and Trinitarians for control of Harvard spilled into the legislature. The predominantly Unitarian merchant class increased its financial support for the college and consolidated their control with the installation of John Thornton Kirkland, an in-law of the wealthy Cabot family, as president. Merchants financed research and education, and they oversaw the new academic initiatives. The wealthy West Indies trader John McLean endowed the Massachusetts General Hospital and the McLean Asylum for the Insane. He also created the McLean Professorship of Ancient and Modern History at Harvard. In 1782 James Perkins of Boston sailed on a ship owned by his mother to Saint-Domingue, where he joined in a slaving partnership. Perkins later brought his younger brothers Thomas and Samuel into the trade. The Perkinses were nearly killed at the outbreak of the Haitian Revolution, and James fled back to Boston, where he again entered the slave trade. That business allowed him to fund the Perkins Professorship in Astronomy and Mathematics at Harvard.[36]

Again, the sources of such generosity mattered. In the decade before the Revolution, John Bard continued investing in lands and slaves, including a black man named Jamaica and a child named Cuffy, whom he included in a 1765 lease. They were among the innumerable enslaved people whose bodies, labor, and lives paid for the rise of Atlantic science. Just months after Harvard opened its medical school with the Royall bequest, "Belinda, an African," recorded the torments of her life after being captured and sold into American slavery. "Fifty years her faithful hands have been compelled to ignoble servitude, for the benefit of Isaac Royall," reads her February 14, 1783, petition to the Massachusetts legislature. Seeking support from the Royall estate, the enslaved woman's appeal reminded the court that her work had augmented the Royalls' fortune. Now more than seventy years old, she had been exploited every moment of her life since being snatched from West Africa by "men whose faces were like the moon." The aged woman was struggling to find a way to maintain herself and her sickly daughter. A week later the General Court allotted Belinda (Royall) a yearly stipend of about £15.[37]

"Is nothing to be allowed for the feelings of the mind?" the Irish jurist William Preston eloquently begged. "Are the *negroes* such mere machines, indeed, that exemption from death and torture, and the necessary sustenance of animal duration are sufficient to their happiness?" Those simple moral questions were difficult for many people in the Americas and Europe to answer.[38]

The conceit of science could and did shift from correcting theology's logical sins to claiming the superior position for legitimating the dominant civilization. Within decades of the *Whistelo* trial, race researchers were actively questioning the unity of humankind. In little time, the political and economic weight of slavery's defenders, beliefs about the inferiority of black people that undergirded inquiries into the nature of mankind, and the fragility of the scientific defense of monogenism combined to doom African Americans to a scientific verdict as harsh and irreversible as that received at the hands of theologians.

THE REGIONAL SPECIFICITY OF KNOWLEDGE

The North-South divide, the sectional crisis, is not a particularly useful template for explaining the course of science or the behavior of college faculties and governors in the antebellum nation.

Academics both were conscripted into these political conflicts and searched for opportunities to apply science to social questions. Eighteenth-century race researchers had largely believed that science could verify Christian monogenism, but nineteenth-century scientists increasingly held that their research would discover the impassable biological distance between the races. Academic science lunged toward polygenism: the theory that the races of humankind had separate origins. Such ideas gained popularity in pre–Civil War colleges, North and South. There were certainly distinct regional strategies and preferences for deploying science in politics; however, throughout the antebellum nation, intellectuals were largely striving toward a single goal: a science that *proved* the inferiority of the Negro and thereby quieted the moral speculations and political agitation of abolitionists, race agnostics, and foreign critics. That ambition alone constituted a revolution within the profession.

Moral philosophers such as Adam Smith of Glasgow and the controversial David Hume of Edinburgh had dominated the intellectual culture of Scotland during Benjamin Rush's student days. The cooperation of theologians and scientists in the greater national project of modernization distinguished Scotland within the European Enlightenment. A vibrant dialogue between theology and science shaped the Scottish Enlightenment and benefited from the mingling of theologians and scientists in learned societies.[39] Moral questions influenced the course of scientific investigation.

Scottish students ventured out to study in the centers of European science. Almost a thousand Scots had enrolled at Leiden in the century before the establishment of the Edinburgh medical college. Scottish theologians encouraged the growth of the science faculties, cultivated the medical programs, and helped give direction to science. By the close of the eighteenth century, medicine was the largest academic program at Edinburgh, and medical missions—linking science and evangelism to address human needs—were among its leading vocations. James Ramsay enrolled at King's College, Aberdeen, and then studied medicine in London. In 1762 he sailed to St. Kitts, where he practiced medicine and where his antislavery convictions were born. When he returned almost two decades later, Ramsay published a thorough

Dr. Benjamin Rush
SOURCE: University Archives, University of Pennsylvania

exposé of the brutality and immorality of slavery in the British possessions in which he also countered the emerging racist defenses of slavery from intellectuals such as David Hume.[40]

A confidence that theology and science had a common social purpose also convinced Rush that the moral currents of human society were converging to end African slavery. "The abolition of domestic Slavery is not a Utopian Scheme," he promised. He saw the institution faltering under its own economic inefficiencies and growing public hostility.[41]

The idea can be pushed further. Rush and many of his peers viewed science as rescuing a theology that had been hijacked in defense of slavery. Theological racism hampered Christians' response to modern social questions. Science could save theology by addressing that failure. The German scientist Carl Vogt, a professor at the University of Geneva, was likely answering this concern

when he concluded that "the term 'race' expresses, perhaps, only a
theological idea." The origins of racialism were to be found in a
theology that had been corrupted by social sins ranging from color
prejudice to human bondage.[42]

"The vulgar notion of their being descended from Cain, who was
supposed to have been marked with this color, is too absurd to need
a refutation," Rush had insisted. It was not difficult to expose religion as the primary offender in the emergence of modern racial
thought, he continued. The moral silence of American ministers on
the issue of slavery was troubling by itself. "But chiefly—ye Ministers of the Gospel, whose dominion over the principles and actions
of men is so universally acknowledged and felt," the doctor demanded, "let your zeal keep pace with your opportunities to put
a stop to slavery." Nor could slavery be rationalized as a mecha-
nism for Christianization, since a just religion could not spread
by unjust means. "A Christian Slave is a contradiction in terms,"
he concluded.[43]

Nonetheless, Rush enjoyed broad intellectual influence over
medical science in the slave states. In June 1813 the members of the
Medical Society of South Carolina gathered in the Circular Church
in Charleston to memorialize Benjamin Rush. The Philadelphia
physician had taught or mentored half the members of the society, a telling measure of his influence, the reach of the Pennsylvania medical program, and the legacies of Scottish universities
in American medicine and science. When Rush began teaching,
he had fewer than two dozen students; the year before his death he
taught more than four hundred. Dr. David Ramsay, a New Jersey
graduate and the son-in-law of John Witherspoon, delivered the
eulogy. He recounted Rush's heroic sacrifices during the yellow fever outbreaks in Philadelphia, his contributions to science and public health, his service in the Continental Congress, and his
educational and humanitarian endeavors.[44]

In fact, southern scholars had routinely and vigorously debated
slavery. Student literary societies at the University of Georgia took
up the question, and such exchanges were fairly common on southern campuses before the escalation of sectional tensions in the antebellum era. In 1828 Georgia's Phi Kappas decided that slavery

was unjust, and a decade later they debated themselves to an abolitionist conclusion. Another campus society, the Demosthenians,
came within a single vote of endorsing abolition. Students at Georgia became more reflexively proslavery as the sectional crisis intensified. In 1832 William Gaston, a graduate of New Jersey, included
an antislavery critique in an address at the University of North
Carolina. The university published the speech and kept it in circulation for decades. Gaston served as a trustee at North Carolina for
forty years.[45]

Scholars became more reluctant to criticize slavery in the face of
the social anxieties that followed Nat Turner's 1831 slave rebellion
in Southampton County, Virginia; the political pressure of an aggressive, organized Atlantic movement to abolish slavery; and the
economic promises of financial speculation in Mississippi cotton
lands and slaves. Professor Thomas R. Dew, a slave owner from a
wealthy plantation family, earned the presidency of the College of
William and Mary in part with his forthright defenses of slavery
in the wake of the Turner uprising. President Thomas Cooper of
South Carolina College (University of South Carolina) ended academic debate of slavery at that institution and insisted upon a full,
positive defense of human bondage. Professor James H. Thornwell, who later served as president of South Carolina, lobbied to
stop Presbyterians from publicly criticizing and opposing slavery,
and he became an architect of a proslavery Christian theology that
asserted the eternal morality of servitude in Judeo-Christian
tradition.[46]

Academics had long exploited political opportunities to demonstrate the validity of science—as in the *Whistelo* trial—and southern scholars were equally adept at using the sectional crisis to
establish their value to the region and the nation. "Are we to have
peace or fratricidal war?" worried Professor William Barton Rogers of William and Mary. In 1819 Hannah Blythe Rogers and Patrick Kerr Rogers, professor of chemistry, had moved to Williamsburg
with their four sons: James Blythe, William Barton, Henry Darwin, and Robert Empie. William and James entered the undergraduate class with young men like Thomas R. Dew. The Rogerses
lived in Brafferton Hall—the old Indian College—which had its

own crew of slaves. William Barton disliked the South. He panned his classmates for their incessant "feasting, dancing, and music," and he predicted that their graduations would hasten the decline of a civilization that was already "fast falling to decay." In 1824 he warned Thomas Jefferson that his alma mater was lost. There was simply something about the place, he explained, that "must forever prevent it from being prosperous or successful." In 1828 William Rogers replaced his father on the faculty. His concerns soon shifted to the political climate of the region. "In this part of the State the politics are ultra-Southern," he lamented to his uncle. Nonetheless, he and his brothers Henry and Robert had substantial careers in tobacco and cotton country.[47]

The region's dependence upon northern and European scholars added to these tensions. The cotton wealth that funded southern education had enticed many ambitious northern- and European-born intellectuals to adapt to the slave regime. The pedigrees of intellectual outsiders came under greater scrutiny as slavery came under greater criticism in Atlantic discourses. The rapid expansion of the southern academy in the decades after the Revolution had brought a migration of scholars from the North and Europe to the plantation states. Academics looking for opportunities found new southern colleges and universities flush with money and students. They also found a growing defensiveness about slavery and a rising insecurity about the migration of people and ideas into the South.[48]

"I am a slaveholder, and, if I know myself, I am 'sound on the slavery question,'" President Frederick A. P. Barnard responded to critics at the University of Mississippi. Toward the end of 1859 several students entered Barnard's house while the president was away, with "shameful designs" upon an enslaved young woman named Jane. They assaulted Jane, beating her so severely that she carried scars and wounds for months, and one of them, Samuel Humphreys, raped her. When the faculty declined to dismiss Humphreys on the testimony of a black woman, the president ordered his expulsion. A divided faculty vote—the northerners voting with the northern-born president—and Barnard's decision to dismiss the student brought accusations of race treason. Detractors accused the president of using "Negro evidence" against a white man.[49]

The faculty response to Barnard constituted a public unpacking and examination of the lineage and quality of the ideas that informed his moral and social judgments; it was an attempt to display the regional specificity of knowledge. "There were scores of thousands of [northern-born] men at the South in much the same position as he," a biographer estimated, and many of them were scholars. Jefferson Davis, soon to be the president of the new Confederate government, sided with Barnard, making a public show of shaking the president's hand during the controversy. Jacob Thompson, a university trustee, sent Barnard a note of support for exercising an honorable "paternalism" over his slaves. If Barnard's actions signaled hostility toward slavery, Thompson added, "then I am a downright abolitionist." Barnard left Mississippi at the outbreak of the Civil War, eventually taking the presidency of Columbia University, where he served for a quarter century. The trustees commemorated his death in 1889 with the dedication of Barnard College.[50]

Despite its troubled reputation, the University of Virginia saw its largest undergraduate classes in the years before the Civil War. Most of these students were southerners bound by the knowledge that they would soon take guardianship over an increasingly isolated region. They solidified their bonds with violent rituals, drunken games, and other passages into manhood. They had a well-known appetite for whiskey. Spirited contests and public disorder on campus—such as the chemistry faculty's annual "Laughing-Gas Day"—were common and taxed the patience of administrations, but the campus soon became infamous for outright insurrections. On Thursday, November 12, 1840, a masked student began shouting and firing a pistol outside the house of John Davis, chairman of the faculty. Earlier that day, the student had borrowed a gun from a classmate, and declared his intention to defend his right to riot. When Davis went to the door to investigate the disturbance, the young man turned and shot him in the stomach. "He died a Christian hero, blessing his family and his weeping colleagues and friends," William Barton Rogers, now a professor in Charlottesville, wrote to his brothers. It was part of a long and dangerous period, during which the administration and prominent alumni struggled to reestablish order. Still, in 1852 John S. Mosby, a sophomore, shot a classmate during an altercation. The following year, Rogers resigned his chair as the undergraduate population at Virginia reached its antebellum peak.[51]

Politicians, editors, and academics in the South urged the necessity of expanding the educational infrastructure of the region to defend slavery. Dr. Samuel A. Cartwright, a Virginian who studied at Philadelphia under Benjamin Rush and then practiced and taught in Mississippi and Louisiana, used Thomas Jefferson's call for the anatomical dissection of colored people to argue for a distinct southern science. The climate, conditions, and history of Europe reduced the value of modern science for southerners, Cartwright argued. The slave states shared more with the ancient civilization of Greece, where Hippocrates had anticipated the peculiar influence of climate and region on medical knowledge. Proslavery thought found academic expression in the desire to free the South from external intellectual influences. Editors cried for southern medical schools to address unique regional realities, and hundreds of southern students withdrew from northern medical colleges in the years before the Civil War.[52]

Southern intellectuals did not conjure the idea that there was knowledge particular to the slave societies of the Americas. For more than a century American and European scholars had presumed that the plantations were distinct environments for understanding natural science, and they assigned unique authority to researchers from those areas. They acknowledged the expertise of doctors from the slave colonies on questions of race. Physicians who practiced in the South and the Caribbean had held sway during the *Whistelo* proceedings. As bondage became peculiar to their region, southerners made a discrete claim to this knowledge and seized upon its political potential.

The sectional crisis hastened the rise of a regional intellectual elite. In the summer of 1857 the Episcopal bishops of ten southern states gathered on Lookout Mountain in Tennessee to approve a plan for the University of the South, which they envisioned as a rival to the elite universities of the world and the headquarters of southern intellectualism. They chose a site on the Cumberland Plateau and began designing the campus. Vermont bishop John Henry Hopkins, a northern apologist for slavery, resided six months in the Tennessee woods while he assisted the engineers and officers in laying out the grounds and buildings. A grand ceremony to place the cornerstone attracted some five thousand guests—including an envoy from Trinity Church in New York City—catered to by a parade of slaves brought from Nashville.[53]

As proslavery ultraism radicalized higher education in the South, northern scholars sought political common ground at the logical extremes of race. They did not retreat; they lagged behind. Faced with an increasingly divided nation and their own ambivalence about the place of black people in American society, a new generation of northern researchers expounded upon the mental and physical gaps between the races—an academic project with immediate relevance to the political conflicts over slavery. New York City became a clearinghouse for translating and circulating new developments in race science, particularly polygenist theories. The physician John Van Evrie ran a small industry translating, reworking, and publishing new scholarship from Europe asserting the distinct origins and development of the races.[54] American scholars constructed two ideological paths to a national reconciliation: positive defenses of slavery grounded in history, theology, and economics; and scientific attacks upon the humanity of the colored races that denied black people the moral status of persons and forced them into the moral sphere of brutes.

The ship *Indian Chief*, Captain Cochran, chartered by the American Colonization Society, sailed from this port on Wednesday last, the 15th inst. for the Society's settlement at Cape Montserado, on the Coast of Africa. She takes out one hundred fifty-four free people of colour, with supplies for the Colony.

—*AFRICAN REPOSITORY AND COLONIAL JOURNAL*, 1826

It is the most ludicrous Society that ever yet was dreamed of. . . . There is no reason for removing the negro from America but his color.

—DANIEL O'CONNELL, M.P., 1833

Heigho! it is a fine thing to be an Indian. One might almost as well be a slave. . . . I greatly doubt that any missionary has ever thought of making the Indian or African his equal. As soon as we begin to talk about equal rights, the cry of amalgamation is set up, as if men of color could not enjoy their natural rights without any necessity of intermarriage between the sons and daughters of the two races. Strange, strange indeed!

—REV. WILLIAM APESS, 1833

When an enlightened and Christianized community shall have, on the shores of Africa, laws, language and literature, drawn from among us, may then the scenes of the house of bondage be to them like the remembrance of Egypt to the Israelite,—a motive of thankfulness to Him who hath redeemed them!

—HARRIET BEECHER STOWE, *UNCLE TOM'S CABIN* (1852)

CHAPTER 8

"Could They Be
Sent Back to Africa"

Colleges and the Quest for a White Nation

In the summer of 1806, several students at Williams College were overtaken by a sense of the presence and grace of God. As a teenager in Torrington, Connecticut, Samuel John Mills Jr. had witnessed the spiritual fervor of the Second Great Awakening. He began praying for a similar rebirth on campus. James Richards, Francis L. Robbins, Harvey Loomis, and Byram Green joined him. During one prayer meeting, they ran into a haystack to seek shelter from a storm. That haystack assembly committed to spreading the Gospel around the world. New colleges—Williams (1793), Bowdoin (1794), Union (1795), and Middlebury (1800)—amplified the social effects of the Awakening. Faculty and students on the older campuses also experienced revivals of faith. "The divine influence seemed to descend like a silent dew of heaven," President Ashbel Green reported from Princeton, "and in about four weeks there were very few individuals in the college edifice who were not deeply impressed with a sense of the importance of spiritual and eternal things." Green noted that every space on the campus was turned over to prayer.[1]

Williams president Edward Dorr Griffin later identified the haystack meeting as the beginning of a religious revolution that led to the American Board of Commissioners for Foreign Missions (1812), the New York–New Jersey Synod's African School (1816), the American Bible Society (1816), the United Foreign Missionary Society (1817), and the American Colonization Society (1817). The Awakening had earlier roused Griffin's church in Newark, New Jersey. "I never before witnessed the communication of a spirit of prayer so earnest and so general," he recalled with awe, "nor observed such evident and remarkable answers to prayer." It began when the deaths of the Reverend Alexander Mc-Whorter—a trustee of the College of New Jersey (Princeton) and a founder of Newark Academy—and other prominent Christians shook the community. A hundred people joined the congregation in a single day, and the converts came from all strata of the society, "including poor negroes," Griffin celebrated. Union College awarded Rev. Griffin an honorary degree for his contributions to this national revival.[2]

This religious renewal sent American Christians crusading across the globe to fulfill the agenda of the compassionate and protective God who had guided them through the Revolution and into political liberty. It also further exposed the moral conflict between their declarations of individual and group freedom and their continued reliance upon the enslavement and dispossession of other peoples. As it swept the campuses, the revival forced intellectual engagement with these social injustices.

The Awakening occurred as the people of the United States were defining themselves as a nation, and it ultimately revealed the social limits of religious humanitarianism in American society. In the aftermath of the American Revolution, white people selected deeply racialized criteria for membership in the United States to defend their material aspirations from the challenges of their political and religious declarations.

The language of race was the vernacular of the campus. The political struggles to decide the composition of the United States marked the first time that college professors and officers occupied the public sphere as an interested class. They exercised expertise over the pressing social question of who belonged in the new nation. "I am not accustomed to speak in public, except on subjects connected with my own profession," Calvin Stowe, a professor of biblical studies and the husband of Harriet Beecher Stowe, confessed at the beginning of a lecture on what to do with the nation's black population.[3]

The greatest domestic questions of the nineteenth century were debated in racial terms, and thus they enhanced the authority of the academy in political affairs. Scholars acquired broad influence as they responded to anxieties about the makeup of the nation and crafted arguments for restricting membership in American society. Academics delineated the social boundaries of the United States and synthesized discordant regional definitions of citizenship into a common dream of a white Christian society.

"O YE AMERICANS"

The American Revolution and the Second Great Awakening had incited a sincere and prolonged critique of slavery on campuses that remained financially dependent upon slave owners and slave traders; however, efforts to challenge and dismantle slavery in the Mid-Atlantic and New England aggravated concerns about the composition of American society. In 1784 the New York State legislature reopened King's College as Columbia, changed its governance to recognize the disconnection from Britain, and named the continuing and new trustees. John Jay, Alexander Hamilton, John Lawrence, and Matthew Clarkson, all slaveholders, were on the new board. All four men were also founding members of the New York Manumission Society, established in January 1785 as the Society for Promoting the Manumission of Slaves, and Protecting Such of Them as Have Been or May Be Liberated.[4]

The founders acknowledged a divine will that black people "share equally with us in that civil and religious liberty with which an indulgent Providence has blessed these states." Such godsends led merchants such as Matthew Clarkson to doubt the morality of human slavery. In 1789 Moses Brown, of the Providence family partnership that had funded the deadly voyage of the *Sally* in 1764 and helped found the College of Rhode Island (Brown), organized the Providence Society for the Abolition of the Slave Trade.[5]

President Ezra Stiles maintained a religious fellowship with the black community of New Haven during his tenure at Yale. He had earlier held services for African Americans in the study of his Newport home, welcoming as many as ninety people at a time. He referred to black people as his brothers and sisters in Christ and fell to his knees with them in prayer. "This day died Phyllis a Negro Sister of our Church," the minister noted with affection in March 1773, adding that Brother Zingo, her husband, had joined the church first and then urged his wife and children to attend. "She was brought hither out of Guinea [in] 1759 aet. 13 or 14 [years old], and has lived in Gov. [Josiah] Lyndon[']s Family ever since." In August 1790 President Stiles and fourteen other men—most of them faculty and officers of Yale—drafted a constitution for the Connecticut Society for the Promotion of Freedom. They began meeting the following month with Rev. Stiles as their president.[6]

A lively antislavery discourse flowered on the young nation's campuses. Ashbel Green penned a position paper against slavery for the General Assembly of the New Jersey Presbytery, and he ministered to black people in the Princeton area. Peter Wilson, professor of Greek and Latin at Columbia, authored an antislavery tract, which he followed with other abolitionist essays. His colleague John Daniel Gros, a German immigrant and professor of the German language, moral philosophy, and geography, also began publicly condemning bondage. In 1789 Columbia awarded Rev. Gros an honorary doctorate of divinity. His fellow honorees included the Reverend Abraham Beach of Somerset, New Jersey, a Yale graduate and slave owner, who served more than a quarter century as a trustee of Columbia and nearly a half century on the board of Rutgers. In an address before President Stiles's antislavery society, the Reverend Jonathan Edwards Jr., later the president of Union College, charged that the slave trade had brought only brutality, inhumanity, bloodshed, warfare, upheaval, and immorality to Africa, Europe, and the Americas.[7]

Manumission societies were encouraging this antislavery dialogue. In 1785 Thomas Clarkson won a medal at Cambridge University for the best Latin dissertation on the morality of slavery. The New York Manumission Society ordered copies of that thesis. The following year the board supplied a similar essay award at Columbia, where the trustees voted that "a gold medal be given to the person who shall deliver the best oration at the next annual commencement of the College in New York, exposing in the best manner the injustice and cruelty of the slave trade, and the oppression and impolicy of holding negroes in slavery." The effect was immediate. "Who gave you a better right, O ye Americans, to go to the coast of Africa, and betray and kidnap its quiet and peaceful inhabitants," a graduate challenged his audience during a 1786 commencement, while reminding them of the evil of holding "your fellow men . . . in hopeless and perpetual slavery." Moses Brown offered an antislavery prize to Rhode Island but learned that it would not be "agreeable" to the slave traders on the board. He then queried President Samuel Hopkins on the possibility of creating competitions at Harvard, Yale, or New Jersey.[8]

The era saw a measurable decline in slaveholding among northern faculty and administrators. In 1788 Timothy Dwight, later the president of Yale, made a contract with an enslaved woman named Naomi for her freedom. In 1807 Ashbel Green manumitted nine-year-old Betsey Stockton after the death of his wife, Elizabeth Stockton. The child continued to live with President Green, who also tutored her. That year Edward Dorr Griffin purchased a black boy named Samuel Skudder and made an emancipation agreement with the child's parents. During the next five years Professor Peter Wilson of Columbia freed two black women, Susan and Isabel. In 1817 the college patron and trustee Henry Rutgers liberated Thomas Boston. In September 1821 the trustee Abraham Beach brought Caesar Jackson before the justices of Franklin Township, New Jersey, to begin the manumission process.[9]

However, these steps toward the regional eradication of slavery aggravated fears of a multiracial future. By the early nineteenth century American Christians were missionizing the Hawaiian

Henry Rutgers's Manumission of Thomas Boston, 1817
SOURCE: New-York Historical Society

Islands, India, Palestine, and China. This enthusiasm for overseas outreach reflected, in part, a fracturing of the consensus for domestic evangelization. Foreign missions allowed white Christians to convert indigenous and colored peoples without strengthening the political and legal claims of nonwhite and non-Christian peoples upon the United States. Students from Yale tutored Henry Obookiah, one of five Hawaiian teenagers brought to Connecticut, and Obookiah later lived and studied with President Timothy Dwight. In 1817 the American Board of Commissioners for Foreign Missions (ABCFM) had established a school in Cornwall, Connecticut, to prepare colored youth for Christian missions. Yale president Jeremiah Day mentored Yung Wing, a Chinese student and the first Asian to graduate from a United States college. The place of people of color in North America was less clear. When Gallegina, or "The Buck," a Scottish and Cherokee student from Georgia, arrived at Cornwall, he was surrounded by youth from Hawaii, India, China, Malaysia, and other nations. Gallegina became a ward of Elias Boudinot, the former president of the Continental Congress, the founding president of the American Bible Society, and a graduate and trustee of the College of New Jersey. At twenty-four years old, Betsey Stockton left Princeton for an ABCFM program—in Hawaii.[10]

BANISHED NEGROES AND VANISHED INDIANS

"Could they be sent back to Africa, a three-fold benefit would arise," the Reverend Robert Finley promised a friend in 1816: "we should be cleared of them:—we should send to Africa a population *partially civilized and christianized* for its benefit:—our blacks themselves would be put in a better situation." His father, James Finley, a Glasgow merchant and a parishioner of John Witherspoon, followed Witherspoon to Princeton. In 1787 Robert graduated from the College of New Jersey, and at fifteen he became a tutor in the South. Finley returned to Princeton to study for the ministry, and he later served as a professor and a trustee. As he began planning African colonization, Robert Finley was called to the presidency of the University of Georgia. He shared the colonization plan with his family and close friends. Finley saw the immediate task as convincing "the rich and benevolent [to] devise means to form a colony on some part of Africa" for the relocation of free black people. In

1817 United States Supreme Court justice Bushrod Washington, the nephew of George Washington, became the charter president of the American Colonization Society (ACS). Elias B. Caldwell recruited Washington power brokers to the cause. Caldwell was clerk of the Supreme Court, Finley's brother-in-law, and a charge of Elias Boudinot. Samuel John Mills, of the haystack communion, helped draw religious radicals to the cause. Charles Fenton Mercer, a 1797 graduate of New Jersey and possibly the originator of the colonization idea, established the Liberia colony in 1822.[11]

The ACS was born on campus. It was conceived from the collision between enthusiastic Christianity and the rigid racial definitions that governed social and political thought in the United States. Colonization was, at its genesis, a compromise between the evangelical urge to solve the moral problem of slavery and the political and social rejection of a multiracial society. It sought to balance the moral economy by answering the religious challenges of the Great Awakening while respecting the solidifying political configuration of the United States. Academics exercised disproportionate influence over this discourse. They advanced colonization as the best, perhaps only, chance to manage the political tensions resulting from the nation's diverging regional economies and demographic transformations.

White Americans had already made ethnic cleansing a preferred solution to their self-constructed racial dilemmas. President Thomas Jefferson ignited speculation about the fate of Native Americans when the Louisiana Purchase opened the possibility of the United States exchanging lands with the eastern Indian nations. The federal government subsequently used coercion, violence, cycles of debt, and deceit to reduce Native territories in the Southeast and displace Indians who stood in the path of white migrations and the expansion of plantation slavery. President James Madison faced increased pressure to dispossess Indians as the price of cotton climbed in international markets and overproduction exhausted the seaboard plantations. In his second inaugural address, President James Monroe belittled the

Certificate of membership in the American Colonization Society
SOURCE: Library of Congress

idea of Indian nations as a dangerous and misleading flattery that inhibited the federal government's administration of Native peoples, whom he cast as perpetual dependents. Monroe urged Congress to vacate Native Americans' land rights and settle Indians in such ways as to encourage the westward expansion of white people.[12]

The image of Indians as a barrier to progress supplanted earlier beliefs that Native peoples could be assimilated through the civilizing institutions of Christian society. Christians had once accused Native people of "savagery" and prescribed conversion as the antidote, but the social meaning of savagery was shifting from a cultural flaw to a fixed biological trait measured in the vulnerabilities of Indians and announced by their complexions. The racial constructs that coalesced in defense of slavery also allowed white people to redefine Native Americans as incapable of civilization. An Indian presence thus became incompatible with progress. Andrew Jackson's military campaigns popularized the image of Indians as defeated peoples. The immediate and complete removal of Indians to areas beyond white settlement, President Jackson later explained, promised to further economic development in the South and end the political conflicts between the national and state governments over the status of Native people and their lands. In 1814 Jackson had led the forces that defeated the Creek and forced them to surrender twenty-three million acres, including most of Alabama and southern Georgia, to the United States.[13]

White southerners were now poised to claim tens of millions of acres from multiple Native nations. The 1830 Indian Removal Act authorized the federal government to treat with Native nations to swap lands in the East for territories across the Mississippi. The following year, Chief Justice John Marshall declared Indians "domestic dependent nations" in *Cherokee Nation v. State of Georgia*. The decision invoked the scientific notion of a hierarchy of the human races to depict the political subordination of all indigenous peoples as inevitable.[14]

Those same political pressures had reshaped evangelical outreach to Native Americans and African Americans. A Bible Society founder and future president of Rutgers College, Philip Milledoler designed missions to Indian nations west of the Mississippi River. Planters and settlers eyeing agricultural lands in the southeastern states helped push national policy toward removal, and missionary activity deferred to their politics. Simultaneously, Rev. Milledoler also joined Williams president Edward Dorr Griffin in promoting African colonization. Father Milledoler and Henry Rutgers served as the founding vice president and president, respectively, of the New York Colonization Society.[15]

Although many northerners opposed Indian removal, it was precisely the success of the racial clearances in the South that offered the most compelling evidence that a campaign to relocate free black people and conduct religious crusades on the African continent and throughout the colored world were viable. The prolonged attack upon Native presences gave millions of Americans reason to believe that all subject peoples could be disappeared. It was through Indian removal that the desire to eliminate nonwhite, non-Christian presences came to dominate the popular culture.

REGIONAL WHITE NATIONALISMS

"Where the Indian always *has been*, he enjoys an absolute right still to *be*," Senator Theodore Frelinghuysen declared in opposition to Georgia's steps to remove the Cherokee nation. The future chancellor of the University of the City of New York (New York University) and future president of Rutgers University was one of the most prominent defenders of the Indians in the southeastern states. It belongs among the great speeches of United States history, if only for its elegant defense of the separation of powers and its articulation of the principle of state subordination to federal authority. Frelinghuysen warned that the violation of treaties with Indian nations would undermine the integrity of the United States government. Even mere contracts constrain all parties, but the Cherokee possessed more than pieces of paper recording ancient promises. They were a sovereign nation, the senator thundered. European powers had recognized their sovereignty throughout the colonial era, and the United States had repeatedly affirmed their national status. "I ask in what code of the law of nation, or by what process of abstract deduction, their rights have been extinguished?" These treaties constituted exchanges of obligations, and now Georgia sought to keep the gains but toss off the responsibilities. "Truth and honor have no citadel on earth—their sanctions are despised and forgotten, and the law of the strongest prevails," Frelinghuysen charged. Raw greed threatened the constitution. Native people had ceded hundreds of millions of acres of land to the United States by purchase and by treaty, "yet we crave more." That hunger was so great, so insatiable, that it could be neither satisfied nor restrained by contract, honor, or principle.[16]

When President Jackson visited Harvard in 1834, the residents of Cambridge sharply divided over whether and how to protest his Indian removal policy. By the time that Jackson left the White House, federal relocation programs had affected virtually every nation east of the Mississippi and north to Lake Michigan. Native peoples from New England, the Mid-Atlantic, and the Midwest—including the Oneida, Winnebago, and Black Hawk—were uprooted, and the policy remapped the South. The "Five Civilized

Senator Theodore Frelinghuysen, president of Rutgers and
New York University
SOURCE: Library of Congress

Tribes"—Chickasaw, Choctaw, Creek, Cherokee, and Seminole—
were cleared. The government cultivated political and economic
conditions that made removal the only option for many communities, and federal troops warred against Native nations that did not
comply. Martin Van Buren of New York was secretary of state in
Andrew Jackson's cabinet and part of the northern bloc that sided
with Georgia. In 1838 President Van Buren concluded this tragic
era with the deadly forced march of the Cherokee along the "Trail
of Tears."[17]

Many northerners condemned Georgians for supporting any
permutation of state and federal power—whatever its constitution-
ality—that promised to clear Indians off rich agricultural lands.
Southerners responded by lampooning these fiery defenses of
Cherokee territorial rights from northerners whose recent family

histories were intertwined with the violent subordination of Indian peoples and whose regional histories included the erasure of scores of Native sovereignties. What if his ancestors were "a bloodthirsty race?" Congressman Edward Everett of Massachusetts cautiously allowed. What if they "treated the Indians barbarously?" A former Harvard professor and a future president and trustee of the college, Everett argued that a prior breach was a poor defense for a new injustice.[18]

President Edward Everett of Harvard
SOURCE: Library of Congress

While northerners could find fault with the necessity and legal-
ity of Indian removal, they could hardly disown the underlying
body of ideas. Countless white people in New England and the
Mid-Atlantic were convinced of not only the possibility of racially
homogenizing their regions but also the value of that project. They
were building a social geography consistent with their political and
economic desires. The presuppositions of removal campaigns—
particularly the biological basis of civilization and citizenship—
were informed by racial ideas that had ascended in every region of
the antebellum nation.

Congressman Everett shared the New Jersey senator's sense of
the potentially tragic consequences of Indian removal. Everett
signed a copy of Frelinghuysen's speech and sent it to the librarian
of Harvard, John Langdon Sibley. "I cannot disguise my impres-
sion, that it is the greatest question which ever came before Congress, short of the question of peace and war," Everett estimated.
He argued that the reputation of the United States in all its foreign
affairs was at issue. Georgia sought to strip a sovereign and friendly
nation of its land and open that territory to white settlement. It
declared the Cherokee its subjects in order to acquire the power to
turn them into exiles and refugees. Its primary justification was
to protect the Cherokee from an aggressively expanding white
population. "Who urges this plea?" asked Frelinghuysen. "They
who covet the Indian lands." Proponents offered a circular explanation that Indians had to be driven away to secure them from
the people driving them away.[19]

Frelinghuysen and Everett made impassioned defenses of the
humanity and equality of the Cherokee. "The Indians are men,
endowed with kindred faculties and powers with ourselves," the
senator appealed, "they have a place in human sympathy, and are
justly entitled to share in the common bounties of benignant Providence." They were no less the children of God and no less a part of
the divine plan. The northerners cited Thomas Jefferson's affirmation of Cherokee civilization. Everett recalled that the Virginian
had helped to organize the Cherokee government. These Indians
had embraced Christianity, commercial trade, farming and advanced agricultural techniques, and democracy. They had skilled

political leaders, successful businessmen and merchants, artisans, and professionals. "Men as competent as ourselves" were being robbed of privilege and property, Everett countered.[20]

These crusades peaked in the 1830s. As Congressman Everett was sending Harvard a copy of Frelinghuysen's speech, Elliot Cresson was forwarding a signed copy of the annual report of the Pennsylvania Colonization Society to Harvard president Josiah Quincy. A wealthy merchant and college benefactor, Cresson was one of four Philadelphians to hold a $1,000 life membership in the American Colonization Society. He worked as an ACS agent, and he had raised funds for the cause in England. "The removal of our coloured population is, I think, a common object," wrote Chief Justice Marshall in 1831, the year of *Cherokee v. Georgia*. "The whole union would be strengthened by it, and relieved from a danger whose extent can scarcely be estimated." Justice Marshall joined former president James Madison in arguing the practicality and constitutionality of selling federal lands to fund African colonization.[21]

The advocates of Indian removal did not always mirror the communities urging the relocation of other peoples. Senator Frelinghuysen's robust defense of the Cherokee led the abolitionist William Lloyd Garrison to invite him to extend that compassion to enslaved black people. The senator fit the profile of an antislavery advocate. He was a leading social and religious activist and was involved in a range of reform movements, including temperance, the improvement of prisons, and public education. Garrison had also been a colonizationist, but, like many people in the humanitarian wing of the ACS, he turned to abolition as the organization became hostile to emancipation and as African Americans expressed unified and strident opposition to the plan. Frelinghuysen seemed to sit in that liberal camp, and he had earlier worked with progressives such as Arthur Tappan and Gerrit Smith, both of whom transitioned from colonizationism to abolitionism.[22]

The editor had reason to believe that the senator could be coaxed toward antislavery. During an 1824 fund-raiser for the New Jersey Colonization Society, Frelinghuysen had rehearsed many of the ideas that later informed his defense of the Cherokee. He emphasized the philanthropic aims of colonization: providing a refuge

for the victims of the slave trade rescued at sea and creating a
"home" for the free black communities of the United States. He
hinted at the association's antislavery potential, however distant.
He declared slavery unjustifiable and rebuked the nation for denying physical and spiritual liberty to millions of people. Frelinghuysen even defended the intellectual and cultural capacity of
African peoples, arguing that suggestions of their inferiority were
erroneous in a society that outlawed their advancement and invoking the Haitian Revolution and its black generals as examples
of their capacity.[23]

Theodore Frelinghuysen simultaneously considered the free black
population "a separate, degraded, scorned, and humbled people."
That bleak assessment closed a lecture that was otherwise sympathetic to the plight of free and enslaved African Americans. Frelinghuysen had grown up in a slaveholding house. His father, Frederick
Frelinghuysen, was the stepson of the Reverend Jacob Hardenbergh,
the president of Queen's College (Rutgers) and a slave owner. After
graduating from New Jersey in 1770, Frederick Frelinghuysen became the first tutor at Queen's. He married Gitty Schenk—of the
wealthy Dutch slaveholding family—and owned slaves throughout his life.[24]

Senator Frelinghuysen's racial beliefs regulated his compassion.
The ideas that grounded his virile defense of the Cherokee also
informed his final judgment against the emancipation of black
people. As Frelinghuysen explained, race was "a line of demarca-
tion drawn deep and broad; and durable as time." No matter how
fully one sympathized with the enslaved, race made abolition, to
quote President Wilbur Fisk of Wesleyan University, an exercise in
"moral quackery." Fisk was complaining that a recent publication
had quoted him in ways that suggested he was an abolitionist. He
publicly rejected abolition and announced his support for colonizing black people. Frelinghuysen also saw removing African Americans as a superior alternative to the "madness of self-destruction"
inherent in abolition. He began his chancellorship at the University of the City of New York with a pro-colonization tour of the
city. Later, as a vice presidential candidate on the Whig ticket in
1844, Frelinghuysen offered his long tenure in the American Colo-

nization Society as evidence of goodwill toward southern slave-holders.[25]

Race constrained the political solutions to the social challenges of the nineteenth century, particularly when those questions concerned the composition of the citizenry. Professor Charles Follen, an abolitionist, provided Harvard's students with evidence of the intellectual and cultural equality of African people extending back to the ancient Egyptians. The belief that the fates of subjugated peoples lay naturally in the hands of the dominant classes could lead down humanitarian or destructive paths. Follen cautioned his undergraduates about the limited value of Jewish history, which, although "the most interesting of all antiquity," was filled with so much superstition and hyperbole that it was largely impenetrable. "The Hist[ory] of the Jews is important only as a hist[ory] of religion," a student in the class jotted, "for they were the most depraved and the most worthy of contempt and censure of all."[26]

Many Christians doubted the biological capacity of Jews for conversion. "In taking leave of the Soc[iet]y I heartily pray that it may be instrumental in promoting the spiritual & temporal welfare of that ancient & wonderful people whose present infidelity is among the strongest evidences of the Religion they reject," wrote Peter Augustus Jay in 1822 upon resigning as director and treasurer of the American Society for Ameliorating the Condition of the Jews (ASACJ). A trustee of Columbia College, Jay also headed the New York Manumission Society as it lobbied to apply revenues from public lands to colonize African Americans in Africa, Haiti, or "such countries as they may choose for their residence." The ASACJ funded efforts to Christianize or deport American Jews. In 1823 John Robert Murray, another Columbia trustee, brokered an agreement with Jacob Van Rensselaer and Hezekiah Pierpont, two of New York State's wealthiest men, to endow the association by transferring some of Pierpont's lands in Jefferson, Lewis, Franklin, and St. Lawrence counties at a significant discount. It was the same year that Pope Leo XII reestablished mandatory Jewish ghettoization in the Papal States.[27]

Christian activists favored relocating or segregating even Jewish converts to Christianity, a medieval stratagem that they revived as they reconciled their faith with race. Missions to Jews emphasized conversion and removal, and the missionaries' weapons included everything from Hebrew editions of the New Testament to political campaigns to uproot recalcitrant Jews. In addition to exiling the unconverted, the ASACJ proposed opening a twenty-thousand-acre reservation in western New York for the settlement of Christianized Jews. Anticipating a growing population of Jewish converts, Elias Boudinot bequeathed four thousand acres in Warren County, Pennsylvania, for their settlement. "For nearly eighteen centuries that people have suffered for the sin of killing the Prince of life," reads the 1823 founding address of the Portland Society for Promoting Christianity Among the Jews. That Israel would embrace Christianity was a promise from "Him who cannot lie." Balancing prophecy with a surrender to racial determinism, the Maine organization then pledged to raise funds to find an American "asylum" for Jewish converts.[28]

ASSIGNING BLACK PEOPLE'S BURDEN

At the emotional height of his speech against Indian removal, Senator Frelinghuysen asked his colleagues: "Do the obligations of justice change with the color of the skin?" The question was an ethical trap in which Frelinghuysen also became entangled once the debate shifted to black people. "We view, with unfeigned astonishment, the anti-christian and inconsistent conduct of those who strenuously advocate our removal from this our native country to the burning shores of Liberia, and who with the same breath contend against the cruelty and injustice of Georgia in her attempt to remove the Cherokee Indians," declared free black residents of Providence, Rhode Island. A public meeting of black Bostonians accused the ACS of using "philanthropy, smooth words, and a sanctified appearance" to further an "absurd" proslavery program. Black leaders such as Henry C. Thompson of Brooklyn, New York, and George C. Willis of Providence, along with white abolitionists including Simeon Jocelyn of New Haven, Connecticut, and Garrison in Boston, condemned this transparent intellectual inconsistency.[29]

Many northerners were attracted to the idea that providence intended black people to Christianize Africa and thereby redeem America from slavery, and they used that belief to distinguish their movement from southerners' anti-Indian furor. For these northerners, Indian removal lived in an uneasy dialogue with African colonization, one that they resolved with the remote promise of a Christianized Africa. Congressman Jabez Huntington asked Connecticut Supreme Court justice David Daggett, a Yale graduate and founder of Yale Law School, for advice on Indian removal. Daggett, who also served as a vice president of the Connecticut Colonization Society, aggressively defended the territorial rights of the Cherokee and dismissed white Georgians as "howling villains."[30] Congressman Isaac Bates of Massachusetts, Senator Peleg Sprague of Maine, and scores of other New England and mid-Atlantic politicians came to parallel conclusions.

An extravagance of sympathy for Africa in colonizationist rhetoric was, in part, a response to this ideological tension. President Milledoler assigned the Rutgers class of 1831 responsibility for fulfilling providence by colonizing black Americans, reversing the history of slavery and the slave trade, and securing the "greatest good out of the greatest evils." He promised that "monumental pillars" would one day be raised for them in Africa if they completed this noble work. "Remember the toil and the tears of black men, and pay your debt to Africa," Frelinghuysen implored. "We have injured, and we must make reparation." President Fisk of Wesleyan declared that Africa was fated for a religious revolution. "And among other cares poor forsaken Africa must not be neglected," cautioned Rev. Griffin. "Her crime of having a sable skin must not exclude her from the kingdom of heaven."[31]

In contrast, northern scholars, ministers, and politicians often bristled at applying the arguments against Indian removal to their own region. The level of Cherokee, Creek, and Choctaw civilization was a consistent protest leveled by opponents of relocation. These nations democratically governed thousands upon thousands of people on millions of acres. They had productive farms, businesses and factories, roads, schools, churches, newspapers, and countless other indicators of civilization. Connecticut representative William

Ellsworth offered a census of Cherokee wagons, sheep, horses, cattle, pigs, and ploughs to prove that "they are the creatures of the same God with ourselves."[32] Opponents of Indian removal rejected not race but the necessity of relocating people who had attained an acceptable level of social accomplishment, were believed to be declining in numbers, and were already spatially isolated.

If property, education, Christianization, and capacity for self-government were evidence of the inhumanity of Indian removal, then it would be hard to ignore the emerging civil and political entitlement embedded in the rapid social development of free African American communities. Free black people in Philadelphia, New York, and Boston, and in even smaller cities such as Providence, Hartford, and Newark, had thriving political and intellectual cultures. Black people paraded through the streets in celebration of markers of social progress such as the 1808 termination of the slave trade to the United States. Print media extended the reach of the African American authors, preachers, and community leaders who began invading the public sphere in the late eighteenth century. In the following decades, sermons, poems, and autobiographies by black authors from throughout the Americas were in regular circulation. In 1827 Samuel Cornish and John Brown Russwurm began publishing *Freedom's Journal*, the nation's first African American newspaper.[33]

It was the success of free black communities that aggravated many white people's fears of a multiracial nation. Black neighborhoods, churches, schools, cemeteries, businesses, benevolent associations, literary clubs, insurance societies, newspapers, and political organizations combined to give African American communities an undeniable presence. As President Jackson was signing the Indian Removal Act into law, African Americans were organizing the first National Negro Convention, to publish their commitment to ending slavery, denounce the American Colonization Society, and forge greater cooperation with white abolitionists.[34]

Thus, colonizationists routinely balanced their estimates of the spiritual needs of Africa with predictions of the eternal persecution of black Americans. President Elihu Baldwin of Wabash College opened an 1836 meeting of Indiana colonizationists by rehearsing the long history of forced migrations, including American colonial history, which, he argued, proved the value of freedom in an unknown land over oppression in a native land. President Milledoler drew upon his decades of experience in the Indian ministries of the Dutch Reformed Church and the ABCFM to justify colonization. Jared Sparks of Harvard harvested the history of English religious and military campaigns among New England Indians to defend assigning black Americans the duty of uplifting Africa.[35]

Biological racism could turn these appeals for relocation into demands for removal. President Sparks gleaned scientific evidence of the cultural and mental limitations of Negroes, and he concluded that race was a fixed and impassable divide between white people and the colored world. Facing what he viewed as the "unfortunate" truth of racial inferiority, Sparks insisted upon exile. Black Americans were misplaced Africans whose color and other physical and mental characteristics ensured their eternal misuse, he declared. Therefore, he proposed the establishment of a single missionary school in the United States—allowing colonizationists to control African Americans' access to education—linked to a network of schools in Africa.[36]

Many intellectuals were certain that there was simply no better use for black people than African missions. Edward Everett defended cleansing even without a pretense of abolition—the spiritual elevation of Africa was justification enough. God intended black Americans to fulfill this destiny, he insisted, because white men had civilized the entire world except Africa, where the climate and conditions made their efforts ineffective. President Fisk of Wesleyan echoed this sentiment when he argued that colonization created "a passage of civilization and salvation into the interior of that dark continent!" A leader of the Massachusetts Colonization Society, Everett recast American slavery as part of a divine plan to Christianize Africa: providence took the "descendants of the torrid clime, children of the burning vertical sun—and fitted them by centuries of stern discipline for this noble work."[37] With that moral renovation, he cleared his mind of the problem of human slavery while clearing black people from his future.

The Janus face of colonization—its benevolent and despotic manifestations—sustained seemingly incompatible communions. The declining antislavery contingent and the growing antiabolition-ist constituency agreed on the necessity of removal. Here, a sincere Christian antislavery withered at the limits of egalitarianism in antebellum American society. For those who opposed human bond-age, colonization contained the rhetorical residue of Christian benevolence toward Africans and Africa generated during the eighteenth-century anti-slave-trade movement. For those who per-ceived the presence of black people as a threat to the political and social health of the nation, it promised a radical alteration of the racial geography. "I am a friend to the Colonization Society, and yet no friend of slavery, and neither a knave nor a dupe," Calvin Stowe responded to critics. Professor Stowe rejected the accusation of rac-ism by invoking what he saw as the moral and scientific truth of race: "I am in favor of colonization, because I suppose it to be right, and agreeable to God's design, that the different races of men should continue to be distinct and each reside in a climate best adapted to their physical and intellectual development."[38]

New Jersey offers a vivid example of this interplay between moral philanthropy and racial animosity. The Presbyterian church in Princeton hosted the 1824 founding meeting of the New Jersey Colonization Society. Captain Robert Field Stockton presided over the state association. A passenger diary includes some of the events and sights as Captain Stockton piloted the schooner *Alliga-tor* from Boston to the African coast during the spring of 1821 to find a location for the colony. "With extensive and apparently luxu-rious forests," a passenger happily reported, "the Coast of Africa [is] a more pleasant spectacle than my expectations had antici-pated." On May 13 the ACS agent Daniel Coker recorded the *Al-ligator's* arrival at Freetown. "We have been visited at our temporary residence by Captain Stockton and some of his officers," Rev. Coker noted. "They appear'd in words to be zealous in the cause." Just a week earlier, an English ship had captured a slaver with five hundred enslaved Africans and brought it to port.[39]

From the early 1820s through the Civil War, the presidents and trustees of the College of New Jersey and Rutgers governed the state and local colonization movements. New Jersey president James Carnahan served as a director of the state society, and Professor John Maclean Jr., his successor, was an officer. Rutgers president John Henry Livingston was a director, and faculty from both schools could be found at all levels of the state and local auxiliaries. Black people continued to serve the students in Princeton and New Brunswick. For example, New Jersey alumni recalled with affection their encounters with "negro Sam," the assistant in Professor Joseph Henry's laboratory, during the height of the colonization campaign.[40]

The organizational meeting in Princeton was telling. Captain Stockton opened the gathering with a lengthy examination of the history and accomplishments of the colonization campaign. He emphasized Robert Finley's original aims: the evangelization of Africa, the end of the slave trade, and, perhaps, laying a path for gradual emancipation. However, in a transition that captured the conflict at the heart of the organization, James S. Green followed with a rant against free black people: "What a mass of ignorance, misery and depravity, is here mingled with every portion of our population, and threatening the whole with a moral and political pestilence," he bitterly roared. "This enormous mass of revolting wretchedness and deadly pollution will, it is believed, be ultimately taken out of her territory, if the plan of the Colonization Society be adopted." Green insisted that white people could never be safe so long as black people shared their nation. "The slave is a mere animal" and free black people were "really but little better." Colored people lacked merit and character, Green added, and the nation would spiral into race war if black freedom was not tied to expatriation. The possibility of failure was unacceptable:

> I seriously doubt, whether there is one white father or mother in New-Jersey, who would be willing, that a son or daughter should contract marriage with the best educated negro, male or female, that now exists. And what do you think, Sir, of a black Governor, a black Chief Justice, a black member of Congress, a black member of the Legislature, a black Justice of the Peace, or even a black Lawyer.[41]

The intellectual cultures of the United States contained little space for the possibility of a heterogeneous society. Theodore Frelinghuysen worried that the history of white injustice toward black people created a cleavage that could never be bridged, and reconciliation, even if possible, remained offensive: it was irresponsible to let loose a "licentious, ignorant, and irritated" population upon white southern communities, which would be the equivalent of asking the white South, "after unsheathing the sword, to place it in the grasp of rapine and murder." When Senator Frelinghuysen authored the ACS response to the declarations of the New York and American Anti-Slavery Societies, he subordinated the humanitarian objectives of colonization to a full assault on free black people. The senator drew the biological boundaries of democracy. "They are a depressed and separate race," he began, "excluded from the privileges of freemen." Frelinghuysen believed that oppression fed a desire for vengeance, and, therefore, black people could be redeemed only through relocation. Justice required that they be uprooted.[42]

As a student, minister, professor, and politician, Edward Everett viewed the world through a racial prism that narrowed throughout his lifetime. At twenty-five years of age he had traveled in Europe, where he befriended the race scientist Johann Friedrich Blumenbach and other scholars, and studied the ruins of the Mediterranean. "In my last letter, I mentioned the practice of depositing the ashes of slaves & freedmen in the Columbaria," Everett wrote to Harvard president John Thornton Kirkland. "These were large tombs of twenty or thirty feet height, length, and breadth." An undergraduate, William Lincoln, found that Professor Everett was fascinated with Africa, especially the regions "where the cradle of the human race was placed by tradition." Lincoln's winter 1821 class included a series of lectures on Ethiopia—"one of the abodes of the human race & of primordial innocence"—and Egypt. However, the imagined divisions between people became more fixed and less permeable with time. Race emboldened Everett to celebrate the conquest and Christianization of nonwhite peoples, and it also allowed him to treat Africa and Africans as mere instruments of white civilization. "No, no, Anglo-Saxon, this is no part of your vocation," Everett came to believe; only black people could Christianize Africa. Blackness, like geography, was a divine limitation.

> Sir you cannot civilize Africa,—you Caucasian—you proud white man—you all-boasting, all-daring, Anglo-Saxon, you cannot do this work. You have subjugated Europe; the native races of this country are melting before you as the untimely snows of April beneath a vernal sun, you have possessed yourselves of India, you threaten China and Japan; the farthest isles of the Pacific are not distant enough to escape your grasp, or insignificant enough to elude your notice: but this great Central Africa lies at your doors and defies your power.[43]

"OUR ENEMIES—THE ABOLITIONISTS"

The American Colonization Society's control of the campus has received little attention, but in an era when barely 1 percent of the population had a college education, this relationship heightened its prestige and influence. By the 1830s colonizationists were active on three-fifths of the approximately sixty colleges operating in the free states. The organization operated on at least three-quarters of the campuses in New England and the Mid-Atlantic. The ACS had an even tighter grip on the old northeastern schools. For example, seven of the eight institutions in the Ivy League—an athletic conference established in the early twentieth century—had been founded by this period. Each was a stronghold of the movement, and Yale and New Jersey largely furnished its leadership. Colonizationists headed every college in New York State, New Jersey, Connecticut, and Massachusetts. Joseph Caldwell, president of the University of North Carolina, brought his institution into the cause. Colonizationists led several schools in Maryland, Virginia, North Carolina, Georgia, and Kentucky, the birthplaces of many of the black émigrés to Liberia, and had strongholds in Ohio. Officers and faculty promoted removal, officiated at ACS meetings, and donated and raised funds for relocation. They also refined the intellectual and political arguments against abolition.[44]

American scholars' ability to articulate the racial limits of the society provided a path to influence. Academics formed an important and boisterous lobby against abolitionism. In 1826 Williams students established an antislavery society to host public debates, sponsor Fourth of July lectures, and encourage emancipation. Williams had housed an earlier antislavery association: a campus society appeared among the supporters of an 1809 petition to Congress. However, President Edward Dorr Griffin soon had students donating to the American Colonization Society. The ACS agent John Danforth carried off a collection from the Congregational parish in Williamstown and an endorsement from the president. Danforth reported to his Washington headquarters that one of the undergraduate classes had even rewarded its instructor with a life membership in the ACS.[45]

Rev. Danforth continued on to the commencement exercises at Amherst College, where President Heman Humphrey, "a warm friend to the cause," addressed the inaugural gathering of a county colonization society. President of that auxiliary, Rev. Humphrey was also a leader of the state colonization association. "On questions relating to slavery, he has always been regarded as conservative," an Amherst historian concludes. In 1833 a small group of faculty began a campus colonization society.[46]

This was no innocent exchange of ideas. The Reverend Ralph Randolph Gurley, Yale class of 1818 and the principal agent of the American Colonization Society, chose colleges as a battlefield in the war to defeat "our enemies—the abolitionists." The leadership collected intelligence on student activism, deployed professors and administrators to promote colonization, and empowered ACS agents to police antislavery organizations. Colonizationists positioned their movement as the socially responsible alternative to abolition. The officers and agents described abolition as the antithesis of colonization, and attacked abolitionists as dangerous advocates of a multiracial future. Moreover, the inner circle of the national organization responded to its financial mismanagement and the struggles of the Liberia colony by seeking public confrontations with American abolitionists.[47]

Rev. Gurley had reason to be concerned. Students and faculty often rejected the ACS despite its influence and its appeals to social order. At Western Reserve College in Ohio, President Charles B. Storrs and Professor Elizur Wright Jr. led a series of debates on slavery that concluded with a decision to affiliate the campus with the New England Anti-Slavery Society. Western Reserve's faculty explained that they "now feel, and feel very deeply too, that they had been blinded by a strange prejudice, which had the effect of infatuation on their minds." President Beriah Green established an abolitionist outpost at the radical Oneida Institute in New York State. Students and faculty at Lane Seminary in Cincinnati toppled their ACS auxiliary after a two-week community debate; the Lane campus judged colonization to be unchristian.

Colonizationists in Ohio promised the ACS headquarters that the greater population opposed emancipation, and that Western Reserve's abolitionists were "women and children, and students." The abolitionist Arnold Buffum saw matters quite differently. That same summer he noted of Amherst: "There are between two and three hundred fine young men, who when they have finished their collegiate studies, will be scattered over the country, exercising a powerful influence in the community, as well as in the various learned professions."[48]

An undergraduate at a New England college agreed that students were an emerging political power. "If they grow up as did the last generation with all their prejudices and blindness, slavery will never be abolished," he warned. In contrast, an editorialist for *Western Monthly Magazine* called on faculties to end the debate of slavery. Colleges belonged to the public, and nothing abrasive to the public harmony or divisive in civil affairs could be tolerated in the curriculum or the culture of a student body, he insisted. The formation of campus antislavery societies insulted the intentions of those who donated money to support education, this writer continued. In his opinion, the ACS was different: its message was appropriate for students, while abolitionism was a sinister institutional plot, "which would have been creditable to the ingenuity of a college of Jesuits."[49]

At Amherst the faculty was "suspicious of the new [abolitionist] movement" and favored colonization. A student in the class of 1830 reported that his professors "disliked negro servitude" but preferred to solve it through a mass removal or "a gradual process of education." When the professors organized a colonization chapter, several undergraduates began exploring abolitionism. Three students traveled to Boston to hear Elizur Wright Jr. debate Robert S. Finley. Wright's argument pulled them to the principle of immediate emancipation. They returned to campus to organize an auxiliary of the New England Anti-Slavery Society. They also committed to raising funds to support a school for colored youth and to providing instruction to black communities in their area.[50]

The struggle for Amherst intensified. In 1833 President Humphrey barred the abolitionist Arnold Buffum from the campus. The Amherst faculty eventually permitted Buffum to speak on the condition that he not criticize colonization. The following year the officers attempted to end all discussions of slavery. The abolitionist students continued meeting. To avoid a controversy over destroying the student organization, the faculty imposed rules that ensured its slow death: the student organization could continue as long as it met no more than once a month, did not solicit members, held no public discussions, and corresponded with no newspapers or other public outlets.[51]

As it had in the South, the sectional crisis made the question of slavery politically sensitive on northern campuses; as they had in the South, college officers responded by silencing the discussion of human bondage. A firestorm erupted when the public learned of a clandestine antislavery society at Hanover College in Indiana. "If you wish to break up your institution," promised the delighted editor of the *Philanthropist*, "pass oppressive laws." In the spring of 1836 the student organization had begun meeting in a college that bordered a slave state and attracted students from slaveholding regions. The school's trustees quickly calmed the public outrage by declaring the antislavery association incompatible with the culture of the school and asserting that it was opposed by "at least nine-tenths of the students connected with the institution." Hanover president James Blythe, himself a slaveholder, insisted that the public affairs of the nation had no place on campus. "They are here taught to *obey*," he remarked of his students, "that in the future they may be prepared to *command*."[52]

Many students rejected Blythe's sociology of learning. Undergraduates at Hamilton College acknowledged that "young men have less of that reverence for old opinions than those in more advanced life." They replied that they had an obligation to prepare themselves for life "beyond these collegiate walls," viewed slavery as an appropriate topic for intellectual and moral debate, and saw this moment as an opportunity to engage the larger community. Rather than retreating, they prayed that every campus would begin examining slavery: "It is not well known that should our College and Seminaries become purified on this subject, an influence would go forth so mighty that very soon the hand of oppression would be stayed, and the groans of its victims be exchanged for the rejoicing of freedom." In the face of restrictions from the faculty, Amherst students claimed a superior status as "disciples of the *compassionate Jesus*" with an obligation to prepare for a future as missionaries and ministers. They then refused to disband a union forged from prayer and collective conscience:

> We look again over two millions of our countrymen—we hear the clanking of their chains—we listen to their moving pleas for deliverance—their deep-toned wailings are borne to us on every breeze. . . . We would gladly comply with your requests, if we *could* do it consistently with the dictates of conscience, and the wants and woes of perishing millions.[53]

Students on numerous campuses rose up in defense of the abolitionist minority. At Colby College in Maine, the boys demanded that the governors recognize their antislavery society. Condemning the "most unwarrantable, virulent, and wicked prejudice" that restrained black people's access to jobs and schools, the founders of the Union College Anti-Slavery Society also took an expansive

view of the fight against slavery. More than forty students joined
the association, declared themselves an auxiliary of the New York
Anti-Slavery Society, committed to immediate emancipation, and
refuted accusations of fanaticism. "I have put my name to the constitution of an Abolition society . . . which labors, which acts, and
which has some efficiency in the great cause of Emancipation,"
William Frederick Wallis, an undergraduate at Dartmouth College, proudly informed a friend. About 150 people joined the Dartmouth society, and, Wallis boasted, they were outfitting the library
with abolitionist newspapers and books, and supporting antislavery work in the state.[54]

THE THIRD PILLAR

In 1834 the American Colonization Society held its annual meeting
in the Hall of the United States Congress in Washington, D.C. Yale
president Jeremiah Day served as a vice president of the convention
under former United States president James Madison. The audience
included justices of the United States Supreme Court, senators, congressmen, a large contingent of state and local officials, and a corps
of scholars. That same year Chief Justice John Marshall loaned the
ACS $500 of the $50,000 it sought to borrow to maintain solvency.
The state and local auxiliaries were equally privileged, enjoying the
patronage of politicians, ministers, and an academic elite. In Connecticut, for example, the governor, college presidents, numerous
professors, the Episcopal bishop and leading clergy, and wealthy
merchants headed the colonization movement.[55]

Shortly after the ACS closed its meetings in the United States
Capitol, white mobs began attacking abolitionists and antislavery
symbols, destroyed their property, and broke up their meetings.
The height of the antiabolitionist and antiblack terror in the North
came as academic influence on the colonization movement peaked.
During a week of violence in New York City, gangs roamed the
streets, assaulted black and white people, raided antislavery institutions, and sacked African American schools and churches. Columbia president William Alexander Duer—the heir of an old

Meeting of the American Colonization Society in Washington, D.C.
SOURCE: Bettmann/Corbis

West Indies plantation family—served as the founding president of the Colonization Society of the City of New York and was a delegate to the national ACS meetings. The affiliate's introductory appeal, which carried Duer's signature, advised that "a numerous free population of a distant and inferior race" threatened the nation's great cities, and the problem of slavery paled before the emergency of this menace.[56]

Violence was not limited to the city streets. The ACS and its auxiliaries were directly involved in a string of wars upon African American students and abolitionist schools, part of a larger struggle to halt the development of free black communities. In the summer of 1831 Justice David Daggett, Congressman Ralph Ingersoll, and other public figures with close ties to Yale conspired to stop a planned black college, the first of its kind, from opening in New Haven. Two years later colonizationists targeted the abolitionist Prudence Crandall's school for African American girls and women in Canterbury, Connecticut. They engineered a sequence of criminal prosecutions, convicted her in a trial presided over by Judge Daggett, and physically destroyed the school. In 1835 New England colonizationists plotted against Noyes Academy in Canaan, New Hampshire, a new school open to both genders and all races.

A mob of three hundred people hunted black students with guns and a cannon, then used oxen and horses to pull the academy's building from its foundations and drag it through town.[57]

Just two weeks after the riot at Noyes Academy, antiabolitionist violence shocked Amherst College. As the undergraduate classes marched to the August 1835 commencement prayers, Robert C. Mc-Nairy, a sophomore from Tennessee, took a heavy club and began bludgeoning John L. Ashby, a junior and abolitionist from New Hampshire. At the time, Rev. Gurley of the ACS was in New England lecturing on the dangers of abolitionism and praising the progress of the colonizationist cause. Moreover, Edward Everett was on the Amherst campus. He was addressing the students on the importance of academic institutions and public education to the diffusion of arts and sciences that sustained the unprecedented liberty of the American people. In the wake of a wave of assaults on African American schools, black students, and abolitionists, Everett prayed that "freedom and knowledge and morals and religion . . . be the birthright of our children to the end of time!"[58]

American scholars who stoked fears of a multiracial future provided a compelling intellectual justification for violence. Academics cannibalized their wayward colleagues and silenced their obstinate students. Professor Benjamin Silliman of Yale cautioned a New Haven audience about the demographic threats underlying the "national anxiety" over slavery. "Who can then, without dismay, contemplate the character of this overwhelming [black] population," Silliman projected, before suggesting inevitable race war and black rule. Silliman blamed abolitionists for the political fracture and pointed to the removal of black people as the most practical solution to the nation's racial dilemma.[59]

The great majority of the crusade's adherents had serious doubts about the spiritual capacity and social potential of black peoples, African or American. Their insistence upon removal revealed a declining faith in Christianity's ability to transform nonwhite peoples, a position bolstered by the popular belief that human beings occupied fixed racial categories with biologically determined fates. Academics were well positioned to make this argument.

In the decades before the Civil War, American scholars claimed a new public role as the racial guardians of the United States. They interpreted race science into national social policy to construct the biological basis of citizenship and to assert that the very presence of nonwhite and non-Christian peoples threatened the republic. They laid the intellectual foundations for a century of exclusion and removal campaigns. The intellectual roots of the cyclical political and social assaults upon Native Americans, African Americans, Jews, Irish, and Asians can be traced back to this scholarly obsession with race.

Of one thing, my friends, you may be sure, that the
diploma which you expect to carry home with you
from this literary institution, though delivered to you
in the most authentic form, unless it be countersigned
and attested in the inner court of the mind and heart
of the receiver, will be nothing to you but a certificate
of a square of years passed within the college walls,
sufficient to prove an *alibi* in a court of justice, but not
sufficient to establish the competency of the bearer to
meet the demands which society has upon every
graduate of Harvard College.

—PROFESSOR CHARLES FOLLEN, SERMON TO
THE STUDENTS OF HARVARD, CA. 1835

Mourn, Christians—mourn—a brother loved
Is stricken from your sight,
Follen, the good—the wise—the pure—
Has heavenward ta'en his flight.

—"THE BURNING OF THE LEXINGTON,"
LIBERATOR, FEBRUARY 21, 1840

Cotton Comes to Harvard

On January 13, 1840, "Rev. Dr. Follen, of Harvard College," sat among 150 passengers aboard the *Lexington*. At 3:00 P.M. the ship left Long Island for Stonington on Connecticut's eastern shore carrying a large cargo of cotton on its upper deck. On any other day it would have been a routine commercial voyage. However, the cotton had been loaded near a smoke pipe, and around 7:00 P.M. it caught fire. Flames swept the ship. The engine failed. Safety boats were lost or flooded as the crew and passengers panicked. The *Lexington* drifted eastward for hours. At about 3:00 A.M. it sank in the waters south of New England. All but a few of the people on board perished in the fire or drowned in Long Island Sound; the three survivors had clung to debris or tied themselves to bales of cotton. Northern businessmen accounted for many but not all of the fatalities. Alice Winslow, a recent widow escorting her husband's corpse back to Providence, Rhode Island, died with her family that night. The Reverend Charles Follen also perished. "I picture him as he ever was in life, calm and resolute amid that scene of danger and death," the Reverend John Pierpont cried. "The flames surround him! the cold depths are below!"[1]

In 1824 Congress had invited the Marquis de Lafayette, the

French general who had fought with the colonists during the American Revolution, to return to the United States in anticipation of the fiftieth anniversary of independence. During this extended celebratory tour, General Lafayette received a letter from Charles Follen in Philadelphia, where the German refugee was studying English and looking to begin his career anew. Five years earlier, in Mannheim, Germany, a young theology student named Karl Ludwig Sand had stabbed the dramatist August von Kotzebue with a dagger in retaliation for the artist's editorial attacks upon political liberalism and academic freedom in the universities. During the investigations into the murder, authorities questioned, arrested, and jailed activists and academics. An open supporter of political and intellectual freedom, Charles Follen was rounded up and driven from the University of Jena. He fled Germany under threat of imprisonment, and eventually left for the United States.[2]

General Lafayette interrupted the national commemoration to introduce the refugee to George Ticknor, Smith Professor of Modern Languages at Harvard and Lafayette's biographer. Ticknor brought Follen to Cambridge, where he was appointed instructor in German. As a teenager Follen had left the University of Giesen to fight against Napoleon. In America, he was immediately attracted to the antislavery movement. He read William Lloyd Garrison's *Liberator*, and then dropped in to meet the editor at his upstairs office in Merchants' Hall, Boston. By 1833 Follen was serving as vice president of the New England Anti-Slavery Society, and the following year he helped organize its first convention in Boston. As mob violence and government intimidation threatened to stall antislavery, Follen argued that morality had to persevere in the face of sin, he rejected the accusation that abolitionists had invited violence, and he pushed the boundaries of radicalism by calling for the equal treatment of black people in antislavery circles. When southern politicians demanded that the New England states silence and outlaw antislavery associations, Follen defended abolitionism before the Massachusetts legislature.[3]

During the 1834 New England Anti-Slavery Society Convention, Professor Follen chaired the committee charged with writing an "Address to the People of the United States," drafted their

Charles Follen
SOURCE: New York Public Library

statement, and appeared first among its signatories. That public document confronted the critics of abolitionism and the defenders of slavery. It judged slavery incompatible with Christian principle and offensive to the basic tenets of republicanism and democracy. Slavery deflated the moral culture of the nation. It encouraged arrogance and fed upon violence. It hid sin under the guise of supremacy. "The law of the land which declares the house of the white man his 'castle,' and guards it against the threats of intruders by imprisonment and death," Follen challenged the nation, "admits to the unguarded dwelling of the colored man, every selfish and brutal passion, if it bears the color of legalized oppression; it licenses the profanation of all that is sacred and dear to the wretched victim of avarice and prejudice."[4]

Charles Follen was equally resolute in the classroom, and Harvard boys judged him quite favorably. "Dr. Follen was the best of teachers," recalled the Reverend Andrew Preston Peabody, an upperclassman when Follen arrived. "One fact is worthy of notice which is that they were negroes—of this there can be no doubt," reads Henry Watson Jr.'s notebook from an 1829 course on ancient history. This future cotton planter also wrote that the ancient Egyptians had the curly hair and other features of the African race and that contemporary Egyptians were only lighter in complexion because of centuries of mixing with Europeans. Professor Follen did not leave it to his students to infer that black Africans cradled civilization. "This fact refutes all the false theories so often advanced in favor of slavery," Follen concluded for them, "since they cannot be so inferior when all we know is due to the superiority of the so much despised Blacks." In 1831 the college collected donations for a new professorship in German. That year Thomas Wigglesworth took a course on moral philosophy in which Follen used the lives of the Christian martyrs to demonstrate the heavy burden of a free will, a rational mind, and a loving but demanding God. "Conscience cannot be considered . . . the creature of circumstances," Wigglesworth recorded at the beginning of one lecture.[5]

But the exile again became a political liability to his institution. Follen had sympathized with student protests of the governance and curriculum, publicly supported abolition, and criticized the administration. Political antislavery was not the only cause of the subsequent backlash, but it was the part of the story that the governors tried to hide. Harvard president Josiah Quincy later admitted that there was little tolerance for antislavery discourse on the Harvard campus during his sixteen-year term. "Harvard College once trampled on Dr. Follen for his anti-slavery principles, and in their pride of place and power, they did it successfully," Wendell Phillips angrily remembered, adding that the Harvard Corporation later worked feverishly to cover up its role in the persecution.[6]

The funds for Follen's professorship came from sensitive sources: the merchant Thomas H. Perkins, whose well-armed ships carried thousands of enslaved people from Africa to the Americas and tons of opium to Asia; Samuel Cabot, a merchant and shipping heir who arranged the appointment; and the merchant Jonathan Phillips, to whom Harvard awarded an honorary degree and whose family gave hundreds of thousands of dollars to the college, the Boston Public Library, Phillips Andover Academy, Massachusetts General Hospital, and other institutions. The donors had more than financial connections to Harvard. President John Thornton Kirkland, who appointed Follen, was married to Elizabeth Cabot, the daughter of George Cabot of the Perkins and Cabot firm. Josiah

Quincy, his successor, was married to Eliza Morton, the daughter of the wealthy New York merchant John Morton. From the end of the Revolution to the outbreak of the Civil War, the presidents of Harvard were almost always the sons or sons-in-law of the commercial elite—beginning with Joseph Willard, who wedded Mary Sheafe, the daughter of a rich West Indies supplier in Portsmouth, New Hampshire, and ending with Cornelius Conway Felton, who married Mary Louisa Cary, the granddaughter of Thomas H. Perkins.[7]

The reaction was swift. In February 1835 the governors discussed the situation. Their March minutes read: "Dr. Follen resigns his Prof[esso]r[ship] Of German Lit[erature]." The donors withdrew their subscriptions, and President Quincy and the officers discontinued his chair. The minutes of a meeting several weeks later include another announcement: "Prof. Ticknor resigns Smith Prof[essorship]." Ticknor's decision to leave responded to the death of his son, the marginalization of his field, and the burdens of the recent upheavals on campus. "We differ, however, very largely, both as to what the College can be, and what it ought to be," Ticknor admitted to a friend. "We therefore separate, as men who go different roads, though proposing the same end, each persuaded the one he prefers is the best, the pleasantest, and the shortest."[8]

In 1828 Eliza Lee Cabot, a childhood neighbor of the Quincys, had married Charles Follen. After her family and friends conspired to end her husband's academic career, she began tutoring boys for entrance to Harvard to support the family. She wrote children's books, contributed to abolitionist journals, and joined the antislavery movement. Follen eventually accepted the pulpit of the First Unitarian Church in New York City—likely with the assistance of the Unitarian cabal within the abolitionist movement—where he was also elected to the executive committee of the American Anti-Slavery Society.[9]

The idea that human slavery was wrong was not new to Harvard Yard. In 1829 the governors appointed the younger Henry Ware to a professorship in the Divinity School despite his advocacy of abolition. Ware was a founder and president of the Cambridge Anti-Slavery Society. Follen had regularly dined at the home of the elder Henry Ware, the Hollis Professor of Divinity, during his early days in Cambridge. The Boston newspapers accused Ware of undermining his value as a teacher and jeopardizing Harvard. Follen also befriended the Unitarian minister William Ellery Channing, the Harvard-trained pastor of Federal Street Church in Boston, who encouraged him to study for the ministry. During his father's presidency of Harvard, Edmund Quincy served as a guest editor of the *Liberator* and an officer of the Massachusetts Anti-Slavery Society—which replaced the New England organization in 1835. Charles Follen, William Lloyd Garrison, Maria Chapman, Charles Stuart, and Sarah and Angelina Grimké were founders.[10] Follen did not enjoy the freedom afforded the son of the man occupying the most prestigious faculty chair at Harvard or the son of its president, but that was not his only vulnerability.

THE AGE OF EUPHEMISM

The northern elite was cleansing the stain of human slavery from the story of its prosperity. Some of the best-educated people in the nation were revising history to romanticize and sanitize their relationship to bondage. They erased their pasts as masters or reimagined their slaves as a lower order of adopted family—trusted, faithful, and beloved servants whom they had treated with dignity and human sympathy. They recast their enslavement of Africans into a tale of decorative servitude.

The descendants of Thomas Perkins took pride in the story of his rescuing a dying African from a brutal slave dealer in Saint-Domingue, getting this man to the hospital, and then giving him to his sister-in-law, with whom he lived a full life. Mousse (Perkins) helped the Perkins family escape the island during the Haitian Revolution, and served them loyally in New England. He was buried in the Perkins family vault at St. Paul's Church. This is a peculiar act of mercy when examined in conjunction with the history of the Perkinses' eighteenth-century slaving voyages, which killed hundreds of human beings and continued after public opinion had turned against the slave trade. The Perkinses

soon graduated into the opium trade with the backing of prominent New Englanders such as Massachusetts governor James
Bowdoin.[11]

The great families distanced themselves rhetorically from the
planters of the West Indies and the South—despite numerous
shared surnames—by claiming histories as merchants, investors,
and insurers, and then elevating underwriting, finance, and trade
to high arts. Slave traders became Atlantic merchants, and the biggest firms received the greatest praise. It was an age of euphemism,
populated with fragile lies, half-truths, and deflections.

If most white northerners found it difficult to tolerate antislavery zealots pointing fingers at the South, they also dreaded the
abolitionists' critique of the social order of New England and the
Mid-Atlantic. The shipping, finance, and manufacturing economies of New England and the Mid-Atlantic remained firmly tied
to human slavery long after the retreat of slaveholding in the
northern states. The elite encouraged the antiabolitionist violence
that began in New York City in the summer of 1834 and continued
through the burning of the American Anti-Slavery Society's
Pennsylvania Hall in Philadelphia four years later. During a memorial for Follen, the Reverend Samuel Joseph May described the
1835 riot in Boston:

> The doors of Faneuil Hall were thrown open, that *the gen-
> tlemen of property and standing* might crowd that *sacred place*
> to execrate the cause of liberty, and prepare their creatures
> to inflict that indelible stain upon the fair fame of our city,
> the mob of October 21, five thousand strong, which broke
> up a meeting of Anti-Slavery women—tore down the signs
> of our Anti-Slavery office—and dragged the Editor of an
> Anti-Slavery paper through the streets with a halter about
> him. Almost every one of the clergy stood aloof. Some
> held the garments of those who were stoning us.[12]

The "sacred" status of Faneuil Hall itself came from cycles of
mythmaking. It was hardly an inappropriate site for an attack upon
abolitionism

A wealthy trader with a taste for grandeur, Peter Faneuil built the hall in 1742. Using a significant inheritance from his merchant uncle, Faneuil had put several slave ships to sea, including the not so modestly named *Jolly Bachelor.* The same year that Faneuil Hall opened, the *Jolly Bachelor* made a fatal trip to the Guinea coast, where the captain and several crewmen were killed in an attack. A skeleton crew completed emergency repairs to the ship and sailed back to Newport, Rhode Island, with twenty enslaved people on board. This too became a story of adventure and progress that obscured the heinous details. Two centuries later, a biographer described Peter Faneuil as a beneficiary of the "race growth" that occurred in the rugged Protestant culture of New England and an exemplar of the superior "racial development" that formed the spine of American history.[13]

The affluent and the powerful did discredit abolitionism, but they failed to stop it. On November 7, 1837, a mob in Alton, Illinois, murdered Elijah P. Lovejoy, editor of the abolitionist *Observer.* The "first martyr" of white abolitionism created a moral stir that shook the nation. In the wake of the Lovejoy killing, undergraduates at Amherst accused the faculty of censoring free thought, while an even larger group of Amherst students demanded the right to reestablish their campus antislavery society. Students at numerous schools charged that "free discussion was forbidden in northern colleges." In the aftermath of the murder, Jonathan Phillips, one of the donors for Follen's professorship, chaired an antislavery gathering at which Wendell Phillips, a distant relative, delivered an impassioned call for immediate emancipation. Amherst's faculty acceded to the students' demand to form an auxiliary of the American Anti-Slavery Society. President Heman Humphrey also reduced, briefly, his public connections to the colonization cause, and by January 1838 the student antislavery society reopened with about sixty members. "I believe we shall all have to become abolitionists, after all," President Humphrey sighed.[14]

Violence against prominent white men aggravated the sectional divide. "My heart has been always much more affected by the slavery to which the Free States have been subjected, than with that of the negro," President Quincy once confessed. In May 1856 Representative Preston Brooks of South Carolina viciously beat Senator Charles Sumner of Massachusetts in the United States Capitol after Sumner delivered a forceful antislavery address. A former congressman, Quincy blasted southerners for stamping out freedom of speech in the capital and threatening the lives of any who opposed the Slave Power. "Their boastful chivalric bravery is, in truth, only disguised cowardice," Quincy continued, while accusing southern politicians of undermining democracy with everything from fawning to bullying.[15]

Although Quincy was genuinely shaken, he acknowledged only a portion of the sin. The issue was quite a bit worse than northern ambivalence toward southern slavery, the ubiquitous call to elevate the union over the question of human suffering, and the cozy relations of the northern, southern, and West Indian aristocracies. The problem of slavery in the antebellum North, like the problem of slavery at Harvard, could not be solved by rhetoric or emotion. It was located in the entangled economies, histories, institutions, and lineages of the South, the free states, Europe, the Caribbean, and Africa. It was a problem so ugly and so personal that it invited dishonesty.

"The soil of New England is trodden by no slave," Quincy asserted in his history of Boston, crediting a commitment to an "equality of rights" that he traced back to the Pilgrims and Puritans. Harvard president Jared Sparks authored a series of books on the lives and letters of the Founding Fathers that raised his prestige and earned him firm friendships in the South. In 1822 Everett had married Charlotte Brooks, the daughter of Peter Chardon Brooks, the wealthy Atlantic maritime insurer and college benefactor. Antebellum presidents often turned to history, producing national and regional studies, and biographies of leading political and economic figures. From Princeton came accounts of the Presbyterian Church, the college, the region's leading families, and the African colonization movement. President William Alexander Duer of Columbia wrote about society and life in New York City

Harvard University Presidents, 1829–1862
SOURCE: Harvard University Libraries

and the heroism of his English and West Indian ancestors.[16] This turn to the past was not peculiar to universities. The antebellum nation saw a broad social concern with history.

Popular fixations with history often reflect popular anxieties about the future. If history is a search for distant truths, then it is also an attempt to regulate the judgments of coming generations. White northerners removed slavery from their accounts and memories by driving the descendants of slaves from view and crafting new explanations for their wealth and regional development. Not coincidentally, President Quincy and the Harvard Corporation dismissed Charles Follen on the eve of Harvard's bicentennial, a moment of ritual historical revision. The attack on abolitionists and abolitionism began the process of hiding the college's long, sordid affair with slavery and the slave trade.

COTTON COMES TO HARVARD

The most active slaving house in the nation, the DeWolfes, opened a firm and purchased plantations in Cuba to circumvent the United States' 1808 prohibition on the slave trade. Such families became the new patrons of higher education. Israel Thorndike, whose fortune came from the Caribbean trade and a Cuban estate acquired from the DeWolfes, gave $500 to endow the Massachusetts Professorship of Natural History at Harvard, the same amount to the theology school, and $100 for the Professorship in Mineralogy and Geology. In 1818 he spent several thousand dollars on the Americana collection—ten thousand maps and more than three thousand books—of the Hamburg professor and librarian Christoph Daniel Ebeling. Thorndike's son, Israel Augustus, graduated from Harvard in 1835, and in 1841 he married Frances Maria Macomb, the daughter of a Cuban sugar planter. In 1838 Elisha Atkins opened a trading house in Boston to import sugar from Cuba, where he also purchased plantations. Edwin Atkins bought Soledad and other sugar estates during the violent and unstable demise of slavery on the island. The family owned one of the largest sugar-producing and -refining operations in Cuba, which they maintained after the 1886 emancipation. Atkins created the Harvard Botanical Garden at Soledad, and later donated the estate to serve as the tropical laboratory for Harvard science faculty and students.[17]

Merchants and manufacturers with economic ties to the cotton and sugar plantations of the South and the Caribbean transformed higher education in the antebellum North. The Boston Associates, a combination of investors and industrialists from roughly forty families, planned dozens of cotton mill towns across New England, and branched into finance and railroads. John Lowell Jr., the son of the cotton textile magnate Francis Cabot Lowell, bequeathed $250,000 to support the Lowell Institute (1839) in Boston. Edward Everett of Harvard gave the inaugural address on the history of the founder. Yale's Benjamin Silliman followed with a lecture on geology, and returned for an introduction to chemistry. In its first years, the institute offered talks on anatomy, Christian philosophy, botany, electromagnetism, religion, optics, American history, and astronomy from scholars such as Jared Sparks of Harvard and Mark Hopkins of Williams.[18]

Industrialists were retooling universities to meet their needs. Under Everett's presidency, the practical sciences significantly expanded at Harvard. In 1847 Abbott Lawrence, the cotton textile manufacturer, gave $50,000 to establish the Lawrence Scientific School, motivated by his own frustrations locating qualified engineers and planners to build his mills and towns. He later bequeathed an additional $50,000. His brother Amos, also a manufacturer and college benefactor, celebrated the historic donation as the "last best work ever done by one of our name." The Lawrences donated to Williams, Amherst, Bowdoin, and other colleges across the nation. This was not detached benevolence. Realizing the vision of an industrialized nation required mechanics and engineers. "Buying up vast stretches of land and water, and plunking down whole cities where none had been before," Robert F. Dalzell writes of this manufacturing elite, displayed the possibilities of technology and capital.[19]

More than a dozen engineering and science schools had opened in the United States before the Civil War. In 1824 Stephen Van Rensselaer chartered Rensselaer Polytechnic Institute in New York. By the 1830s William and Mary and the University of Virginia, where William Barton Rogers held professorships, were offering practical science courses. In 1846 Rogers sent an outline for a polytechnic school to John A. Lowell, of the cotton manufacturing empire. His influences came from the more advanced technical schools in France and Germany. Among the founding trustees of the Brooklyn Polytechnic Institute (1855) were James C. Brevoort, who had finished his education at the École Centrale des Arts et Manufactures in Paris, and James Stranahan, a civil engineer who had planned the manufacturing town of Florence, New York, for the abolitionist Gerrit Smith. Charles Pratt's oil refinery and the Havemeyer sugar works were driving a production revolution that transformed Brooklyn from a small town to an industrial city. "Among the people themselves," Frederick Barnard, then of the University of Mississippi, said in a speech in New York City that year, "there has sprung up a demand for something more practical" in education. In 1859 the iron

Awful Conflagration of the Steam Boat Lexington
SOURCE: Library of Congress

industrialist and abolitionist Peter Cooper opened the Cooper Union for the Advancement of Science and Art in New York City. Two years later, Rogers became the president of the new Massachusetts Institute of Technology, with support from the Lowells.[20]

"STRICKEN FROM YOUR SIGHT"

On January 13, 1840, Rev. Follen left New York for New England to preach the dedicatory sermon at a new church in East Lexington, Massachusetts, which he helped to build and was to pastor. If not for his humility, he might have touted it as a triumphant return. He and his family had survived Harvard's punishment, he had sustained his moral and political opposition to human slavery, and he had grown his reputation. But his career ended on the ill-fated *Lexington*.[21] Slavery shaped much of Follen's life in the United

States, and it also influenced his death: a professor, minister, and abolitionist was consumed in a fire that began in a cargo of slave-grown cotton steaming toward free New England.

Even as the sun began setting on Atlantic slavery, the leaders of American colleges were chasing the darkness.

Acknowledgments

Brown University president Ruth Simmons's courageous articulation of the academic obligation to pursue truth and the forthright presentations of James T. Campbell, Anthony Bogues, Evelyn Hu-Dehart, and the committee that authored *Slavery and Justice* (2006), the report on Brown's ties to the slave trade, came at a time when I was considering giving up on what then seemed to be too massive an undertaking. Brown's self-study was not the first of these recent investigations. Graduate students and staff at Yale had authored *Yale, Slavery, & Abolition* (2001) during the university's three hundredth anniversary. But President Simmons's call for a reckoning with this past resonated well beyond the walls of her campus.

Leslie M. Harris, James T. Campbell, and Alfred L. Brophy organized a historic conference on slavery and the university at Emory. Sven Beckert and Katherine Stevens's seminars at Harvard led to the collection *Harvard & Slavery* (2011). Terry L. Meyers has published on slavery at William and Mary. Mark Auslander has been researching and teaching the history of slavery at Emory. Deborah K. King is recovering the lives of enslaved people at the northern New England colleges. Shanti M. Singham has guided students in discovering these connections at Williams College.

Martha Sandweiss is leading an undergraduate research seminar on slavery at Princeton. Faculty, librarians, and students at other schools—including William and Mary, Duke, Amherst, North Carolina, South Carolina, Virginia, Alabama, and Maryland—have been producing detailed studies of the relationship between colleges and slavery. Campus by campus, they are providing complex portraits of slavery and the university at a speed that is difficult to follow. They are also beginning to synthesize this scholarship online, in museum exhibits, and in major publications like the forthcoming *Slavery and the University* volume from the Emory conference.

I took an unusual path to this subject. A decade ago, I began research for an article on how black abolitionists entered the professions given the racial barriers at American colleges. I had just arrived at Dartmouth College, a perfect site for exploring stories that often began or concluded in New England. The work of Colin G. Calloway, Celia Naylor, Dale Turner, and other colleagues and students in Dartmouth's Native American Studies Program reshaped my interests. I became more curious about the uneven statuses of Native people and Africans on early American campuses, and the differing ideas about their educability. The contrasts are striking. The first attempt to establish an Indian college in the British colonies came more than two centuries before the first movement to found a black college. The first Native student to graduate from a college in what is now the United States did so nearly one hundred and seventy years before the first African American graduated. The first ordained Native minister in the Protestant colonies preceded the first black clergyman by about a century and a half. These differences do not signal a privileging of Native Americans over Africans; rather, they reflect the troubling role of colleges and education in the colonial world.

James Wright, president emeritus of Dartmouth, and Ozzie Harris, now at Emory, were sources of constant support during the early years of this project. I presented some of this work at the Black New England Conference at the University of New Hampshire, where James T. Campbell offered concrete advice and encouragement. Jonathan Veitch, now the president of Occidental

College, arranged for a visiting professorship at the New School, where I benefited immeasurably from workshops and exchanges with David Plotke, Robin Blackburn, Ferentz Lafargue, Frederico Finchelstein, Sam Haselby, and Oz Frankel. I also enjoyed a semester as a visitor in the history department at University College London. Simon Renton, Bernhard Rieger, John Sabapathy, Nicola Miller, Adam Smith, and the graduate students at UCL invited me to present material and they gave me good guidance on locating British and European sources. My thanks to the Urban History Seminar, Chicago History Museum, where I discussed an early version of the chapter on race science. Kate Fermoile and Deborah Schwartz hosted a talk on the medical sciences and slavery at the Brooklyn Historical Society. Colin G. Calloway generously reviewed the first full draft of the book, certainly a difficult assignment.

Numerous friends have read or listened to parts of the book on more than one occasion. My departmental colleagues Harriet Ritvo and Elizabeth Wood read chapters. Graham Russell Hodges, Joseph Cullon, John Ehrenberg, Jonathan Soffer, and Diana Linden were kind enough to critique parts of the manuscript. Michael Green and Deborah K. King read final versions of the book. I have presented this work with colleagues and students in the Bard Prison Initiative and on the Bard campus. Jeff Ravel, Jack Tchen, David Gerwin, and other friends have provided opportunities for me to share this material. As this project expanded, I had to give up the fantasy that I could acknowledge in writing all the librarians and archivists who have assisted me during a decade of research, but I have thanked them all in person.

I could not have completed this project without Zoë Pagnamenta, who placed the book with Peter Ginna and the Bloomsbury Press USA group. Several years ago, Zoë and I bonded over a cup of coffee and a long chat that drifted from British sitcoms to colonial history. She has been a reliable advocate for my work ever since. Peter Ginna patiently permitted the project to evolve and skillfully helped me move ideas into words. He allowed me to make mistakes and discoveries. I deeply appreciate his dedication to telling this story.

Finally, I have to thank my sister. For two decades, Dr. Gloria has provided medical care to thousands of children living in Washington, D.C. I have had the honor of sitting in audiences to watch my sister receive awards, but I have not had a chance to acknowledge her influence on me. Long before these successes, she protected me, time and time again, from the dangers of growing up black, male, and poor in the United States. Gloria believed that we had something to offer. I was, truthfully, quite doubtful. This is a little tribute to my first and best friendship.

Notes

❦❦❦❦❦

PROLOGUE: A CONNECTICUT YANKEE
AT AN ANCIENT INDIAN MOUND

1. Henry Watson Jr. to Henry Watson, 10 November 1830, 16 November 1830, and 16 December 1830, Henry Watson Family Papers, 1803–1823, in the John Spencer Bassett Papers, Box 32, Folder 23, Manuscript Division, Library of Congress; Chandos Michael Brown, *Benjamin Silliman: A Life in the Young Republic* (Princeton: Princeton University Press, 1989), 35–49.

2. Henry Watson Jr. to Henry Watson, 10 November 1830; Brown, *Benjamin Silliman*, 35–49.

3. On 18 May 1705, Tamar, a slave, was accepted into First Church in Hartford. *Historical Catalogue of the First Church in Hartford, 1633–1885* (Hartford, CT: By the Church, 1885), 26; Bushrod Washington, "Address of the American Colonization Society to the People of the United States," *Christian Herald*, 13 September 1817; *Memorial of the President and the Board of Managers of the American Society for Colonizing the Free People of Colour of the United States: January 14, 1817. Read and Ordered to Lie upon the Table* (Washington, DC: William A. Davis, 1817).

4. Henry Watson Jr., "Dr. [J. C.] Warren's Anatomical Lectures, Harvard College, May 1829," in Henry Watson Jr. Lecture Notes, 1829, II:139, Rare Books and Special Collections, Neilson Library, Smith College; Samuel J. May, *Discourse on the Life and Character of the Rev. Charles Follen, L.L.D., Who Perished, Jan. 13, 1840, in the Conflagration of the Lexington. Delivered*

Before the Massachusetts Anti-Slavery Society, in the Marlborough Chapel, Boston, April 17, 1840 (Boston: Henry L. Devereux, 1840), 7–22; "Biographical Notices of the Late Dr. Charles Follen," *Monthly Miscellany of Religion and Letters*, February 1840.

5. Henry Watson Jr. to Henry Watson, 16 December 1830, 30 December 1830, John Spencer Bassett Papers, Box 32, Folder 23, Library of Congress.

6. *General Catalogue of Dartmouth College and the Associated Schools, 1769–1900, Including a Historical Sketch of the College Prepared by Marvin Davis Bisbee, the Librarian* (Hanover, NH: For the College, 1900), 169; Henry Watson Jr. to My Dear Father, 19 June 1830, John Spencer Bassett Papers, Box 32, Folder 23, Library of Congress; Henry Watson Jr., "Journal of Horseback Ride from Erie, Alabama, to East Windsor Hill, Conn[ecticut], May 20th to July 8th, 1831," Rare Books and Special Collections, Neilson Library, Smith College.

7. Roger G. Kennedy, *Hidden Cities: The Discovery and Loss of Ancient North American Civilization* (New York: Free Press, 1994), 7–22; Gregory D. Wilson, *The Archaeology of Everyday Life at Early Moundville* (Tuscaloosa: University of Alabama Press, 2008); William Leete Stone, *The Moundbuilders: Were They Egyptian, and Did They Ever Occupy the State of New York?* (New York: A. S. Barnes, 1878); Paul Kelton, *Epidemics and Enslavement: Biological Catastrophe in the Native Southeast, 1492–1715* (Lincoln: University of Nebraska Press, 2007), 1–46, 101–59.

8. Watson, "Journal of Horseback Ride from Erie, Alabama, to East Windsor Hill, Conn[ecticut]."

9. James Kent was a charter member of the Yale chapter. In 1793 Kent began lecturing on law at Columbia. Chief Justice John Jay, Justice John S. Hobart of the New York State Supreme Court, Dr. Samuel Bard, and Edward Livingston helped secure him an appointment as professor of law. The trustees approved a law school in 1858. The abolitionist William Jay eventually drew Kent out of the colonization movement. James Kent, *An Address Delivered at New Haven, Before the Phi Beta Kappa Society, September 13, 1831* (New Haven: Hezekiah Howe, 1831), 14–15; James Kent, *Dissertations: Being the Preliminary Part of a Course of Law Lectures* (New York: George Forman, 1795); Theodore W. Dwight, "Columbia College Law School, New York," *The Green Bag*, 1889, 141–60; John Theodore Horton, *James Kent: A Study in Conservatism, 1763–1847* (1939; Union, NJ: Lawbook Exchange, 2000), 310n; Robert A. Trendel, *William Jay: Churchman, Public Servant, and Reformer* (New York: Arno, 1982), 188; William Kent, *Memoirs and Letters of James Kent, LL.D., Late Chancellor of the State of New York, Author of "Commentaries on American Law," Etc.* (Boston: Little, Brown, 1898), 54–59, 99–100, 180, 229.

10. *A Connecticut Yankee in King Arthur's Court* is a novel about slavery; perhaps more accurately, it is about a people who had failed to acknowledge their long reliance upon the enslavement of other human beings. Mark Twain assures his readers that the history beneath his story is factually if not chronologically accurate. He wrote and published the novel a quarter century after the Civil War, while he was living in Hartford, Connecticut, in a house neighboring that of his friend Harriet Beecher Stowe. A postbellum American would not likely imagine a journey through time that did not include encounters with Africans and Native Americans. "Negroes" and "Indians" are present throughout this ironic juxtaposition of the sixth and nineteenth centuries. Struck on the head in his Connecticut workshop, Hank Morgan wakes to find himself shackled and sold alongside the king of England, who is shocked to discover how easily a free man can be converted to chattel, offended by the injustice of his own laws, and humbled by his unflattering market value. Twain uses the fictionalized world of Morgan's enslavement to unleash a passionate indictment of the real slavery that had only recently existed in the United States. This abolitionist lament, however eloquent, was merely retrospective. Moreover, Twain's references to Native peoples treat them as romantic primitives, noble savages, and cultural artifacts. Morgan describes King Arthur's Camelot as a barbaric society governed by bravado, force, and honor, but never intelligence. The Round Table is "just a sort of polished up court of Comanches, and there isn't a squaw in it who doesn't stand ready at the dropping of a hat to desert to the buck with the biggest string of scalps at his belt." James Oakes, *The Ruling Race: A History of American Slaveholders* (New York: Vintage, 1983), 121, 125, 199–209; James L. Roark, *Masters Without Slaves: Southern Planters in the Civil War and Reconstruction* (New York: Norton, 1977), 71–72, 132; Kenneth M. Stampp, *The Peculiar Institution: Slavery in the Ante-Bellum South* (New York: Vintage, 1956), 386; Herbert G. Gutman, *The Black Family in Slavery and Freedom, 1750–1925* (New York: Vintage, 1976), 155–67; Mark Twain, *A Connecticut Yankee in King Arthur's Court* (New York: Harper, 1917), esp. 102, 119, 186–90, 298–99.

11. Gutman, *Black Family in Slavery and Freedom*, 155–59; Eric Foner, *Reconstruction: America's Unfinished Revolution, 1863–1877* (New York: Harper and Row, 1988), 376.

CHAPTER I: THE EDGES OF THE EMPIRE

1. This was not the first time that Europeans gave Native Americans as gifts. In March 1493 Christopher Columbus returned to Lisbon with Indian

prisoners and advice for the king and queen on enslaving the indigenous peoples of the Americas. As early as 1500 Bristol merchants had brought home three men from Newfoundland. French sailors seized a woman and a child in 1567 and brought them to Zeeland. In 1576 Captain Martin Frobisher took an Inuit man to London, where the prisoner committed suicide. A year later Frobisher returned to Bristol with a young Inuit woman called Arnaq, her infant child, Nutaaq, and a young man named Kalicho. In 1584 English adventurers presented Manteo and Wanchese, two men from coastal Carolina, to Elizabeth I, whose reign saw the spread of public spectacles involving American Indians. By 1603, the year of her death, Londoners watched two Powhatans from Virginia row the Thames in canoes. Kidnapped Indians worked as guides and interpreters for colonial proprietors such as Walter Raleigh, of Virginia and Guyana, and Ferdinando Gorges, director of Maine. Tisquantum from Patuxet (Plymouth) was a victim of serial kidnappings. He was the fabled Squanto in the Pilgrim Thanksgiving story. After the 1603 ascendance of James I over Scotland, England, and Ireland—the grandfather of Sophia of Hanover—such "exotic souvenirs" were regularly exchanged. James's daughter, Princess Elizabeth, had a "Red Indian" theme for her marriage. In 1616 Pocahontas arrived in London as a dignitary, marking a shift in the perception and treatment of Native delegations. *Publications of the Colonial Society of Massachusetts* (Boston: By the Society, 1920), XX:99–100; Alden T. Vaughan, *Transatlantic Encounters: American Indians in Britain, 1500–1776* (Cambridge: Cambridge University Press, 2006), 1–112; Robert Zemsky, *Merchants, Farmers, and River Gods: An Essay on Eighteenth-Century American Politics* (Boston: Gambit, 1971), 102–4; Susi Colin, "The Wild Man and the Indian in Early 16th Century Book Illustration," in Christian F. Feest, ed., *Indians and Europe: An Interdisciplinary Collection of Essays* (Lincoln: University of Nebraska Press, 1999), 5–29; Oliver Dunn and James E. Kelley Jr., trans., *The Diario of Christopher Columbus's First Voyage to America, 1492–1493, Abstracted by Fray Bartolomé De Las Casas* (Norman: University of Oklahoma Press, 1989), 394–95; Luis N. Rivera, *A Violent Evangelism: The Political and Religious Conquest of the Americas* (Louisville, KY: Westminster/John Knox, 1991), 93–98; William C. Sturtevant and David Beers Quinn, "This New Prey: Eskimos in Europe in 1567, 1576, and 1577," in Feest, ed., *Indians and Europe*, 61–112, 113n; Dagmar Wernitznig, *Europe's Indians, Indians in Europe: European Perceptions and Appropriations of Native American Cultures from Pocahontas to the Present* (Lanham, MD: University Press of America, 2007), esp. 1–5; William Bradford, *Of Plimoth Plantation, 1620–1647* (Boston: Wright and Potter, State Printers, 1898), 114–23; James Rosier, *A True Relation of the Most Prosperous Voyage Made This Present Yeere 1605, by Captaine George Waymouth, in the Discovery of the Land of Virginia: Where He Discovered 60*

Miles Up a Most Excellent River; Together with a Most Fertile Land (London: George Bishop, 1605); Thomas Gorges to Sir Ferdinando Gorges, 19 May 1642, in Robert E. Moody, ed., *The Letters of Thomas Gorges: Deputy Governor of the Province of Maine, 1640–1643* (Portland: Maine Historical Society, 1978), 94–95; Walter Raleigh, *The Discoverie of the Large, Rich and Beautiful Empire of Guiana, with a Relation of the Great and Golden City of Manoa (Which the Spaniards Call El Dorado)* . . . (London: Robert Robinson, 1596); Paula Gunn Allen, *Pocahontas: Medicine Woman, Spy, Entrepreneur, Diplomat* (New York: HarperCollins, 2004); Camilla Townsend, *Pocahontas and the Powhatan Dilemma* (New York: Hill and Wang, 2004); 107–58; Christian F. Feest, "Pride and Prejudice: The Pocahontas Myth and the Pamunkey," in James A. Clifton, ed., *The Invented Indian: Cultural Fictions and Government Policies* (New Brunswick, NJ: Transaction, 1990), 49–52.

2. Boston's Latin School opened in 1635. Lorenzo J. Greene, "Slave-holding New England and Its Awakening," *Journal of Negro History*, October 1928, 496–97. The college was under its 1642 organization, which included the governor among the overseers. Obituary for Andrew Belcher, *Boston News-Letter*, 4 November 1717; Henry F. Jenks, *Catalogue of the Boston Public Latin School, Established in 1635, With an Historical Sketch* (Boston: Boston Latin School Association, 1886), 41–43; *Harvard University Quinquennial Catalogue of the Officers and Graduates, 1636–1920* (Cambridge, MA: By the University, 1930), 13, 141; Michael C. Batinski, *Jonathan Belcher, Colonial Governor* (Lexington: University Press of Kentucky, 1996), 167–70.

3. John Langdon Sibley, *Biographical Sketches of the Graduates of Harvard University, in Cambridge, Massachusetts* (1881; Boston: Massachusetts Historical Society, 1996), IV:446–48; Zemsky, *Merchants, Farmers, and River Gods*, 99–128; entries for 13 October 1748 and 24 September–7 May 1755, "The Minutes of the Proceedings of the Trustees of the College of New Jersey," vol. I, Seeley G. Mudd Manuscript Library, Princeton University.

4. The college in Cambridge (Newtown) was renamed Harvard in 1639. Yale was founded in Killingsworth (Clinton), Connecticut, in 1701, removed to Saybrook in 1707, and then relocated to New Haven in 1716. The College of New Jersey was founded in Elizabethtown (Elizabeth), New Jersey, in 1746. It was moved to Newark the following year, and then relocated to Princeton in 1756. Donald G. Tewksbury, *The Founding of American Colleges and Universities Before the Civil War with Particular Reference to the Religious Influences Bearing upon the College Movement* (New York: Teachers College, 1932), 32–33; Frank B. Dexter, "The Removal of Yale College to New Haven in October, 1716," *Papers of the New Haven Colony Historical Society* (New Haven: For the Society, 1918), IX:70–89; entries from the founding of the Collegiate School to its removal to New Haven, "Yale

University Corporation and Prudential Committee Minutes," 2–23, Manuscripts and Archives, Yale University Library.

5. John Tate Lanning, *Academic Culture in the Spanish Colonies* (New York: Oxford University Press, 1940), 3–15; *Discurso del Licenciado Julio Ortega Frier, Rector de la Universidad de Santo Domingo, Pronunciado en el Acto Académico Celebrado el 28 de Octubre de 1938 con Motivo del Cuarto Centenario de la Erección de la Universidad* (Santo Domingo: Listin Diario, 1938), 3–9; Antonio Valle Llano, *La Compañía de Jesús en Santo Domingo durante el Período Hispanico* (1950; Santo Domingo: Academia Dominicana de la Historia, 2011), 51–75; Sergio Mendez-Arceo, *La Real y Pontificia Universidad de Mexico: Antecedentes, Tramitacion y Despacho de las Reales Cedulas de Ereccion* (Mexico: Consejo de Humanidades, 1952), 13–39; Alberto Maria Carreño, *La Real y Pontificia Universidad de México, 1536–1865* (Mexico: Universidad Nacional Autónoma de México, 1961), 13–39; John J. Martinez, *Not Counting the Cost: Jesuit Missionaries in Colonial Mexico—A Story of Struggle, Commitment, and Sacrifice* (Chicago: Loyola Press, 2001); Luis Martin, *The Intellectual Conquest of Peru: The Jesuit College of San Pablo, 1568–1767* (New York: Fordham University Press, 1968), 1–6, 25–31; *La Universidad Nacional Mayor de San Marcos: IV Centenario de la Fundacion de la Universidad Real y Pontificia y de Su Vigorosa Continuidad Historia* (Lima: 1950), 7–31; David Rubio, *La Universidad de San Marcos de Lima durante la Colonización Española* (Madrid: Juan Bravo, 1933), 7; Luis Antonio Eguiguren, *Catalogo Historico del Claustro de la Universidad de San Marcos, 1576–1800* (Lima: Progreso Editorial, 1912); Instituto Colombiano para el Fomento de la Educacion Superior, *La Educacion Superior en Colombia: Documentos Basicos para Su Planeamiento* (Bogota, 1970).

6. Hugh Thomas, *The Slave Trade: The Story of the Atlantic Slave Trade, 1440–1870* (New York: Simon and Schuster, 1997), 98–103; Edward Gaylord Bourne, *Spain in America, 1450–1850* (New York: Harper and Brothers, 1904), 269–73; Jesús Guanche, "Cuba en el Tráfico Esclavista Transamericano y Caribeño a Través de las Denominaciones de Procedencia," 57–73, in *La Ruta del Esclavo* (Santo Domingo: Comisión Nacional de la Ruta del Esclavo, 2006); Marta Espejo-Ponce Hunt, "Colonial Yucatán: Town and Region in the Seventeenth Century," Ph.D. diss., University of California, Los Angeles, 1974, 91–98; Mathew Restall, *The Black Middle: Africans, Mayas, and Spaniards in Colonial Yucatan* (Stanford, CA: Stanford University Press, 2009), 26–33; Herbert S. Klein, *African Slavery in Latin America and the Caribbean* (New York: Oxford University Press, 1986), 28–33.

7. African students attended San Pablo in the sixteenth century and the faculty even made attempts at codifying and teaching African languages, but the protests of leading Spanish families soon drove black people from

the student body. By the eighteenth century colonists and clergy had elaborated racial barriers, including purity tests, at all of the colleges and universities in New Spain. Martin, *Intellectual Conquest of Peru*, 36–70; Frederick P. Bowser, *The African Slave in Colonial Peru, 1524–1650* (Stanford, CA: Stanford University Press, 1974), 90, 230–32, 245, 269, 312–13; Kendall W. Brown, "Jesuit Wealth and Economic Activity within the Peruvian Economy: The Case of Colonial Southern Peru," *The Americas*, July 1987, 26–41; Nicholas P. Cushner, "Slave Mortality and Reproduction on Jesuit Haciendas in Colonial Peru," *Hispanic American Historical Review*, May 1975, 178, 180–99; K. V. Fox, "Pedro Muniz, Dean of Lima, and the Indian Labor Question (1603)," *Hispanic American Historical Review*, February 1962, 63–68; Lanning, *Academic Culture in the Spanish Colonies*, 38–42; Rivera, *A Violent Evangelism*, 90–112, 180–95.

8. Henry Warner Bowden, *American Indians and Christian Missions: Studies in Cultural Conflict* (Chicago: University of Chicago Press, 1981), 75–78; Rev. P. F. X. De Charlevoix, *History and General Description of New France*, trans. John Gilmary Shea (New York: Francis P. Harper, 1900), II:55–90; J. M. Le Moine, "Jesuits' College, Quebec," *Canadian Antiquarian and Numismatic Journal*, October 1878, 58; Daniel Royot, *Divided Loyalties in a Doomed Empire: The French in the West from New France to the Lewis and Clark Expedition* (Newark: University of Delaware Press, 2007), 20–23; A. J. Macdougall, "Classical Studies in Seventeenth-Century Quebec," *Phoenix*, Spring 1952, 6–21; Samuel Eliot Morison, *Samuel de Champlain: Father of New France* (Boston: Little, Brown, 1972), 216–17; David Hackett Fischer, *Champlain's Dream: The Visionary Adventurer Who Made a New World in Canada* (New York: Simon and Schuster, 2008), 345–478; Thomas Guthrie Marquis, *The Jesuit Missions: A Chronicle of the Cross in the Wilderness* (Toronto: Glasgow, Brook, 1916), 44–67; Francis Parkman, *The Jesuits in North America in the Seventeenth Century* (Boston: Little, Brown, 1867), 167–68; Nöel Baillargeon, *Le Séminaire de Québec sous L'Épiscopat de Mgr de Laval* (Québec: Presses de l'Université Laval, 1972), 4–88.

9. Earlier in the century, a free African Portuguese man, Mathieu da Costa, served as interpreter for the governor of Acadia, Nova Scotia, to the Micmac nation. There is a disagreement over whether Olivier Le Jeune was sold or presented to Father Le Jeune. David Geggus, "The French Slave Trade: An Overview," *William and Mary Quarterly*, January 2001, 119–38; Robert Harms, *The Diligent: A Voyage Through the Worlds of the Slave Trade* (New York: Basic Books, 2002), 32–41; Robin W. Winks, *The Blacks in Canada: A History*, 2nd ed. (Montreal: McGill-Queen's University Press, 1997), 2–6; Paul Le Jeune, *Brief Relation of the Journey to New France, Made in the Month of April Last by Father Paul le Jeune, of the Society of Jesus* (Paris: Sebastian Cramoisy, 1632), in Reuben Gold Thwaites, *Jesuit*

Relations and Allied Documents (Cleveland: Burrows Brothers, 1897), V:62–63; Morison, *Samuel de Champlain*, 216–17; George Hendrick and Willene Hendrick, *Black Refugees in Canada: Accounts of Escape During the Era of Slavery* (Jefferson, NC: McFarland, 2010), 4.

10. Brett Rushforth, "'A Little Flesh We Offer You': The Origins of Indian Slavery in New France," *William and Mary Quarterly*, October 2003, 777–808; Le Jeune, *Brief Relation of the Journey to New France*, 70–73; James Cleland Hamilton, "The Panis—An Historical Outline of Canadian Indian Slavery in the Eighteenth Century," *Proceedings of the Canadian Institute*, February 1897, 19–27; Francis Parkman, *France and England in North America: A Series of Historical Narratives*, (Boston: Little, Brown, 1877), IV:388; James Cleland Hamilton, "Slavery in Canada," *Transactions of the Canadian Institute* 1 (1889–90): 102–8; H. Clare Pentland, *Labour and Capital in Canada, 1650–1860* (Toronto: James Lorimer, 1981), 1–2; Brett Rushforth, *Bonds of Alliance: Indigenous and Atlantic Slaveries in New France* (Chapel Hill: University of North Carolina Press, 2012), esp. 9–10.

11. Scott Mandelbrote, "All Souls from Civil War to Glorious Revolution," in S. J. D. Green and Peregrine Horden, eds., *All Souls Under the Ancien Régime: Politics, Learning and the Arts, c. 1600–1850* (Oxford: Oxford University Press, 2007), 60–65; Thomas Richards, *The Puritan Visitation of Jesus College Oxford and the Principalship of Dr. Michael Roberts, 1648–1657* (London: Honourable Society of Cymmrodorion, 1924); G. B. Tatham, *The Puritans in Power: A Study in the History of the English Church from 1640–1660* (Cambridge: University Press, 1913), 93–197; Rebecca Seward Rolph, "Emmanuel College, Cambridge, and the Puritan Movements of Old and New England," Ph.D. diss., University of Southern California, Department of History, June 1979, esp. 321–26.

12. James I, 26 February 1615, and Archbishop Tobias Matthew, 26 April 1616, in Paul Walne, "The Collections for Henrico College, 1616–1618," *Virginia Magazine of History and Biography*, July 1972, 259–66; Lyon Gardiner Tyler, *The College of William and Mary in Virginia: Its History and Work, 1693–1907* (Richmond: Whittet and Shepperson, 1907), 3; Alexander Whitaker, *Good Newes from Virginia: Sent to the Counsell and Company of Virginia. From Alexander Whitaker, the Minister of Henrico in Virginia. Wherein Also Is a Narration of the Present State of that Countrey, and Our Colonies There. Perused and Published by Direction from that Counsell. And a Preface Prefixed of Some Matters Touching that Plantation, Very Requisite to Be Made Knowne* (London: Felix Kyngston, 1613); Robert Hunt Land, "Henrico and Its College," *William and Mary Quarterly*, October 1938, 459–87.

13. "By His Maiesties Counseil for Virginia," 6, "A Note of the Shipping, Men, and Provisions Sent to Virginia, by the Treasurer and Company in the Yeere, 1619," 3, "Orders and Constitutions, Partly Collected Out of

His Maiesties Letters Patents, and Partly Ordained upon Mature Delib-
eration, by the Treasuror, Counseil and Companie of Virginia for the
Better Governing of the Actions and Affaires of the Said Companie Here
in England Residing. Anno 1619 and 1620," 13, 36–37, all in *A Declaration
of the State of the Colonie and Affaires in Virginia: With the Names of the Ad-
venturors, and Summes Adventured in that Action* (London: T. S., 1620); see
the 26 May 1619 order of the Virginia Company relating to the Henrico
college, in R. A. Brock, ed., *Abstract of the Proceedings of the Virginia Company of London, 1619–1624, Prepared from the Records in the Library of Congress by Conway Robinson* (Richmond: Virginia Historical Society, 1888),
I:6–9, 50n–51n; Land, "Henrico and Its College," 469–98; John S. Flory,
"The University of Henrico," *Publications of the Southern History Association*, January 1904, 40–52; Edmund S. Morgan, *American Slavery, American Freedom: The Ordeal of Colonial Virginia* (New York: Norton, 1975), 98;
Tyler, *College of William and Mary*, 3–6; *The History of the College of William
and Mary from Its Foundation, 1660, to 1874* (Richmond: J. W. Randolph
and English, 1874), 34; Edward D. Neill, *Memoir of Rev. Patrick Copland:
Rector Elect of the First Projected College in the United States, A Chapter of the
English Colonization of America* (New York: Charles Scribner, 1871), 15–21,
81–82; H. C. Porter, *The Inconstant Savage: England and the North American Indian, 1500–1660* (London: Duckworth, 1979), 434–50.

14. Land, "Henrico and Its College," 469–98; Neill, *Memoir of Rev. Patrick
Copland*, 15–21, 81–82; Patrick Copland, *Virginia's God be Thanked, or A
Sermon of Thanksgiving for the Happie Successe of the Affayres in Virginia This
Last Yeare. Preached by Patrick Copland at the Bow-Church in Cheapside,
before the Honorable Virginia Company, on Thursday, the 18. Of April 1622.
And Now Published by the Commandment of the Said Honorable Company.
Hereunto are adjoyned some Epistles, written first in Latine (and now En-
glished in the East Indies by Peter Pope, an Indian Youth, borne in the Bay of
Bengala, who was first taught and converted by the said P.C. And after bap-
tized by Master John Wood, Dr. in Divinitie, in a famous Assembly before the
Right Worshipful East India Company, at S. Dems in Fan-Church Streete in
London, December 22, 1616* (London: I.D., 1622); J. Frederick Fausz, "The
Powhatan Uprising of 1622: A Historical Study of Ethnocentrism and
Cultural Conflict," Ph.D. diss., Department of History, College of Wil-
liam and Mary, 1977; Harry Thomas Stock, "A Résumé of Christian Missions Among the American Indians," *American Journal of Theology*, July
1920, 369.

15. Increase Mather, father of Cotton Mather, served Harvard College as
acting president from 1685 to 1686, as rector from 1686 to 1692, and again
as president from 1692 to 1701. Richard Hofstadter, *Academic Freedom in
the Age of the College* (New York: Columbia University Press, 1961), 82–83;
Robert H. Murray, *Dublin University and the New World: A Memorial*

Discourse Preached in the Chapel of Trinity College, Dublin, May 23, 1921 (London: Society for Promoting Christian Knowledge, 1921); Samuel Eliot Morison, *Builders of the Bay Colony* (Boston: Houghton Mifflin, 1930), 269–88.

16. Samuel Eliot Morison, "The History of Harvard College," in *The History and Traditions of Harvard College* (Cambridge, MA: Harvard Crimson, 1936), esp. 11–12; Rolph, "Emmanuel College, Cambridge, and the Puritan Movements," 334.

17. *New England's First Fruits; In Respect, First of the Conversion of Some, Conversion of Divers Others, Preparation of Sundry of the Indians. 2. Of the Progresse of Learning, in the Colledge at Cambridge in Massachusetts Bay. With Other Special Matters Concerning that Country* (London: R.O. and G.D. for Henry Overton, 1643); Michael P. Clark, *The Eliot Tracts: With Letter from John Eliot to Thomas Thorowgood and Richard Baxter* (Westport, CT: Praeger, 2003); George Parker Winship, *The Eliot Indian Tracts* (Cambridge, MA: Harvard University Press, 1925).

18. Kathleen J. Bragdon, *Native People of Southern New England, 1500–1650* (Norman: University of Oklahoma Press, 1996), 23–28; John D. Daniels, "The Indian Population of North America," *William and Mary Quarterly*, April 1992, 298–320; S. F. Cook, *The Indian Population of New England in the Seventeenth Century* (Berkeley: University of California Press, 1976), 1–12; John Eliot and Thomas Mayhew, *Tears of Repentance: Or, a Further Narrative of the Progress of the Gospel Amongst the Indians in New England . . .* (London: Peter Cole, 1653), esp. 33–36.

19. "An Act for the Promoting and Propagating the Gospel of Jesus Christ in New England" (1649).

20. Charles Firth, *Oliver Cromwell and the Rule of the Puritans in England* (New York: G. P. Putnam, 1900), 394–406; "Cash in the Hands of Mr. Richard Floyd, Trea[sur]er of the Corporation for New England," Corporation for New England Records, 1653–1685, Box 1, Massachusetts Historical Society; William Kellaway, *The New England Company, 1649–1776* (London: Longmans, 1961); see "To the Christian Reader," in Henry Whitfield, *Strength out of Weaknesse; Or a Glorious Manifestation of the Further Progresse of the Gospel among the Indians of New-England. Held Forth in Sundry Letters from Divers Ministers and Others to the Corporation Established by Parliament for Promoting the Gospel among the Heathen in New-England; And to Particular Members thereof Since the Last Treatise to that Effect* (London: M. Simmons for John Blague, 1652); C. V. Wedgwood, *A Coffin for King Charles: The Trial and Execution of Charles I* (New York: Macmillan, 1964); Maurice Ashley, *Charles I and Oliver Cromwell: A Study in Contrasts and Comparisons* (London: Methuen, 1987); Jill Lepore, *The Name of War: King Philip's War and the Origins of American Identity* (New York: Knopf, 1998), 34–35.

21. Harvard College was incorporated in 1650. William B. Weeden, *Economic and Social History of New England, 1620–1789* (New York: Hillary House, 1963), I:41, 140; William B. Weeden, *Indian Money as a Factor in New England Civilization* (Baltimore: Johns Hopkins University Studies in Historical and Political Science, 1884), 24; *The Day-Breaking, If Not the Sun-Rising of the Gospell with the Indians in New-England* (London: Rich Cotes for Fulk Clifton, 1647), 24; Thomas Shepard, *The Clear Sun-shine of the Gospel Breaking Forth upon the Indians in New-England. Or, an Historicall Narration of Gods Wonderful Workings upon Sundry of the Indians, Both Chief Governors and Common-People, in Bringing Them to a Willing and Desired Submission to the Ordinances of the Gospel; and Framing Their Hearts to an Earnest Inquirie after the Knowledge of God the Father, and of Jesus Christ the Saviour of the World* (London: R. Cotes for John Bellamy, 1648), 6; Stock, "Résumé of Christian Missions Among the American Indians," 370; Benjamin Pierce, *A History of Harvard University, from Its Foundation, in the Year 1636, to the Period of the American Revolution* (Cambridge, MA: Brown, Shattuck, 1833), 28; Alden T. Vaughan, *New England Frontier: Puritans and Indians, 1620–1675* (1965; Norman: University of Oklahoma Press, 1995), 280–88; "Historical Sketches of Harvard College," *Harvard Register*, October 1827, 248; Samuel Eliot Morison, *Harvard College in the Seventeenth Century* (Cambridge, MA: Harvard University Press, 1936), I:5–8, 42–44, 340–60.

22. Charles Chauncy, *God's Mercy, Shewed to His People in Giving Them a Faithful Ministry and Schooles of Learning for the Continual Supplyes Thereof* (Cambridge: Samuel Green, 1655), esp. 20. The boys were tested in 1659 and 1660. John Eliot, *A Further Accompt of the Progresse of the Gospel amongst the Indians in New-England, and of the Means used Effectually to Advance the Same. Set Forth in Certaine Letters Sent from Thence Declaring a Purpose of Printing the Scriptures in the Indian Tongue into Which They Are Already Translated* (London: M. Simmons for the Corporation of New-England, 1659), postscript; John Eliot, *A Further Account of the Progress of the Gospel amongst the Indians in New England: Being a Relation of the Confessions Made by Several Indians (in the Presence of the Elders and Members of Several Churches) in Order to Their Admission into Church-Fellowship* (London: John Macock, 1660), postscript; Morison, *Harvard College in the Seventeenth Century*, I:354.

23. Daniel Mandell, "'To Live More Like My Christian English Neighbors': Natick Indians in the Eighteenth Century," *William and Mary Quarterly*, October 1991, 555; *New England's First Fruits*, 2–3; Edward Winslow, *The Glorious Progress of the Gospell, Amongst the Indians of New England. Manifested by Three Letters, under the Hand of That Famous Instrument of the Lord Mr. John Eliot, and Another from Mr. Thomas Mayhew Jun: Both Preachers of the Word, as Well to the English as Indians in New England* (London: For

Hannah Allen, 1649), 7–8; Neal Salisbury, "Red Puritans: The 'Praying Indians' of Massachusetts Bay and John Eliot," *William and Mary Quarterly*, January 1974, 32–48; Stock, "Résumé of Christian Missions Among the American Indians," 372–73; Harral Ayres, *The Great Trail of New England* (Boston: Meador, 1940), 33–34; John Eliot, *A Late and Further Manifestation of the Progress of the Gospel amongst the Indians in New-England. Declaring Their Constant Love and Zeal to the Truth: With a Readinesse to Give Accompt of Their Faith and Hope; as of Their Desires in Church Communion to Be Partakers of the Ordinances of Christ* (London: M.S., 1655), 4; Daniel Gookin, *Historical Collections of the Indians in New England, of Their Several Nations, Numbers, Customs, Manners, Religion and Government, before the English Planted There* (Boston: Belknap and Hall, 1792), 55–67; John Eliot to Robert Boyle, 6 July 1669, in Michael Hunter, et al., eds., *The Correspondence of Robert Boyle* (London: Pickering and Chatto, 2001), IV:137–40.

24. "The Lawes of the Colledge Published Publiquely Before the Students of Harvard College, May 4, 1655," *Publications of the Colonial Society of Massachusetts* (Boston: By the Society, 1935), XXXI:229–33; Ann M. Little, "'Shoot That Rogue, for He Hath an Englishman's Coat On!': Cultural Cross-Dressing on the New England Frontier, 1620–1760," *New England Quarterly*, June 2001, 239–48; Timothy J. Shannon, "Dressing for Success on the Mohawk Frontier: Hendrick, William Johnson, and the Indian Fashion," *William and Mary Quarterly*, January 1996; Gookin, *Historical Collections of the Indians in New England*, 32–36.

25. The trustees buried Benjamin Larnel with money from the fund for Indian education. Peter Burke, *Languages and Communities in Early Modern Europe* (Cambridge: Cambridge University Press, 2004), 15–33; Benedict Anderson, *Imagined Communities: Reflections on the Origin and Spread of Nationalism* (London: Verso, 1991), 77–80; Morison, *Harvard College in the Seventeenth Century*, I:352–57; Josiah Quincy, *The History of Harvard University* (Cambridge, MA: J. Owen, 1840), I:443–44; entry for 27 September 1714, Records of the Harvard Corporation, 1650–1992, I:96, Harvard University Archives. On the manipulations and deception in the publication of these Indian addresses and letters, see Wolfgang Hochbruck and Beatrix Dudensing-Reichel, "'Honoratissimi Benefactores': Native American Students and Two Seventeenth-Century Texts in the University Tradition," *Studies in American Indian Literatures*, Summer/Fall 1992, 42–44.

26. Samuel G. Drake, ed., *The History of King Philip's War, by the Rev. Increase Mather D.D. Also, a History of the Same War, by the Rev. Cotton Mather, D.D.* (Albany, NY: J. Munsell, 1862), 37–43. The translation is available in Hochbruck and Dudensing-Reichel, "'Honoratissimi Benefactores,'" 38–39.

27. George Francis Dow, *Slave Ships and Slaving* (1927; Mineola, NY: Dover, 2002), 267; "Notes on Early Ship-Building in Massachusetts, Communicated by Capt. George Henry Preble," *New-England Historical and Genealogical Register and Antiquarian Journal*, January 1871, 17; James Kendall Hosmer, ed., *Winthrop's Journal, 1630–1649* (New York: Charles Scribner's Sons, 1908), I:227–28; Greene, "Slave-holding New England and Its Awakening," 496; David Jaffee, *People of the Washusett: Greater New England in History and Memory, 1630–1860* (Ithaca, NY: Cornell University Press, 1999), 64–68; Henry C. Kittredge, *Cape Cod: Its People and Their History* (1930; Boston: Houghton Mifflin, 1968), 63; Katherine A. Grandjean, "New World Tempests; Environment, Scarcity, and the Coming of the Pequot War," *William and Mary Quarterly*, January 2011, 75–100.

28. Samuel Maverick—an Anglican minister from a family that settled Noddle's Island and Dorchester—bought three of these enslaved black people. Hosmer, ed., *Winthrop's Journal*, I:260; Peter Oliver, *The Puritan Commonwealth: An Historical Overview of the Puritan Government in Massachusetts in Its Civil and Ecclesiastical Relations from Its Rise to the Abrogation of Its First Charter* (Boston: Little, Brown, 1856), 419; Dow, *Slave Ships and Slaving*, 267; Daniel C. Eaton, "The Family of Nathaniel Eaton, of Cambridge, Mass." *Papers of the New Haven Colony Historical Society* (New Haven: For the Society, 1888), IV:185–92; Samuel Eliot Morison, *The Founding of Harvard College* (Cambridge, MA: Harvard University Press, 1935), 231–40, 389; Morison, "History of Harvard College," 11–13.

29. Morison, *Founding of Harvard College*, 231–40; Hosmer, ed., *Winthrop's Journal*, I:310–14; Morison, *Builders of the Bay Colony*, 188–92.

30. Morison, *Harvard College in the Seventeenth Century*, I:31–39; Vaughan, *Transatlantic Encounters*, 99; Hosmer, ed., *Winthrop's Journal*, I:221–28.

31. Hosmer, ed., *Winthrop's Journal*, II:227; George Downing to John Winthrop Jr., 26 August 1645, *Collections of the Massachusetts Historical Society*, Series 4 (Boston: For the Society, 1863), VI:536; Robert C. Winthrop, *Life and Letters of John Winthrop, from His Embarkation for New England in 1630, with the Charter Company of the Massachusetts Bay, to His Death in 1649* (Boston: Little, Brown, 1869), II:263, 360–61; Quincy, *History of Harvard University*, I:459; *Sibley's Harvard Graduates*, I:1; E. T. Fisher, trans., *Report of a French Protestant Refugee, in Boston, 1687* (Brooklyn, NY, 1868), 20.

32. George Downing to John Winthrop Jr., 26 August 1645; Karen Ordahl Kupperman, "Errand to the Indies: Puritan Colonization from Providence Island Through the Western Design," *William and Mary Quarterly*, January 1988, 70–99; Karen Ordahl Kupperman, *Providence Island, 1630–1641: The Other Puritan Colony* (Cambridge: Cambridge University Press, 1993), esp. 171–80; *Sibley's Harvard Graduates*, I:28–51; Richard S. Dunn, *Sugar and Slaves: The Rise of the Planter Class in the English West Indies,*

1624–1713 (New York: Norton, 1973), 84–87, 336; Winthrop, *Life and Letters of John Winthrop*, II:360–61.

33. George Downing to John Winthrop Jr., 26 August 1645; Jeremiah Dummer, *A Defence of the New-England Charters* (Boston: B. Green, 1745), 6–7; Weeden, *Economic and Social History of New England*, I:148–49, 244–45.

34. Edgar J. McManus, *Black Bondage in the North* (Syracuse, NY: Syracuse University Press, 1973), 72–87; Cotton Mather, *An Abstract of the Lawes in the Province of the Massachusetts-Bay, New-England, Against those Disorders, the Suppression whereof is Desired and Pursued by Them that Wish Well to the Worthy Designs of Reformation* (Boston: Timothy Green, 1704); *A Report of the Record Commissioners of the City of Boston, Containing the Records of Boston Selectmen, 1716–1736* (Boston: Rockwell and Churchill, 1885), 8–9, 42–43, 59–60, 82–83, 109; Charles J. Hoadly, ed., *The Public Records of the Colony of Connecticut, from May, 1762, to October, 1767, inclusive* (Hartford, CT: Case, Lockwood, and Brainard, 1850–), IV:32–41, 375–76, 437–38, V:52–53, VI:390–91; Abner Cheney Goodell Jr., *The Trial and Execution, for Petit Treason, of Mark and Phillis, Slaves of Capt. John Codman, Who Murdered Their Master at Charlestown, Mass., in 1755; for Which the Man Was Hanged and Gibbeted, and the Woman Was Burned to Death. Including, also, Some Account of Other Punishments by Burning in Massachusetts* (Cambridge, MA: John Wilson and Son, 1883), 30–33; "The Case of Maria in the Court of Assistants in 1681," *Transactions: Publications of the Colonial Society of Massachusetts* (Boston: By the Society, 1904), VI:323–36; see entries for slave sales in the *Boston News-Letter* from April 1704 through April 1714.

35. At the outbreak of the Haitian Revolution, the New England merchant George Cabot, a Harvard benefactor, warned Alexander Hamilton that the United States economy could not survive the loss of its French West Indian markets, where "nearly one half of the whole fish is consumed." W. E. B. DuBois, *The Suppression of the African Slave-Trade to the United States of America 1638–1870* (New York: Longmans, Green, 1904), 27–29; Samuel Eliot Morison, *The Maritime History of Massachusetts, 1783–1860* (Boston: Houghton Mifflin, 1921), 11–12; John Romeyn Brodhead, *History of the State of New York* (New York: Harper and Brothers, 1871), II:337; Henry W. Cunningham, "Note on William Sanford," *Publications of the Colonial Society of Massachusetts* (Boston: Privately published, 1905), VII:203; Eugene Aubrey Stratton, *Plymouth Colony: Its History and People, 1620–1691* (Salt Lake City, UT: Ancestry, 1986), 187–89; Greene, "Slaveholding New England and Its Awakening," 496–97; S. D. Smith, *Slavery, Family, and Gentry Capitalism in the British Atlantic: The World of the Lascelles, 1648–1834* (Cambridge: Cambridge University Press, 2006), esp. 21; Cabot to Hamilton, 18 December 1791, in Henry Cabot Lodge, *Life and Letters of George Cabot* (Boston: Little, Brown, 1877), 48–51; Quincy, *History of Harvard University*, vol. II, appendices.

36. H. P. Biggar, *The Early Trading Companies of New France* (New York: Argonaut, 1965), 66–93.

37. Brock, ed., *Abstract of the Proceedings of the Virginia Company of London, 1619–1624*, I:9n–10n; Fausz, "Powhatan Uprising of 1622," esp. 278–343.

38. *New England's First Fruits*, Parts 1–2.

39. George F. Willison, *Saints and Strangers: Being the Lives of the Pilgrim Fathers & Their Families, with Their Friends & Foes; & an Account of Their Posthumous Wanderings in Limbo, Their Final Resurrection & Rise to Glory, & the Strange Pilgrimages of Plymouth Rock* (New York: Reynal and Hitchcock, 1945), 198–99; Morison, *Builders of the Bay Colony*, 13; Bradford Smith, *Bradford of Plymouth* (Philadelphia: J. B. Lippincott, 1951), 166–67; J. Franklin Jameson, ed., *Johnson's Wonder-Working Providence, 1628–1651* (New York: Charles Scribner's Sons, 1910), 33–36. The latter was originally published in England as Edward Johnson, *A History of New-England, From the English Planting in the Yeere 1628 Until the Yeere 1652* . . . (London: Nathaniel Brooke, 1654).

40. Ian K. Steele, *Warpaths: Invasions of North America* (New York: Oxford University Press, 1994), 91–93; Laurence M. Hauptman, "The Pequot War and Its Legacies," in Laurence M. Hauptman and James D. Wherry, eds., *The Pequots in Southern New England: The Fall and Rise of an American Indian Nation* (Norman: University of Oklahoma Press, 1990), 69–80; Colin G. Calloway, *New Worlds for All: Indians, Europeans, and the Remaking of Early America* (Baltimore: Johns Hopkins University Press, 1997), 92–98; John Underhill, *Newes from America; or, a New and Experimentall Discoverie of New England; Containing a True Relation of Their War-like Proceedings these Two Years Last Past, with a Figure of the Indian Fort, or Palizado* (London: J.D. for Peter Cole, 1638), 39.

41. Samuel de Champlain used firearms during the Battle of Lake Champlain in 1609, likely the first use of such weapons in the Northeast. David E. Jones, *Native North American Armor, Shields, and Fortifications* (Austin: University of Texas Press, 2004), 48–49; Captain John Underhill, "The Pequot War (1635)," in John Gould Curtis, ed., *American History Told by Contemporaries: Era of Colonization, 1492–1689* (New York: Macmillan, 1917), I:439–44; Alfred A. Cave, *The Pequot War* (Amherst, MA: University of Massachusetts Press, 1996), esp. 13–48; Harold L. Peterson, *Arms and Armor in Colonial America, 1526–1783* (Harrisburg, PA: Stackpole, 1956), 7–49, 69–82; Steele, *Warpaths*, 91–93; Margaret Connell Szasz, *Scottish Highlanders and Native Americans: Indigenous Education in the Eighteenth-Century Atlantic World* (Norman: University of Oklahoma Press, 2007), 187–89; Hauptman, "The Pequot War and Its Legacies," 69–80; James Shepard, *Connecticut Soldiers in the Pequot War of 1637, with Proof of Service, a Brief Record for Identification, and References to Various Publications in Which Further Data May Be Found* (Meriden, CT: Journal

Publishing, 1913); Calloway, *New Worlds for All*, 92–98; Carl Parcher Russell, *Guns on the Early Frontiers: A History of Firearms from Colonial Times Through the Years of the Western Fur Trade* (Berkeley: University of California Press, 1957); Otis Tufton Mason, *North American Bows, Arrows, and Quivers*, Smithsonian Report for 1893 (Washington, DC: Government Printing Office, 1894). On the impact of guns on military institutions and social life in West Africa, see John K. Thornton, *Warfare in Atlantic Africa, 1500–1800* (London: University College London Press, 1999).

42. Morison, *Harvard College in the Seventeenth Century*, I:31–34; Margaret Ellen Newell, "The Changing Nature of Indian Slavery in New England, 1670–1720," in Colin G. Calloway and Neal Salisbury, eds., *Reinterpreting New England Indians and the Colonial Experience* (Boston: Colonial Society of Massachusetts, 2003), 107–9.

43. Salisbury, "Red Puritans," 29–36; Elise M. Brenner, "To Pray or Be Prey: That Is the Question: Strategies for Cultural Autonomy of Massachusetts Praying Towns," *Ethnohistory*, Spring 1980, 137–48.

44. John Winthrop to Robert Boyle, ca. 1662, and John Winthrop to Robert Boyle, 15 October 1674, in Hunter et al., eds., *Correspondence of Robert Boyle*, II:57–58, IV:393–94; Kellaway, *New England Company*, 173–74.

45. For a comprehensive account of the war, see Lepore, *Name of War*; John Easton, "A Relacion of the Indyan Warre" (1675), in Charles Henry Lincoln, ed., *Narratives of the Indian Wars, 1675–1699* (New York: Charles Scribner's Sons, 1913), 7–12; Morison, *Harvard College in the Seventeenth Century*, I:349, II:422n; David Pulsifer, ed., *Records of the Colony of New Plymouth in New England: Deeds, &c., 1620–1651* (Boston: William White, 1861), I:237.

46. In his history of the conflict, Cotton Mather praised an enslaved African for alerting the English of the Wampanoag plot. After the Wampanoag killed Thomas Willett, they captured his servant. Knowing Algonquian, the black man discovered their military plans. In July 1674 he escaped and alerted the English that the Indians were preparing to attack Taunton. "There was a special providence in that Negroes escape," Rev. Mather wrote, without reflecting upon the moral tension created by a captive slave escaping his captors to rescue his enslavers. Of course, such providence by definition favored the English, not Africans. Lepore, *Name of War*, 23–26; Drake, ed., *History of King Philip's War*, 177–78; Thomas Church, *The Entertaining History of King Philip's War, Which Began in the Month of June, 1675. As Also of Expeditions More Lately Made Against the Common Enemy, and Indian Rebels, in the Eastern Parts of New-England: With Some Account of the Divine Providence Towards Col. Benjamin Church* (Boston, 1716); "The Book of Indian Records for Their Lands," in Pulsifer, ed., *Records of the Colony of New Plymouth in New England*, I:237; Easton,

"Relacion of the Indyan Warre," 7–17; Samuel G. Drake, *The Book of the Indians of North America: Comprising Details in the Lives of About Five Hundred Chiefs and Others, the Most Distinguished among Them. Also, a History of Their Wars; their Manners and Customs; Speeches of Orators, &c., From Their First Being Known to Europeans to the Present Time. Exhibiting Also an Analysis of the Most Distinguished Authors Who Have Written upon the Great Question of the Peopling of America* (Boston: Josiah Drake, 1835), III:9–12; James P. Ronda and Jeanne Ronda, "The Death of John Sassamon: An Exploration in Writing New England Indian History," *American Indian Quarterly*, Summer 1974, 91–102; Jenny Hale Pulsipher, *Subjects unto the Same King: Indians, English, and the Contest for Authority in Colonial New England* (Philadelphia: University of Pennsylvania Press, 2007), 95–100; William Apess, *Eulogy on King Philip, as Pronounced at the Odeon, in Federal Street, Boston, by the Rev. William Apes, an Indian* (Boston: By the author, 1836); see the account book and notes, "Thomas Chesholme, His Booke, June 5 1655," *Publications of the Colonial Society of Massachusetts* (Boston: By the Society, 1935), XXXI:150n; Morison, *Harvard College in the Seventeenth Century*, I:352–54; minutes of the New England Company, 5 February 1659–19 March 1659, in *The New England Company of 1649 and John Eliot: The Publications of the Prince Society* (Boston: For the Society, 1920), 51–54.

47. Calloway, *New Worlds for All*, 96–97; Charles I, *By the King: A Proclamation Forbidding the Disorderly Trading with the Salvages in New England in America, Especially the Furnishing of the Natives in Those and Other Parts of America by the English with Weapons, and Habiliments of War* (London: Robert Barker, 1630); David Pulsifer, ed., *Records of the Colony of New Plymouth in New England: Laws, 1623–1682* (Boston: William White, 1861); Franklin Bowditch Dexter, ed., *Ancient Town Records: New Haven Town Records, 1649–1662* (New Haven: For the Society, 1917), I:174–75; "Ordinance of the Directors of New Netherland, Prohibiting the Sale of Firearms, etc., to Indians, and Requiring Vessels Sailing to or from Fort Orange, the South River, or Fort Hope, to Take Out Clearances," passed 31 March 1639, in E. B. O'Callaghan, comp., *Laws and Ordinances of New Netherland, 1638–1674. Compiled and Translated from the Original Dutch Records in the Office of the Secretary of State, Albany, N.Y.* (Albany, NY: Weed, Parsons, 1868), 18–19; Russell, *Guns on the Early Frontiers*, 10–12; Don Higginbotham, "The Military Institutions of Colonial America: The Rhetoric and the Reality," in John A. Lynn, ed., *Tools of War: Instruments, Ideas, and Institutions of Warfare, 1445–1871* (Urbana: University of Illinois Press, 1990), 136; Patrick M. Malone, "Changing Military Technology Among the Indians of Southern New England, 1600–1677," *American Quarterly*, March 1973, 50–63.

48. Morison, *Harvard College in the Seventeenth Century*, II:420–23. Also see Urian Oakes, "Salutatory Oration: Commencement 1677," *Publications of the Colonial Society of Massachusetts*, XXXI:405–36.

49. Several veterans of the Pequot Massacre participated in King Philip's War. Carole Doreski, ed., *Massachusetts Officers and Soldiers in the Seventeenth-Century Conflicts* (Boston: New England Historic Genealogical Society, 1982), 241; *Sibley's Harvard Graduates*, I:1, 194–208, II:13–36, 489–98; John Mason to Capt. Allyn, 27 April 1676, Wyllys Papers, 1633–1829, I:58B, Connecticut Historical Society; Eric B. Schultz and Michael J. Tougias, *King Philip's War: The History and Legacy of America's Forgotten Conflict* (Woodstock, VT: Countryman, 1999), 210–18; William Bradford, *A Letter from Major William Bradford to the Reverend John Cotton, Written at Mount Hope on July 21, 1675* . . . (Providence: Society of Colonial Wars in the State of Rhode Island and Providence Plantations, 1914); George Madison Bodge, *Soldiers in King Philip's War: Being a Critical Account of That War with a Concise History of the Indian Wars of New England from 1620–1677* . . . (Boston: For the author, 1906), 119–26, 218–31, 261–65.

50. *Sibley's Harvard Graduates*, I:318–19, 395, II:138–39, 193–95, 522–23; Bodge, *Soldiers in King Philip's War*, esp. 325–41; Mary White Rowlandson, *The Sovereignty and Goodness of God, together, with the Faithfulness of His Promises Displayed: Being a Narrative of the Captivity and Restauration of Mrs. Mary Rowlandson: Commended by Her, to all that Desires to Know the Lords Doings to, and Dealings with Her. Especially to Her Dear Children and Relations/ Written by Her Own Hand for Her Private Use, and Now Made Public at the Earnest Desire of Some Friends, and for the Benefits of the Afflicted* (Cambridge: Samuel Green, 1682); June Namias, *White Captives: Gender and Ethnicity on the American Frontier* (Chapel Hill: University of North Carolina Press, 1993), 7–29; Alden T. Vaughan and Edward W. Clark, eds., *Puritans Among the Indians: Accounts of Captivity and Redemption, 1676–1724* (Cambridge, MA: Belknap Press, 1981), 1–28.

51. In the aftermath of that deadly conflict, the praying towns declined in number. The English even neglected the Natick mission. In the next century, Cotton Mather visited the village "that we may Inspect the Condition of the Christian Indians there, and Revive Religion, and Good Order among them, which have been under a grievous Decay." Douglas William Leach, *A Rhode Islander Reports on King Philip's War: The Second William Harris Letter of August, 1676* (Providence: Rhode Island Historical Society, 1963), esp. 82–86; Richard Slotkin and James K. Folsom, eds., *So Dreadful a Judgment: Puritan Responses to King Philip's War, 1676–1677* (Middletown, CT: Wesleyan University Press, 1978), 370–76; *Plymouth Church Records, 1620–1859* (Baltimore: Genealogical Publishing Company, 1975), I:152–53; Church, *Entertaining History of King Philip's War*, esp. 190–94; Lyle Koehler, *A Search for Power: The "Weaker Sex" in*

Seventeenth Century New England (Urbana: University of Illinois Press, 1980), 112; Colin Calloway, ed., *After King Philip's War: Presence and Persistence in Indian New England* (Hanover, NH: University Press of New England, 1997), 1–3; Kristina Bross, *Dry Bones and Indian Sermons: Praying Indians in Colonial America* (Ithaca, NY: Cornell University Press, 2002), 186; *Report of a French Protestant Refugee, in Boston, 1687*, 40; William R. Manierre, ed., *The Diary of Cotton Mather D.D., F.R.S. for the Year 1712* (Charlottesville: University of Virginia Press, 1964), 53; Mandell, "'To Live More Like My Christian English Neighbors,'" 552–53; Increase Mather, *A Relation of the Troubles Which Have Happened in New-England, by Reason of the Indians There: From the Year 1614 to the Year 1675. Wherein the Frequent Conspiracies of the Indians to Cut Off the English, and the Wonderfull Providence of God, in Disappointing Their Devices, is Declared* (Boston: John Foster, 1677); Samuel A. Green, ed., *Diary of Increase Mather, March, 1675–December, 1676, Together with Extracts from Another Diary by Him, 1674–1687* (Cambridge, MA: John Wilson and Son, 1900), 50–52.

52. Nathaniel Saltonstall, *A Continuation of the State of New-England; Being a Farther Account of the Indian Warr, and the Engagement betwixt the Joynt Forces of the United English Collonies and the Indians, on the 19th of December, 1675, with the True Number of the Slain and Wounded, and the Transactions of the English Army since the Said Fight. With All Other Passages That Have Hapned from the 10th of November, 1675 to the 8th of February 1676. Together with an Account of the Intended Rebellion of the Negroes in Barbadoes* (London: T.M., 1676), reprinted in Lincoln, ed., *Narratives of the Indian Wars, 1675–1699*, 71–74.

53. John Saffin kept a rather eclectic daybook that includes some material on Bristol. As the town was being established, Saffin attempted a tribute to Harvard's Charles Chauncy, who had died a few years before the war: "Chancey the School-man: Great Divine whose faime / First took its Rise, and from Grand Cambridg[e] came / Who in his pregnant Braine was wont to carrie / Arts Master-pieces like a liberarie." Patricia E. Rubertone, *Grave Undertakings: An Archaeology of Roger Williams and the Narragansett Indians* (Washington, DC: Smithsonian Institution Press, 2001), esp. 16; Benjamin Bourne, *An Account of the Settlement of the Town of Bristol, in the State of Rhode-Island: And of the Congregational Church Therein, with the Succession of Pastors from Its Origin to the Present Times; Together with the Act of Incorporation of the Catholic Congregational Society, and the Rules Established in Said Society* (Providence: Bennett Wheeler, 1785), 2–4; Wilfred H. Munro, *The History of Bristol, R.I.: The Story of the Mount Hope Lands, from the Visit of the Northmen to the Present Time* (Providence: J. A. and R. A. Reid, 1880), 53–93; George Howe, *Mount Hope: A New England Chronicle* (New York: Viking, 1959), 21–102; Newell, "Changing Nature of Indian Slavery in New England," 118–27; Samuel

Sewall, *The Selling of Joseph: A Memorial* (Boston: Bartholomew Green and John Allen, 1700); John Saffin, *Brief Candid Answer to a Late Printed Sheet, Entituled, the Selling of Joseph: Whereunto is Annexed, a True and Particular Narrative by Way of Vindication of the Author's Dealing with and Prosecution of His Negro Man Servant, for His Vile and Exorbitant Behaviour Towards His Master, and His Tenant Thomas Shepard; Which Hath Been Wrongfully Represented to Their Prejudice and Defamation* (Boston, 1701); John Saffin, "Notebook, 1665–1708," 13–14, 76, American Antiquarian Society.

54. William Kellaway argued that the very decision to emphasize Indian education in the college mission was "likely opportunist," intended to increase support in Parliament and allow Harvard to access funds from the New England Company. Samuel Eliot Morison disdainfully described the Indian Bible as the "least useful" publication that came from the Indian College, this "unwanted structure." Gookin, *Historical Collections of the Indians in New England*, 34–36; Quincy, *History of Harvard University*, I:352–56; Minutes of the New England Company, 30 September 1685, in *New England Company of 1649 and John Eliot*, xliii, 206–9; Increase Mather to John Leusden, 12 July 1687, in Cotton Mather, *Magnalia Christi Americana: Or, the Ecclesiastical History of New-England, from Its First Planting in the Year 1620 unto the Year of Our Lord, 1698* (London, Thomas Parkhurst 1702), III:194–95; Morison, *Harvard College in the Seventeenth Century*, I:26–34, 345–60; Albert Ehrenfried, *A Chronicle of Boston Jewry: From the Colonial Settlement to 1900* (Privately printed, 1963), 99–101; Jaspar Dankers and Peter Sluyter, *Journal of a Voyage to New York and a Tour in Several of the American Colonies in 1679–80*, trans. and ed. Henry C. Murphy (Brooklyn: Long Island Historical Society, 1867), 382–84; John Wright, *Early Bibles of America* (London: Gay and Bird, 1893), 24. Kellaway, *New England Company*, 109–10.

55. Entries for 6 November 1693, 2 September 1695, and 7 April 1698, Records of the Harvard Corporation, I:20, 27, 34.

56. Wilcomb E. Washburn, *The Governor and the Rebel: A History of Bacon's Rebellion in Virginia* (Chapel Hill: University of North Carolina Press, 1957); Alfred A. Cave, *Lethal Encounters: Englishmen and Indians in Colonial Virginia* (Santa Barbara, CA: Praeger, 2011), 147–65.

57. See the Royal Charter of the College of William and Mary in Virginia, 8 February 1693, Miscellaneous American Materials from the Lambeth Palace Library, Virginia Historical Society; Records of James Blair's education from Marischal College, Folder 3, Box 1, Special Collections, Swem Library, College of William and Mary; "Earliest Extant Land Patents (and Leases) of the Colony of Virginia," *The Researcher* (1927), I and II; "Copies of the Rent Rolls of the Several County's [*sic*] for the Year 1704," Virginia Historical Society; Wilford Kale, "Educating a Colony:

The First Trustees of the College of William and Mary in Virginia," *Colonial Williamsburg*, Autumn 2000, 25–28; Thomas Jefferson, *Notes on the State of Virginia* (Boston: H. Sprague, 1802), 207–8; land survey for the College of William and Mary and map of the town of Williamsburg, 2 June 1699, MR 1/2067, National Archives, United Kingdom.

58. As he was establishing Indian education on campus, President Blair proposed new uses for enslaved Africans, including shifting silk production to Virginia, where this labor-intensive process "might be perform'd by Negro Children, that are now so many useless Hands." Henry Hartwell, James Blair, and Edward Chilton, *The Present State of Virginia, and the College* (London: John Wyat, 1727), 4, 60–77, 93; Col. Francis Nicholson to Archbishop Tenison, 22 May 1710, Misc. American Materials from the Lambeth Palace Library; Gov. Francis Nicholson to John Locke, 30 March 1697, James Blair Papers, Box 1, Folder 4, Special Collections, Swem Library, College of William and Mary; Douglas Sloan, *The Scottish Enlightenment and the American College Ideal* (New York: Teachers College Press, 1971), 20n–21n; Margaret Connell Szasz, *Indian Education in the American Colonies, 1607–1783* (Lincoln: University of Nebraska Press, 1988), 68–74; Tyler, *College of William and Mary*, 12–67.

59. Later in the century, the governors of William and Mary began affording some educational training to the college slaves. Hugh Jones, *The Present State of Virginia. Giving a Particular and Short Account of the Indian, English, and Negroe Inhabitants of that Colony. Shewing Their Religion, Manners, Government, Trade, Way of Living, &c. With a Description of the Country. From Whence is Inferred a Short View of Maryland and North Carolina. To Which are Added, Schemes and Propositions for the Better Promotion of Learning, Religion, Inventions, Manufactures, and Trade in Virginia, and the Other Plantations. For the Information of the Curious, and for the Service of Such as are Engaged in the Propagation of the Gospel and Advancement of Learning, and for the Use of All Persons Concerned in the Virginia Trade and Plantation* (London: J. Clarke, 1724), 1–94; Tyler, *College of William and Mary*, 21–23; "The Humble Petition [to Lieutenant Governor Edmund Andros] of the Clergy of Virginia at a General Meeting at James City, June 25th, 1696," James Blair Papers, Box 1, Folder 3; Terry L. Meyers, "A First Look at the Worst: Slavery and Race Relations at the College of William and Mary," *William & Mary Bill of Rights Journal*, April 2008, 1141–68.

60. "Present Rules and Methods setled and agreed on by us the Rt honble Richd Earle of Burlington and the Rt Reverend father in God Henry Lord Bishop of London for the disposition of the Rents and profits of the Mannor of Brafferton in the County of York towards the propagateing the Gospel in Virginia in persuance of an authority to us given in and by a decree in the high court of Chancery beareing date the 8th day of Aug 1695 . . . ," and "Accounts Folder," Brafferton Estate Collection, Box 3,

Folder 1, and Box 1, Special Collections, Swem Library, College of William and Mary.

61. "The Memorial of What Col. Spotswood, Gov. of Virginia Sent to the Bishop of London in Relacion to the Education of Indian Children at William & Mary Colledge and ye Conversion of the Neighboring Nations, to be Laid before the Queen," 8 November 1712, Brafferton Estate Collection; Tyler, *College of William and Mary*, 21–22; "Notes from the Journal of the House of Burgesses, 1712–1726," *William and Mary Quarterly*, April 1913, 249.

CHAPTER 2: "BONFIRES OF THE NEGROS"

1. Alexander Hamilton to Edward Stevens, 11 November 1769, the correspondence between Alexander Hamilton and Nicholas, John, Henry, and Tileman Cruger, 1771–1772, and the scattered records of Hamilton's matriculation in Elizabethtown and at King's College, in Harold C. Syrett, ed., *The Papers of Alexander Hamilton* (New York: Columbia University Press, 1961), I:4–42; *Catalogue of the Governors, Trustees, and Officers and of the Alumni and Other Graduates, of Columbia College (Originally King's College), in the City of New York, from 1754 to 1882* (New York: Printed for the College, 1882), 7–10; Milton Halsey Thomas, comp., *Columbia University Officers and Alumni, 1754–1857* (New York: Columbia University Press, 1936), 8, 98; Ron Chernow, *Alexander Hamilton* (New York: Penguin, 2004), 29–38; Willard Sterne Randall, *Alexander Hamilton: A Life* (New York: HarperCollins, 2003), 45–50.

2. Virginia D. Harrington, *The New York Merchant on the Eve of the Revolution* (Gloucester, MA: Peter Smith, 1964), 22–38; James Thomas Flexner, *John Singleton Copley* (Boston: Houghton Mifflin, 1948), 51–52; Cynthia A. Kierner, *Traders and Gentlefolk: The Livingstons of New York, 1675–1790* (Ithaca, NY: Cornell University Press, 1992), 157–59. Gabriel Ludlow was born in New Castle, Somerset, England, in 1663. On 24 November 1694, he arrived in New York to claim a 4,000-acre grant in Orange County. He became one of the leading merchants of New York City, a founding vestryman of Trinity Church, clerk of the assembly, and a slaveholder. See the papers of "Ludlow, Gabriel, 1663–1736, and descendants," entries 34–37, Franklin Delano Roosevelt Presidential Library and Museum, Hyde Park, New York.

3. Kierner, *Traders and Gentlefolk*, 152–53; Jon Butler, *Becoming America: The Revolution before 1776* (Cambridge, MA: Harvard University Press, 2001).

4. The founding of the College of Philadelphia has traditionally been dated at 1755, when the college charter was granted. I am using the date when the academy was first founded, which conflicts with the University of

Pennsylvania's preference, 1740. I have no desire to resolve the intercollegiate contest to claim ancient status and any attendant historical flatteries. In 1740 the evangelist George Whitefield began an ephemeral school for the poor in Philadelphia, but the project failed for a lack of funds. In 1749 the trustees of a new academy drew up a constitution, and purchased and renovated the "New Building" that Whitefield had raised. The constitution included provisions for admitting destitute children to a charity school under the board's governance. The trustees later announced that their academy would open in January 1751, and the charity school opened later that year. The 1740 founding date rests on overlap between the two boards, the purchase of the Whitefield building, the decision to reserve space for Whitefield's use, and the agreement to reestablish the charity school.

Numerous colleges have claims to founding moments that predate their charters. In the 1740s the Reverend Eleazar Wheelock began his English and Indian school in Connecticut, and formalized the academy a decade later. His Connecticut school had direct ties to and continuities with Dartmouth College. However, the history of Dartmouth College begins in 1769, when the charter was issued. Similarly, the University of Delaware (1921) has a long and complicated lineage with New Ark Academy (1743). The Penn family had proprietorship over Delaware and governed from Philadelphia, which had its own college. This colonial structure also kept the New Ark Academy trustees from elevating the school beyond the preparatory grades.

While the claim to a 1740 founding is a reach, the Philadelphians were running a college course well before their 1755 charter and before King's College opened in New York City. Charters are imperfect tools for dating colleges. Many colleges were chartered several years before the establishment of a course of study and the admission of scholars. In contrast, students at the Philadelphia academy were taking a college course quite a few years before the trustees decided to augment their 1749 charter to empower the professors to grant degrees. In December 1754 the board casually ordered two of their number "to draw up a Clause to be added to the Charter for that Purpose," having already agreed that offering degrees "would probably be a Means of advancing the Reputation of the Academy." The trustees brought the revised charter to the governor, who approved their plan. In June 1755 they reelected Benjamin Franklin to the presidency and "assume[d] the Name and Stile of The Trustees of the College, Academy and Charitable School of Philadelphia in the Province of Pennsylvania, by which Name they are incorporated."

The College of New Jersey, the College of Philadelphia, and the College of Rhode Island had colonial charters. King's College, Queen's College, and Dartmouth College had royal charters.

The trustees originally located the College of Rhode Island in the rural town of Warren, and then moved it to Providence in 1770.

"Constitutions of the Publick Academy in the City of Philadelphia" and entries from 13 November 1749 to 10 June 1755, in *Minutes of the Trustees of the College, Academy and Charitable Schools of the University of Pennsylvania, vol. 1, 1749–1768* (Wilmington, DE: Scholarly Resources, 1974), vi, 1–53; Thomas Penn and Richard Penn, Charter of Incorporation for the Academy of Newark, 10 November 1769, reprinted in "Board of Trustees, Minute Book, June 5, 1783–June 24, 1952," University Archives, University of Delaware; John S. Whitehead, *The Separation of College and State: Columbia, Dartmouth, Harvard, and Yale, 1776–1876* (New Haven: Yale University Press, 1973).

5. K. G. Davies, *The Royal African Company* (London: Longmans, Green, 1957), 15, 38–39, 65.

6. *Ecclesiastical Records of the State of New York* (Albany, NY: James B. Lyon, 1901), I:79; Richard C. Simmons "Mrs. Morris and the Philipse Family, American Loyalists," *Winterthur Portfolio*, 1965, 14–16; see order for Abraham Martensen Clock and Frederick Philipse to report on work, 11 May 1660, Historic Hudson Valley Library; Jean Zimmerman, *The Women of the House: How a Colonial She-Merchant Built a Mansion, a Fortune, and a Dynasty* (Orlando, FL: Harcourt, Harvest Books, 2006), esp. 86–111.

7. The *Margarit* was built in New York in 1695. Two versions of the orders were drafted. "Orders for Capt. Samuel Burgos Com[m]ander of the Barcque Maragarit bound to Madagascar &c Second Voyage," 9 June 1698; also see the register record for the ship dated 9 April 1698, in Frederick Philipse, Merchant Books and Correspondence, 2 Books, HCA 1/98, National Archives, United Kingdom.

8. Jacob Judd, "Frederick Philipse and the Madagascar Trade," *New-York Historical Society Quarterly*, October 1971, 354–74; Oscar and Mary Handlin, "Origins of the Southern Labor System," *William and Mary Quarterly*, April 1950, 214–15; Davies, *Royal African Company*, 122–35; Dixon Ryan Fox, *Caleb Heathcote, Gentleman Colonist: The Story of a Career in the Province of New York, 1692–1721* (New York: Charles Scribner's Sons, 1926), 23–32; Zimmerman, *Women of the House*, 179–85; Patricia U. Bonomi, *Factious People: Politics and Society in Colonial New York* (New York: Columbia University Press, 1971).

9. Serena R. Zabin, *Dangerous Economies: Status and Commerce in Imperial New York* (Philadelphia: University of Pennsylvania Press, 2009), 34–37; Lawrence H. Leder and Vincent P. Carosso, "Robert Livingston (1654–1728): Businessman of Colonial New York," *Business History Review*, March 1956, 18–27; Clare Brandt, *An American Aristocracy: The Livingstons* (Garden City, NY: Doubleday, 1986), 2; Kierner, *Traders and Gentlefolk*, 39, 71–72; Randall, *Alexander Hamilton*, 54–55; Thomas Clap, *The Annals or*

History of Yale-College, in New-Haven, in the Colony of Connecticut, from the First Founding thereof, in the Year 1700, to the Year 1766: with an Appendix, Containing the Present State of the College, the Method of Instruction and Government, with the Officers, Benefactors and Graduates (New Haven: John Hotchkiss and B. Mecom, 1766), 109–11; Milton M. Klein, ed., *The Independent Reflector, or Weekly Essays on Sundry Important Subjects More Particularly Adapted to the Province of New-York by William Livingston and Others* (Cambridge, MA: Harvard University Press, 1963), 6–7.

10. Davies, *Royal African Company*, 123–51; Hugh Thomas, *The Slave Trade: The Story of the Atlantic Slave Trade: 1440–1870* (New York: Simon and Schuster, 1997), 201–6; C. M. MacInnes, *Bristol and the Slave Trade* (Bristol: Bristol Branch of the Historical Association, 1963), 3–9; Bristol Museums and Art Gallery, *Slave Trade Trail Around Central Bristol* (Bristol, 1999); James A. Rawley and Stephen A. Behrendt, *The Transatlantic Slave Trade: A History* (Lincoln, NE: University of Nebraska Press, 2005), 129–65.

11. By the 1740s Bristol's claim to being England's "premier slaving port" had slipped, argues David Richardson, but it remained an important center for organizing and financing the Africa trade, and for coordinating investors, ship owners, buyers, and factors in England, Africa, the Caribbean, and North America. The Bristol traders maintained a consistently profitable commerce in people despite the financial power of London and a rivalry with Liverpool.

    In September 1770 Henry Cruger Jr.'s *Nancy* returned to New York City after a journey to Africa that took more than a year. It carried 239 captives, and the venture killed 54 people. Cruger registered this ship in Bristol.

    Jaspar Dankers and Peter Sluyter, *Journal of a Voyage to New York and a Tour in Several of the American Colonies in 1679–80*, trans. and ed. Henry C. Murphy (Brooklyn: Long Island Historical Society, 1867), 30, 37; W. E. Minchinton, ed., *Politics and the Port of Bristol in the Eighteenth Century: The Petitions of the Society of Merchant Venturers, 1698–1803* (Bristol: Bristol Record Society, 1963); "Waste [Account] Book of Henry and John Cruger, June 28, 1762–January 15, 1768," Henry and John Cruger manuscript collection, New-York Historical Society; Harrington, *New York Merchant on the Eve of the Revolution*, 12–13, 194–97; "Van Schaack Family Genealogical Notes," Van Schaack Family Papers, Box 1, Rare Book and Manuscript Library, Columbia University.

12. Peter Van Brugh Livingston insurance papers for the sloop *Good Intent*, 31 March 1737, Storke and Gainsborough, Correspondence with American Merchants, NYS Miscellaneous Collections, Box 5, New York State Archives; David Richardson, ed., *Bristol, Africa and the Eighteenth Century Slave Trade to America* (Bristol: Bristol Record Society, 1986–1996),

III:xiv–xxxi, 233; Harrington, *New York Merchant on the Eve of the Revolution*, 16–17, 194–97.

13. Elizabeth Donnan, ed., *Documents Illustrative of the History of the Slave Trade to America* (Washington, DC: Carnegie Institution, 1930–35), III:492, 511; Marcus Rediker, *The Slave Ship: A Human History* (New York: Viking, 2007), 94–97; Joseph C. Miller, *Way of Death: Merchant Capitalism and the Angolan Slave Trade, 1730–1830* (Madison: University of Wisconsin Press, 1988).

14. Rediker, *Slave Ship*, 73–78.

15. Miller, *Way of Death*, 695–96; T. Aubrey, *The Sea-Surgeon, Or the Guinea Man's Vade Mecum. In Which is Laid Down, The Method of Curing Diseases as Usually Happen Abroad, Especially on the Coast of Guinea; With the Best Way of Treating Negroes, Both in Health and in Sickness* (London: John Clarke, 1729), 127–29; Kenneth F. Kipple and Brian T. Higgins, "Mortality Caused by Dehydration During the Middle Passage," in Joseph E. Inikori and Stanley L. Engerman, eds., *The Atlantic Slave Trade: Effects on Economies, Societies, and Peoples in Africa, the Americas, and Europe* (Durham, NC: Duke University Press, 1994), 322–30; Wyndham B. Blanton, "Epidemics, Real and Imaginary, and Other Factors Influencing Seventeenth Century Virginia's Population," *Symposium on Colonial Medicine in Commemoration of the 350th Anniversary of the Settlement of Virginia* (Williamsburg: Jamestown-Williamsburg-Yorktown Celebration Commission and the Virginia 350th Anniversary Commission, 1957), 64–72.

16. Jasper Farmar, "A Journal of the Proceedings of the Ship Catherine, Jasp[er] Farmar Master[,] from New York and by God's Grace Toward One Part of ye Coast of Africa This Second Voyage Begun Sept 6th 1732," Ship Logs, 1732–1861, MG 49, collection of the New Jersey Historical Society.

17. *Boston News-Letter*, 7–14 April 1712, 14–21 April 1712, 21–28 April 1712; Kenneth Scott, "The Slave Insurrection in New York in 1712," *The New-York Historical Society Quarterly*, January 1961, 47–52, 62–67; Butler, *Becoming America*, 8–46; Evarts B. Greene and Virginia D. Harrington, *American Population Before the Federal Census of 1790* (New York: Columbia University Press, 1932), 92–99; "An Act for Preventing Suppressing and Punishing the Conspiracy and Insurrection of Negroes and Other Slaves," 10 December 1712, and "An Act for the More Effectual Preventing and Punishing the Conspiracy and Insurrection of Negro and Other Slaves; for the Better Regulating Them and for Repealing the Acts Herein Mentioned Relating Thereto," 29 October 1730, *The Colonial Laws of New York, from the Years 1664 to the Revolution* (Albany, NY: James B. Lyon, 1894), I:761–67, II:679–88; "A Law for Regulating Negro and Indian Slaves in the Night Time," 10 March 1713, *Minutes of the Common Council of the City of New York, 1675–1776* (New York: Dodd, Mead, 1905), III:30–31.

18. Daniel Horsmanden, *The New York Conspiracy* (1744; Boston: Beacon, 1971), 395–405.

19. Ibid., 22–31.

20. A British lawyer ruined when the South Sea Bubble collapsed, Horsmanden had fled to the colonies to rebuild his life. His remaining connections in England and William Byrd, a Virginia cousin, helped him secure an appointment to New York governor William Cosby's council. The governor rewarded Horsmanden's loyalty with serial assignments, including a 1737 appointment to the Supreme Court. Graham Russell Hodges, *Root and Branch: African Americans in New York and East Jersey, 1613–1863* (Chapel Hill: University of North Carolina Press, 1999), 88–98; Jill Lepore, *New York Burning: Liberty, Slavery, and Conspiracy in Eighteenth-Century Manhattan* (New York: Knopf, 2005), esp. 19–26; Zabin, *Dangerous Economies*, 132–58; Thelma Wills Foote, *Black and White Manhattan: The History of Racial Formation in Colonial New York* (New York: Oxford University Press, 2004), 159–86; Leslie M. Harris, *In the Shadow of Slavery: African Americans in New York City, 1626–1863* (Chicago: University of Chicago Press, 2003), 43–46; David Barry Gaspar, *Bondmen and Rebels: A Study of Master-Slave Relations in Antigua* (Baltimore: Johns Hopkins University Press, 1985), 21–30; Peter H. Wood, *Black Majority: Negroes in Colonial South Carolina from 1670 through the Stono Rebellion* (New York: Norton, 1974).

21. Thomas J. Davis, "Introduction," to Horsmanden, *New York Conspiracy*, ix–xi; George Clarke, 17 April 1741, *General Magazine, and Historical Chronicle, for All the British Plantations*, April 1741; Mrs. Peter DeLancey to Cadwallader Colden, 1 June 1741, in *The Letters and Papers of Cadwallader Colden* (New York: New-York Historical Society, 1937), VIII:264–66, and anonymous letter, 269–72.

22. Horsmanden, *New York Conspiracy*, 31–33. The lieutenant governor confirmed the rewards and pardons for voluntary witnesses. See letters from George Clarke, 17 April 1741 and 19 June 1741, *General Magazine, and Historical Chronicle, for All the British Plantations*, April and June 1741.

23. Horsmanden, *New York Conspiracy*, 37–39, 200; Mrs. Peter DeLancey to Cadwallader Colden, 1 June 1741; *American Weekly Mercury*, 23 July 1741.

24. Donnan, ed., *Documents Illustrative of the History of the Slave Trade*, III:507; New York Colony Treasurer's Office, "Reports of Goods Imported (Manifest Books) to New York," Boxes 1–2, New York State Archives; James G. Lydon, "New York and the Slave Trade, 1700–1774," *William and Mary Quarterly*, April 1978, 388–89; Horsmanden, *New York Conspiracy*, esp. 395–96.

25. William Dunlap, *History of the New Netherlands, Province of New York, and State of New York, to the Adoption of the Federal Constitution* (New York: Carter and Thorp, 1839), 324–29; Horsmanden, *New York Conspiracy*, 88–114, 227–28.

26. Emphasis added. Copy of Frederick Philipse's last will and testament, 26 October 1700, Historic Hudson Valley Library.

27. Ibid.

28. See the lists of those taken into custody and the record of their disposition, in Horsmanden, *New York Conspiracy*, appendices.

29. New York Colony Treasurer's Office, "Reports of Goods Imported (Manifest Books) to New York," Boxes 3–12; Donnan, ed., *Documents Illustrative of the History of the Slave Trade*, III:462–508. Also see Henry Cuyler's 14 June 1734 protest with petition of affirmation from Mayor Robert Livingston on the seizure of the *Mary*, Storke and Gainsborough, Correspondence with American Merchants, NYS Miscellaneous Collections, Box 4; Historical Manuscripts Commission, *The Manuscripts of the Earl of Dartmouth: American Papers* (London: Eyre and Spottiswoode, 1895), II:5.

30. *New-York Gazette*, 13 May 1751; "The Diary of William Chancellor: A Ship's Doctor on a Slaving Expedition to Africa, 1749–1751," IV:9–12, Edward Anderson Williams Papers, Maryland Historical Society; Alexander Falconbridge, *An Account of the Slave Trade on the Coast of Africa* (London: J. Phillips, 1788), 25–28; Darold D. Wax, "A Philadelphia Surgeon on a Slaving Voyage to Africa, 1749–1751," *Pennsylvania Magazine*, October 1968, 465–93.

31. Rediker, *Slave Ship*, esp. 187–99; entries for the seventh day, Thomas Prince, "Journal of Voyages to Barbados, 1709–1711," Massachusetts Historical Society; Thomas Prince, *A Chronological History of New-England, in the Form of Annals* . . . (Boston: Kneeland and Green, 1736).

32. "Diary of William Chancellor," IV:1–12.

33. Darold D. Wax, "Negro Imports into Pennsylvania, 1720–1766," *Pennsylvania History*, July 1965, 274; Theophilus Conneau, *A Slaver's Log Book, or 20 Years' Residence in Africa* (1854; Englewood Cliffs, NJ: Prentice-Hall, 1976), 81–87; Falconbridge, *Account of the Slave Trade*, 23–25; Benjamin Silliman, *A Journal of Travels in England, Holland and Scotland, and of Two Passages over the Atlantic in the Years 1805 and 1806* (New York: D. and G. Bruce, 1810), I:3–4, 47; Benjamin Silliman, *A Visit to Europe in 1851* (New York: George P. Putnam, 1853), I:29.

34. "Diary of William Chancellor," 9–12, 50; Wax, "Philadelphia Surgeon on a Slaving Voyage," 465–93.

35. Lydon, "New York and the Slave Trade," 393; John Watts to Gedney Clarke, Esq., 30 March 1762, *The Letter Book of John Watts: Merchant and Councillor of New York, January 1, 1762–December 22, 1765*, vol. LXI of *The Collections of the New-York Historical Society for the Year 1928* (New York: Printed for the Society, 1928), 31–32; Joyce Lee Malcolm, *Peter's War: A New England Slave Boy and the American Revolution* (New Haven: Yale University Press, 2009), 5; Phillis Wheatley, *Memoir and Poems of Phillis*

Wheatley: A Native African and a Slave. Dedicated to the Friends of the Africans, 2nd ed. (Boston: Light and Horton, 1835), 9–10.

36. Kenneth P. Minkema, "Jonathan Edwards's Defense of Slavery," *Massachusetts Historical Review* IV (2002): 23–30; Edmund S. Morgan, *The Gentle Puritan: A Life of Ezra Stiles, 1727–1795* (New Haven: Yale University Press, 1962), 125; Justin Winsor, ed., *The Memorial History of Boston, Including Suffolk County, Massachusetts, 1630–1880* (Boston: James R. Osgood, 1882), II:262; William B. Weeden, *Economic and Social History of New England, 1620–1789* (New York: Hillary House, 1963), II:627; Peter Faneuil to Capt. Peter Buckley (Bulkeley), 3 February 1738, *Proceedings of the Massachusetts Historical Society, 1863–1864* (Boston: Printed for the Society, 1864), 7:418–19; William Vassall to James Wedderburn, 22 April 1771, "Letter Book 1, November 27th, 1769–July 24th, 1786," 23–24, Vassall Letter Books, 1769–1800, collection of the Boston Public Library; Frank Edward Manuel and Fritzie P. Manuel, *James Bowdoin and the Patriot Philosophers* (Philadelphia: American Philosophical Society, 2004), 46; *Historical Register of Harvard University, 1636–1926* (Cambridge, MA: Harvard University Press, 1937), 70; *Annual Reports of the President and Treasurer of Harvard College, 1860–61* (Cambridge, MA: Welch, Bigelow, 1862), 45; Daniel C. Littlefield, "Plantations, Paternalism, and Profitability: Factors Affecting African Demography in the Old British Empire," *Journal of Southern History*, May 1981, 167–82.

37. "Diary of William Chancellor," 12–34.

38. Ibid., 23–25, 35–53; Wax, "Philadelphia Surgeon on a Slaving Voyage," 465–93.

39. "Diary of William Chancellor," 84–86; *New-York Gazette*, 13 May 1751; New York Colony Treasurer's Office, "Reports of Goods Imported (Manifest Books) to New York," Box 11; Wax, "Philadelphia Surgeon on a Slaving Voyage," 465–93.

40. Klein, ed., *Independent Reflector*, 6–33; Milton M. Klein, *The Politics of Diversity: Essays in the History of Colonial New York* (Port Washington, NY: Kennikat, 1974), 97–107.

41. William Smith, *A General Idea of the College of Mirania; With a Sketch of the Method of Teaching Science and Religion, in the Several Classes: And Some Account of Its Rise, Establishment and Building. Address'd More Immediately to the Consideration of the Trustees Nominated, by the Legislature, to Receive Proposals, &c. Relating to the Establishment of a College in the Province of New-York* (New York: J. Parker and W. Weyman, 1753); Benjamin Franklin to Samuel Johnson, 19 August 1750, Samuel Johnson Papers, Letter Books, vol. I, Rare Book and Manuscript Library, Columbia University; *Additional Charter of the College, Academy, and Charity-School of Philadelphia, in Pennsylvania* (Philadelphia: B. Franklin and D. Hall, 1755), 10; George B. Wood, *Early History of the University of Pennsylvania: From Its*

Origin to the Year 1827, 3rd ed. (Philadelphia: J. B. Lippincott, 1896), 222–30; William D. Carrell, "Biographical List of American College Professors to 1800," *History of Education Quarterly,* Autumn 1968, 359; Elizabeth DeLancey to Cadwallader Colden, 24 June 1755, *Letters and Papers of Cadwallader Colden,* IX:152–53.

42. Klein, ed., *Independent Reflector,* 36–46; Beverly McAnear, "College Founding in the American Colonies, 1745–1775," *Mississippi Valley Historical Review,* June 1955, 24–26.

43. Just months before the granting of the college charter, New York's merchants petitioned to move the administrative center of Jamaica—including the governor's house, the courts, and the public records office—from St. Jago de la Vega to Kingston in order to facilitate trade, particularly the commerce in slaves and the products of slavery. The governor conceded, but the capital was not formally moved until the next century. The regular trustees of the new college were a significant subset of these signatories. *Catalogue of the Governors, Trustees, and Officers and of the Alumni and Other Graduates, of Columbia College.* The original trustees and sponsors were checked against the New York Colony Treasurer's Office, "Reports of Goods Imported (Manifest Books) to New York," and Donnan, ed., *Documents Illustrative of the History of the Slave Trade to America,* III:462–512. See also Harrington, *New York Merchant on the Eve of the Revolution,* 23–24, 134; "To the Right Honourable the Lords Commissioners for Trade and Plantations—May it Please Your Lordships—The Merchants residing in the city of New York and trading to the Island of Jamaica . . . ," 30 July 1754, EST 9/74, National Archives, United Kingdom.

44. Harrington, *New York Merchant on the Eve of the Revolution,* 34; New York Colony Treasurer's Office, "Reports of Goods Imported (Manifest Books) to New York," Box 12; Donnan, ed., *Documents Illustrative of the History of the Slave Trade,* 462–512; Lydon, "New York and the Slave Trade," 379–81.

45. King's College was bounded by Murray Street to the north, Barclay to the south, and Church and Chapel to the east and west, respectively. Robinson Street intersected east-west but did not run through the campus. See "Plan for the City of New-York, with Recent and Intended Improvements. Drawn from an Actual Survey by William Bridges, City Surveyor, A.D. 1807," New York Public Library Map Room. See also Thomas Bradbury Chandler, *The Life of Samuel Johnson, D.D. The First President of King's College, in New-York* (New York: T. and F. Swords, 1805), 87–90; Clement Clarke Moore, *The Early History of Columbia College: An Address Delivered Before the Alumni on May 4, 1825, by Clement Clarke Moore of the Class of 1798, Author of "'Twas the Night Before Christmas"* (New York: Columbia University Press, 1940), 5; Klein, ed., *Independent Reflector,* 34–35; Nathaniel Fish Moore, *An Historical Sketch of Columbia College, in the City of New-York* (New York, 1846), 12–20; E. B. O'Callahan, M.D., LL.D.,

Documents Relative to the Colonial History of the State of New-York; Procured in Holland, England and France, by John Romeyn Brodhead, Esq., Agent, Under and by Virtue of an Act of the Legislature Entitled "An Act to Appoint an Agent to Procure and Transcribe Documents in Europe Relative to the Colonial History of the State," Passed May 2, 1839 (Albany, NY: Weed, Parson, 1853–), VII:528n.

46. Last wills and testaments of Peter Van Brugh, 23 May 1740, and James Alexander, 13 March 1745, in Peter Van Brugh Livingston, "Record Book of Deeds, Mortgages, etc, 1667–1803," New York State Library. See the correspondence of Robert Livingston and Peter Van Brugh Livingston, Storke and Gainsborough, Correspondence with American Merchants, NYS Miscellaneous Collections, Box 5.

47. Brendan McConville, *These Daring Disturbers of the Public Peace: The Struggle for Property and Power in Early New Jersey* (Ithaca, NY: Cornell University Press, 1999), 31–36.

48. The last wills and testaments of Philip Livingston, 15 July 1748, and James Alexander, March 13, 1745, in Livingston, "Record Book of Deeds, Mortgages, etc, 1667–1803"; New York Colony Treasurer's Office, "Reports of Goods Imported (Manifest Books) to New York"; John Watts to James Napier, 1 June 1765, *Letter Book of John Watts*, 354–56.

49. "Report of the Meeting of the Governors of the College of New York (King's College), Reading of the Royal Charter of Incorporation, and Report of the Governors' Taking the Oath of Office, New York, 1755," *The New-York Post-Boy, or Weekly Gazette*, May 12, 1755, Rare Book and Manuscript Library, Columbia University.

50. *Pennsylvania Gazette*, 16 September 1742; Peter Fryer, *Staying Power: The History of Black People in Britain* (London: Pluto, 1984), 46; D. M. Joslin, "London Private Bankers, 1720–1785," *Economic History Review* 7, no. 2 (1954): 184; entry for 25 June 1750, in *Minutes of the Trustees of the College, Academy and Charitable Schools of the University of Pennsylvania*, vol. 1, *1749–1768*, 7; Frederick B. Tolles, *Meeting House and Counting House: The Quaker Merchants of Colonial Philadelphia* (New York: Norton, 1948), 151; Allen B. Ballard, *One More Day's Journey: The Story of a Family and a People* (Bloomington, IN: iUniverse, 2011), 18–20; George E. Thomas and David B. Brownlee, *Building America's First University: An Historical and Architectural Guide to the University of Pennsylvania* (Philadelphia: University of Pennsylvania Press, 2000), 26–27; William Smith, *A Poem on Visiting the Academy of Philadelphia, June 1753* (Philadelphia, 1753), 15n; Gaspar, *Bondmen and Rebels*, 21–30; Richard B. Sheridan, *Sugar and Slavery: An Economic History of the British West Indies, 1623–1775* (Kingston, Jamaica: University of the West Indies Press, 2000), 200–203; *Catalogue of the Governors, Trustees, and Officers and of the Alumni and Other Graduates, of Columbia College*, 8.

51. Cheesman A. Herrick, *White Servitude in Pennsylvania: Indentured and Redemption Labor in the Colony and Commonwealth* (Philadelphia: John Joseph McVey, 1926), esp. 57–99.

52. A founder of Bethlehem Steel, Joseph Wharton began his manufacturing career as one of many Quakers in the iron industry of Pennsylvania. He also joined Samuel Willetts, the New York merchant and Quaker, in founding Swarthmore College (1864), and he later became the founder of the Wharton School of Business (1881) at the University of Pennsylvania, the nation's first such university program. Willets also left Swarthmore a major gift in his will. Thomas M. Doerflinger, *A Vigorous Spirit of Enterprise: Merchants and Economic Development in Revolutionary Philadelphia* (Chapel Hill: University of North Carolina Press, 1986), 152–57; Samuel M. Janney, *The Life of William Penn: With Selections from His Correspondence and Auto-Biography* (Philadelphia: Hogan, Perkins, 1852), 422; Herrick, *White Servitude in Pennsylvania*, 92–94; Wax, "Negro Imports into Pennsylvania, 1720–1766," 254–87; Sheryllynne Haggerty, *The British-Atlantic Community, 1760–1810* (Leiden: Brill, 2006), esp. 170; Darold D. Wax, "Africans on the Delaware: The Pennsylvania Slave Trade, 1759–1765," *Pennsylvania History*, January 1983, 38–39; see the voluminous correspondence with David Barclay in William Allen, Letterbook Commencing 31 July 1753, Shippen Family Papers, 1749–1860, Box 3, Historical Society of Pennsylvania; *Pennsylvania Gazette*, 8 June 1749, 30 August 1750, 10 October 1754, 23 November 1752; *American Weekly Mercury*, 13–20 June 1728; W. Ross Yates, *Joseph Wharton: Quaker Industrial Pioneer* (Bethlehem, PA: Lehigh University Press, 1987), esp. 211–26; *New York Times*, 14 February 1883.

53. Wax, "Africans on the Delaware," 41–44; Wax, "Negro Imports into Pennsylvania, 1720–1766," 254–87; *Pennsylvania Gazette*, 25 June 1747; Doerflinger, *A Vigorous Spirit of Enterprise*, 38, 48.

54. Wax, "Africans on the Delaware," 42; Wax, "Negro Imports into Pennsylvania, 1720–1766," 254–87; *American Weekly Mercury*, 19–26 April 1739, 7 May 1741, 18–25 June 1741.

55. Wax, "Negro Imports into Pennsylvania, 1720–1766," 254–87; *Pennsylvania Gazette*, 8–15 March 1739, 5–12 July 1739, 15 October 1741, 1 July 1742, 26 October 1749, 26 September 1751, 11 June 1752; *American Weekly Mercury*, 7 May 1741, 6–13 September 1744; Herrick, *White Servitude in Pennsylvania*, esp. 57–99.

56. Gertrude Selwyn Kimball, *Providence in Colonial Times* (Boston: Houghton Mifflin, 1912), 270–71; Wax, "Negro Imports into Pennsylvania, 1720–1766," 285.

57. James T. Campbell et al., *Slavery and Justice: Report of the Brown University Steering Committee on Slavery and Justice* (Providence: Brown University, October 2006), 12–25; orders and letters from Nicholas Brown and

Company to Esek Hopkins, dated 10 September 1764, 9 November 1765, 16 November 1765, and 8 January 1766, and "Brig. Salley's Account Book, 1765," 16–86, University Steering Committee on Slavery and Justice, Brown University Library.

58. Graham Russell Hodges, *Slavery and Freedom in the Rural North: African Americans in Monmouth County, New Jersey, 1665–1865* (Madison, WI: Madison House, 1997), 1–32; Charles R. Foy, "Ports of Slavery, Ports of Freedom: How Slaves Used Northern Seaports' Maritime Industry to Escape and Create Transatlantic Identities, 1713–1783," Ph.D. diss., Rutgers University, 2008, 215n; *The Charter of Queen's College, in New-Jersey* (New Brunswick, NJ: Abraham Blauvelt, 1810); John Howard Raven, comp., *Catalogue of the Officers and Alumni of Rutgers College (Originally Queen's College) in New Brunswick, N.J., 1766–1909* (Trenton, NJ: State Gazette Publishing, 1909), 5–25, 66; Maria Farmar, last will and testament, 18 March 1788, "Abstracts of Wills on File in the Surrogates Office, City of New York, Volume XIV, June 12, 1786–February 13, 1796. With Letters of Administration, January 5, 1786–December 31, 1795," *Collections of the New-York Historical Society for the Year 1905* (New York: Printed for the Society, 1906), 136–38; Charles Farmar Billopp, comp., *A History of Thomas and Anne Billopp Farmar and Some of Their Descendants in America* (New York: Grafton, 1907), 33–50; John P. Wall, *The Chronicles of New Brunswick, New Jersey, 1667–1931* (New Brunswick, NJ: Thatcher-Anderson, 1931), 58–59; Lydon, "New York and the Slave Trade," 389.

59. William Bentinck-Smith, "Nicholas Boylston and His Harvard Chair," *Proceedings of the Massachusetts Historical Society*, 1981, 17–39; *Boston Evening-Post*, 17 February 1772; *Historical Register of Harvard University, 1636–1926*, 44; "Nicholas Boylston," *Harvard Graduates' Magazine*, December 1895, 205–9; Donnan, ed., *Documents Illustrative of the History of the Slave Trade*, III:72–76, 257; epitaph for John Richardson Bayard, 15 July 1756, and the last will and testament of Peter Bayard, Cecil County, Maryland, 25 June 1765, #1377 and 1381–2, Box 1, Henley Smith Collection, Library of Congress; last will and testament of Cornelius Van Schaack, 31 July 1775 (in hand of his son Peter Van Schaack), Van Schaack Family Papers; Peyton Farrell Miller, *A Group of Great Lawyers of Columbia County, New York* (Privately printed, 1904), 75–76.

60. Just a few years earlier, while serving the Presbyterian communion in Virginia, Rev. Davies had accused the planters of neglecting and preventing the spiritual salvation of enslaved people. In unequivocal language, he charged them with offending providence. It was not just immoral but a sin that put white people's souls in jeopardy, he judged. The Society in Scotland for Propagating Christian Knowledge had supported Davies' Virginia ministry. In New Jersey, the SSPCK supported the Indian mission, but slave traders and slave owners governed the college. Samuel

Davies, Nassau Hall, to Mr. [Peter Van Brugh] Livingston, 18 January 1760, *Proceedings of the New Jersey Historical Society* 1, no. 2 (1845): 78; Samuel Davies, *The Duty of Christians to Propagate Their Religion among Heathens, Earnestly Recommended to the Masters of Negroe Slaves in Virginia. A Sermon Preached in Hanover, January 8, 1757* (London: J. Oliver, 1758).

61. *General Catalogue of the College of New Jersey, 1746–1896* (Princeton: Princeton University Press, 1896), 43–52; Thomas, *Columbia University Officers and Alumni*, 97–105; Kierner, *Traders and Gentlefolk*, 163–64.

62. Donnan, ed., *Documents Illustrative of the History of the Slave Trade*, III:494; Theodore Thayer, *As We Were: The Story of Old Elizabethtown* (Elizabeth, NJ: Grassmann for the New Jersey Historical Society, 1964), 78–79; David Ogden, *The Claim of the Inhabitants of the Town of Newark, in Virtue of the Indian Purchase Made by the First Settlers of Newark, in 1667, Stated and Considered* (Woodbridge, NJ: Samuel F. Parker, 1766); David Ogden of Newark, NJ, to Jonathan Sergeant, 16 November 1759, 23 May 1760, and 24 July 1761, Box 2, Folder 8, Robert Ogden of Elizabethtown, NJ, to Jonathan Sergeant, 10 June 1771, Box 2, Folder 20, Abraham Ogden of Newark, NJ, to Nicholas Low, 31 December 1783, Box 2, Folder 1, Ogden Family Papers, Manuscripts Division, Firestone Library, Princeton University; Franklin Bowditch Dexter, *Biographical Sketches of the Graduates of Yale College with Annals of the College History, October, 1701–May, 1745* (New York: Henry Holt, 1885), 373–75; *General Catalogue of the College of New Jersey*, 42–50; Thomas, *Columbia University Officers and Alumni*, 97, 102–3; Thomas Harrison Montgomery, *A History of the University of Pennsylvania from Its Foundation to A.D. 1770* (Philadelphia: George W. Jacobs, 1900), 547; see also William Ogden Wheeler, comp., *The Ogden Family in America: Elizabethtown Branch and Their Ancestry: John Odgen, the Pilgrim and His Descendants, 1640–1906, Their History, Biography and Genealogy* (Philadelphia: J. B. Lippincott, 1907), esp. 67–84.

63. Entry for 16 April 1746, "Yale University Corporation and Prudential Committee Minutes," Manuscripts and Archives, Yale University Library; Clap, *Annals or History of Yale-College, in New-Haven*, esp. 54; *Historical Register of Yale University, 1701–1937* (New Haven: Yale University, 1939), 63; Wheeler, *Ogden Family in America*, 52.

64. Ebenezer Baldwin, *Annals of Yale College in New Haven, Connecticut, from Its Foundation, to the Year 1831* (New Haven: Hezekiah Howe, 1831), 308; Fryer, *Staying Power*, 46–47; the letter appointing John Lloyd Jr. is reprinted in "John Leverett's Diary, 1707–1723," 145, Papers of John Leverett, Box 8, Harvard University Archives; *Virginia Magazine of History and Biography*, July 1903, 310–11.

CHAPTER 3: "THE VERY NAME OF
A WEST-INDIAN"

1. Jonathan Swift, *Travels into Several Remote Nations of the World. In Four Parts by Lemuel Gulliver, First a Surgeon, and then a Captain of Several Ships* (London: Benj. Motte, 1726), 194; Elaine L. Robinson, *Gulliver as Slave Trader: Racism Reviled by Jonathan Swift* (Jefferson, NC: McFarland, 2006); Daniel Defoe, *The Farther Adventures of Robinson Crusoe: Being the Second and Last Part of His Life, and of the Strange Surprising Accounts of His Travels Round Three Parts of the Globe. Written by Himself; to Which is Added a Map of the World, in Which is Delineated the Voyages of Robinson Crusoe* (London: W. Taylor, 1719); Tim Severin, *Seeking Robinson Crusoe* (London: Macmillan, 2002); Daniel Defoe, *A New Voyage Round the World, by a Course Never Sailed Before. Being a Voyage Undertaken by Some Merchants, Who Afterwards Proposed the Setting up an East-India Company in Flanders* (London: A. Bettesworth, 1725).

2. Pierre Carlet de Chamblain de Marivaux reversed the master-slave relationship in his 1725 comedy *L'isle des esclaves: Comèdie en un acte* (Paris: Noel Pissot, 1725). See also John Witherspoon, *The History of a Corporation of Servants, Discovered a Few Years Ago in the Interior Parts of South America, Containing Some Very Surprising Events and Extraordinary Characters* (Glasgow: John Gilmour, 1765), esp. 57; Jonathan Swift, *Directions to Servants in General; and in Particular to the Butler, Cook, Footman, Coachman, Groom, House-Steward, and Land-Steward, Porter, Dairy-Maid, Chamber-Maid, Nurse, Laundress, House-Keeper, Tutoress, or Governess* (London: R. Dodsley, 1745).

3. Virginia's Arthur Lee, a graduate of the Edinburgh medical program whose family patronized the College of New Jersey, responded to Adam Smith with a rabid assault upon the humanity of black people, a ridiculing of the lives of peasants in Ireland and Scotland, and a reminder that England had transported Africans to the colonies. Adam Smith, *The Theory of Moral Sentiments* (London, 1759), 402; Adam Smith, *An Inquiry into the Nature and Causes of the Wealth of Nations* (London: W. Strahan and T. Cadell, 1776), ch. 3; County Tax Ratables, Somerset County, Western Precinct, 1780–1786, reel 18, New Jersey State Archives; Arthur Lee, *An Essay in Vindication of the Continental Colonies of America, from a Censure of Mr. Adam Smith, in His Theory of Moral Sentiments. With Some Reflections on Slavery in General. By an American* (London: For the author, 1764).

4. Rev. Witherspoon emerged as a major intellectual and political champion of colonial resistance to English rule and his college helped define a new national culture. During his tenure in the presidency, John Witherspoon completed two terms in the New Jersey legislature, and served with Benjamin Rush in the Continental Congress. John Witherspoon of Paisley,

Scotland, to Benjamin Rush, 29 April 1767, 22 May 1767, 3 June 1767, 7 July 1767, 4 August 1767, and John Witherspoon, New York City, to Benjamin Rush, 8 October 1768, John Witherspoon Collection, Box 1, Folder 13, Manuscripts Division, Firestone Library, Princeton University; Benjamin Rush, Edinburgh, to Jonathan Smith, 30 April 1767, Box 1, Henley Smith Collection, Manuscript Division, Library of Congress.

5. Christopher Codringon's last will and testament, 1702, also see his wills of 1700 and 1710, PROB 20/540, National Archives, United Kingdom; William Gordon, *A Sermon Preach'd at the Funeral of the Honourable Colonel Christopher Codrington, Late Captain General and Governor in Chief of Her Majesty's Carribbee Islands; Who Departed Life at His Seat in Barbadoes, on Good-Friday the 7th of April 1710. and Was Interr'd the Day Following in the Parish Church of St. Michael* (London: G. Strahan, 1710), 3–4, 20–23; Frank J. Klingberg, *Codrington Chronicle: An Experiment in Anglican Altruism on a Barbados Plantation, 1710–1834* (Berkeley: University of California Press, 1949), 24–35; Sylvester Hovey, *Letters from the West Indies: Relating Especially to the Danish Island St. Croix, and to the British Islands Antigua, Barbadoes and Jamaica* (New York: Gould and Newman, 1838), 110–12.

6. J. M. Hone and M. M. Rossi, *Bishop Berkeley: His Life, Writings, and Philosophy* (London: Faber and Faber, 1931), 165; A. A. Luce, *The Life of George Berkeley, Bishop of Cloyne* (London: Thomas Nelson and Sons, 1949), 131–32; George Berkeley, *A Proposal for the Better Supplying of Churches in Our Foreign Plantations, and for Converting the Savage Americans to Christianity* (London: H. Woodfall, 1724), 8–9.

7. Samuel E. Morison, "The Letter-Book of Hugh Hall: Merchant of Barbados, 1716–1720," *Transactions, 1933–1937: Publications of the Colonial Society of Massachusetts* (Boston: By the Society, 1937), XXXII: 514–21; *New-England Weekly Journal*, 27 May 1728.

8. "Hugh Hall Account Book, 1728–1733," 5–36, Hugh Hall Papers, Massachusetts Historical Society; Elizabeth Donnan, ed., *Documents Illustrative of the History of the Slave Trade to America* (Washington, DC: Carnegie Institution, 1930–35), III:50; John Langdon Sibley, *Biographical Sketches of Graduates of Harvard University, in Cambridge, Massachusetts* (Cambridge, MA: Charles William Sever, 1873–), IV:120–28; Ebenezer Turell, *The Life and Character of the Reverend Benjamin Colman* (Boston: Rogers and Fowle, 1749), esp. 53–59.

9. *Sibley's Harvard Graduates*, esp. I:597–98, V:432; Andrew P. Peabody, *Memoir of John Langdon Sibley* (Cambridge, MA: John Wilson and Son, 1886).

10. *Sibley's Harvard Graduates*, IV:128, 359, V:341–68; entries for 12 June 1709, Thomas Prince, "Journal of Voyages to Barbados, 1709–1711," Massachusetts Historical Society; "Hugh Hall Account Book," 29.

11. The intervention of Spanish ships destroyed Woodbridge's scheme and left the company with thousands of enslaved black people whom he sold at a significant loss in a weak market. L. Vernon Briggs, *History of Shipbuilding on North River, Plymouth County, Massachusetts, with Genealogies of the Shipbuilders, and Accounts of the Industries upon Its Tributaries, 1640–1872* (Boston: Coburn Brothers, 1889), 261, 285; Josiah Quincy, *The History of Harvard University* (Cambridge, MA: J. Owen, 1840), I:421–22; *Sibley's Harvard Graduates*, IV:318–20; Morison, "Letter-Book of Hugh Hall," 517–18.

12. Dudley Woodbridge to Benjamin Colman, 10 July 1711, 10 April 1718, Benjamin Colman Papers, Massachusetts Historical Society; Franklin Bowditch Dexter, *Biographical Sketches of the Graduates of Yale College with Annals of the College History, October, 1701–May, 1745* (New York: Henry Holt, 1885), 520; last will and testament of Timothy Woodbridge, 1 April 1732, *The Woodbridge Record: Being an Account of the Descendants of the Rev. John Woodbridge of Newbury, Mass. Compiled from the Papers Left by the Late Louis Mitchell, Esquire* (New Haven: Privately printed, 1883), 10–24, 234; Ebenezer Baldwin, *Annals of Yale College in New Haven, Connecticut, from Its Foundation, to the Year 1831* (New Haven: Hezekiah Howe, 1831), 308.

13. Hugh Hall Jr., Barbados, to Benjamin Colman, 30 March 1720, Benjamin Colman Papers; Klingberg, *Codrington Chronicle*, 24–35.

14. Nathaniel Saltonstall, *A Continuation of the State of New-England; Being a Farther Account of the Indian Warr, and the Engagement betwixt the Joynt Forces of the United English Collonies and the Indians, on the 19th of December, 1675, with the True Number of the Slain and Wounded, and the Transactions of the English Army since the Said Fight. With All Other Passages That Have Hapned from the 10th of November, 1675 to the 8th of February 1676. Together with an Account of the Intended Rebellion of the Negroes in Barbadoes* (London: T.M., 1676), reprinted in Charles H. Lincoln, ed., *Narratives of the Indian Wars, 1675–1699* (New York: Charles Scribner's Sons, 1913), 71–74; David Eltis, *The Rise of African Slavery in the Americas* (Cambridge: Cambridge University Press, 2000), 243; Winthrop D. Jordan, *White over Black: American Attitudes Toward the Negro, 1550–1812* (New York: Norton, 1977), 156; Hugh Hall Jr. to Benjamin Colman, 30 March 1720, Benjamin Colman Papers; Mr. Sharpe to the Secretary, 23 June 1712, vol. VII, no. 33, Archives of the Society for the Propagation of the Gospel in Foreign Parts.

15. Several years later, Gore died of smallpox. Cotton Tufts became a physician and a founder of the Massachusetts Medical Society. *Boston News-Letter*, 2 July 1711; *Harvard Graduates' Magazine*, March 1914, 555–56; William Cooper, *A Sermon Concerning the Laying the Deaths of Others to Heart, Occasion'd by the Lamented Death of the Ingenious & Religious Gentleman, John Gore M.A. of Harvard College in Cambridge, N.E., Who Died of Small-pox, November 7, 1720, in the 38th Year of His Age* (Boston:

B. Green, 1720); Morison, "Letter-Book of Hugh Hall," 514–21; "Instructions to Captain Pollipus Hammond, 1746," in Donnan, ed., *Documents Illustrative of the History of the Slave Trade*, III:138–39; entries dated 30 January 1749 at the back of Cotton Tufts's diary in Ames' Almanac, 1748, "Cotton Tufts Diaries, 1748–1794," Massachusetts Historical Society.

16. S. D. Smith, *Slavery, Family, and Gentry Capitalism in the British Atlantic: The World of the Lascelles, 1648–1834* (Cambridge: Cambridge University Press, 2006), 11–26; William Vassall to James Wedderburn, 8 January 1770, 22 April 1771, William Vassall to Dear Gentlemen, 2 January 1770, "Letter Book 1, November 27th, 1769–July 24th, 1786," 5–6, 23–24, Vassall Letter Books, 1769–1800, Boston Public Library.

17. William M. Fowler Jr., "Marine Insurance in Boston: The Early Years of the Boston Marine Insurance Company, 1799–1807," in Conrad Edick Wright and Katheryn P. Viens, eds., *Entrepreneurs: The Boston Business Community, 1700–1850* (Boston: Massachusetts Historical Society, 1997), 162–78; Edward Everett, "Peter Chardon Brooks," in Freeman Hunt, *Lives of American Merchants* (New York: Hunt's Merchants' Magazine, 1856), I:133–83; New England Historic Genealogical Society, *Proceedings of the New England Historic Genealogical Society at the Annual Meeting, 1 February 1922 with Memoirs of Deceased Members, 1921: Supplement to the April Number, 1922* (Boston: By the Society, 1922), lxv–lxvii; S. D. Smith, "Gedney Clarke of Salem and Barbados: Transatlantic Super-Merchant," *New England Quarterly*, December 2003, 499–549.

18. Richard S. Dunn, *Sugar and Slaves: The Rise of the Planter Class in the English West Indies, 1624–1713* (New York: Norton, 1973), 110–16, 239; Peter H. Wood, *Black Majority: Negroes in Colonial South Carolina from 1670 Through the Stono Rebellion* (New York: Norton, 1974), 13–28.

19. Alan Gallay, *The Indian Slave Trade: The Rise of the English Empire in the American South, 1670–1717* (New Haven: Yale University Press, 2002), esp. 48–49; Patrick Minges, "Beneath the Underdog: Race, Religion, and the Trail of Tears," *American Indian Quarterly*, Summer 2001, 453–56; W. L. McDowell, *Journals of the Commissioners of the Indian Trade, September 20, 1710–August 29, 1718* (Columbia: South Carolina Archives Department, 1955), esp. 160–61, 233, 263, 269; Wood, *Black Majority*, 35–62.

20. Gallay, *Indian Slave Trade*, 74–79, 129–54, 299–301.

21. McDowell, *Journals of the Commissioners of the Indian Trade*, 5–16, 27–33, 49–50, 103.

22. *Sibley's Harvard Graduates*, IV:101–5, 121, 168, 297, 322–25.

23. Ibid., IV:446–48, V:528, VII:575–80.

24. Josiah Quincy, Edenton, North Carolina, to Samuel Quincy, Boston, 6 April 1773, Quincy, Wendell, Holmes, Upham Papers, Massachusetts Historical Society; "Journal of a Voyage to South Carolina, &c.," in Josiah Quincy, *Memoir of the Life of Josiah Quincy Jun. of Massachusetts, by His Son,*

Josiah Quincy (Boston: Cummings, Hilliard, 1825), 74–125; S. Max Edelson, *Plantation Enterprise in Colonial South Carolina* (Cambridge, MA: Harvard University Press, 2006), 153–56; Arney R. Childs, ed., *Rice Planter and Sportsman: The Recollections of J. Motte Alston, 1821–1909* (Columbia: University of South Carolina Press, 1999), 143–44; Robert Olwell, *Masters, Slaves, and Subjects: The Culture of Power in the South Carolina Low Country, 1740–1790* (Ithaca, NY: Cornell University Press, 1998), 33–34.

25. Deed of sale from Joseph and Sarah Whipple to George Berkeley, D.D., 18 February 1728, Berkeley Papers, 1724–1801, Whitehall and Berkeley Scholarship Folder, Beinecke Rare Book and Manuscript Library, Yale University; Berkeley, *Proposal for the Better Supplying of Churches in Our Foreign Plantations, and for Converting the Savage Americans to Christianity*, 6–7; John Wild, *George Berkeley: A Study of His Life and Philosophy* (Cambridge, MA: Harvard University Press, 1936), 280–330; Hone and Rossi, *Bishop Berkeley*, 130–63; Luce, *Life of George Berkeley*, 94–135; Alice Brayton, *George Berkeley in Newport* (Newport: Privately printed, 1954), 3–30.

26. By the Author of American Fables [William Smith], *Indian Songs of Peace with a Proposal, in a Prefatory Epistle, for Erecting Indian Schools, and a Postscript by the Editor, Introducing Yariza, an Indian Maid's Letter, to the Principal Ladies of the Province and City of New-York* (New York: J. Parker and W. Wayman, 1752), 3–12; Samuel Davies, *Letters from the Rev. Samuel Davies, &c. Shewing the State of Religion in Virginia, Particularly among the Negroes* . . . (London, 1757), 39–40.

27. Berkeley, *Proposal for the Better Supplying of Churches in Our Foreign Plantations, and for Converting the Savage Americans to Christianity*, 3–16; Bertha Borden Davis, *Bishop Berkeley: Notes Compiled from Many Sources* (1946), 8–9.

28. Wheelock and Benjamin Pomeroy, his future brother-in-law, shared the first award. Deed of transfer from George Berkeley to Yale College, 26 July 1732, Berkeley Papers, 1724–801, Beinecke Library, Yale; Hone and Rossi, *Bishop Berkeley*, 163–65; Luce, *Life of George Berkeley*, 136–52; Wild, *George Berkeley*, 308–30; James Dow McCallum, *Eleazar Wheelock: Founder of Dartmouth College* (Hanover, NH: Dartmouth College Publications, 1939), 5–7; Edwin S. Gaustad, *George Berkeley in America* (New Haven: Yale University, 1979), 83–87; *Boston News-Letter*, 1–8 March 1733; *Rhode Island Gazette*, 25 October 1732.

29. The July 1751 letter and the catalogue of books are reprinted in Daniel C. Gilman, "Bishop Berkeley's Gifts to Yale College: A Collection of Documents Illustrative of 'The Dean's Bounty,'" *Papers of the New Haven Colony Historical Society* (New Haven: For the Society, 1865), I:147–70; Thomas Clap, *The Annals or History of Yale-College, in New-Haven, in the Colony of Connecticut, from the First Founding thereof, in the Year 1700, to the Year 1766; with an Appendix, Containing the Present State of the College,*

the Method of Instruction and Government, with the Officers, Benefactors and Graduates (New Haven: John Hotchkiss and B. Mecom, 1766), 59–60, 97; Jonathan F. Stearns, *Historical Discourses, Relating to the First Presbyterian Church in Newark; Originally Delivered to the Congregation of that Church During the Month of January, 1851* (Newark: Daily Advertiser Office, 1853), 151–52.

30. Gilman, "Bishop Berkeley's Gifts to Yale College," 157; Ezra Stiles, *A Funeral Sermon, Delivered Thursday, July 26, 1787, at the Internment of the Reverend Chauncey Whittelsey, Pastor of the First Church in the City of New-Haven, Who Died July 24th, 1787 in the LXXth Year of His Age, and XXXth of His Ministry* (New Haven: T. and S. Green, 1787), 26.

31. Entries for 2 October 1759, 15 April 1762, and 20 May 1773, in "Minutes of the Governors of King's College," vol. I, Rare Book and Manuscript Library, Columbia University.

32. Samuel Johnson to William Samuel Johnson, 1 February 1762, Samuel Johnson Papers, Letter Books, vol. II, Rare Book and Manuscript Library, Columbia University; *Catalogue of the Governors, Trustees, and Officers, and of the Alumni and Other Graduates, of Columbia College (Originally King's College), in the City of New York, from 1754 to 1867* (New York: D. Van Nostrand, 1868), 41; David C. Humphrey, *From King's College to Columbia, 1746–1800* (New York: Columbia University Press, 1976), 126–30; John B. Pine, "King's College and the Early Days of Columbia College," *Proceedings of the New York State Historical Association* (1919), XVII:118.

33. Walter Barrett, *The Old Merchants of New York City* (New York: Carleton, 1864), 61–63.

34. Scott Bryant, *The Awakening of the Freewill Baptists: Benjamin Randall and the Founding of an American Religious Tradition* (Macon, GA: Mercer University Press, 2011), 57–58; see the broadside from the convention in New Jersey recommending the Reverend Eleazar Wheelock and his academy, dated September 5, 1765; *New-Hampshire Gazette*, 21 June 1765; W. DeLoss Love, *Samson Occom and the Christian Indians of New England* (Boston: Pilgrim Press, 1899), 130–34; Alden T. Vaughan, *Transatlantic Encounters: American Indians in Britain, 1500–1776* (New York: Cambridge University Press, 2006), 190–94; Frederick Chase, *A History of Dartmouth College and the Town of Hanover, New Hampshire*, ed. John K. Lord (Cambridge, MA: John Wilson and Son, 1891), I:32–33, 300–301.

35. George B. Wood, *Early History of the University of Pennsylvania from Its Origin to the Year 1827* (1833; Philadelphia: J. B. Lippincott, 1896), 57–58.

36. William Smith, "A General Evening Prayer," in *Prayers, For the Use of the Philadelphia Academy* (Philadelphia: B. Franklin and D. Hall, 1753), 14–17.

37. *Pennsylvania Chronicle*, 9–16 March 1772; David Hosack, *Biographical Memoir of Hugh Williamson, M.D., LL.D., . . . Delivered on the First Day of November, 1819, at the Request of the New-York Historical Society* (New

York: C. S. Van Winkle, 1820), 18–23; Whitfield J. Bell Jr., "Some American Students of 'That Shining Oracle of Physic,' Dr. William Cullen of Edinburgh, 1755–1766," *Proceedings of the American Philosophical Society*, 20 June 1950, 281; Hugh Williamson, "To the Human and Liberal, Friends of Learning, Religion and Public Virtue, in the island of Jamaica. The Memorial and Humble Address of Hugh Williamson, M.D. One of the Trustees of the Academy of New-Ark, in Behalf of That Institution," *Philadelphia Packet*, 15 June 1772.

38. Hugh T. Lefler and William S. Powell, *Colonial North Carolina: A History* (New York: Scribner's Sons, 1973), 208–12; Joseph Caldwell, 1791 salutary address in Latin, Joseph Caldwell Papers, Folder 1, Manuscripts Department, Wilson Library, University of North Carolina at Chapel Hill; Indenture from Col. Benjamin Smith to the Trustees of the University, 18 December 1789, Folder 3, letter from Joseph Caldwell, June 1796, Folder 9, and records of lands, stocks, assets, and donations, and slave inventories, Folders 1–10, UNC Papers, Box 1, Wilson Library, UNC; David Ker and Mary Boggs Ker Papers, Wilson Library, UNC; George Dames Burtchaell and Thomas Ulick Sadleir, *Alumni Dublinenses: A Register of the Students, Graduates, Professors and Provosts of Trinity College in the University of Dublin (1593–1860)* (Dublin: Alex. Thom, 1935), 464.

39. Franklin W. Knight, *The Caribbean: The Genesis of a Fragmented Nationalism* (New York: Oxford University Press, 1990), 284; Walter Pilkington, ed., *The Journals of Samuel Kirkland: 18th-Century Missionary to the Iroquois, Government Agent, Father of Hamilton College* (Clinton, NY: Hamilton College Press, 1980), 280.

40. John Witherspoon, New York City, to Benjamin Rush, 8 September 1768, John Witherspoon Collection, Box 1, Folder 14.

41. John Witherspoon, *Address to the Inhabitants of Jamaica, and other West-India Islands, in Behalf of the College of New-Jersey* (Philadelphia: William and Thomas Bradford, 1772), 6–27; entries from 11 March to 30 September 1772, "The Minutes of the Proceedings of the Trustees of the College of New Jersey," vol. I, Seeley G. Mudd Manuscript Library, Princeton University; Varnum Lansing Collins, *President Witherspoon: A Biography* (Princeton: Princeton University Press, 1925), I:143–45.

42. Richard Stockton, a signer of the Declaration of Independence, was also invested in Nova Scotia lands. Last will and testament of Richard Stockton (signer), 20 May 1780, Stockton Family Additional Papers, Box 2, Folder 22, Manuscripts and Archives, Princeton University. After the *New York Gazette* published Witherspoon's *Address to the Inhabitants of Jamaica*, "Causidicus" objected to the minister's negative comments on the colleges in New York and Philadelphia, which the respondent saw as part of a pattern of self-interest and duplicity. "A Wellwisher to Old Scotland" replied to Witherspoon's advertisements in Scotland with similar concerns, accusing

the proprietors of rent gouging and hiding the actual cost of settlement. The lands were not cleared, a considerable expense that would fall upon the tenants. Renters would have to fend for themselves while preparing and planting farms. Moreover, if and when these farms became productive, there were no local markets for surpluses. Emigrants, this critic concluded, would need considerable capital to execute such an agreement, would lose much of what they produced to rents, and would fare better if they remained in Scotland. J. M. Bumsted, *The People's Clearances: Highland Emigration to British North America* (Edinburgh: Edinburgh University Press, 1982), 20–21, 61–65, 72; Winthrop Pickard Bell, *The "Foreign Protestants" and the Settlement of Nova Scotia: The History of a Piece of Arrested British Colonial Policy in the Eighteenth Century* (Toronto: University of Toronto Press, 1961), 9–17; *New-York Gazette; and the Weekly Mercury*, 7 December 1772, with Witherspoon's reply appearing on 28 December 1772; David Walker Woods Jr., *John Witherspoon* (London: Fleming H. Revel, 1906), 185–89.

43. C. Vann Woodward, ed., *Mary Chesnut's Civil War* (New Haven: Yale University Press, 1981), 195–212; Ben Ames Williams, ed., *A Diary from Dixie by Mary Boykin Chesnut* (Cambridge, MA: Harvard University Press, 1980), 138–48; C. Vann Woodward and Elisabeth Muhlenfeld, eds., *The Private Mary Chesnut: The Unpublished Civil War Diaries* (New York: Oxford University Press, 1984), 162–67.

44. Joseph Bailey Witherspoon, *The History and Genealogy of the Witherspoon Family (1400–1972)* (Fort Worth, TX: Miran, 1973), 18–156; Daniel Walker Hollis, *University of South Carolina* (Columbia: University of South Carolina Press, 1951–56), I:7–8, 98–99; Edwin L. Green, *A History of the University of South Carolina* (Columbia: State Company, 1916), 388, 441, 445.

45. On the spread of Presbyterian academies in Mississippi, see David G. Sansing, *The University of Mississippi: A Sesquicentennial History* (Oxford: University of Mississippi Press, 1999), 3–19.

46. Witherspoon, *History and Genealogy of the Witherspoon Family*; David Dobson, *Scottish Emigration to Colonial America, 1607–1785* (Athens: University of Georgia Press, 1994), 66–80; Woodward, ed., *Mary Chesnut's Civil War*, 195n–210n.

47. Witherspoon, *History and Genealogy of the Witherspoon Family*, 18–109; *Heads of Family at the First Census of the United States Taken in the Year 1790: North Carolina* (Washington, DC: Government Printing Office, 1908), 131; Virginia D. Harrington, *The New York Merchant on the Eve of the Revolution* (Gloucester, MA: Peter Smith, 1964), 51, 209; John Witherspoon to David Witherspoon, Hampden Sydney, Virginia, 17 March 1777, John Witherspoon Collection, Box 1, Folder 20; Richard A. Harrison, *Princetonians, 1769–1775: A Biographical Dictionary* (Princeton: Princeton University Press, 1980), 442–45; Samuel A. Ashe, ed., *Biographical History of North Carolina: From Colonial Times to the Present* (Greensboro, NC:

Charles L. Van Noppen, 1906), V:487–88. A valuable census of Scots emigrants in the Carolinas is compiled in David Dobson, *Directory of Scots in the Carolinas, 1680–1830* (Baltimore: Genealogical Publishing, 1986).

48. Patrick Griffin, *The People with No Name: Ireland's Ulster Scots, America's Scots Irish, and the Creation of a British Atlantic World, 1689–1764* (Princeton: Princeton University Press, 2001), 1–3, 65–124; Charles W. J. Withers, *Urban Highlanders: Highland-Lowland Migration and Urban Gaelic Culture, 1700–1900* (East Linton, Scotland: Tuckwell, 1998), 4; Lefler and Powell, *Colonial North Carolina*, 210–12; Bumsted, *The People's Clearances*, 2–80; Robert A. Dodgshon, *From Chiefs to Landlords: Social and Economic Change in the Western Highlands and Islands, c. 1493–1820* (Edinburgh: Edinburgh University Press, 1998), 102–18, 237–43; T. M. Devine, *Clanship to Crofter's War: The Social Transformation of the Scottish Highlands* (Manchester: Manchester University Press, 1994), 177–84; Duane Gilbert Meyer, *The Highland Scots of North Carolina, 1732–1776* (Chapel Hill: University of North Carolina Press, 1961). On the scope and pattern of Highland outmigration in the nineteenth century, see T. M. Devine, *The Great Highland Famine: Hunger, Emigration and the Scottish Highlands in the Nineteenth Century* (Edinburgh: John Donald, 1988).

49. Douglas Sloan, *The Scottish Enlightenment and the American College Ideal* (New York: Teachers College Press, 1971), 109–10; John Witherspoon to Benjamin Rush, 21 December 1767, 9 February 1769, John Witherspoon Collection, Box 1, Folder 13; *New-York Gazette*, 20 March 1769; Samuel Miller, *Memoir of the Rev. John Rodgers, D.D.: Late Pastor of the Wall Street and Brick Churches, in the City of New York* (Philadelphia: Presbyterian Board of Publication, 1840), 19–26, 140. John Rodgers delivered the eulogy at the memorial for John Witherspoon in Princeton. *Argus*, 22 June 1795.

50. By the 1770s, New Jersey residents were less than a quarter of the student body, and Madison's class included only one person from the colony. Collins, *President Witherspoon*, II:216–17; Edward C. Mead, ed., *Genealogical History of the Lee Family of Virginia and Maryland from A.D. 1300 to A.D. 1866 with Notes and Illustrations* (New York: Richardson, 1868), appendix; Gaillard Hunt, *The Life of James Madison* (New York: Doubleday, Page, 1902), 14–15; Harrison, *Princetonians, 1769–1775*, 301–8. Members of the classes of 1770 and 1771, respectively, Wallace and Madison, both Virginians, became close friends while in Princeton and even visited while home in Virginia. Richard Harrison, *Princetonians, 1776–1783: A Biographical Dictionary* (Princeton: Princeton University Press, 1981), xxix–xxxii, 116–22, 160–65; John Witherspoon to Colonel Henry Lee, 20 December 1770, John Witherspoon Collection, Box 1, Folder 11.

51. Robert Polk Thomson, "Colleges in the Revolutionary South: The Shaping of a Tradition," *History of Education Quarterly*, Winter 1970, 399; Sloan, *Scottish Enlightenment and the American College Ideal*, 20–21n, 36–41;

Donald G. Tewksbury, *The Founding of American Colleges and Universities Before the Civil War with Particular Reference to the Religious Influences Bearing upon the College Movement* (New York: Teachers College, 1932), 69.

52. Elizabeth Brown Pryor, "An Anonymous Person: The Northern Tutor in Plantation Society, 1773–1860," *Journal of Southern History*, August 1981, 363–92; J. Blake Scott, "John Witherspoon's Normalizing Pedagogy of Ethos," *Rhetoric Review*, Autumn 1997, 63–64.

53. Hunter Dickinson Farish, ed., *Journal and Letters of Philip Vickers Fithian, 1773–1774: A Plantation Tutor of the Old Dominion* (Williamsburg, VA: Colonial Williamsburg, 1943), esp. 3–12; Harrison, *Princetonians, 1769–1775*, 216–21. On Fithian's graduation and commencement, see *Providence Gazette*, 24 October 1772.

54. Farish, ed., *Journal and Letters of Philip Vickers Fithian*, esp. 351, 113–14; Harrison, *Princetonians, 1769–1775*, 420–22.

55. Robert Donald Come, "The Influence of Princeton on Higher Education in the South Before 1825," *William and Mary Quarterly*, October 1945, 359–96; John D. Wright Jr., *Transylvania: Tutor to the West* (Lexington, KY: Transylvania University, 1975), 1–18; Thomas G. Dyer, *The University of Georgia: A Bicentennial History, 1785–1985* (Athens: University of Georgia Press, 1985), 1–45; *Boston Post Boy*, 25 July 1768; Lefler and Powell, *Colonial North Carolina*, 212–13; Marshall DeLancey Haywood, "The Story of Queen's College or Liberty Hall in the Province of North Carolina," *North Carolina Booklet*, January 1912, 169–75; William D. Snider, *Light on the Hill: A History of the University of North Carolina at Chapel Hill* (Chapel Hill: University of North Carolina Press, 1992), 3–37; Walter Clark, ed., *The State Records of North Carolina: Published Under the Supervision of the Trustees of the Public Libraries, by Order of the General Assembly* (1903; Wilmington, NC: Broadfoot, 1994), XXI:265, 325, 415–17, 709, 718.

56. Tewksbury, *Founding of American Colleges and Universities*, 69–71; James McLachlan, *Princetonians, 1748–1768: A Biographical Dictionary* (Princeton: Princeton University Press, 1976), 21–23, 157–60, 289–92.

57. Witherspoon, *History and Genealogy of the Witherspoon Family*, 103–4; Come, "Influence of Princeton on Higher Education," 365–76; Pryor, "An Anonymous Person," 389.

58. Harrison, *Princetonians, 1769–1775*, 116–22; "Negroes for Hire," bill dated 19 December 1826, Washington College, Lexington, Virginia, John Spencer Bassett Papers, Box 32, Folder 13, Manuscripts Division, Library of Congress; "Old College," Tusculum College, no. Tenn-157, Historic American Buildings Survey, Library of Congress.

59. Edward Long, *The History of Jamaica, or, General Survey of the Antient and Modern State of that Island: With Reflections on Its Situation, Settlements, Inhabitants, Climate, Products, Commerce, Laws, and Government* (London: T. Lowndes, 1774), I:278–79; Hollis, *University of South Carolina*, I:7–8;

Eric Williams, *From Columbus to Castro: The History of the Caribbean* (New York: Vintage, 1984), 132–33.

60. Witherspoon, *History and Genealogy of the Witherspoon Family,* 59, 71; Marion Mills Miller, *American Debate: A History of Political and Economic Controversy in the United States, with Critical Digests of Leading Debates,* part 1, *Colonial, State, and National Rights, 1761–1861* (New York: G. P. Putnam's Sons, 1916), 164–65.

CHAPTER 4: EBONY AND IVY

1. Wheelock arrived with some thirty scholars, most of them charity students supported under funds raised in Britain. Many of these boys were not in the college course. In 1771, the first graduating class comprised four students, including Wheelock's son John, who transferred from Yale.

Dow died in 1817 at age one hundred. Governor Wentworth was so generous that Wheelock proposed naming the college after him, but the honoree declined. The minister then recognized another benefactor: William Legge, Earl of Dartmouth. One of the early campus buildings was named for Wentworth.

Professor Deborah K. King of Dartmouth College is producing new work on gender and enslavement in colonial and early national New England, which she has generously shared over the years. Deborah K. King, "Still Embattled, Yet Emboldened: Contesting Black Female Embodiments," Black Womanhood Symposium, 12 April 2008, Hood Museum, Dartmouth College; Eleazar Wheelock, *A Continuation of the Narrative of the Indian Charity School, Begun in Lebanon, in Connecticut; Now Incorporated with Dartmouth-College in Hanover, in the Province of New-Hampshire* (New Hampshire, 1773), esp. 3–5; Samson Occom to Eleazar Wheelock, 4 October 1765, #765554.2, Dartmouth College Archives; Eleazar Wheelock to George Whitefield, 27 August 1770, in Baxter Perry Smith, *The History of Dartmouth College* (Boston: Houghton, Osgood, 1878), 55–56; John King Lord, *A History of the Town of Hanover, N.H.* (Hanover, NH: Dartmouth College Press, 1928), 148–49, 301–2; Leon Burr Richardson, *History of Dartmouth College* (Hanover, NH: Dartmouth College Publications, 1932), I:102–7; Lawrence Shaw Mayo, *John Wentworth: Governor of New Hampshire, 1767–1775* (Cambridge, MA: Harvard University Press, 1921), 110; *The Records of the Town of Hanover, New Hampshire, 1761–1818: The Records of the Town Meetings, and of the Selectmen, Comprising All of the First Volume of Records and Being Volume 1 of the Printed Records of the Town* (Hanover, NH: By the town, 1905), 6–9; Elizabeth Forbes Morison and Elting E. Morison, *New Hampshire: A Bicentennial History* (New York: Norton, 1976), 22

2. Eleazar Wheelock to Sachem Gill at St. Francis, 1 November 1777, #777601, and "Roster of Names of Pupils Attending Charity School, Chiefly 1760–1775," Rauner Library, Dartmouth College; Colin G. Calloway, ed., *Dawnland Encounters: Indians and Europeans in Northern New England* (Hanover, NH: University Press of New England, 1991), 243–45; Colin G. Calloway, *The Indian History of an American Institution: Native Americans and Dartmouth* (Hanover, NH: Dartmouth College Press, 2010), esp. 1–37; Dartmouth College, "Catalogus eorum qui in Collegio-Dartmuthensi (a Reverendo Eleazaro Wheelock S.T.D divinis auspiciis) Nov-Hantoniae . . ." (Hanover, NH: Alden Spooner, 1779); *The General Catalogue of Dartmouth College and Associated Schools, 1769–1940* (Hanover, NH: Dartmouth College Publications, 1940), esp. 70.

3. John and Isaac Lawrence owned land and slaves in New Jersey and New York. They supported the regional colleges. "Rutgers University Board of Trustees Records, 1778–1956, Series I: Queens College Board of Trustees, 1778–1829," Folder 1, Special Collections and University Archives, Alexander Library, Rutgers University.

4. Evarts B. Greene and Virginia D. Harrington, *American Population Before the Federal Census of 1790* (New York: Columbia University Press, 1932), 5; Herbert S. Klein, *A Population History of the United States* (Cambridge: Cambridge University Press, 2004), 20, 139–40; Graham Russell Hodges, "Ethnicity in Eighteenth-Century North America, 1701–1788," in Ronald H. Bayor, ed., *Race and Ethnicity in America* (New York: Columbia University Press, 2003), 21–40; *Return of the Whole Number of Persons within the Several Districts of the United States, According to "An Act Providing for the Enumeration of the Inhabitants of the United States," Passed March the First, One Thousand Seven Hundred and Ninety-One* (Philadelphia: Childs and Swaine, 1791), esp. 3; Russell Thornton, *American Indian Holocaust and Survival* (Norman: University of Oklahoma Press, 1987), esp. 60–90.

5. Greene and Harrington, *American Population Before the Federal Census of 1790*, esp. 15–17, 49–50, 63, 71–72, 115–19; *Boston News-Letter*, 3 July 1704, in Charles J. Hoadly, ed., *The Public Records of the Colony of Connecticut, from May, 1762, to October, 1767, inclusive* (Hartford, CT: Case, Lockwood, and Brainard, 1850–), V:516, 534, VII:580–85; "Answers returned to the Queries sent the Governor and Company of His Majesty's Colony of Connecticut from the Right Honourable the Lords Commissioners for Trade and Plantations, A.D. 1762," Massachusetts Historical Society.

6. Graham Russell Hodges, *Root and Branch: African Americans in New York and East Jersey, 1613–1863* (Chapel Hill: University of North Carolina Press, 1999), esp. 272–75; Greene and Harrington, *American Population Before the Federal Census of 1790*, 92–100; Gary B. Nash, "Slaves and Slaveowners in Colonial Philadelphia," *William and Mary Quarterly*, April 1973, 223–56; Jean R. Soderlund, "Black Importation and Migration to

Southeastern Pennsylvania, 1682–1810, *Proceedings of the American Philosophical Society*, June 1989, 144–53.

7. Robert V. Wells, *The Population of the British Colonies in America Before 1776: A Survey of Census Data* (Princeton: Princeton University Press, 1975), 147; Marvin L. Michael Kay and Lorin Lee Cary, *Slavery in North Carolina, 1748–1775* (Chapel Hill: University of North Carolina Press, 1995), 19; Peter H. Wood, "The Changing Population of the Colonial South: An Overview by Race and Region, 1685–1790," in Gregory A. Waselkov, Peter H. Wood, and Tom Hatley, eds., *Powhatan's Mantle: Indians in the Colonial Southeast* (Lincoln: University of Nebraska Press, 2006), 57–76; Peter H. Wood, *Black Majority: Negroes in Colonial South Carolina from 1670 Through the Stono Rebellion* (New York: Norton, 1975), 131–66; Betty Wood, *Slavery in Colonial Georgia, 1730–1775* (Athens: University of Georgia Press, 1984), 59–87; Russell Thornton, *The Cherokees: A Population History* (Lincoln: University of Nebraska Press, 1990), 30–32; Greg O'Brien, *Choctaws in a Revolutionary Age, 1750–1830* (Lincoln: University of Nebraska Press, 2005), 121n; Governor William Gooch, "Report to the Lords of Trade," 1749, Virginia Governor, 1741–1749, Virginia Historical Society.

8. See Bishop François de Laval's deeds transferring his property to the seminary and the trustees' acknowledgment of his donations, April–November 1680, Archives du Séminaire de Québec, Séminaire 1, no. 17B, and Séminaire 2, no. 68 and 69, Centre de référence de l'Amérique française, Musée de l'Amérique française, Quebec, Canada. The deeds recording Laval's land acquisitions are also available in the collection. Noël Baillargeon, *Le Séminaire de Québec sous l'Épiscopat de Mgr de Laval* (Quebec: Les Presses de L'Université Laval, 1972), 65–88, 193–97; H. Clare Pentland, *Labour and Capital in Canada, 1650–1860* (Toronto: James Lorimer, 1981), 1–2; Marcel Trudel, *Les Débuts du Régime Seigneurial au Canada* (Montreal: Fides, 1974), 90–101, 275, 279; Gur Frégault and Marcel Trudel, *Histoire du Canada: par les textes* (Montreal: Fides, 1963), I:38–43. Also see William B. Munro, *The Seigneurs of Old Canada: A Chronicle of New World Feudalism* (Toronto: Brook, 1914); Richard Colebrook Harris, *The Seigneurial System in Early Canada: A Geographical Study* (Madison: University of Wisconsin Press, 1966).

9. Nathaniel Byfield owned multiple slaves and at least one Scottish indentured servant, James Furdize, a nineteen-year-old. "John Leverett's Diary, 1707–1723," 64–72, 106–8, Papers of John Leverett, Box 8, Harvard University Archives; Samuel A. Bates, ed., *Records of the Town of Braintree, 1640–1793* (Randolph, MA: Daniel H. Huxford, 1886), 725; Edward Field, ed., *State of Rhode Island and Providence Plantations at the End of the Century: A History* (Boston: Mason, 1902), II:476; Thomas Williams Bicknell, *The History of the State of Rhode Island and Providence Plantations* (New York: American Historical Society, 1920), III:1179; Nathaniel

Byfield, *An Account of the Late Revolution in New-England: Together with the Declaration of the Gentlemen, Merchants, and Inhabitants of Boston, and the Country Adjacent. April 18, 1689* (London: Richard Chiswell, 1689); Harriette M. Forbes, ed., *The Diary of Ebenezer Parkman, of Westborough, Mass.* (Westborough, MA: Westborough Historical Society, 1899), esp. vi; *Boston News-Letter*, 30 September 1706, 25 November 1706, 17 Feb 1707; *New-England Weekly Journal*, 25 March 1728.

10. Yale's estates were in slaveholding regions, and its tenants included slave owners. Entries on the leasing of the college farms, "Yale University Corporation and Prudential Committee Minutes," Manuscripts and Archives, Yale University Library; Ebenezer Baldwin, *Annals of Yale College in New Haven, Connecticut, from Its Foundation, to the Year 1831* (New Haven: Hezekiah Howe, 1831), 308; *An Account of the Number of Inhabitants, in the Colony of Connecticut, January 1, 1774: Together with An Account of the Number of Inhabitants, Taken January 1, 1756* (Hartford, CT: Ebenezer Watson, 1774); A. G. Hibbard, *History of the Town of Goshen, Connecticut with Genealogies and Biographies* (Hartford, CT: Case, Lockwood, and Brainard, 1897), 22–25; Bureau of the Census, *Heads of Families at the First Census of the United States Taken in the Year 1790: Connecticut* (Washington, DC: Government Printing Office, 1908), 57; entries for 25 January 1742, 15 August 1758, College of William and Mary, "Faculty Minutes, 1729–1784," and College of William and Mary, "Bursars Books, 1743–1770," Special Collections, Swem Library, College of William and Mary; "College Negroes," *William and Mary Quarterly*, January 1908, 170.

11. Edward Field, ed., *State of Rhode Island and Providence Plantations at the End of the Century: A History* (Boston: Mason, 1902), I:584; Silas Cooke to Aaron Lopez, 27 August 1776, 7 and 16 September 1776, Aaron Lopez Papers, Box 14, Folder 7, American Jewish Historical Society; entries for 16 April 1746, 10 September 1760, 30 November 1762, 22 October 1766, 13 September 1769, "Yale University Corporation and Prudential Committee Minutes"; Susan Stanton Brayton, "Whitehall during the War of Revolution," n.d., Rhode Island Historical Society; *Census of the Inhabitants of the Colony of Rhode Island and Providence Plantations, Taken by Order of the General Assembly, in the Year 1774; and by the General Assembly of the State Ordered to be Printed* (Providence: Anthony Knowles, 1858), 10; Jay Mack Holbrook, *Rhode Island 1782 Census* (Oxford, MA: Holbrook Research Institute, 1979), 36; *Census Record of the State of Rhode Island for 1782*, copied by Mrs. Lewis A. Waterman, historian, Rhode Island Daughters of Founders and Patriots of America, 1941–1945, and typed by Mrs. Louis Oliver and Mrs. Albert Congdon, president and past president of the RIDFPA, 16, Rhode Island Historical Society.

12. A conflict between Jay and the trustees of King's College undermined the appeal for a royal grant. These grants were largely in the disputed area

that became Vermont. Lieutenant Governor Cadwallader Colden apportioned a twenty-four-thousand-acre tract west of the Connecticut River
to King's. The trustees secured twenty thousand acres to the north. Governor William Tryon then gave the college ten thousand acres of his own
estate. Because of the location of these lands and the sparse populations
in these areas, the board had trouble attracting tenants. "The Memorial
and Humble Petition of Sir James Jay, Knight, in behalf of the Govrs of
King's College in the City of New York in America" and "To the Right
Honble Lords of the Committee of His Majesty's Most Honble Privy
Council for Plantation Affairs," in E. B. O'Callahan, ed., *Documents Relative to the Colonial History of the State of New-York* (Albany, NY: Weed,
Parsons, 1853–), VII:643–46; David C. Humphrey, *From King's College to
Columbia, 1746–1800* (New York: Columbia University Press, 1976), 132–34.

13. Governor Belcher was urging the trustees to choose a location and begin
constructing a campus. Entries for 15 May 1751 and 27 September 1752,
"The Minutes of the Proceedings of the Trustees of the College of New
Jersey," vol. 1, Seeley G. Mudd Manuscript Library, Princeton University;
Gerald Breese, *Princeton University Land, 1752–1984* (Princeton: Prince-
ton University Press, 1986), 3–34; "University Land Records" (AC028),
Folder 12, Seeley G. Mudd Manuscript Library, Princeton University;
Brendan McConville, *These Daring Disturbers of the Public Peace: The
Struggle for Property and Power in Early New Jersey* (Ithaca, NY: Cornell
University Press, 1999), 31–36, 51; T. B. Chandler to Samuel Johnson, 26
February 1753, in "Some Early Princeton History," *Princeton Alumni Weekly*,
7 January 1914; James Manning to Rev. Dr. Samuel Stennett, 5 June 1771,
James Manning Papers, 1761–1827, Box 1, Folder 5 (A753), John Hay
Library, Brown University.

14. William W. H. Davis, *The History of Bucks County, Pennsylvania, from the
Discovery of the Delaware to the Present Time* (Doylestown, PA: Democrat
Book and Job Office, 1876), 181–83, 789–97; Samuel M. Janney, *The Life of
William Penn: With Selections from His Correspondence and Auto-Biography*
(Philadelphia: Hogan, Perkins, 1852), 184–85; entries for 9 October 1759, 9
November 1762, 11 October 1763, and 14 June 1764, in *Minutes of the Trustees of the College, Academy and Charitable Schools of the University of Pennsylvania*, vol. 1, *1749–1768* (Wilmington, DE: Scholarly Resources, 1974),
108, 174–75, 224, 269; Thomas Harrison Montgomery, *A History of the
University of Pennsylvania: From Its Foundation to A.D. 1770* (Philadelphia: W. Jacobs, 1900), 380–82, 415–16; George B. Wood, *Early History of
the University of Pennsylvania: From Its Origin to the Year 1827* (Philadelphia: J. B. Lippincott, 1896), 49–50, 60–61.

15. Onesimus is the slave in Paul's Epistle to Philemon. Henry Louis Gates Jr.
and Evelyn Brooks Higginbotham, eds., *African American Lives* (New York:
Oxford, 2004), 640–41; Donald G. Tewksbury, *The Founding of American*

Colleges and Universities Before the Civil War with Particular Reference to the Religious Influences Bearing upon the College Movement (New York: Teachers College, 1932), 84–87; Thomas Symmes, "Notebook, 1696–1774," American Antiquarian Society; Cotton Mather, *Diary of Cotton Mather* (New York: Frederick Ungar, 1957), I:579. Quoted in John Langdon Sibley, *Biographical Sketches of the Graduates of Harvard University in Cambridge, Massachusetts* (Cambridge: Charles William Sever, 1873–) V:esp. 432.

16. "Benjamin Wadsworth's Book (A. Dom. 1725) Relating to the College," *Publications of the Colonial Society of Massachusetts* (Boston: By the Society, 1935), XXXI:461, 470.

17. The board comprised James Noyes, Stonington; Israel Chauncy, Stratford; Thomas Buckingham, Saybrook; Abraham Pierson, Kenilworth; Samuel Mather, Windsor; Timothy Woodbridge, Hartford; James Pierpont, New Haven; Samuel Andrew, Milford; Joseph Webb, Fairfield; and Noadiah Russell, Middletown. Edwin Oviatt, *The Beginnings of Yale* (New Haven: Yale University Press, 1916), 196, 333; "Act for a Collegiate School," October 1701, in Hoadly, ed., *Public Records of the Colony of Connecticut*, IV:363–64; last will and testament of Timothy Woodbridge, 1 April 1732, *The Woodbridge Record: Being an Account of the Descendants of the Rev. John Woodbridge of Newbury, Mass. Compiled from the Papers Left by the Late Louis Mitchell, Esquire* (New Haven: Privately printed, 1883), 234.

18. David Lawrence Pierson, *Narratives of Newark (in New Jersey) from the Days of Its Founding: 1666–1916* (Newark: Pierson, 1917), 18–46, 88; Abraham Pierson, *Some Helps for the Indians: Shewing Them How to Improve Their Natural Reason, to Know the True God, and the True Christian Religion . . .* (London: M. Simmons, 1659); Rev. Joseph F. Folsom, "Church History," *A History of the City of Newark, New Jersey: Embracing Practically Two and a Half Centuries, 1666–1913* (New York: Lewis Historical Publishing, 1913), II:949–52; Sibley, *Harvard University Graduates*, II:253–58; *Sketches of Yale College, with Numerous Anecdotes, and Embellished with More Than Thirty Engravings* (New York: Saxton and Miles, 1843), 20–22; John Fiske, *The Dutch and Quaker Colonies in America* (Cambridge: Riverside, 1903), II:17–18.

19. The last will and testament of Benjamin Pierpont, and the last will and testament of John Pierpont, *Acts and Resolves of the General Court*, vol. 17, 27–28, Massachusetts State Archives; R. Burnham Moffat, *Pierrepont Genealogies from Norman Times to 1913, with Particular Attention Paid to the Line of Descent from Hezekiah Pierpont, Youngest Son of Rev. James Pierpont of New Haven* (New York: Privately printed, 1913), 34–37; John S. Whitehead, *The Separation of College and State: Columbia, Dartmouth, Harvard, and Yale, 1776–1876* (New Haven: Yale University Press, 1973), 13–14.

20. *Sibley's Harvard Graduates*, IV:192–95, V:588–97, VII:496.

21. President Francis Wayland of Brown, for instance, used the story during one of his own commentaries on slavery. The various accounts disagree on

whether Stiles traded a barrel of rum or a hogshead of whiskey. Franklin Bowditch Dexter, ed., *The Literary Diary of Ezra Stiles, D.D., LL.D., President of Yale College* (New York: Charles Scribner's Sons, 1901), I:521, 525, II:271, 272; Edmund S. Morgan, *The Gentle Puritan: A Life of Ezra Stiles, 1727–1795* (New Haven: Yale University Press, 1962), 124–25; Richard Fuller, *Domestic Slavery Considered as a Scriptural Institution: In a Correspondence Between the Rev. Richard Fuller, of Beaufort, S.C., and the Rev. Francis Wayland, of Providence, R.I. Revised and Corrected by the Authors*, 5th ed. (New York: Lewis Colby, 1847), 38.

22. The Pennsylvania Society for Promoting the Abolition of Slavery and the Relief of Negroes Unlawfully Held in Bondage was founded in 1775. Edmund S. Morgan, *Benjamin Franklin* (New Haven: Yale University Press, 2002), 105; Alan Houston, *Benjamin Franklin and the Politics of Improvement* (New Haven: Yale University Press, 2008), 200–201; Benjamin Franklin to Mrs. Abiah Franklin, undated, in Jared Sparks, ed., *A Collection of the Familiar Letters and Miscellaneous Papers of Benjamin Franklin* (Boston: Charles Bowen, 1833), 17–19; David Waldstreicher, *Runaway America: Benjamin Franklin, Slavery, and the American Revolution* (New York: Hill and Wang, 2004), 25–26, 144; *Publications of the Rhode Island Historical Society* (Providence: By the Society, 1899), VII:140–41; William G. McLoughlin, *Rhode Island: A History* (New York: Norton, 1986), 78–80, 106–7.

23. Bill for Jonathan Dickinson's purchase of Genny, "a Negro Girl," 9 June 1733, in Anson Phelps Stokes, *Memorials of Eminent Yale Men: A Biographical Study of Student Life and University Influences During the Eighteenth and Nineteenth Centuries* (New Haven: Yale University Press, 1914), I:196; bill for Aaron Burr's purchase of Caesar, a black man, 2 September 1756, in Milton Meltzer, *Slavery: A World History* (Boston: Da Capo, 1993), 142; Samuel Davies, *Letters from the Rev. Samuel Davies, &c. Shewing the State of Religion in Virginia, Particularly among the Negroes . . .* (London, 1757), esp. 28–31; Samuel Davies, *The Duty of Christians to Propagate Their Religion among Heathens, Earnestly Recommended to the Masters of Negroe Slaves in Virginia. A Sermon Preached in Hanover, January 8, 1757* (London: J. Oliver, 1758); notice for Finley estate auction, 31 July 1766, in Francis Bazley Lee, ed., *Genealogical and Personal Memorial of Mercer County, New Jersey* (New York: Lewis, 1907), I:27; Kenneth P. Minkema, "Jonathan Edwards's Defense of Slavery," *Massachusetts Historical Review* IV (2002): 23–30; Morgan, *Gentle Puritan*, 125; County Tax Ratables, Somerset County, Western Precinct, 1780–1786, reel 18, New Jersey State Archives; Samuel Stanhope Smith, *Essay on the Causes of the Variety of Complexion and Figure in the Human Species. To Which are Added Strictures on Lord Kaims' Discourse, on the Original Diversity of Mankind* (Edinburgh: C. Elliot, 1788), 181; Constance K. Escher, "She Calls Herself Betsey

Stockton," *Princeton History*, 1991, 98–102. Jennifer Epstein produced a full study of slaveholding patterns at the college and in the larger community in Princeton. See Jennifer Epstein, "Slaves and Slavery at Princeton," thesis, Princeton University, 2008.

24. County Tax Ratables, Somerset County, Eastern Precinct, 1793–1795, reel 18, New Jersey State Archives.

25. Bills of sale from William Clark, 7 February 1757 (#757157), Timothy Kimball, 22 April 1760 (#761477), and Peter Spencer, 26 April 1760 (#760276), Dartmouth College Archives, Rauner Library.

26. Bills of sale from Ann Morrison to Eleazar Wheelock, 13 May 1762 (#762313), Eleazar Wheelock to Gideon Buckingham, 23 December 1770 (#775673), and Gideon Buckingham to Eleazar Wheelock, 17 February 1772 (#772167), Dartmouth College Archives.

27. Eleazar Wheelock to Capt. Moses Little, 6 May 1773 (#773306), and Eleazar Wheelock to Asa Foot, 28 January 1776 (#776128), Dartmouth College Archives.

28. See the letter announcing John H. Livingston's acceptance of the call to the Dutch Reformed Church of New York, 10 May 1770, in *Ecclesiastical Records, State of New York* (Albany, NY: James B. Lyon, 1905), VI:4184; William R. Davie, agreement for the sale of "a negroe girl slave called Dinah," 9 August 1793, William R. Davie Papers, Folder 13, Manuscripts Department, Wilson Library, University of North Carolina at Chapel Hill.

29. Eleazar Wheelock to John Wheelock, student at Yale College, 24 August 1769 (#769474.2), and last will and testament of Eleazar Wheelock, 4 June 1779 (#779252.6), Dartmouth College Archives.

30. "Benjamin Wadsworth's Journal Concerning the Five Nations Commission, 1694," 51–53, Benjamin Wadsworth Diary, 1692–1737, Massachusetts Historical Society.

31. Frederick Lewis Weis, *The Colonial Clergy of Virginia, North Carolina, and South Carolina* (Baltimore: Genealogical Publishing, 1976), 22; John Fiske, *Old Virginia and Her Neighbours* (Boston: Houghton Mifflin, 1897–1902), II:227; Philip Alexander Bruce, *Institutional History of Virginia in the Seventeenth Century: An Inquiry into the Religious, Moral, Educational, Legal, Military, and Political Condition of the People* (New York: G. P. Putnam's Sons, 1910), I:213; Rev. John Moncure, "Christ Church, Middlesex, County, Virginia," in *Colonial Churches in the Original Colony of Virginia* (Richmond: Southern Churchman Company, 1908), 246; Herbert Aptheker, *American Negro Slave Revolts* (1943; New York: International Publishers, 1987), 134; Wilford Kale, "Educating a Colony: The First Trustees of the College of William and Mary in Virginia," *Colonial Williamsburg*, Autumn 2000, 25–27.

32. Benjamin Wadsworth, *The Well-Ordered Family: Or, Relative Duties. Being the Substance of Several Sermons, About Family Prayer, Duties of*

Husbands & Wives, Duties of Parents & Children, Duties of Masters & Servants (Boston: B. Green, 1712), 103–21. The reference is to Proverbs 29:19.

33. "The Case of Maria in the Court of Assistants in 1681," *Transactions: Publications of the Colonial Society of Massachusetts, 1899, 1900* (Boston: By the Society, 1904), VI:330.

34. Abner Cheney Goodell Jr., *The Trial and Execution, for Petit Treason, of Mark and Phillis, Slaves of Capt. John Codman, Who Murdered Their Master at Charlestown, Mass., in 1755; for Which the Man Was Hanged and Gibbeted, and the Woman Was Burned to Death. Including, also, Some Account of Other Punishments by Burning in Massachusetts* (Cambridge, MA: John Wilson and Son, 1883), 4–30; Elise Lemire, *Black Walden: Slavery and Its Aftermath in Concord, Massachusetts* (Philadelphia: University of Pennsylvania Press, 2009), 42–69; *Sibley's Harvard Graduates*, XIII:99, 230; John Winthrop, 1755 Almanac, entry for 18 September 1755, Almanacs of Professor John Winthrop, Papers of John and Hannah Winthrop, Box 4, Vol. 14, Harvard University Archives; "Portrait of Professor John Winthrop," *Publications of the Colonial Society of Massachusetts: Transactions, 1900–1902* (Boston: By the Society, 1905), VII:325–27; entries for 12 April 1754, 18 September 1755, in "Rev. Edward Brooks Journal, 1753–1762," 9, 27, Massachusetts Historical Society; entry for 10 April 1754, "The Diary of Ebenezer Parkman, 1754–1755," ed. Francis G. Walett, in *Proceedings of the American Antiquarian Society at the Semi-annual Meeting Held in Boston, April 20, 1966* (Worcester, MA: American Antiquarian Society, 1966), 76:95–96; *Boston Weekly News-Letter*, 14 March 1754, 11 April 1754.

35. *New-York Mercury*, 16 April 1764; Thomas Bradbury Chandler, D.D., *The Life of Samuel Johnson, D.D., the First President of King's College, in New-York* (New York: T. and F. Swords, 1805), 106–8.

36. Entries for 9 February 1763 and 16 November 1769, College of William and Mary, "Faculty Minutes, 1729–1784"; Terry L. Meyers, "A First Look at the Worst: Slavery and Race Relations at the College of William and Mary," *William & Mary Bill of Rights Journal*, April 2008, 1144–45; *Records of the Town of Hanover, New Hampshire, 1761–1818*, 6–8; Lord, *History of the Town of Hanover*, 148–49.

37. Entry for 19 February 1759, Augustus Van Horne, "Account Book," New-York Historical Society; *New-York Mercury*, 22 January 1759; Elizabeth Donnan, ed., *Documents Illustrative of the History of the Slave Trade to America* (Washington, DC: Carnegie Institution, 1931–), III:463–87; Cynthia A. Kierner, *Traders and Gentlefolk: The Livingstons of New York, 1675–1790* (Ithaca, NY: Cornell University Press, 1992), 254, 259.

38. John Watts to Isaac Young-Husband, 27 November 1762, and John Watts to John Riddell, 27 November 1762, 21 February 1763, 13 July 1763, *The Letter Book of John Watts: Merchant and Councillor of New York, January 1, 1762–December 22, 1765*, vol. LXI of *The Collections of the New-York Historical*

Society for the Year 1928 (New York: Printed for the Society, 1928), 97–98, 126, 154.

39. In 1812 the New Jersey trustees decided to reduce the faculty and reemphasize theology. Maclean had turned down an offer from South Carolina College several years earlier and now found himself in need of a position, which he found at the College of William and Mary. Professor Maclean died in 1814, just a couple of years before his son graduated from New Jersey.

   The New York merchant John Delafield, closely tied to Columbia, sold a number of black children, often into black households, with the condition that they be freed by age twenty-one or twenty-five. Bill of sale between John Maclean and William Gulick, 1 January 1809, Gulick Family Papers, Box 1, Folder 65, C0436, Firestone Library, Princeton University; Edwin L. Green, *A History of the University of South Carolina* (Columbia: State Company, 1916), 22–23; William D. Carrell, "Biographical List of American College Professors to 1800," *History of Education Quarterly*, Autumn 1968, 365; John Delafield's bills of sale and indenture, dated 14 May 1798, 21 May 1798, 10 June 1805, and 25 November 1807, Delafield Family Papers, Box 102, Folder 10, C0391, Firestone Library, Princeton University.

40. George P. Fisher, *Life of Benjamin Silliman, M.D., LL.D., Late Professor of Chemistry, Mineralogy, and Geology in Yale College, Chiefly from His Manuscript Reminiscences, Diaries, and Correspondence* (New York: Charles Scribner, 1866), I:21–23, 87–107; Benjamin Silliman, *An Introductory Lecture, Delivered in the Laboratory of Yale College, October, 1828* (New Haven: Hezekiah Howe, 1828).

41. Fisher, *Life of Benjamin Silliman*, 22–23; Chandos Michael Brown, *Benjamin Silliman: A Life in the Young Republic* (Princeton: Princeton University Press, 1989), 3–61.

42. Barbara S. Lindemann, "'To Ravish and Carnally Know': Rape in Eighteenth-Century Massachusetts," *Signs*, Autumn 1984, 79–82; Catherine Adams and Elizabeth H. Pleck, *Love of Freedom: Black Women in Colonial and Revolutionary New England* (New York: Oxford University Press, 2010), ch. 1.

43. Philip Alexander Bruce, *History of the University of Virginia, 1819–1919: The Lengthened Shadow of One Man* (New York: Macmillan Company, 1920), II:208–10; "Benjamin Wadsworth's Book (A. Dom. 1725) Relating to the College," 470; Constance M. Greiff and Wanda S. Gunning, "Tusculum: The History of a House," *Princeton History*, 1998, 37–40.

44. Hugh Jones, *The Present State of Virginia. Giving a Particular and Short Account of the Indian, English, and Negroe Inhabitants of that Colony. Shewing Their Religion, Manners, Government, Trade, Way of Living, &c. With a Description of the Country. From Whence is Inferred a Short View of Maryland*

and North Carolina. To Which are Added, Schemes and Propositions for the Better Promotion of Learning, Religion, Inventions, Manufactures, and Trade in Virginia, and the Other Plantations. For the Information of the Curious, and for the Service of Such as are Engaged in the Propagation of the Gospel and Advancement of Learning, and for the Use of All Persons Concerned in the Virginia Trade and Plantation (London: J. Clarke, 1724), 88; Samuel K. Lothrop, Life of Samuel Kirkland, Missionary to the Indians (Boston: Charles C. Little and James Brown, 1848), 208.

45. Wheelock, Continuation of the Narrative of the Indian Charity School, 3–5; Lord, History of the Town of Hanover, 301–2; see the sworn statement of Nathaniel Hovey, 12 May 1783, Papers of Richard Hovey, Box 1, Folder 6, Rauner Library, Dartmouth College.

46. Jacob Rodriguez de Rivera to Nicholas Brown and Company, 21 March 1770, and "Rough Draft of the Rev. Mr. Smith's Authorization, 1769," University Steering Committee on Slavery and Justice, Brown University Library; James T. Campbell et al., Slavery and Justice: Report of the Brown University Steering Committee on Slavery and Justice (Providence: Brown University, October 2006), esp. 11–15.

47. For two decades before the Civil War, the trustees of Wake Forest College (1838) in North Carolina kept a death watch over an ill widow, Rebecca Blount. In 1836 her husband died. He gave one enslaved black girl to each of his two nieces and an enslaved black boy to his nephew. Nine enslaved adults, a house and lots in Edenton, a plantation with house and furnishings outside town, and all other furnishings, carriages, and equipment went into trust to support Rebecca Blount. Upon her death, the executors were to transfer the estate to support "poor and indigent young men destined for the ministry" at a planned local Baptist college. For twenty-three years, the trustees anxiously awaited that inheritance, even hiring lawyers to protect the college's interests by challenging Rebecca Blount's financial decisions. In November 1859 she died. Wake Forest's governors immediately convened to seize the property, especially the slaves. They listed six men (Isaac, Jim, Pompie, Joseph, Thomas, and Harry), seven women (Lucy, Caroline, Emma, Nancy, Harriet, Ann, and May), and three children, an increase from the number transferred in the Blount will. Two enslaved people had died but some of the women had given birth, and the trustees claimed these children, or the "natural increase," as part of the entitlement. Over the college's objections, Rebecca Blount had sold a few of the children, and the treasurer now negotiated for their return. The latter decision was not intended to reunite families but to maximize profits. On 7 May 1860, the board placed the women, men, and children on sale. The adults were dispersed to various buyers in North Carolina and Virginia. The youngest children were discarded with their mothers. The trustees did not get to sell Mary, a girl who, according

to a historian of Wake Forest, had run away, "probably because she feared the ordeal of the auctioneer's block." Mary was soon captured in Norfolk. The board paid the bounty and jail fees. They then rid themselves of her at public sale, receiving less than anticipated because of her new reputation for absconding. Altogether, Wake Forest acquired about $12,000 from the sales. It was not its first transaction of this type. For instance, in 1847, Celia Wilder bequeathed roughly $600 to the college: "the sale price of two negro women, and the residue of her estate." "With the exception of a supervisor of grounds and a single campus policeman, all the workers at Vanderbilt [University] seem to have been black," notes Paul Conkin. "They cared for grounds, cleaned and maintained buildings, cooked food in the student messes, and worked as porters or servants in professors' homes. They remained hidden, even resented components of the campus." Lyon Gardiner Tyler, *The College of William and Mary in Virginia: Its History and Work, 1693–1907* (Richmond: Whittet and Shepperson, 1907), 22–23, 37; "Boarding Accounts, 1743–1891," Office of the Bursar Records, 1745–1875, Special Collections, Swem Library, College of William and Mary; William Gooch to Thomas Gooch, 1727, 1–2, Gooch Letters, James Blair Papers, Box 1, Folder 3, Special Collections, Swem Library, College of William and Mary; Paul K. Conkin, *Gone with the Ivy: A Biography of Vanderbilt University* (Knoxville: University of Tennessee Press, 1985), 82–83; George Washington Paschal, *History of Wake Forest College* (Wake Forest, NC: Wake Forest College, 1935), I:213–19, 217–18n.

48. Ron Chernow, *Washington: A Life* (New York: Penguin, 2010), 155–64; Helen Bryan, *Martha Washington: First Lady of Liberty* (New York: John Wiley and Sons, 2002), 162–66; Henry Wiencek, *An Imperfect God: George Washington, His Slaves, and the Creation of America* (New York: Farrar, Straus and Giroux, 2003), 282–88; John Parke Custis to Dear Mama, 5 July 1773, in Joseph E. Fields, comp., *"Worthy Partner": The Papers of Martha Washington* (Westport, CT: Greenwood, 1994), 152–53; entries for May and April 1773, in Donald Jackson, ed., *The Diaries of George Washington* (Charlottesville: University of Virginia Press, 1978), III:178–83; Patricia Brady, *Martha Washington: An American Life* (New York: Viking, 2005), 74–89.

49. William R. Davie to Spruce Macay, 3 September 1793, William R. Davie Papers, Folder 13, UNC; William D. Snider, *Light on the Hill: A History of the University of North Carolina at Chapel Hill* (Chapel Hill: University of North Carolina Press, 1992), 3–23; Green, *History of the University of South Carolina*, 19–20.

50. Bruce, *History of the University of Virginia*, I:258–59, 284.

51. Christopher Grant Champlin eventually represented Rhode Island in the United States Senate. See the Champlin brothers' correspondence with their captains and factors, and Christopher Grant Champlin to Christopher

Champlin, 6 September 1784, *Commerce of Rhode Island, 1726–1800* (Boston: Massachusetts Historical Society, 1914–15), esp. II:227–28.

52. Unsigned letter to Samuel Johnson (ca. 1760), Samuel Johnson Papers, Box 1, Rare Book and Manuscript Library, Columbia University; "Constitutions of the Publick Academy in the City of Philadelphia," in *Minutes of the Trustees of the College, Academy and Charitable Schools of the University of Pennsylvania*, vol. 1, *1749–1768*, 9; Christopher J. Lucas, *American Higher Education: A History* (New York: St. Martin's Griffin, 1994), 108; Virginia D. Harrington, *The New York Merchant on the Eve of the Revolution* (Gloucester, MA: Peter Smith, 1964), 33–34; Donnan, ed., *Documents Illustrative of the History of the Slave Trade*, III:131; Edward Peterson, *History of Rhode Island* (New York: J. S. Taylor, 1853); Estate Papers of the Malbone Family, and Godfrey Malbone Sr.'s Account Book, Malbone Family Collection, Rhode Island Historical Society.

53. "Census of Negro Slaves of 16 Years Age or Upward, in Each Town in Massachusetts, 1754," Massachusetts State Archives; Edgar J. McManus, *Black Bondage in the North* (Syracuse, NY: Syracuse University Press, 1973), 72–87; John Winthrop, 1754 Almanac, Almanacs of Professor John Winthrop, Box 4, Vol. 13, Harvard University Archives; *Account of the Number of Inhabitants, in the Colony of Connecticut, January 1, 1774, Together with An Account of the Number of Inhabitants, Taken January 1, 1756* ; *A Return of the Number of Inhabitants in the State of Connecticut, February 1, 1782, and Also of the Indians and Negroes* (Connecticut, 1782); "A List of the Ratables of the Several Townships & Precincts in the County of Somerset in the State of New Jersey, of July 1784 with the Assessments Made Upon," and the county lists, reel 18, New Jersey State Archives.

54. Lucius R. Paige, *History of Cambridge, Massachusetts, 1630–1877* (Boston: H. O. Houghton, 1877), 286–92; Stephen Paschall Sharples, *Records of the Church of Christ at Cambridge in New England 1632–1830: Comprising the Ministerial Records of Baptisms, Marriages, Deaths, Admission to the Covenant and Communion, Dismissals and Church Proceedings* (Boston: Eben. Putnam, 1906).

55. Samuel Curwen, "His Colledge Laws, 1731," Curwen Family Papers, 1637–1808, American Antiquarian Society; entries for 4 April 1737, 21 March 1740, and 3 September 1751, Records of the Harvard Faculty, I:90, 125, 342–43, Harvard University Archives; *Sibley's Harvard Graduates*, XIII:410–13, 458–59; Samuel Eliot Morison, *Three Centuries of Harvard, 1636–1936* (Cambridge, MA: Harvard University Press, 1936), 115.

56. "The Lawes of the Colledge Published Publiquely Before the Students of Harvard College, May 4, 1655," *Publications of the Colonial Society of Massachusetts* (Boston: By the Society, 1935), XXXI:330–40; "John Leverett's Diary, 1707–1723," 14–15, 44, Papers of John Leverett, Box 8; David Cressy, "Gender Trouble and Cross Dressing in Early Modern England," *Journal*

of British Studies, October 1996, 438–65; "Benjamin Wadsworth's Book (A. Dom. 1725) Relating to the College," 454–58; John Burton, "Collegiate Living and Cambridge Justice: Regulating the Colonial Harvard Student Community in the Eighteenth Century," *History of Higher Education Annual*, 2007, XXIII:86; entries for 30 March 1753 and 26 October 1753, Harvard University, Faculty Minutes, 1725–1890, II:6, 12–13, Harvard University Archives; entry for 1 October 1754 in "Rev. Edward Brooks Journal, 1753–1762," 15.

57. Entry for 20 February 1753, Judgments of the President and Tutors of Yale College, 1751–1768, in Faculty of Yale College Records; "Yale University Corporation and Prudential Committee Minutes," esp. entries for 16 October 1723, 10 September 1760, 22 November 1763, 31 July 1765.

58. Entry for 9 November 1748, "Minutes of the Proceedings of the Trustees of the College of New Jersey," vol. I; entries for 3 June 1755, 1 March 1763, 23 April 1763, and 2 September 1773, in "Minutes of the Governors of King's College," vol. I, Rare Book and Manuscript Library, Columbia University.

59. Columbia University, *The Black Book, or Book of Misdemeanors in King's College, New-York, 1771–1775* (New York: Columbiana at the University Press, 1931), 3, New-York Historical Society; *Catalogue of the Governors, Trustees and Officers, and of the Alumni and Other Graduates, of Columbia College (Originally King's College), in the City of New York, from 1754 to 1882* (New York: Printed for the College, 1882), 9, 14.

60. Leverett Wilson Spring, *A History of Williams College* (Boston: Houghton Mifflin, 1917), 306.

61. George Moses Horton, *The Poetical Works of George M. Horton: The Colored Bard of North-Carolina: To Which Is Prefixed the Life of the Author* (Hillsborough, NC: D. Heartt, 1845), 12–18; Joseph Caldwell to Samuel Stanhope Smith, President of the College of New Jersey, 5 September 1811, Joseph Caldwell Papers, Folder 1, Wilson Library, UNC; Kemp P. Battle, *History of the University of North Carolina: From Its Beginnings to the Death of President Swain, 1789–1868* (Raleigh, NC: Edwards and Broughton, 1907), I:261–62.

62. See also, Mark Auslander, "The Other Side of Paradise: Glimpsing Slavery in the University's Utopian Landscapes," *Southern Spaces*, May 2010. Clifton K. Shipton, *Biographical Sketches of Those Who Attended Harvard College in the Classes 1761–1763* (Boston: Massachusetts Historical Society, 1970), XV:56–67; Freeman Hunt, *Lives of American Merchants* (New York: Hunt's Merchants' Magazine, 1856), I:556–57; Justin Winsor, ed., *The Memorial History of Boston, Including Suffolk County, Massachusetts, 1630–1880* (Boston: James R. Osgood, 1882), IV:155n.

63. Betsey Stockton developed her expertise in Mosaic institutions, early Judaism, and biblical geography by studying in the president's library at Princeton. "Betsey Stockton" clipping file and biographical file, library of

the New York State Historical Association; obituary, Cooperstown *Freeman's Journal*, 3 November 1865; Escher, "She Calls Herself Betsey Stockton," 98–102.

64. Phebe Jacobs was working at Bowdoin when John Brown Russwurm, the third black person to graduate from an American college, gave the commencement address in 1826. Málaga is a Moorish city on the southern coast of Spain. King, "Still Embattled, Yet Emboldened"; "An Honored Negress," *Farmer's Cabinet*, 11 April 1850; John B. Russwurm, "The Condition and Prospects of Hayti," ed. Philip S. Foner, *Journal of Negro History*, October 1969, 395–97; Mrs. T[homas]. C. Upham, *Narrative of Phebe Ann Jacobs* (London: W. and F. G. Cash, 1850); Louis C. Hatch, *The History of Bowdoin College* (Portland, Maine: Loring, Short, and Harmon, 1927), 41–45; Maria Wheelock's obituary, *Haverhill Gazette*, 21 June 1828; George Augustus Wheeler and Henry Warren Wheeler, *History of Brunswick, Topsham, and Harpswell, Maine, Including the Ancient Territory Known as Pejepscot* (Boston: Alfred Mudge and Son, 1878), 104–6, 206; William D. Williamson, *The History of the State of Maine; From Its First Discovery, A.D. 1602, to the Separation, A.D. 1820, Inclusive* (Hallowell, ME: Glazier, Masters, and Smith, 1839), 373; William David Barry, "The Shameful Story of Malaga Island," *Reunion*, 30 April 1996; John King Lord, *A History of Dartmouth College, 1815–1909: Being the Second Volume of A History of Dartmouth College and the Town of Hanover, New Hampshire, begun by Frederick Chase* (Concord, NH: Rumford Press, 1913), 629–30; Frederick Chase, *A History of Dartmouth College and the Town of Hanover, New Hampshire*, ed. John K. Lord (Cambridge, MA: John Wilson and Son, 1891), I:163.

65. Maria Suhm owned "several slaves." Last will and testament of Eleazar Wheelock, 4 June 1779; see the letters of John Wheelock, Maria Suhm, and the extended families, in John Wheelock Family Correspondence, MS 934, Rauner Library, Dartmouth College. More than three dozen black people were buried in Hanover during this era. Dartmouth Cemetery Association, "Record of Deaths, Interment and Inscriptions," March 1929, Baker Library, Dartmouth College. David Ogden of Newark, NJ, to Jonathan Sergeant, 24 July 1761, Ogden Family Papers, Box 2, Folder 8, Firestone Library, Princeton University; Lord, *History of the Town of Hanover*, 148–89, 301–2.

CHAPTER 5: WHITENING THE PROMISED LAND

1. H. Frank Eshleman, *Lancaster County Indians: Annals of the Susquehannocks and Other Indian Tribes of the Susquehanna Territory from About the Year 1500–1763, the Date of Their Extinction* (Lancaster, PA, 1908), 373–87; Benjamin Franklin, *A Narrative of the Late Massacres, in Lancaster County, of a Number of Indians, Friends of this Province, by Persons Unknown With*

Some Observations on the Same (Philadelphia, 1764), 3–8; C. Hale Sipe, *The Indian Wars of Pennsylvania: An Account of the Indian Events, in Pennsylvania, of the French and Indian War, Pontiac's War, Lord Dunmore's War, the Revolutionary War and the Indian Uprising from 1789–1795* (Harrisburg, PA: Telegraph Press, 1929), 462–69.

2.   Eshleman, *Lancaster County Indians*, 375–86; Franklin, *Narrative of the Late Massacres*, 8–13; Sipe, *Indian Wars of Pennsylvania*, 463–67; Wayland F. Dunaway, *The Scotch-Irish of Colonial Pennsylvania* (Chapel Hill: University of North Carolina Press, 1944), 50–71; George W. Franz, *Paxton: A Study of Community Structure and Mobility in the Colonial Pennsylvania Backcountry* (New York: Garland, 1989), 3–83.

3.   Kevin Kenny, *Peaceable Kingdom Lost: The Paxton Boys and the Destruction of William Penn's Holy Experiment* (New York: Oxford University Press, 2009), 140–46; Sipe, *Indian Wars of Pennsylvania*, 463–67.

4.   Kenny, *Peaceable Kingdom Lost*, 40–49, 89–90, 217; Franz, *Paxton*, 340–45; Wilson Armistead, *Memoirs of James Logan; A Distinguished Scholar and Christian Legislator; Founder of the Loganian Library at Philadelphia; Secretary of the Province of Pennsylvania; Chief Justice; Commissioner of Property; and (as President of the Council) for Two Years Governor of the Province* (London: Charles Gilpin, 1851), 78–91; Frederick B. Tolles, *James Logan and the Culture of Provincial America* (Boston: Little, Brown, 1957), 159–85. On the background of the colony, see Edwin B. Bronner, *William Penn's "Holy Experiment": The Founding of Pennsylvania, 1681–1701* (New York: Columbia University Press [for Temple University], 1962); Steven C. Harper, "Delawares and Pennsylvanians After the Walking Purchase," in William A. Pencak and Daniel K. Richter, eds., *Friends and Enemies in Penn's Woods: Indians, Colonists, and the Racial Construction of Pennsylvania* (University Park: Pennsylvania State University Press, 2004), 167–72.

5.   In 1711 Robert Livingston sold several thousand acres of Mohawk Valley land to Governor Robert Hunter for the settlement of eighteen hundred Palatines: German Protestants from the Rhine Valley. These immigrants received permission from Queen Anne to come to the Americas, and the governor situated them in a strategically important slice of Indian country. Hunter and Livingston abused this group to a point where they depended upon the charity of the Mohawk, while the governor bound out their children to English families and tradesmen. Among these apprenticed children was John Peter Zenger, later embroiled in the famous freedom-of-speech case after he was arrested for publishing libelous statements against Governor William Cosby of New York. The New Jersey land speculator and attorney James Alexander, a Livingston in-law, represented him in that controversy. Alexander and Lewis Morris had funded Zenger's *New-York Weekly Journal* and had editorial control over its content.
       Brendan McConville, *These Daring Disturbers of the Public Peace: The*

Struggle for Property and Power in Early New Jersey (Ithaca, NY: Cornell University Press, 1999), 30–31; Nathaniel S. Benton, *A History of Herkimer County, Including the Upper Mohawk Valley, from the Earliest Period to the Present Times: With a Brief Notice of the Iroquois Indians, the Early German Tribes, the Palatine Immigrations into the Colony of New York, and Biographical Sketches of the Palatine Families, the Patentees of Burnetsfield in the Year 1725* (Albany, NY: J. Munsell, 1856), esp. 32–49; J. David Hoeveler, *Creating the American Mind: Intellect and Politics in Colonial Colleges* (Lanham, MD: Rowman and Littlefield, 2002), 155–62; Bronner, *William Penn's "Holy Experiment,"* 59–65; Marianne S. Wokeck, *Trade in Strangers: The Beginnings of Mass Migration to North America* (University Park: Pennsylvania State University Press, 1999), 59–112; "Account of Servants Bound & Assigned Before James Hamilton, Mayor, 1745," Historical Society of Pennsylvania; Aaron Spencer Fogleman, *Hopeful Journeys: German Immigration, Settlement, and Political Culture in Colonial America, 1717–1775* (Philadelphia: University of Pennsylvania Press, 1996), 69–99; Evarts B. Greene and Virginia D. Harrington, *American Population Before the Federal Census of 1790* (New York: Columbia University Press, 1932), 114–27; Stella H. Sutherland, *Population Distribution in Colonial America* (New York: Columbia University Press, 1936), 154–58; Allen S. Fisher, *Lutheranism in Bucks County, 1734–1934: With a Restudy of the Indians of the Eastern United States to More Definitely Prove Lutheran Missions Among the Lenape of the Delaware Valley, 1638–1740* (Tinicum, PA: Allen S. Fisher, 1935); Lucy Simler, "Tenancy in Colonial Pennsylvania: The Case for Chester County," *William and Mary Quarterly*, October 1986, 542–69; see surveyor's reports for Nathan Levy and David Franks, 4 October 1765, on warrant granted 13 April 1752, Pennsylvania Counties Papers, 1708–1882, Lancaster County, Box 3, Folder 1, Historical Society of Pennsylvania.

6. Rosalind J. Beiler, "From the Rhine to the Delaware Valley: The Eighteenth-Century Transatlantic Trading Channels of Caspar Wistar," in Hartmut Lehmann et al., eds., *In Search of Peace and Prosperity: New German Settlements in Eighteenth-Century Europe and America* (University Park: Pennsylvania State University Press, 2000), 172–88; I. Daniel Rupp, *A Collection of Upwards of Thirty Thousand Names of German, Swiss, Dutch, French and Other Immigrants in Pennsylvania from 1727 to 1776, with a Statement of the Names of Ships, Whence They Sailed, and the Date of Their Arrival at Philadelphia, Chronologically Arranged, Together with the Necessary Historical and Other Notes, Also, an Appendix Containing Lists of More than One Thousand German and French Names in New York Prior to 1712* (Philadelphia: Leary, Stuart, 1898), esp. 4–18; Barbara Ann Chernow, *Robert Morris, Land Speculator, 1790–1801* (New York: Arno, 1978), 8–12.

7. See the Berkshire Furnace Ledgers, 145–46, Folder 1, Box 1, GM-0003, and Berkshire Furnace Ledgers, 96–97, Folder 2, Box 1, GM-0004, in

Accounts of Iron Forges and Plantations, MG–2, Business Records Collection, 1681–1963, Pennsylvania State Archives; John Heckwelder, *A Narrative of the Mission of the United Brethren Among the Delaware and Mohegan Indians, from Its Commencement, in the Year 1740, to the Close of the Year 1808. Comprising All the Remarkable Incidents Which Took Place at Their Missionary Stations During that Period. Interspersed with Anecdotes, Historical Facts, Speeches of Indians, and Other Interesting Matter* (Philadelphia: M'Carty and David, 1820), 17–19.

8. Jonathan Edwards, *The Life of Rev. David Brainerd, Chiefly Extracted from His Diary* (1765; New York: American Tract Society, 1844), 30–32; John Hall, *History of the Presbyterian Church in Trenton, N.J. from the First Settlement of the Town* (New York: Anson D. F. Randolph, 1859), 116–17; *The Testimony of the President, Professors, Tutors and Hebrew Instructor of Harvard College in Cambridge, Against the Reverend Mr. George Whitefield, and His Conduct* (Boston: T. Fleet, 1744); entries for 13 November 1749, 2 February 1749, and 10 September 1751, in *Minutes of the Trustees of the College, Academy and Charitable Schools of the University of Pennsylvania*, vol. 1, *1749–1768* (Wilmington, DE: Scholarly Resources, 1974), x, 1, 3–4, 15.

9. Jon Butler, *Becoming America: The Revolution before 1776* (Cambridge, MA: Harvard University Press, 2001), 187–203.

10. A bequest from Thomas Hollis underwrote the cost of Indian education at the Sergeants' mission. E. Pemberton, *A Sermon Preach'd in New-Ark, June 12, 1744, at the Ordination of Mr. David Brainerd, A Missionary among the Indians upon the Borders of the Provinces of New-York, New-Jersey, and Pennsylvania* (Boston: Roger and Fowle, 1744), 22–32; Jonathan Edwards, Stockbridge, to the Hon. Thomas Hubbard, esq., Boston, 31 August 1751, Historical Society of Pennsylvania; John Sergeant to William Johnson, 1 July 1749, Joseph Dwight to William Johnson, 13 October 1751, Martin Kellogg to Hendrick, 23 December 1751, in John Sullivan, ed., *The Papers of Sir William Johnson* (Albany: University of the State of New York, 1921–1965), I:233–39, 353–58; Stephen West, Stockbridge, to Andrew Oliver, Boston, 2 July 1763, Massachusetts Historical Society; William Kellaway, *The New England Company, 1649–1776* (London: Longmans, 1961), 272–76; Lion G. Miles, "The Red Man Dispossessed: The Williams Family and the Alienation of Indian Land in Stockbridge, Massachusetts, 1736–1818," in Alden T. Vaughan, ed., *New England Encounters: Indians and Euroamericans, ca. 1600–1850* (Boston: Northeastern University Press, 1999), 276–97; Colonel Ephraim Williams, last will and testament, 22 July 1755, Archives and Special Collections, Williams College; Leverett Wilson Spring, *A History of Williams College* (Boston: Houghton Mifflin, 1917), 22; Robert H. Romer, "Higher Education and Slavery in Western Massachusetts," *Journal of Blacks in Higher Education*, Winter 2004.

11. Land-hungry farmers crossed the sound and established new villages on Long Island. Robert Treat and his congregation left New Haven and settled in Newark, New Jersey. Connecticut settlers raised villages east of the Hudson, where they gained the attention of the Dutch, Mohawk, and Anglicans as they trespassed the river. They journeyed up the Connecticut River and constructed settlements in the contested lands that became "New Connecticut," or Vermont. They also traversed across New York in the aftermath of the Revolution to create a beachhead of Yankee radicalism in the Western Reserve of Ohio. Edith Anna Bailey, "Influences Toward Radicalism in Connecticut, 1754–1775," *Smith College Studies in History* V, no. 4 (July 1920): 179–248; Julian Parks Boyd, *The Susquehannah Company: Connecticut's Experiment in Expansion* (New Haven: Yale University Press for the Tercentenary Commission of the State of Connecticut, 1935), XXXIV:1–48; Julian P. Boyd, ed., *The Susquehannah Company Papers* (Wilkes-Barre, PA: Wyoming Historical and Geological Society, 1930), I:lxx–lxxxix; on the resolution of the land claims, see Simeon E. Baldwin, "Connecticut in Pennsylvania," *Papers of the New Haven Colony Historical Society* (New Haven: For the Society, 1914), VIII:1–19.

12. Annette Gordon-Reed, *Thomas Jefferson and Sally Hemings: An American Controversy* (Charlottesville: University Press of Virginia, 1997), 197–98; Fawn McKay Brodie, *Thomas Jefferson: An Intimate History* (New York: Norton, 1974), 36–38; Anthony F. C. Wallace, *Jefferson and the Indians: The Tragic Fate of the First Americans* (Cambridge, MA: Harvard University Press, 1999), 21–40.

13. Albert Cook Myers, *The Boy George Washington, Aged 16: His Own Account of an Iroquois Indian Dance, 1748* (Philadelphia: Albert Cook Myers, 1932), 1–17; Louis Knott Koontz, *The Virginia Frontier, 1754–1763* (Baltimore: Johns Hopkins University Press, 1925), 39–41; Rufus Blanchard, *History of Illinois* (Chicago: National School Furnishing Company, 1883), 29; Washington Irving, *Life of George Washington* (New York: G. P. Putnam, 1855), I:47–63; Shelby Little, *George Washington* (New York: J. J. Little and Ives, 1929), 14; William Addison Phillips, *Labor, Land, and Law: A Search for the Missing Wealth of the Working Poor* (New York: Charles Scribner's Sons, 1886), 321–24; Wallace, *Jefferson and the Indians*, 21–40, 50.

14. William Smith, *A Discourse Concerning the Conversion of the Heathen Americans, and the Final Propagation of Christianity and the Sciences to the Ends of the Earth* (Philadelphia: W. Dunlap, 1760), 14–22; John Brown, *On Religious Liberty: A Sermon at St. Paul's Cathedral, on Sunday the 6th of March, 1763. On Occasion of the Brief for the Establishment of the Colleges of Philadelphia and New-York. Published at the Request of the Managers of the Charity. To which is prefixed An Address to the Principal Inhabitants of the North American Colonies, on Occasion of the Peace* (Philadelphia: Andrew Steuart, 1763), 22–23.

15. Benjamin Franklin, "Observations Concerning the Increase of Mankind and the Peopling of Countries," written in Pennsylvania, 1751, in Jared Sparks, ed., *The Works of Benjamin Franklin; Containing Several Political and Historical Tracts Not Included in Any Former Edition, and Many Letters Official and Private Not Hitherto Published; with Notes and a Life of the Author by Jared Sparks* (Boston: Hilliard, Gray, 1836), II:320–21; Franklin, *Narrative of the Late Massacres*, 13; Kenny, *Peaceable Kingdom Lost*, 184–85; Ezra Stiles, *The United States Elevated to Glory and Honor: A Sermon, Preached before His Excellency Jonathan Trumbull, Esq. L.L.D., Governor and Commander in Chief, and the Honorable the General Assembly of the State of Connecticut, Convened at Hartford, at the Anniversary Election, May 8th, 1783* (New Haven: Thomas and Samuel Green, 1783), 8–10; Eshleman, *Lancaster County Indians*, 383–86; Ezra Stiles to Pelatiah Webster, 21 May 1763, in Boyd, ed., *Susquehannah Company Papers*, II:221–33.

16. Alan Houston, *Benjamin Franklin and the Politics of Improvement* (New Haven: Yale University Press, 2008), esp. 201; David Waldstreicher, "Capitalism, Slavery, and Benjamin Franklin's American Revolution," in Cathy Mason, ed., *The Economy of Early America: Historical Perspectives and New Directions* (University Park: Pennsylvania State University, 2006), 202–3; Douglas R. Egerton, *Death or Liberty: African Americans and Revolutionary America* (New York: Oxford, 2009), 237; Wallace, *Jefferson and the Indians*, 34–49; Phillips, *Labor, Land, and Law*, 324.

17. Franklin, "Observations Concerning the Increase of Mankind and the Peopling of Countries," 234; William Smith, *A Brief History of the Rise and Progress of the Charitable Scheme, Carrying on by a Society of Noblemen and Gentlemen in London, for the Relief and Instruction of Poor Germans, and Their Descendents, Settled in Pennsylvania, and the Adjacent British Colonies in North-America* (Philadelphia: B. Franklin and D. Hall, 1755), esp. 5–7; Hoeveler, *Creating the American Mind*, 162–65.

18. Joseph Henry Dubbs, *History of Franklin and Marshall College* (Lancaster, PA: Franklin and Marshall College Alumni Association, 1903), 15–23; *A Letter by Dr. Benjamin Rush Describing the Consecration of the German College at Lancaster in June, 1787* (Lancaster, PA: Franklin and Marshall College, 1945), 16; Donald G. Tewksbury, *The Founding of American Colleges and Universities Before the Civil War with Particular Reference to the Religious Influences Bearing upon the College Movement* (New York: Teachers College, 1932), 34.

19. The children of the eighteenth century New York City slave traders Moses Levy and David Franks established themselves as prominent merchants and society figures in Philadelphia. They also drifted away from religious orthodoxy. Some even married out of the faith or abandoned Judaism. In 1742 Jacob and Abigail Franks's daughter, Phila, eloped with Oscar DeLancey, whose older brother was the chief justice of New York

colony and the incoming lieutenant governor. Her parents, Orthodox Jews, protested her marriage to a Christian by ceasing contact with her for a year. The Franks' concerns were affirmed seven years later when Oliver DeLancey joined a group of men in terrorizing a Dutch Jewish immigrant. Blackening their faces, they broke into the man's home and destroyed his property. Oliver DeLancey then threatened to rape his wife, telling her that she favored Sarah Tappen, the wife of Governor George Clinton, and that he would take her since the First Lady was out of reach. George Clinton was delaying James DeLancey's appointment as lieutenant governor in retaliation for DeLancey's decision to support the legislature in a dispute over his salary as governor. Naomi W. Cohen, *Jews in Christian America: The Pursuit of Religious Equality* (New York: Oxford University Press, 1992), 11–30; Jacob Katz, *From Prejudice to Destruction: Anti-Semitism, 1700–1933* (Cambridge, MA: Harvard University Press, 1980), 23–33; John Watts to Moses Franks, 21 May 1762, *The Letter Book of John Watts: Merchant and Councillor of New York, January 1, 1762–December 22, 1765*, vol. LXI of *The Collections of the New-York Historical Society for the Year 1928* (New York: Printed for the Society, 1928), 28, 59; Morris A. Gutstein, *Aaron Lopez and Judah Touro: A Refugee and a Son of a Refugee* (New York: Behrman's Jewish Book House, 1939), 68–70; George Alexander Kohut, "Ezra Stiles and the Jews," *The American Hebrew*, serialized from 29 November 1901 to 13 June 1902; Albert Ehrenfried, *A Chronicle of Boston Jewry: From the Colonial Settlement to 1900* (Privately printed, 1963), 722–27. The Rhode Island college received gifts from three Jews in South Carolina, including Moses Lindo of Charleston, whose small donation led the governors to officially welcome Jewish students. Moses Lindo to Sampson and Solomon Simson, 17 April 1770, and corporation of the College of Rhode Island to Moses Lindo, 1 January 1771, Rhode Island College Miscellaneous Papers, 1763–1804, Box 1, Folder 1, Brown University. Also, Jacob R. Marcus, *The Colonial American Jew, 1492–1776* (Detroit: Wayne State University Press, 1970), 1243–48; Jacob R. Marcus, *Early American Jewry: The Jews of New York, New England, and Canada, 1649–1794* (Philadelphia: Jewish Publication Society of America, 1951), I: 64–72.

20. In 1800 Sampson Simson delivered a Hebrew lecture during the Columbia College commencement at St. Paul's Episcopal Chapel. "Your request to open my mouth in the Hebrew language," Simson confessed, left me struggling to find a subject worthy of "so great—so respectable an audience." He chose to offer a history of the oldest Jewish community in North America. Simson later founded Mount Sinai Hospital in New York City. He descended from Nathan Simpson, a merchant who brought more than two hundred enslaved Africans into New York in two of the larger local ventures of the early eighteenth century. In 1822 Aaron Lopez, the

grandson of the Newport slave trader, took the doctor of medicine degree at the College of Physicians and Surgeons, Columbia.

Jews had traditionally used tutors and religious academies to educate their children. The descendants of the Gratz family established Gratz College in Philadelphia in 1897. Diane King, "Jewish Education in Philadelphia," in Murray Friedman, ed., *Jewish Life in Philadelphia, 1830–1940* (Philadelphia: Institute for the Study of Human Issues, 1983), 246–48; Ehrenfried, *Chronicle of Boston Jewry*, 722–27; William D. Carrell, "Biographical List of American College Professors to 1800," *History of Education Quarterly*, Autumn 1968, 367; Malcolm H. Stern, *First American Jewish Families: 600 Genealogies, 1654–1977* (Cincinnati: American Jewish Archives, 1978), 87, 272; Diane Ashton, *Rebecca Gratz: Women and Judaism in Antebellum America* (Detroit: Wayne State University Press, 1997), 38; Sampson Simson, "Some Historical Traits of the American Jews from Their First Settlement in North America," Delivered in St. Paul's Church on Wednesday, August 6th, 1800, Anno Mundi 5560, Simson Family Papers, American Jewish Historical Society; Oscar Reiss, *The Jews in Colonial America* (New York: McFarland, 2004), 174–77; Marcus, *Colonial American Jew*, III:1198–201; Jacob Katz, *Out of the Ghetto: The Social Background of Jewish Emancipation, 1770–1870* (Syracuse, NY: Syracuse University Press, 1998), 42–103.

21. The residents of the village of Amherst in western Massachusetts named their town for the victorious general and sought to attract funding from the Williams' estate for a college. The move reflected Amherst's popularity among the colonists, but it was also a strategic step to counter anticipated objections from Harvard to another college in the commonwealth. General Amherst declined the town's petition for a college and instead sent its residents to appeal to the Massachusetts legislature, where their cause died, largely from the interference of Harvard. Williams College descended from the original endowment. Later the faculty and students at Williams divided over the religious orientation of the school, and the defectors established Amherst College (1821) in Amherst. Williams, last will and testament, 22 July 1755; Spring, *History of Williams College*, 22; Miles, "Red Man Dispossessed," 276–97; J. C. Long, *Lord Jeffrey Amherst: A Soldier of the King* (New York: Macmillan, 1933), 168–78.

22. Last will and testament of George Washington, in Jared Sparks, ed., *The Writings of George Washington: Being His Correspondence, Addresses, Messages, and Other Papers, Official and Private, Selected and Published from the Original Manuscripts* (Boston: Ferdinand Andrews, 1839), I:569–73.

23. William Smith's introductory letter, "Concerning the Office and Duties of a Protestant Ministry, Especially During Times of Public Calamity and Danger," in Thomas Barton, *Unanimity and Public Spirit: A Sermon*

Preached at Carlisle, and Some Other Episcopal Churches, in the Counties of York and Cumberland, Soon after General Braddock's Defeat (Philadelphia: B. Franklin and D. Hall, 1755); Thomas Barton, *The Conduct of the Paxton-Men, Impartially Represented: With Some Remarks on the Narrative* (Philadelphia: Andrew Steuart, 1764).

24. Samuel Davies, *Religion and Patriotism the Constituents of a Good Soldier: A Sermon Preached to Captain Overton's Independent Company of Volunteers, Raised in Hanover Country, Virginia, August 17, 1755* (Philadelphia: James Chattin, 1755), 3–5, 22; George Whitefield, *A Short Address to Persons of All Denominations, Occasioned by the Alarm of an Intended Invasion* (Philadelphia: B. Franklin and D. Hall, 1756); Samuel Finley, *The Curse of Meroz: Or, the Danger of Neutrality, in the Cause of God, and Our Country: A Sermon, Preached the 2nd of October, 1757* (Philadelphia: James Chattin, 1757), 5–25; Samuel Richardson to the Rev. Mr. Sam[ue]l Davies, secretary of the Society for Managing the Mission and School among ye Indians, 22 May 1759, Folder 1, William Richardson Davie Papers, 1758–1819, Manuscript Department, Wilson Library, University of North Carolina at Chapel Hill; Samuel Davies, *The Duty of Christians to Propagate Their Religion among Heathens, Earnestly Recommended to the Masters of Negroe Slaves in Virginia. A Sermon Preached in Hanover, January 8, 1757* (London: J. Oliver, 1758), 18–37.

25. William Smith, *The Christian Soldier's Duty; the Lawfulness and Dignity of his Office; and the Importance of the Protestant Cause in the British Colonies, state and explained. A Sermon, Preached April 5, 1757. In Christ-Church, Philadelphia, To the first Battalion of his Majesty's Royal American Regiment; at the Request of their Colonel and Officers* (Philadelphia: James Chattin, 1757), 26–27; entry for 4 February 1758, in *Minutes of the Trustees of the College, Academy and Charitable Schools of the University of Pennsylvania*, vol. 1, *1749–1768*, 93; Samuel Davies, *The Curse of Cowardice: A Sermon Preached to the Militia of Hanover County, in Virginia, at a General Muster, May 8, 1758, with a View of the Company for Captain Samuel Meredith* (London: J. Buckland, 1758), 11; By the Author of American Fables [William Smith], *Indian Songs of Peace with a Proposal, in a Prefatory Epistle, for Erecting Indian Schools, and a Postscript by the Editor, Introducing Yariza, an Indian Maid's Letter, to the Principal Ladies of the Province and City of New-York* (New York: J. Parker and W. Wayman, 1752), 3–12.

26. John Witherspoon, *The Absolute Necessity of Salvation Through Christ: A Sermon, Preached Before the Society in Scotland for the Propagating Christian Knowledge, In the High Church of Edinburgh, On Monday, January 2, 1758. To Which is Subjoined, a Short Account of the Present State of the Society* (Edinburgh: W. Miller, 1758), 39–41.

27. Letter from Benjamin Franklin, 12 December 1755, Box 1, #1376, Henley Smith Collection, Library of Congress; *New-York Mercury*, 1 October

1759; Varnum Lansing Collins, *President Witherspoon: A Biography* (Princeton: Princeton University Press, 1925), 217; David Walker Woods Jr., *John Witherspoon* (London: Fleming H. Revel, 1906), 185–89; "Minutes of the Synod of New York and Philadelphia," May 18–25, 1774, in *Records of the Presbyterian Church in the United States of America* (Philadelphia: Presbyterian Board of Publication, 1841), 453.

28. Certificate dated 9 May 1765, and affidavit dated 9 May 1765, in Sylvester K. Stevens and Donald H. Kent, eds., *The Papers of Col. Henry Bouquet*, Series 21651 (Harrisburg: Commonwealth of Pennsylvania and Pennsylvania Historical Commission, 1943), 207.

29. Col. Henry Bouquet to Sir Jeffrey Amherst, 25 June 1763, 13 July 1763, 26 July 1763, 27 August 1763, and Sir Jeffrey Amherst to Col. Henry Bouquet, 16 July 1763, 25 September 1763, in Stevens and Kent, eds., *Papers of Col. Henry Bouquet*, 203, 214–19, 222–23, 250–51, 276–77.

30. John Watts to Moses Franks, John Watts to General Robert Monckton, John Watts to James Napier, 23 July 1763 and 11 June 1764, *Letter Book of John Watts*, 156–58; Gregory Evans Dowd, *War Under Heaven: Pontiac, the Indian Nations, and the British Empire* (Baltimore: Johns Hopkins University Press, 2002); Daniel G. Brinton, *The Lenâpé and Their Legends; with the Complete Text and Symbols of the Walam Olum, a New Translation and an Inquiry into Its Authenticity* (1884; New York: AMS, 1969), 9–73; Samuel Bard to John Bard, 1 August 1764, Miscellaneous Manuscripts, Health Sciences Library, Archives and Special Collections, Columbia University.

31. A Lover of This Country [William Smith], *An Historical Account of the Expedition Against the Ohio Indians, in the Year MDCCLXIV. Under the Command of Henry Bouquet, Esq. Colonel of Foot and Now Brigadier General in America. Including His Transactions with the Indians, Relative to the Delivery of Their Prisoners, and the Preliminaries of Peace. With an Introductory Account of the Preceding Campaign, and Battle at Bushy-Run. To Which are Annexed Military Papers, Containing Reflections on the War with the Savages; a Method of Forming Frontier Settlements; Some Account of the Indian Country; with a List of Nations, Fighting Men, Towns, Distance, and Different Routes. The Whole with a Map and Copper-Plates* (Philadelphia, 1766); Edward Shippen, Lancaster, to son, 13 April 1765, Shippen Family Papers, Cartons 3–4, Manuscript Division, Library of Congress; William Trent's correspondence and records of claims, in Papers on Indian Losses, 1766–1770, 14–39, collection of the Historical Society of Pennsylvania.

32. Hugh Williamson, "To the Human and Liberal, Friends of Learning, Religion and Public Virtue, in the island of Jamaica. The Memorial and Humble Address of Hugh Williamson, M.D. One of the Trustees of the Academy of New-Ark, in Behalf of That Institution," *Philadelphia Packet*, 15 June 1772.

33. "Additional Memoir of the Mohegans, and of Uncas, Their Ancient Sachem," *Collections of the Massachusetts Historical Society* (Boston: Hall and Hiller, 1804), IX:89–90; Long, *Lord Jeffrey Amherst*, 168–78; Samuel Johnson to William Samuel Johnson, 1 February 1762, Samuel Johnson Papers, Letter Books, vol. II, Rare Book and Manuscript Library, Columbia University; minutes for 10 May 1763, "Minutes of the Governors of King's College," vol. 1, Rare Book and Manuscript Library, Columbia University; W. DeLoss Love, *Samson Occom and the Christian Indians of New England* (Boston: Pilgrim Press, 1899), 130.

34. Sir William Johnson to Eleazar Wheelock, 16 October 1762, Sir Jeffrey Amherst to Sir William Johnson, 17 October 1762, Nathaniel Whitaker to Eleazar Wheelock, 1 March 1766, Sir William Johnson to Daniel Burton, 8 October 1766, and Minutes of a Meeting of the Susquehannah Company, 28 December 1768, in Bond, ed., *Susquehannah Company Papers*, I:9–15, II:175–176, 312, 317–18, III:43–47.

35. George William Pilcher, ed., *The Reverend Samuel Davies Abroad: The Diary of a Journey to England and Scotland* (Urbana: University of Illinois Press, 1967), xi, 6; Hall, *History of the Presbyterian Church in Trenton, N.J.*, 121–23.

36. Jay had a conflict with the college over the funds, and the issue ended up in the courts. It was eventually settled with the college issuing a statement clearing Jay of all accusations. "The Memorial and Humble Petition of Sir James Jay, Knight, in Behalf of the Govrs of King's College in the City of New York in America," in E. B. O'Callahan, ed., *Documents Relative to the Colonial History of the State of New-York* (Albany, NY: Weed, Parsons, 1853–), VII:643–45; entries for 23 May 1763 and 27 May 1763, in *Minutes of the Trustees of the College, Academy and Charitable Schools of the University of Pennsylvania*, vol. 1, *1749–1768*, 208, 211; Samson Occom, "Journal, Dec. 6, 1743–Nov. 29, 1748," 77, Samson Occom Diaries, Rauner Library, Dartmouth College; Alden T. Vaughan, *Transatlantic Encounters: American Indians in Britain, 1500–1776* (New York: Cambridge University Press, 2006), 203; Leon Burr Richardson, ed., *An Indian Preacher in England: Being Letters and Diaries Relating to the Mission of the Reverend Samson Occom and the Reverend Nathaniel Whitaker to Collect Funds in England for the Benefit of Eleazar Wheelock's Indian Charity School, from Which Grew Dartmouth College* (Hanover, NH: Dartmouth College Publications, 1933), 14–15. On the controversy between Jay and King's College, see "The Corporation of the Governors of the College &c. of New York against Sir James Jay," and "The Answer of Sir James Jay Knight Defendant to the Bill of Complaint of the Corporation and the Governors of the College of the Province of New York," 6 May 1767, C12/855/19, National Archives, United Kingdom; "Power of Attorney to Thomas Maunsel authorizing him to raise funds for King's college, New York," May

1774, James Jay Manuscript Collection, Rare Book and Manuscript Library, Columbia University. On the resolution, see the statement releasing the governors of King's College from all claims and the governors' unpublished statement admitting the misunderstanding and confirming Jay's good standing and name, James Jay Manuscript Collection, Rare Book and Manuscript Library, Columbia University.

37. "On savage Lands she showers her Beams divine / Their rugged Passions soften and refine," wrote Levi Frisbie, a student from Branford, Connecticut, in celebration of the college charter. "The Veil of Darkness droops from off their Minds / And Gospel Truth in awful glory shines." *State of the Society in Scotland for Propagating Christian Knowledge, in the year 1769* (Edinburgh, 1769), 15–16; Levi Frisbie, *Cohos. The Wilderness Shall Blossom as the Rose. To His Excellency John Wentworth, Esq.; Captain-General, Governor and Commander in Chief, in and over His Majesty's Province of New-Hampshire, On His Grant of a Very Generous Charter of Incorporation of Dartmouth College* (New London, CT: Timothy Green, 1769); *The Society for Propagating the Gospel Among the Indians and Others in North America, 1787–1887* (Cambridge, MA: University Press, 1887), esp. 33–40.

38. Eleazar Wheelock to Captain Arent DePeyster, 10 May 1773 (#773318), and Eleazar Wheelock to Captain Arent DePeyster, 15 June 1774 (#774365), Dartmouth College Archives, Rauner Library; Rev. Levi Frisbie, "A Short Account of the Mission of the Reverend Mr. Levi Frisbie, Mr. James Dean, Mr. Thomas Kendall, to the Indians in the Province of Quebec. Being, An Abstract from the Journal of the Former, 1774," appended to the later editions of Eleazar Wheelock, *A Continuation of the Narrative of the Indian Charity School, Begun in Lebanon, in Connecticut; Now Incorporated with Dartmouth-College in Hanover, in the Province of New-Hampshire* (Hartford, CT, 1775), 44–54.

39. Colin G. Calloway, *The Western Abenakis of Vermont, 1600–1800: War, Migration, and the Survival of an Indian People* (Norman: University of Oklahoma Press, 1990), 30–31; Col. Samuel Stevens to Eleazar Wheelock, 13 June 1775 (#775363), Rauner Library, Dartmouth College; Frederick Chase, *A History of Dartmouth College and the Town of Hanover, New Hampshire*, ed. John K. Lord (Cambridge, MA: John Wilson and Son, 1891), I:300–301.

40. Dr. Wheelock continued to search for a better deal years after the 1769 chartering of Dartmouth College in New Hampshire. As the colonial army marched through Iroquoia, Wheelock was in correspondence with General Philip Schuyler about securing government support for Indian education at his school, although Native education was now a minor part of his vocation. In 1790 an English court directed that the Brafferton Fund, which had nearly £1,000 immediately available, be used to convert African slaves in the British West Indies. James Manning to Rev. Dr. Samuel Stennett, 5 June 1771, James Manning Papers, 1761–1827, Box 1,

Folder 5 (A753), John Hay Library, Brown University; Franklin Bowditch Dexter, ed., *The Literary Diary of Ezra Stiles, D.D., LL.D., President of Yale College* (New York: Charles Scribner's Sons, 1901), I:364; *The Two Charters of the Society for Advancing the Christian Faith in the British West India Islands, and Elsewhere, with the Diocese of Jamaica and of Barbadoes, and the Leeward Island, and in the Mauritius: To Which Is Prefixed, a Short Account of the Charitable Fund* (London: Richard Clay, 1836), 5–7; Samuel Eliot Morison, *Harvard College in the Seventeenth Century* (Cambridge, MA: Harvard University Press, 1936), I:345; Lyon Gardiner Tyler, *The College of William and Mary in Virginia: Its History and Work, 1693–1907* (Richmond: Whittet and Shepperson, 1907), 62; Love, *Samson Occom and the Christian Indians of New England*, 159; Eleazar Wheelock to General Schuyler, 18 February 1777, in the "Duane Letters," *Publications of the Southern History Association*, September 1903, 362–68.

41. Samuel Johnson to Sir William Johnson, 16 January 1767, Samuel Johnson to William Samuel Johnson, 11 February 1767, remarks recorded on the back of printed publication "At a General Assembly of the Governor and Company of the Colony of Connecticut, holden at Hartford, on the Eighth Day of May A.D. 1766," Samuel Johnson Papers, Letter Books, vol. III.

42. Samuel Auchmuty to William Johnson, 14 November 1768, in Sullivan, ed., *Papers of Sir William Johnson*, VI:455–58; Colin G. Calloway, *The Indian History of an American Institution: Native Americans and Dartmouth* (Hanover, NH: Dartmouth College Press, 2010), 8, 23–24.

43. William Johnson to Eleazar Wheelock, 8 August 1766, "To the Clergy of the Church of England Lately Assembled in Convention," December 1766, Guy Johnson to Myles Cooper, 1 December 1767, William Johnson to William Smith, 18 December 1767, in Sullivan, ed., *Papers of Sir William Johnson*, V:342–44, 460–62, 837–39, VI:18, VIII:857.

44. Speech of Captain Onoonghwandekha at the funeral of a Seneca, in Walter Pilkington, ed., *The Journals of Samuel Kirkland: 18th-Century Missionary to the Iroquois, Government Agent, Father of Hamilton College* (Clinton, NY: Hamilton College Press, 1980), 23–25, 37–38. On the Iroquois dialogue about race, see David J. Silverman, "The Curse of God: An Idea and Its Origins among the Indians of New York's Revolutionary Frontier," *William and Mary Quarterly*, July 2009, 495–534.

45. "Journal of Lieutenant Thomas Blake," "Journal of Lieutenant-Colonel Henry Dearborn," and "Journal of Captain Daniel Livermore," in Frederick Cook, ed., *Journals of the Military Expedition of Major General John Sullivan* (Auburn, NY: Knapp, Peck, and Thomson, 1887), 39, 64, 182; Lt. Col. Adam Hubley Jr., "Orderly Book, July to October 1779" (transcribed by Brandon Rapp), Revolutionary War Collection, MG-98, Folder 11, Lancaster County Historical Society, 16, 18; General George Washington

to Major-General Sullivan, 31 May 1779, in Sparks, ed., *Writings of George Washington*, VI:264–67.

46. Dunmore appointed a resident of Pennsylvania as a Virginia militia captain and ordered him to seize Pittsburgh. Captain John Connolly then occupied the ruins of Fort Pitt, declared Fort Dunmore, and issued orders to the local residents to muster in service of Virginia. He was arrested. In the struggle that followed with Penn, Murray argued that he had an obligation to protect the western frontier from Indian attacks and the charter authority to make policy in the disputed region. He sent surveyors into the area and instigated conflicts with the Lenape and Shawnee to encourage settler violence as a pretense for war. He readied an army of more than two thousand men. Henry Melchior Muhlenberg Richards, *The Pennsylvania-German in the Revolutionary War, 1775–1783* (1908; Baltimore: Genealogical Publishing, 1978), 308–38; Glenn F. Williams, *Year of the Hangman: George Washington's Campaign Against the Indians* (Westholme, 2006), 19–30; Colin G. Calloway, *The American Revolution in Indian Country: Crisis and Diversity in Native American Communities* (New York: Cambridge University Press, 1995), 36–40.

47. General George Washington to the President of Congress, 29 March 1777, General George Washington to Philip Schuyler, James Duane, and Volkert P. Duow, Commissioners of Indian Affairs, 13 March 1778, in Sparks, ed., *Writings of George Washington*, IV:369–71, V:273–74; statement of Captain Solomon, Chief of the Stockbridge Indians, 15 January 1776, delivered to Jonathan Edwards, Wyllys Papers, 1633–1829, V:8, Connecticut Historical Society; Nathanael Greene to George Washington, 5 January 1779, in Richard K. Showman et al., eds., *The Papers of General Nathanael Greene* (Chapel Hill: University of North Carolina Press, 1983), III:144–45; Terry Golway, *Washington's General: Nathanael Greene and the Triumph of the American Revolution* (New York: Henry Holt, 2005), 198.

48. General George Washington to Colonel Daniel Brodhead, 22 March 1779, in Sparks, ed., *Writings of George Washington*, VI:205–7.

49. William Shippen Jr., White Plains, New York, 11 August 1778, Shippen Family Papers, Cartons 3–4; Walter Stahr, *John Jay: Founding Father* (New York: Hambledon, 2005), 347–48; William Livingston to James Duane, 3 November 1779, *Publications of the Southern History Association*, January 1904, 55–56.

50. Book of Nehemiah, 4:14; "Journal of Rev. William Rogers, D.D.," in Cook, ed., *Journals of the Military Expedition of Major General John Sullivan*, 6n, 103, 246–51, 346n, 385.

51. General George Washington to the Marquis de Lafayette, 20 October 1779, in Sparks, ed., *Writings of George Washington*, VI:382–86; Robert F. Dalzell Jr. and Lee Baldwin Dalzell, *George Washington's Mount Vernon: At Home in Revolutionary America* (New York: Oxford, 1998), 174; Isabel Thompson Kelsay, *Joseph Brant, 1743–1807: Man of Two Worlds* (Syracuse, NY:

Syracuse University Press, 1984), 279; "Journal of Lieut. Erkuries Beatty," in Cook, ed., *Journals of the Military Expedition of Major General John Sullivan*, 17; Barbara Alice Mann, *George Washington's War on Native America* (Lincoln: University of Nebraska Press, 2008), 27–36.

On Africans and African Americans living among and with Indians, see Celia E. Naylor, *African Cherokees in Indian Territory: From Chattel to Citizens* (Chapel Hill: University of North Carolina Press, 2008); Laura L. Lovett, "'African and Cherokee by Choice': Race and Resistance Under Legalized Segregation," *American Indian Quarterly*, Winter/Spring 1998, 203–229; Patrick N. Minges, *Slavery in the Cherokee Nation: The Keetoowah Society and the Defining of a People* (New York: Routledge, 2003); Tiya Miles, *Ties That Bind: The Story of an Afro-Cherokee Family in Slavery and Freedom* (Berkeley: University of California Press, 2005); Claudio Saunt, *Black, White, and Indian: Race and the Unmaking of an American Family* (New York: Oxford University Press, 2005); Daniel F. Littlefield Jr., *Africans and Creeks: From the Colonial Period to the Civil War* (Westport, CT: Greenwood, 1979); Gary Zellar, *African Creeks: Estelvste and the Creek Nation* (Norman: University of Oklahoma Press, 2007).

52. "Journal of Major Jeremiah Fogg," in Cook, ed., *Journals of the Military Expedition of Major General John Sullivan*, 98; Mrs. A. J. Fogg and J. L. M. Willis, eds., *The Fogg Family of America: The Reunions of the Fogg Families, 1902–3–4–5–6* (Eliot, ME: Historical Press, 1907), 81–84, 112.

53. "Journal of Lieut. Erkuries Beatty," "Journal of Dr. Jabez Campfield," and "Journal of Lieut. Charles Nukerck," in Cook, ed., *Journals of the Military Expedition of Major General John Sullivan*, 23, 58, 217; John Frelinghuysen Hageman, *History of Princeton and Its Institutions* (Philadelphia: J. B. Lippincott, 1878), 221.

54. "Journal of Lieut. Col. Adam Hubley," "Journal of Lieut. John Jenkins," and "Journal of Captain Daniel Livermore," in Cook, ed., *Journals of the Military Expedition of Major General John Sullivan*, 151–63, 168–74, 178–88; entry for 16 August 1779, "Journal of William McKendry, July 1778 to January 1780," Robert Gorham Davis Papers, MS 0330, Rare Book and Manuscript Library, Columbia University.

55. "Journal of Major Jeremiah Fogg," 92–101.

56. "Journal of Lieut. William Barton," "Journal of Lieut. Erkuries Beatty," "Journal of Major John Burrowes," "Journal of Major Jeremiah Fogg," "Journal of Serg't Major George Grant," "Journal of Lieut. Adam Hubley," and "Journal of Sergeant Thomas Roberts," in Cook, ed., *Journals of the Military Expedition of Major General John Sullivan*, 8, 27–30, 44–45, 95, 112–13, 156–57, 165, 244; entry for 17 August 1779, "Journal of William McKendry."

57. Philip Van Cortlandt to Gilbert Van Cortlandt, 22 August 1779, in Jacob Judd, ed., *The Revolutionary War Memoir and Selected Correspondence of*

Philip Van Cortlandt (Tarrytown, NY: Sleepy Hollow Restorations, 1976), 141–43; entries for 8 and 9 November 1779, "Journal of William Mc-Kendry"; Philip Schuyler to James Duane, 5 February 1781, *Publications of the Southern History Association*, September 1904, 384–86.

58. Stiles, *United States Elevated to Glory and Honor*, 8–10.

59. Ibid., 5–14.

60. Laurence M. Hauptman, *Conspiracy of Interests: Iroquois Dispossession and the Rise of New York State* (Syracuse, NY: Syracuse University Press, 1999).

61. Pilkington, ed., *The Journals of Samuel Kirkland*, 189–93, 245–49; Samuel Kirkland to Joseph Brant, 3 January 1792 (#144a), and John Kemp to Samuel Kirkland, 5 February 1794 (#165a), Correspondence of Samuel Kirkland, Samuel Kirkland Papers, College Archives, Burke Library, Hamilton College.

CHAPTER 6: "ALL STUDENTS & ALL AMERICANS"

1. The American Philosophical Society was founded in 1743. Anthony F. C. Wallace, *Jefferson and the Indians: The Tragic Fate of the First Americans* (Cambridge, MA: Belknap Press, 1999), 241–48; Stephen E. Ambrose, *Undaunted Courage: Meriwether Lewis, Thomas Jefferson, and the Opening of the American West* (New York: Simon and Schuster, 2002), 59–151; James P. Ronda, "'To Acquire What Knowledge You Can': Thomas Jefferson as Exploration Patron and Planner," *Proceedings of the American Philosophical Society*, September 2006, 409–13; J. Diane Pearson, "Medical Diplomacy and the American Indian: Thomas Jefferson, the Lewis and Clark Expedition, and the Subsequent Effects on American Indian Health and Public Policy," *Wicazo Sa Review*, Spring 2004, 105–11.

2. Joseph Foster, *Alumni Oxonienses: The Members of the University of Oxford: Their Parentage, Birthplace, and Year of Birth, with a Record of Their Degrees*, vol. IV (Oxford: James Parker, 1891); W. W. Rouse Ball and J. A. Venn, *Admissions to Trinity College, Cambridge* (London: Macmillan, 1911–13), II:591, III:3; John Venn and J. A. Venn, *Alumni Cantabrigienses: A Biographical List of All Known Students, Graduates and Holders of Office at the University of Cambridge, from the Earliest Times to 1900* (Cambridge: Cambridge University Press, 1922–54); Peter John Anderson, *Roll of Alumni in Arts of the University and King's College of Aberdeen, 1596–1860* (Aberdeen: Printed for the University, 1900); George Dames Burtchaell et al., eds., *Alumni Dublinenses: A Register of the Students, Graduates, Professors and Provosts of Trinity College, in the University of Dublin* (London: Williams and Norgate, 1924); John D. Harbreaves, *Academe and Empire: Some Overseas Connections of Aberdeen University, 1860–1970* (Aberdeen: Aberdeen University Press, 1994), v; Edward C. Mead, ed., *Genealogical History of the*

Lee Family of Virginia and Maryland from A.D. 1300 to A.D. 1866 with Notes and Illustrations (New York: Richardson, 1868), 57–58, appendix; W. Innes Addison, ed., *The Matriculation Albums of the University of Glasgow from 1728 to 1858* (Glasgow: James Maclehose and Sons, 1913), 2–3.

3. Douglas Sloan, *The Scottish Enlightenment and the American College Ideal* (New York: Teachers College Press, 1971), 190–93; Guenter B. Risse, *New Medical Challenges During the Scottish Enlightenment* (Amsterdam: Rodopi, 2005), 69–70; Gulielmo Shippen, Juniore, "Oratio Salutatoria Habita In Comitus Academicis Novarcae in Nova-Caesaria Sexto Calendas Octobris 1754," Shippen Family Papers, Cartons 3–4, Manuscript Division, Library of Congress; Betsey Copping Corner, "Day Book of an Education: William Shippen's Student Days in London (1759–1760) and His Subsequent Career," *Proceedings of the American Philosophical Society*, April 21, 1950, esp. 134–36.

4. Benjamin Rush, Edinburgh, to Jonathan Smith, 30 April 1767, Henley Smith Collection, Box 1, Manuscripts Division, Library of Congress; David Hosack, *Biographical Memoir of Hugh Williamson, M.D., LL.D., . . . Delivered on the First Day of November, 1819, at the Request of the New-York Historical Society* (New York: C. S. Van Winkle, 1820), 18–23; Risse, *New Medical Challenges*, 84. Rush dedicated his dissertation to Benjamin Franklin. Benjaminus Rush, *Dissertatio Physica Inauguralis, de Coctione Ciborum in Ventriculo: Quam, Annuente Summo Numine, Ex Auctoriate Reverendi admodum Viri, Gulielmi Robertson, S.S.T.P. Academiae Edinburgenai Praefecti . . .* (Edinburgh: Balfour, Auld, and Smellie, 1768).

5. Samuel Bard to John Bard, 28 November 1761, 25 September 1762, and Samuel Bard to Hon[ored] Parents, 23 January 1762, Bard Family Papers, Box 1, Folders 7 and 8, Archives and Special Collections, Stevenson Library, Bard College; Michael Sappol, *A Traffic of Dead Bodies: Anatomy and Embodied Social Identity in Nineteenth-Century America* (Princeton: Princeton University Press, 2002), 48–50; Samuel Bard to John Bard, 30 January 1763, Bard Collection, Malloch Rare Book Room, New York Academy of Medicine; Samuel Bard, *A Discourse upon the Duties of a Physician, with Some Sentiments on the Usefulness and Necessity of a Public Hospital: Delivered before the President and Governors of King's College, at the Commencement Held on the 16th of May 1769. As Advice to Those Gentlemen Who then Received the First Medical Degrees Conferred by that University . . .* (New York: A. and J. Robertson, 1769); Samuel Bard, *A Discourse on the Importance of Medical Education, Delivered on the Fourth of November, 1811, at the Opening of the Present Session of the Medical College of Physicians and Surgeons* (New York: C. S. Van Winkle, 1812); Alfred R. Hoermann, *Cadwallader Colden: A Figure of the American Enlightenment* (Westport, CT: Greenwood, 2002), 31; Abraham Ernest Helffenstein, *Pierre Fauconnier and His Descendants with Some Account of the*

Allied Valleaux (Philadelphia: S. H. Burbank, 1911), 82–83; Samuel Bard, *Tentamen Medicum Inaugurale, De Viribus Opii* . . . (Edinburgh: A. Donaldson and J. Reid, 1765); John Bard to Samuel Bard, 15 August 1765, Miscellaneous Manuscripts, Box 1, John Bard and Samuel Bard Correspondence Folder, Health Sciences Library, Archives and Special Collections, Columbia University.

6. Benjamin Smith Barton, *Observations on Some Parts of Natural History: To Which is Prefixed an Account of Several Remarkable Vestiges of an Ancient Date, Which Have Been Discovered in Different Parts of North America* (London: Printed for the author, 1787); Benjamin Smith Barton, *New Views of the Origin of the Tribes and Nations of America* (Philadelphia: Printed for the author, 1797); Samuel Bard to John Bard, 9 April 1764, Bard Family Papers, Box 1, Folder 8, Bard College.

7. David Dary, *Frontier Medicine: From the Atlantic to the Pacific, 1492–1941* (New York: Knopf, 2008), 19–25; John Wesley, *Primitive Physick: Or, an Essay and Natural Method of Curing Most Diseases* (London: Thomas Tyre, 1747); Virgil J. Vogel, *American Indian Medicine* (Norman: University of Oklahoma Press, 1970), 148–53; Samuel Bard to John Bard, 16 February 1764, Bard Family Papers, Box 1, Folder 8, Bard College.

8. Kevin Berland, Jan Kirsten Gilliam, and Kenneth A. Lockeridge, eds., *The Commonplace Book of William Byrd II of Westover* (Chapel Hill: University of North Carolina Press, 2001), 7–9, 48, 235n; William Byrd, "An Account of a Negro-Boy that is Dappel'd in Several Places of His Body with White Spots," *Philosophical Transactions* (1695–1697), XIX:781–82. Cotton Mather, *Some Account of What is Said of Inoculating or Transplanting the Small Pox. By the Learned Dr. Emanuel Timonius, and Jacobus Pylarinus. With Some Remarks Thereon. To Which Are Added, a Few Queries in Answer to The Scruples of Many About the Lawfulness of This Method* (Boston: Dr. Zabdiel Boylston, 1721); Margot Minardi, "The Boston Inoculation Controversy of 1721–1722: An Incident in the History of Race," *William and Mary Quarterly*, January 2004, 47–76; Increase Mather, *Some Further Account from London, of the Small-Pox Inoculated. With Some Remarks on a Late and Scandalous Pamphlet Entitled, Inoculation of the Small Pox as Practis'd in Boston* (Boston: J. Edwards, 1721); Eldridge G. Cutler, "A Short Abstract of the Early History of Medicine in Massachusetts to the Year 1800," *Boston Medical and Surgical Journal*, 24 January 1901, 79–80.

9. See, for instance, Alexander Monro, secundus, 1770, Operations of Surgery, lecture book; The Physiology or an Account of the Natural Functions of the Humane Body taken from the Lectures of Mr. Alexr. Monro, Edinburg, undated; The History of the Rise and Progress of Anatomy (ca. 1735); Lectures on the Practice of Medicine Delivered at Edinburgh

in the Session 1785–6 by Doctor Andrew Duncan; Physiological Observa-
tions from Dr. William Cullen's Lectures, 1766–7, University Archives,
Center for Research Collections, University of Edinburgh. Rush to
Smith, 30 April 1767, Henley Smith Collection, Library of Congress.

10. Samuel Stanhope Smith, *Essay on the Causes of the Variety of Complexion
and Figure in the Human Species. To Which are Added Strictures on Lord
Kaims's Discourse, on the Original Diversity of Mankind* (Philadelphia:
Robert Aitken, 1787).

11. Ibid.

12. Ibid., 20–21; Hugh Williamson, *Observations on the Climate in Different Parts
of America, Compared with the Climate in Corresponding Parts of the Other Continent. To Which Are Added, Remarks on the Different Complexions of the Human
Race; With Some Account of the Aborigines of America. Being an Introductory
Discourse to the History of North Carolina* (New York: T. and J. Swords, 1811),
64–69; Cotton Mather, *The Negro Christianized: An Essay to Excite and Assist
That Good Work, the Instruction of Negro-Servants in Christianity* (Boston: B.
Green, 1706), 24; Georges-Louis Leclerc, *Buffon's Natural History. Containing
a Theory of the Earth, a General History of Man, of the Brute Creation, and of
Vegetables, Minerals, &c.* (London: J. S. Barr, 1792), IV:262–63.

13. Smith, *Essay on the Causes of the Variety of Complexion*, 60–62; Peter Silver,
Our Savage Neighbors: How Indian War Transformed Early America (New
York: Norton, 2008), 116–17; Gary B. Nash, *The Unknown American Revolu-
tion: The Unruly Birth of Democracy and the Struggle to Create America* (New
York: Penguin, 2005), 376.

14. Edward Long, *The History of Jamaica, or, General Survey of the Antient and
Modern State of that Island: With Reflections on Its Situation, Settlements,
Inhabitants, Climate, Products, Commerce, Laws, and Government* (Lon-
don: T. Lowndes, 1774), I:336.

15. Thomas Jefferson, *Notes on the State of Virginia; Written in the Year 1781,
Somewhat Corrected and Enlarged in the Winter of 1782, for the Use of a For-
eigner of Distinction, in Answer to Certain Queries Proposed by Him . . .*
(Paris, 1782), 263–65.

16. Cotton Mather, *Magnalia Christi Americana: Or, the Ecclesiastical History
of New-England, from Its First Planting in the Year 1620 unto the Year of Our
Lord, 1698* (London: Thomas Parkhurst, 1702), III:199; George Lyman
Kittredge, *Letter of Samuel Lee and Samuel Sewall Relating to New England
and the Indians* (Cambridge, MA: John Wilson and Son, 1912), 153; Jefferson, *Notes on the State of Virginia*, 173–79; Debra L. Gold, *The Bioar-
chaeology of Virginia Burial Mounds* (Tuscaloosa: University of Alabama
Press, 2004), 6–7; Lyon Gardiner Tyler, *The College of William and Mary
in Virginia: Its History and Work, 1693–1907* (Richmond: Whittet and
Shepperson, 1907), 37, 53; Garry Wills, *Mr. Jefferson's University* (Washington, DC: National Geographic Society, 2002), 57–60; John S. Haller

Jr., *American Medicine in Transition, 1840–1910* (Urbana: University of Illinois Press, 1981), 195; Edward B. Krumbhaar, "The Early History of Anatomy in the United States," in Francis Randolph Packard, ed., *Annals of Medical History* (New York: Paul B. Hoeber, 1922), IV:283.

17. T. Aubrey, *The Sea-Surgeon, Or the Guinea Man's Vade Mecum. In Which is Laid Down, The Method of Curing Diseases as Usually Happen Abroad, Especially on the Coast of Guinea; With the Best Way of Treating Negroes, Both in Health and in Sickness* (London: John Clarke, 1729), 102–5.

18. Hume argued that history showed white to be the color of civilization. Africans lacked intelligence, he continued, and any arguments to the contrary were flattery. Hume went to the effort of adding these thoughts to a later edition of his essays. David Hume, *Essays and Treatises on Several Subjects, Containing Essays, Moral and Political* (London: A. Millar, 1753), 291; Long, *History of Jamaica*, I:376.

19. Jefferson, *Notes on the State of Virginia*, 112–17, 257–63; Franklin B. Sawvel, *Logan the Mingo* (Boston: Gorham, 1921), 82–85.

20. Jefferson, *Notes on the State of Virginia*, 252–54; Long, *History of Jamaica*, 360–64; George M. Fredrickson, *White Supremacy: A Comparative Study in American and South African History* (Oxford: Oxford University Press, 1981), 141–43.

21. Leclerc, *Buffon's Natural History*, 271–352.

22. Samuel Eliot Morison, *Three Centuries of Harvard* (Cambridge, MA: Harvard University Press, 1936), 96; Lawrence Shaw Mayo, *John Wentworth: Governor of New Hampshire, 1767–1775* (Cambridge, MA: Harvard University Press, 1921).

23. Lyman Spalding to William Neil, 28 November 1808 (#808628.2), Rauner Library, Dartmouth College; *General Catalogue of Dartmouth College and the Associated Schools, 1769–1900, Including a Historical Sketch of the College Prepared by Marvin Davis Bisbee, the Librarian* (Hanover, NH: For the College, 1900), 54–55; William Allen, *An Address, Occasioned by the Death of Nathan Smith, M.D., First Lecturer in the Medical School of Maine at Bowdoin College, Delivered by Appointment of the Faculty of Medicine, March 26, 1829* (Brunswick, ME: G. Griffin, 1829); John King Lord, *A History of the Town of Hanover, N.H.* (Hanover, NH: Dartmouth Press, 1928), 135; Frederick Chase, *A History of Dartmouth College and the Town of Hanover, New Hampshire*, ed. John K. Lord (Cambridge, MA: John Wilson and Son, 1891), I:616; James Alfred Spalding, *Dr. Lyman Spalding: The Originator of the United States Pharmacopoeia, Co-Laborer with Dr. Nathan Smith in the Founding of the Dartmouth Medical School and Its First Chemical Lecturer; President and Professor of Anatomy and Surgery of the College of Physicians and Surgeons of the Western District, at Fairfield, N.Y.* (Boston: W. M. Leonard, 1916), 148–65; Daniel C. Gilman, "Bishop Berkeley's Gifts to Yale College: A Collection of Documents Illustrative of 'The Dean's Bounty,'" *Papers of*

the New Haven Colony Historical Society (New Haven: For the Society, 1865), I:162–65; Catalog of New England Indian Relics in the Gilbert Museum at Amherst College, 2nd ed. (1904); Samuel George Morton, Crania Americana; or, A Comparative View of the Skulls of Various Aboriginal Nations of North and South America. To Which Is Prefixed an Essay on the Varieties of the Human Species (Philadelphia: J. Dobson, 1839).

24. See essay on the establishment of an American science academy in "Samuel Bard Lectures at Columbia," ca. 1790, vol. 2, Bard Family Papers, Bard College; William George Nice, "Notes Taken from the Lectures of Benjamin Smith Barton, Professor of the Institutes & Practice of Phisic in the University of Pennsylvania . . . from the First Monday in November 1814 to the First of March 1815," esp. 95, 131, Rare Books, Center for History of Medicine, Countway Library of Medicine, Harvard University.

25. Andrew Fyfe, A Compendium of the Anatomy of the Human Body, Intended Principally for the Use of Students, 2nd American ed. (Philadelphia: James Humphreys, 1807), I:23–34.

26. In 1632 William Gordon assumed a chair in medicine at Aberdeen, where he established the medical program. In 1662 John Stearne became Public Professor of Medicine at Trinity College in Dublin, where his society of physicians later formed the medical college. In 1705 the Edinburgh town council hired Robert Elliot, a surgeon, to teach anatomy. Just a few years later, the anatomy rooms at Oxford were busy enough to lead one antiquarian to protest about the foul smells invading the Bodleian Library. Trinity also opened a laboratory and dissection theater. In 1719 James Gregory began his family's long tenure in the anatomy professorship at Aberdeen, where he shifted science instruction from Latin to English. Alexander Monro and Alexander Monro Jr. established anatomy at Edinburgh. William Cheselden offered dissections in London, where the brothers William and John Hunter later provided regular anatomical instruction. In the first three decades of his career, the elder Alexander Monro alone taught more than 3,500 students. Even at St. Andrews University—where the governors had long neglected medicine in favor of philosophy and mathematics—Thomas Simson arrived from Glasgow to fill a new anatomy chair. Leo M. Zimmerman and Ilza Veith, Great Ideas in the History of Surgery (San Francisco: Norman, 1993), 113–14; Charte de Charles IX, Roy de France, 1567: Privileges octroyez aux professeurs du College & Faculte de Chirugie (Paris, 1644); Alexander Bower, The History of the University of Edinburgh; Chiefly Compiled from Original Papers and Records, Never Before Published (Edinburgh: Alex. Smellie, 1817), II:145–47. This section benefits from material in the collections of the Musée d'Histoire de la Médecine, Université Paris Descartes, France; Museum Vrolik, Amsterdam Medical Center, Netherlands; Hunterian Museum,

Royal College of Surgeons, London, UK; Anatomy Museum, Edinburgh University, Scotland. Rembrandt van Rijn, *The Anatomy Lesson of Dr. Nicolaes Tulp*, 1632, Mauritshuis Museum, Netherlands. Also see Nicolaes Eliasz Pickenoy, *The Osteology Lesson of Dr. Sebastiaen Egbertsz*, 1619, Amsterdam Museum, Netherlands; Rembrandt van Rijn, *The Anatomy Lesson of Dr. Jan Deijman*, 1656, Rijksmuseum, Amsterdam, Netherlands. Andrew Dalzel, *History of the University of Edinburgh from Its Foundations* (Edinburgh: Edmonston and Douglas, 1862), II:291–92; Constantia Maxwell, *A History of Trinity College Dublin 1591–1892* (Dublin: University Press, Trinity College, 1946), 80, 93; Robert G. Frank Jr., "Medicine," in Nicholas Tyacke, ed., *The History of the University of Oxford* (Oxford: Clarendon, 1997), IV:543; John Malcolm Bulloch, *A History of the University of Aberdeen 1495–1895* (London: Hodder and Stoughton, 1895), 156–57; Bower, *History of the University of Edinburgh*, II:179; Ronald Gordon Cant, *The University of St. Andrews: A Short History* (Edinburgh: Scottish Academic Press, 1970), 88, 129.

27. Thomas Shepard, *The Clear Sun-shine of the Gospel Breaking Forth upon the Indians in New-England. Or, an Historicall Narration of Gods Wonderful Workings upon Sundry of the Indians, Both Chief Governors and Common-People, in Bringing Them to a Willing and Desired Submission to the Ordinances of the Gospel; and Framing Their Hearts to an Earnest Inquirie after the Knowledge of God the Father, and of Jesus Christ the Saviour of the World* (London: R. Cotes for John Bellamy, 1648), 25–26; Samuel Eliot Morison, *The Founding of Harvard College* (Cambridge, MA: Harvard University Press, 1935), 378; "John Leverett's Diary, 1707–1723," 60, Papers of John Leverett, Box 8, Harvard University Archives.

28. Shippen, Morgan, and Rush were all students of Samuel Finley. Sloan, *Scottish Enlightenment and the American College Ideal*, 185–89; Corner, "Day Book of an Education: William Shippen's Student Days in London," esp. 134–36; Krumbhaar, "Early History of Anatomy in the United States," 276–79; *Catalogue of All Who Have Held Office in or Have Received Degrees from the College of New Jersey at Princeton in the State of New Jersey* (Princeton: Princeton University Press, 1896), 7; entries for 3 May 1765 and 12 May 1767, in *Minutes of the Trustees of the College, Academy and Charitable Schools of the University of Pennsylvania*, vol. 1, *1749–1768* (Wilmington, DE: Scholarly Resources, 1974), 288–89, 318–20; John Morgan, *A Discourse upon the Institution of Medical Schools in America; Delivered at a Public Anniversary Commencement, Held in the College of Philadelphia, May 30 and 31, 1765. With a Preface Containing, Amongst Other things, the Author's Apology for Attempting to Introduce the Regular Mode of Practicing Physic in Philadelphia* (Philadelphia: William Bradford, 1765), xii–xiii, 28–33; last will and testament of Richard Stockton (signer), 20 May 1780, Stockton Family Additional Papers, Box 2, Folder 22, Manuscripts and Archives,

Princeton University; Whitfield J. Bell Jr., "Some American Students of 'That Shining Oracle of Physic,' Dr. William Cullen of Edinburgh, 1755–1766," *Proceedings of the American Philosophical Society*, 20 June 1950, esp. 277–81.

29. Krumbhaar, "The Early History of Anatomy in the United States," 276; Thomas G. Morton and Frank Woodbury, *The History of the Pennsylvania Hospital, 1751–1895* (Philadelphia: Times Printing House, 1895), 212, 493; Jefferson, *Notes on the State of Virginia*, 263; Reuben Aldridge Guild, *History of Brown University, with Illustrative Documents* (Providence: By subscription, 1867), 177–87.

30. Morgan, *Discourse upon the Institution of Medical Schools in America*, 6–7, 11–13; *Pennsylvania Mercury*, 16 January 1790; Josiah Bartlett, *An Historical Sketch of the Progress of Medical Science, in the Commonwealth of Massachusetts, Being the Substance of a Discourse Read at the Annual Meeting of the Medical Society, June 6, 1810, with Alterations and Additions to January 1, 1813* (1813), 5–6; Francis D. Moore, "Two Hundred Years Ago: Origins and Early Years of the Harvard Medical School," Annual Meeting of the American Surgical Association, Boston, Massachusetts, April 21–23, 1982, 527.

31. George B. Wood, *Early History of the University of Pennsylvania: From Its Origin to the Year 1827*, 3rd ed. (Philadelphia: J. B. Lippincott, 1896), 222–30; Samuel Bard, Edinburgh, to Dr. John Bard, New York City, 29 December 1762, Bard Collection, Malloch Rare Book Room New York Academy of Medicine; William D. Carrell, "Biographical List of American College Professors to 1800," *History of Education Quarterly*, Autumn 1968, 359; John Shrady, *The College of Physicians and Surgeons, New York, and Its Founders, Officers, Instructors, Benefactors and Alumni: A History* (New York: Lewis, 1903), 18–19; Samuel Bard, *A Discourse upon the Duties of a Physician, With Some Sentiments on the Usefulness and Necessity of a Public Hospital: Delivered before the President and Governors of King's College, at the Commencement Held on the 15th of May, 1769. As Advice to Those Gentlemen Who then Received the First Medical Degrees Conferred by That University* (New York: A. and J. Robertson, 1769); Helffenstein, *Pierre Fauconnier and His Descendants*, 88–89.

Students trained at Edinburgh also established the first medical program in Canada. In 1819 Andrew Holmes and John Stephenson graduated from Edinburgh and returned to Montreal after visiting London and Paris. Four years later, they became founding faculty of the new Montreal Medical Institute, an adjunct teaching facility for the Montreal General Hospital; in fact, four of the six original instructors were trained at Edinburgh. In 1828 the Medical Institute reorganized as the medical department of McGill College (1821), which the wealthy merchant James McGill had endowed with a £10,000 bequest and a campus at the base of Mont Royal. Francis J. Shepherd, "The First Medical School in Canada:

Its History and Founders, with Some Personal Reminiscences," *Canadian Medical Association Journal*, April 1925, 418–22.

32. William Nisbet, *The Edinburgh School of Medicine; Containing the Preliminary of Fundamental Branches of Professional Education, viz. Anatomy, Medical Chemistry, and Botany. Intended as an Introduction to the Clinical Guide. The Whole Forming a Complete System of Medical Education and Practice According to the Arrangement of the Edinburgh School* (London: A. Strahan, 1802), I:11, 137–38.

33. Josiah Quincy, *Memoir of the Life of Josiah Quincy Jun. of Massachusetts, by His Son, Josiah Quincy* (Boston: Cummings, Hilliard, 1825), 132–34.

34. There were no enslaved people recorded for the twenty-year period beginning 1810. New Hampshire had about a thousand free black people by the end of that era. Ralph Nading Hill, *The College on the Hill: A Dartmouth Chronicle* (Hanover, NH: Dartmouth Publications, 1964), 102–3; draft chapters with written notes, Samuel Sterns Morse Papers, 1964–1976, Box 1, Rauner Library, Dartmouth College (also see the Ralph Nading Hill Papers, Box 1); Dick Hoefnagel and Virginia L. Close, *Eleazar Wheelock and the Adventurous Founding of Dartmouth College* (Hanover, NH: Durand, 2002), 95; M. E. Goddard and Henry V. Partridge, *A History of Norwich, Vermont* (Hanover, NH: Dartmouth Press, 1905), 219–21; Emily A. Smith, *The Life and Letters of Nathan Smith, M.B., M.D.* (New Haven: Yale University Press, 1914), 51–52, 99; *General Catalogue of Dartmouth College and the Associated Schools, 1769–1900,* 62; Dr. Charles Knowlton's unfinished autobiography was published in two parts under the title "The Late Charles Knowlton, M.D.," *Boston Medical and Surgical Journal,* 10 September 1851 and 24 September 1851, 109–120 and 149–57; *The Seventh Census of the United States: 1850* (Washington, DC: Robert Armstrong, 1853), 22; Dartmouth Cemetery Association, "Record of Deaths, Interment and Inscriptions" (copied March 1929).

35. Alexander Grant, *The Story of the University of Edinburgh During Its First Three Hundred Years* (London: Longmans, Green, 1884), I:298–304; James Coutts, *A History of the University of Glasgow: From Its Foundation in 1451 to 1909* (Glasgow: J. Maclehose and Sons, 1909), 517–19; A. W. Bates, *The Anatomy of Robert Knox: Murder, Mad Science and Medical Regulation in Nineteenth-Century Edinburgh* (Eastbourne, UK: Sussex Academic Press, 2010); Tim Marshall, *Murdering to Dissect: Grave-robbing, Frankenstein and the Anatomy Literature* (Manchester: Manchester University Press, 1995).

36. By 1796 the municipal government and private brokers were seeking to seize the African cemetery to accommodate the expanding white population. The city offered a new burial ground, vacated black people's claims to the property, and resorted to coercion. However, the black community's

desire to protect their deceased also seems to have played a role in shaping the agreement that was finalized in 1800. The new burial ground was in Potter's Field. *Minutes of the Common Council of the City of New York, 1784–1831* (New York: By the City of New York, 1917), II:221, 264, 626, IV:522–25; T. Maerfchalckm, "A Plan of the City of New York, Reduced from an Actual Survey" (1763; New York: Valentine's Manual, 1850); Sappol, *Traffic of Dead Bodies*, 44–45, 106–7; Jaspar Dankers and Peter Sluyter, *Journal of a Voyage to New York and a Tour in Several of the American Colonies in 1679–80*, trans. and ed. Henry C. Murphy (Brooklyn: Long Island Historical Society, 1867), 136–37. On the social meaning and function of funerary ritual in black New York, see Leslie M. Alexander, *African or American? Black Identity and Political Activism in New York City, 1784–1861* (Urbana: University of Illinois Press, 2008).

37. *Providence Gazette*, 24 April 1773.

38. John Watts to the Honorable General Robert Monckton, 16 May 1764, *The Letter Book of John Watts: Merchant and Councillor of New York, January 1, 1762–December 22, 1765*, vol. LXI of *The Collections of the New-York Historical Society for the Year 1928* (New York: Printed for the Society, 1928), 254–56; Jared Sparks, ed., *The Writings of George Washington: Being His Correspondence, Addresses, Messages, and Other Papers, Official and Private, Selected and Published from the Original Manuscripts* (Boston: Ferdinand Andrews, 1839), I:559.

39. Maria Farmer, last will and testament, 18 March 1788, "Abstracts of Wills on File in the Surrogates Office, City of New York, Volume XIV, June 12, 1786–February 13, 1796. With Letters of Administration, January 5, 1786–December 31, 1795," *Collections of the New-York Historical Society for the Year 1905* (New York: Printed for the Society, 1906), 136–38; Charles Farmar Billopp, comp., *A History of Thomas and Anne Billopp Farmar and Some of Their Descendants in America* (New York: Grafton, 1907), 46–49.

40. Edward Warren, *The Life of John Warren, M.D., Surgeon-General During the War of the Revolution; First Professor of Anatomy and Surgery in Harvard College; President of the Massachusetts Medical Society, Etc.* (Boston: Noyes, Holmes, 1874), 11–12, 227–29; Edward Mussey Hartwell, *The Study of Anatomy, Historically and Legally Considered: A Paper Read at the Meeting of the American Social Science Association, September 9, 1880* (Boston: Tolman and White, 1881), 17–19; Moore, "Two Hundred Years Ago," 527–29; Henry Bronson, "Medical History and Biography," *Papers of the New Haven Colony Historical Society* (New Haven: For the Society, 1877), II:239–55.

41. The Rutgers Medical College (1792–93; 1812–16; 1826–30) enjoyed remarkable periods of success that were interrupted by attacks from Columbia College and Physicians and Surgeons. *Maryland Journal*, 26 October 1787; Sappol, *Traffic of Dead Bodies*, 109–10; see the 1826 advertisement in David I. Cowen, *Medical Education: The Queen's-Rutgers Experience, 1792–1830*

(New Brunswick: Rutgers Medical School, 1966); Steven Robert Wilf, "Anatomy and Punishment in Late Eighteenth-Century New York," *Journal of Social History*, Spring 1989, 510–16; minutes for 16 December 1793, in Columbia College Faculty of Medicine, Minutes 1792–1813, Health Sciences Library, Archives and Special Collections, Columbia University.

42. Sappol, *Traffic of Dead Bodies*, 44–45, 48–49, 106–7; *New York Journal and Daily Patriotic Register*, 19 April 1788.

43. *New-York Morning Post*, 15 October 1787; *Catalogue of the Governors, Trustees, and Officers, and of the Alumni and Other Graduates, of Columbia College (Originally King's College), in the City of New York, from 1754 to 1882* (New York: Printed for the College, 1882), 11–12.

44. *New-York Packet*, 25 April 1788; *American Herald*, 1 May 1788; *Pennsylvania Packet, and Daily Advertiser*, 18 April 1788; *Independent Gazetteer*, 18 April 1788; *Pennsylvania Mercury and Universal Advertiser*, 19 April 1788; Paul A. Gilje, *The Road to Mobocracy: Popular Disorder in New York City, 1763–1834* (Chapel Hill: University of North Carolina Press, 1987), 78–83; Sappol, *Traffic of Dead Bodies*, 107–9; Wilf, "Anatomy and Punishment in Late Eighteenth-Century New York," 508–13; Edward Robb Ellis, *The Epic of New York City* (New York: Coward-McCann, 1966), 181–83; *Minutes of the Common Council of the City of New York, 1784–1831*, I:363, 393, 623.

45. *American Herald*, 1 May 1788; *New York Journal and Daily Patriotic Register*, 19 April 1788; Joel Tyler Headley, *The Great Riots of New York, 1712–1873* (New York: E. B. Treat, 1873), 57.

46. President John Wheelock to the Hon. Benjamin J. Gilbert, 18 December 1809 (#809668), Resolutions made at a meeting of the President and other officers of Dartmouth College, 18 December 1809 (#809668.1), Henry Fish, William Tully, John R. Martin, Daniel Lyman, and Ira Bascom (Committee for the Class) to the Honorable President and Professors of Dartmouth College, ca. 1810 (810900.6), Rauner Library, Dartmouth College.

47. Minutes for 18 January 1814, College of Physicians and Surgeons, Faculty Minutes, I:109, Health Sciences Library, Archives and Special Collections, Columbia University; John C. Dalton, *History of the College of Physicians and Surgeons in the City of New York; Medical Department of Columbia College* (New York: By order of the College, 1888), 35–36. The stable also appears in the humorous unpublished poem "To Quackery," in Joseph Rodman Drake and Fitz Greene Halleck, *The Croakers* (New York: Privately printed, 1860), 129–31, 177. Moses Champion to Dr. Reuben Champion Jr., 11 November 1818 and 7 February 1819, Moses Champion Letters, 1818–1819, Box 1, Folder 32, Health Sciences Library, Archives and Special Collections, Columbia University.

48. Sappol, *Traffic of Dead Bodies*, 111–16; "The Late Charles Knowlton, M.D.," 115–20, 151; "Charles Knowlton" and "Dixi Crosby," Dartmouth Medical

School Student Files, Rauner Library, Dartmouth College; Hill, *College on the Hill*, 104–5.

49. Edward H. Dixon, *Scenes in the Practice of a New York Surgeon* (New York: DeWitt and Davenport, 1855), esp. 28, 231–33; Charles Knowlton, *Two Remarkable Lectures Delivered in Boston, by Dr. C. Knowlton, on the Day of His Leaving the Jail at East Cambridge, March 31, 1833, Where He Had Been Imprisoned, for Publishing a Book* (Boston: A. Kneeland, 1833). The controversy was over his book on contraception and morals: *Fruits of Philosophy: or, the Private Companion of Young Married People* (Boston, 1833), which was also published through London. John William Draper, *Petition of the Medical Faculty of the University of the City of New-York, to the Honorable the [sic] Senate and Assembly of the State of New-York, for the Legalization of Anatomy. Also an Introductory Lecture, Delivered at the Opening of the Medical Department of the University, for Session 1853–4, and Entitled an Appeal to the People of the State of New-York, to Legalize the Dissection of the Dead* (New York: Published by the faculty, 1853). On the history of the medical college of Queen's College (Rutgers), see Cowen, *Medical Education*.

50. Sappol, *Traffic of Dead Bodies*, 3–5; Wilf, "Anatomy and Punishment in Late Eighteenth-Century New York," 508–13; Gerard N. Burrow, *A History of Yale's School of Medicine: Passing Torches to Others* (New Haven: Yale University Press, 2002), 26–27; Margaret M. Coffin, *Death in Early America: The History and Folklore of Customs and Superstitions of Early Medicine, Funerals, Burials, and Mourning* (Nashville, TN: Thomas Nelson, 1976), 189–94.

51. *New-York Morning Post*, 15 October 1787; Sappol, *Traffic of Dead Bodies*, 18. For instance, an account of a dissection published the inhumane effects of whippings on a slave. *Independent American*, 10 May 1810. David Hosack's permit to attend at the almshouse for the year beginning 1 January 1789 and samples of tickets to his and other professors' lectures and demonstrations are available in the College of Physicians and Surgeons, Written and Printed Documents, John Dalton Scrapbook, Health Sciences Library, Archives and Special Collections, Columbia University.

Southern medical colleges followed the northern pattern. The disproportionate use of black people for training and research captured white southerners' discomfort with human dissection and medical experimentation. In 1807 local physicians organized a medical school in Baltimore, the first in the South. Physicians multiplied the number of southern medical programs in the decades before the Civil War by drawing upon the region's large black populations for subjects. Forming close ties to poorhouses, city hospitals, and plantations, these medical colleges raked the slave system for patients and specimens. Students at some of the best medical programs in the region, such as those in Charleston and Atlanta, did most of their training on the bodies of African Americans, living and dead.

The living had other uses. In 1852 the seven faculty members of the Georgia College of Medicine (1835) in Augusta pooled their money and purchased Grandison Harris for $700 at the slave market in Charleston, South Carolina. Harris was then put to work as the medical college's resurrectionist, digging up new corpses in the evening and carting them back to the laboratories. To hide the illegal seizures and dissections, he scattered the remains in the basement of the medical school, covered them with dirt, and coated the floor with lime to mask the odor. William G. Rothstein, *American Medical Schools and the Practice of Medicine: A History* (New York: Oxford University Press, 1987), 28–29; Todd L. Savitt, "The Use of Blacks for Medical Experiments in the Old South," *Journal of Southern History*, August 1982, 331–40; Tanya Telfair Sharpe, "Grandison Harris: The Medical College of Georgia's Resurrection Man," in Robert L. Blakely and Judith M. Harrington, eds., *Bones in the Basement: Postmortem Racism in Nineteenth-Century Medical Training* (Washington, DC: Smithsonian Institution Press, 1997), 3–6, 206–15.

52. Johann Friedrich Blumenbach, *Natural Varieties of Mankind*, 3rd ed. (Göttingen, Germany, 1795), in Thomas Bendyshe, ed. and trans., *The Anthropological Treatises of Johann Friedrich Blumenbach* (London: Longman, Green, Longman, Roberts, and Green, 1865), 247–49; Fyfe, *Compendium of the Anatomy of the Human Body*, I:24; Charles White, *An Account of the Regular Gradation in Man, and in Different Animals and Vegetables; and from the Former to the Latter* (London: C. Dilly, 1799), esp. 61–67.

CHAPTER 7: "ON THE BODILY AND MENTAL INFERIORITY OF THE NEGRO"

1. *The Commissioners of the Almshouse v. Alexander Whistelo, a Black Man*, General Sessions—New York, August Term, 1808, 1–7, Schomburg Center, New York Public Library. A complete transcript of the trial was immediately available in New York. *The Commissioners of the Alms-House, vs. Alexander Whistelo, A Black Man; Being a Remarkable Case of Bastardy, Tried and Adjudged by the Mayor, Recorder, and Several Alderman of the City of New-York, Under the Act Passed 6th March 1801, for the Relief of Cities and Towns from the Maintenance of Bastard Children* (New York: David Longworth, 1808). One Baltimore editor noted that the trial "contains the opinions of so many learned men" on the question of generation that it deserved to be reprinted without commentary. See *Medical and Philosophical Register*, 1 October 1808. On the law and violence against women in colonial society, see Ruth H. Bloch, *Gender and Morality in Anglo-American Culture, 1650–1800* (Berkeley: University of California Press, 2003). On the social and legal culture of Whistelo's New York, see Shane

White, "'We Dwell in Safety and Pursue Our Honest Callings': Free Blacks in New York City, 1783–1810," *Journal of American History*, September 1988, 445–70.

2. *Almshouse v. Whistelo*, 2–5; David Hosack, *An Inaugural Dissertation, on Cholera Morbus Submitted to the Examination of the Rev. John Ewing, S.T.P. Provost; the Trustees and Medical Professors of the University of Pennsylvania; for the Degree of Doctor of Medicine: On the Twelfth Day of May, A.D. 1791* (New York: Samuel Campbell, 1791); David Hosack, *Syllabus of the Courses of Lectures on the Theory and Practice of Physic and on Obstetrics and the Diseases of Women and Children, Delivered in the University of New-York* (New York: Van Winkle, Wiley, 1816); David Hosack, *An Inaugural Discourse, Delivered at the Opening of the Rutgers Medical College, in the City of New-York, on Monday the 6th Day of November, 1826* (New York: J. Seymour, 1826), 156–59; John Howard Raven, comp. *Catalogue of the Officers and Alumni of Rutgers College (Originally Queen's College) in New Brunswick, N.J., 1766–1916* (Trenton, NJ: State Gazette Publishing, 1916), 64. Jotham Post dedicated his 1793 dissertation to Professor Post. See *An Inaugural Dissertation, to Disprove the Existence of Muscular Fibres in the Vessels. Submitted to the Public Examination of the Faculty of Physic, Under the Authority of the Trustees of Columbia College in the State of New-York: William Samuel Johnson, LL.D. President; for the Degree of Doctor of Physic; on the Thirtieth Day of April, 1793* (New York: T. and J. Swords, 1793).

3. *Almshouse v. Whistelo*, 5; see Edvardus Miller, M.B., *Dissertatio Medica, Inauguralis, de Physconia Splencia. Quam Sub Moderamine Viri Admodum Reverendi D. Joannis Ewing, S.S.T.P. Universitatis Pennsylvaniensis Praefecti* . . . (Philadelphia: G. Young, 1789); see Samuel Latham Mitchill, Edward Miller, and E. H. Smith, *Address [to Physicians]* (New York: November 15, 1796); *Report of the Proceedings of the Medical and Surgical Society of the University of the State of New-York. During the Winter of 1809–10. Being the Third Session of the Society* (New York: George Long, 1810), 3–4; Hosack, *Inaugural Discourse, Delivered at the Opening of the Rutgers Medical College*, 24–33.

4. *Almshouse v. Whistelo*, 7–8; Benjaminus Kissam, *Dissertatio Medica Inauguralis, Amplectens Quadam de Utero Gravido. Quam, Annuente Summo Numine, Ex Auctoritate Reverendi admondum Viri D. Gulielmi Robertson, S.S.T.P. Academiae Edinburgenae Praelecti* . . . (Edinburgh: Balfour and Smellie, 1783), British Library; Herman Le Roy Fairchild, *A History of the New York Academy of Sciences, Formerly the Lyceum of Natural History* (New York: By the author, 1887).

5. Hosack, for instance, was a member of the Linnaean Society of London and the Royal Medical and Physical Society of Edinburgh. *Almshouse v. Whistelo*, 8–9; David Hosack, *Syllabus of the Course of Lectures, on Botany, Delivered in Columbia College* (New York: John Childs, 1795); *Catalogue of*

the Officers and Alumni of Rutgers College, 63. Valentine Seaman, of New-York, *An Inaugural Dissertation on Opium Submitted to the Examination of John Ewing, S.T.P. Provost; and to the Trustees and Medical Professors of the University of Pennsylvania; for the Degree of Doctor of Medicine: On the Second Day of May, A.D. 1792* (Philadelphia: Johnston and Justice, 1792); Valentine Seaman, *The Midwives Monitor, and Mothers Mirror: Being Three Concluding Lectures of a Course of Instruction on Midwifery. Containing Directions for Pregnant Women; Rules for the Management of Natural Births, and for Early Discovering When the Aid of a Physician is Necessary; and Cautions for Nurses Respecting Both the Mother and Child. To Which is Prefixed a Syllabus of Lectures on That Subject* (New York: Isaac Collins, 1800).

6. Andrew Duncan, *Heads of Lectures on Medical Jurisprudence, or the Institutiones Medicinae Legalis, Delivered at the University of Edinburgh* (Edinburgh: Neill, 1792), iii, 12–14. The first volume was on anatomy and the second covered the dissection and mapping of the human body. See William Nisbet, *The Edinburgh School of Medicine; Containing the Preliminary of Fundamental Branches of Professional Education, viz. Anatomy, Medical Chemistry, and Botany. Intended as an Introduction to the Clinical Guide. The Whole Forming a Complete System of Medical Education and Practice According to the Arrangement of the Edinburgh School*, 4 vols. (London: T. N. Longman and O. Rees, 1802).

7. *Almshouse v. Whistelo*, 9; David Hosack, *A Funeral Address, Delivered on the Twenty-Sixth of May, 1818, at the Interment of Doctor James Tillary, Late President of the St. Andrew's Society of the City of New-York* (New York: C. S. Van Winkle, 1818), 6–9; Hosack, *Inaugural Discourse, Delivered at the Opening of the Rutgers Medical College*, 93, 158, 161; *Catalogue of the Officers and Alumni of Rutgers College*, 62.

8. *Almshouse v. Whistelo*, 9; Matthias H. Williamson, *An Inaugural Dissertation on the Scarlet Fever, Attended with an Ulcerated Sore-Throat. Submitted to the Examination of the Rev. John Ewing, S.T.P. Provost; the Trustees and Medical Professors of the University of Pennsylvania; for the Degree Doctor of Medicine: On the Tenth Day of May, A.D. 1793* (Philadelphia: Johnston and Justice, 1793); Hosack, *Inaugural Discourse, Delivered at the Opening of the Rutgers Medical College*, 158–61; *Report of the Proceedings of the Medical and Surgical Society of the University of the State of New-York*, 3.

9. *Mulatto* was defined as the offspring of a white and a black person, a *quadroon* as the child of a white person and a mulatto, and a *sambo* as the product of a black person and a mulatto. *Almshouse v. Whistelo*, 10–22.

10. In 1825 several Physicians and Surgeons faculty resigned and formed a new medical program. They bought a building in New York City for $25,000 and sought affiliation with Geneva, Rutgers, and other colleges. Letter from Wright Post, president, et al., College of Physicians and Surgeons, New York, 25 March 1825, Rutgers Medical College Records,

1792–1793, Box 2, Folder 12, RG 29/A, Rutgers University Archives; *Documents in the Matter of an Application to the Honourable The Legislature of the State of New-York, for a Charter for Manhattan College* (New York: J. Seymour, 1829); 3–17; *Catalogue of the Officers and Alumni of Rutgers College*, 63; Samuel L. Mitchill, "A Sketch of the Mineralogical History of the State of New-York," *Medical Repository* (1798) I., no. 3; Milton Halscy Thomas, comp., *Columbia University Officers and Alumni, 1754–1857* (New York: Columbia University Press, 1936), 282; DeWitt Clinton, *A Memoir on the Antiquities of the Western Parts of the State of New-York, Read Before the Literary and Philosophical Society of New-York* (Albany, NY: I. W. Clark, 1818); Hosack, *Inaugural Discourse, Delivered at the Opening of the Rutgers Medical College.* Also see David Hosack, *Memoir of De Witt Clinton, with an Appendix, Containing Numerous Documents, Illustrative of the Principal Events of His Life* (New York: J. Seymour, 1829).

11. *Almshouse v. Whistelo*, 16, 20. Earlier, David Hosack had drawn up the curriculum and discipline for a short-lived medical college. See David Hosack, *Course of Studies Designed for the Private Medical School Established in New-York* (New York: Van Winkle, Wiley, 1816).

12. *Almshouse v. Whistelo*, 22–24; [Felix Pascalis Ouvriere], *Medico-Chymical Dissertations on the Causes of the Epidemic Called Yellow Fever; and on the Best Antimonial Preparations for the Use of Medicine* (Philadelphia: Snowden and M'Corkle, 1796); Felix Pascalis Ouvriere, *An Account of the Contagious Epidemic Yellow Fever, Which Prevailed in Philadelphia in the Summer and Autumn of 1797; Comprising the Questions of Its Causes and Domestic Origin, Characters, Medical Treatment, and Prevention* (Philadelphia: Snowden and M'Corkle, 1798), 5–7; Nisbet, *Edinburgh School of Medicine*, I:137; Hosack, *Inaugural Discourse, Delivered at the Opening of the Rutgers Medical College*, 24–33.

13. *Almshouse v. Whistelo*, 24–40.

14. Ibid.

15. Ibid., 40–42.

16. Vitto alleged that Comecho got his aunt, Mary Ephraim, to sell the land, used the money to get out of jail, joined the military, and then refused to honor the deed. Charles Francis Adams, *Some Phases of Sexual Morality and Church Discipline in Colonial New England* (Cambridge, MA: John Wilson and Son, 1891); David Flaherty, "Law and the Enforcement of Morals in Early America," in Lawrence M. Friedman and Harry N. Scheiber, eds., *American Law and the Constitutional Order: Historical Perspectives* (Cambridge, MA: Harvard University Press, 1988), 52–65; Graham Russell Hodges, "The Pastor and the Prostitute: Sexual Power Among African Americans and Germans in Colonial New York," in Martha Hodes, ed., *Sex, Love, Race: Crossing Boundaries in North American History* (New York: New York University Press, 1999), 60–71; "The Petition of Prince Vitto, late a Negro man servant to the

Rev[eren]d Oliver Peabody of Natick," 26 August 1755, *Acts and Resolves of the General Court*, vol. 9: 390–91, Massachusetts State Archives; Charles J. Hoadly, ed., *The Public Records of the Colony of Connecticut* (Hartford, CT: Case, Lockwood, and Brainard, 1850–), 273–74; Arthur W. Calhoun, *The American Family in the Colonial Period* (1917; New York: Dover, 2004), 132–33.

17. Joseph Hawkins, *A History of a Voyage to the Coast of Africa: And Travels into the Interior of That Country; Containing Particular Descriptions of the Climate and Inhabitants, and Interesting Particulars Concerning the Slave Trade* (Troy, NY: Luther Pratt, 1797), iii–ix.

18. Nancy Stepan, *The Idea of Race in Science: Great Britain, 1800–1960* (London: Macmillan, 1982), esp. xiii–xix; Thomas Church, D.D., *A Sermon Preached Before the Royal College of Physicians, London, in the Parish-Church of St. Mary-le-Bow, On Wednesday, September 20, 1752. Being One of the Anniversary Sermons, Appointed by the Will of the Lady Sadlier, Pursuant to the Design of Her First Husband, William Croune, M.D.* (London: John and James Rivington, 1752).

19. Such facilities had contributed to the leading medical programs of Europe, including Leiden and Edinburgh. Harvard's overseers organized a garden five years later. Hosack's project enjoyed the liberal support of well-placed New Yorkers such as Morgan Lewis. Assisted by his marriage to Gertrude Livingston, Lewis became a prominent attorney, slave owner, and public official. He was chief justice of New York until 1804, when he became governor. While serving as a trustee of Columbia College, Lewis adopted Hosack's endeavor. The garden eventually received state support under the condition that the other colleges in the state could use the facility. In 1807 a medical student from Versailles, France, dedicated his dissertation to Hosack, thanking the professor for purchasing and sustaining the garden and, thereby, raising the reputation of Columbia. The state eventually bought Elgin Garden from Hosack for about $75,000. It was transferred to Columbia in 1814. Columbia held the land as real estate for the next century, when it became part of the site of Rockefeller Center. David Hosack, *The Establishment and Progress of the Elgin Botanic Garden, and the Subsequent Disposal of the Same to the State of New-York* (New York: C. S. Van Winkle, 1811); Josiah Quincy, *The History of Harvard University* (Cambridge, MA: J. Owen, 1840), II:328–29; Richard A. Harrison, *Princetonians, 1769–1775: A Biographical Dictionary* (Princeton: Princeton University Press, 1980), 308–16; Simon Schaffer, "The Glorious Revolution and Medicine in Britain and the Netherlands," *Notes and Records of the Royal Society of London*, June 1989, 167; Alire Raffeneau Delile, *An Inaugural Dissertation on Pulmonary Consumption. Submitted to the Public Examination of the Faculty of Physic Under the Authority of the Trustees of Columbia College, in the State of New-York, the Right Rev. Benjamin Moore,*

D.D., President; for the Degree of Doctor of Medicine, on the 5th Day of May, 1807 (New York: T. and J. Swords, 1807); David Hosack, *An Inaugural Discourse, Delivered Before the New-York Horticultural Society at Their Anniversary Meeting, on the 31st of August 1824* (New York: J. Seymour, 1824); "An Act Instituting a Lottery for the Promotion of Literature and for Other Purposes," passed 13 April 1814, *Collections of the New York Historical Society, for the Year 1814* (New York: Van Winkle and Wiley, 1814), II:xi; John S. Whitehead, *The Separation of College and State: Columbia, Dartmouth, Harvard, and Yale, 1776–1876* (New Haven: Yale University Press, 1973), 26–27.

20. On the training, education, and specializations of nineteenth-century American scientists, see Donald deB. Beaver, *The American Scientific Community, 1800–1860: A Statistical-Historical Study* (New York: Arno, 1980). *The Constitution and Bye-Laws of the New-York Historical Society, Instituted in the City of New-York the 10th Day of December, 1804* (New York: T. and J. Swords, 1805); *The Charter and By-Laws of the New-York Dispensary, Instituted, 1790* (New York: C. S. Van Winkle, printer to the University, 1818).

21. Published in 1801, Dr. Hosack's lecture on medical education outlined much of the science literature being used in American colleges. David Hosack, *An Introductory Lecture on Medical Education; Delivered at the Commencement of the Annual Course of Lectures on Botany and the Materia Medica* (New York: T. and J. Swords, 1801); Stepan, *Idea of Race in Science*, 8–12; Johann Friedrich Blumenbach, *Elements of Physiology*, trans. Charles Caldwell (Philadelphia: Thomas Dobson, 1795). See especially Johann Friedrich Blumenbach, *De l'unité du genre humain, et de ses variétés, ouvrage précédé d'une lettre à Joseph Banks*, trans. Fred Chardel (Paris: Allut, 1804); Johann Friedrich Blumenbach, *A Short System of Comparative Anatomy*, trans. William Lawrence (London: Longman, Hurst, Rees, and Orme, 1807).

22. Stepan, *Idea of Race in Science*, xii–19; Georges Cuvier, *Lectures on Comparative Anatomy*, trans. William Ross (London: Wilson, 1802); James Cowles Prichard, *Researches into the Physical History of Man* (London: John and Arthur Arch, 1813); William Lawrence, *Introduction to Comparative Anatomy and Physiology; Being the Two Introductory Lectures Delivered at the Royal College of Surgeons, on the 21st and 25th of March, 1816* (London: J. Callow, 1816); W[illiam] Lawrence, *Lectures on Physiology, Zoology, and the Natural History of Man, Delivered at the Royal College of Surgeons* (Salem: Foote and Brown, 1828).

23. *List of Members, Laws, and Library Catalogue, of the Medical Society of Edinburgh. Instituted MDCCXXXVII; Incorporated by Royal Charter, December 14, MDCCLXXVIII* (Edinburgh: William Aitken, 1820), iii–lxiv and appendices; Douglas Sloan, *The Scottish Enlightenment and the American College Ideal* (New York: Teachers College Press, 1971), 26.

24. Hosack, *Inaugural Discourse, Delivered at the Opening of the Rutgers Medical College*, 24; John Morgan, *A Discourse Upon the Institution of Medical Schools in America; Delivered at a Public Anniversary Commencement, Held in the College of Philadelphia, May 30 and 31, 1765. With a Preface Containing, Amongst Other Things, the Author's Apology for Attempting to Introduce the Regular Mode of Practicing Physic in Philadelphia* (Philadelphia: William Bradford, 1765), 28–33; Whitfield J. Bell Jr., "Some American Students of 'That Shining Oracle of Physic,' Dr. William Cullen of Edinburgh, 1755–1766," *Proceedings of the American Philosophical Society*, 20 June 1950, 279; Donald J. D'Elia, "Dr. Benjamin Rush and the American Medical Revolution," *Proceedings of the American Philosophical Society*, August 23, 1966, 227–34; Betsey Copping Corner, "Day Book of an Education: William Shippen's Student Days in London (1759–1760) and His Subsequent Career," *Proceedings of the American Philosophical Society*, April 21, 1950, 135–36.

25. Valentine Seaman, M.D., *Account of the Yellow Fever, as it Appeared in the City of New-York in the Year 1795, Containing Besides its History, &c. the Most Probable Means of Preventing its Return, and of Avoiding it, in Case it Should Again Become Epidemic* (New York: Hopkins, Webb, 1796).

26. *Almshouse v. Whistelo*, 14; Felix Pascalis, *Eulogy on the Life and Character of the Hon Samuel Latham Mitchill, M.D. Delivered at the Request of the New-York City and County Medical Society, in the Superior Court Room, City Hall, October 15th, 1831* (New York: American Argus Press, 1831), 6–7.

27. Harry B. Yoshpe, "Record of Slave Manumissions in New York During the Colonial and Early National Periods," *Journal of Negro History*, January 1941, 80, 84, 87; Samuel Mitchill's manumission contract for Betsy, 18 June 1816, Records of the New York Manumission Society, New-York Historical Society.

28. Samuel Stanhope Smith, *Essay on the Causes of the Variety of Complexion and Figure in the Human Species. To Which are Added Strictures on Lord Kaims's Discourse, on the Original Diversity of Mankind* (Philadelphia: Robert Aitken, 1787), 22–25, 35n–36n, 48–53. For instance, one scholar has found a large number of students from the South in the courses of the prominent chemist William Cullen. See Bell, "Some American Students of 'That Shining Oracle of Physic,' Dr. William Cullen," 279–81; Sloan, *Scottish Enlightenment and the American College*, 27.

29. *Almshouse v. Whistelo*, 22–23; George Cuvier, *The Animal Kingdom, Arranged after Its Organization, Forming a Natural History of Animals, and an Introduction to Comparative Anatomy* (1817; London: Wm. S. Orr, 1849), 50.

30. Augustus K. Gardner, *Eulogy on John W. Francis, M.D., LL.D. Delivered Before the New York Medico-Chirurgical College, March 7, 1861* (New York:

By order of the College, 1861), 6–9, Special Collections and University Archives, Alexander Library, Rutgers University. *Catalogue of the Officers and Alumni of Rutgers College*, 65.

31. *Report of the Proceedings of the Medical and Surgical Society of the University of the State of New-York, During the Winter of 1807–1808; Being the First Session of the Society* (New York: C. S. Van Winkle, 1808).

32. Richard Hofstadter, *Academic Freedom in the Age of the College* (New York: Columbia University Press, 1961), 149; George B. Wood, *Early History of the University of Pennsylvania from Its Origin to the Year 1827* (1833; Philadelphia: J. B. Lippincott, 1896), 57–58; Rev. Thomas Ball's marriage certificate for William Shippen Jr. and Alice Lee, 3 April 1762, and the last will and testament of William Shippen Jr., 25 July 1807, Shippen Family Papers, Cartons 3–4, Manuscript Division, Library of Congress.

33. John Bard, New York City, to Samuel Bard, Edinburgh, 9 April 1763, and 19 September 1764, Bard Collection, Malloch Rare Book Room, New York Academy of Medicine; John Bard to Samuel Bard, 19 October 1761, Bard Family Papers, Box 1, Folder 7, Archives and Special Collections, Stevenson Library, Bard College; Philip K. Wilson, "Acquiring Surgical Know-How: Occupational and Lay Instruction in Early Eighteenth-Century London," in Roy Porter, ed., *The Popularization of Medicine, 1650–1850* (London: Routledge, 1992), 42–43.

34. Articles of agreement between John Bard, Mr. Stovenby, Esqr. of Dutchess County, and Lucus Lazeire of Dutchess County, 4 May 1763, Bard Collection, New York Academy of Medicine; advertisement for Hyde Park, 12 May 1768 and surveyors reports, Box 2, Folder 1, and the records relating to St. Stephen's College and New York Life Insurance and Trust, Box 3, Folder 2, Bard Family Papers, Bard Collection; Abraham Ernest Helffenstein, *Pierre Fauconnier and His Descendants with Some Account of the Allied Valleaux* (Philadelphia: S. H. Burbank, 1911), 86–99; G. O. Seilhamer, *The Bard Family: A History and Genealogy of the Bards of "Carroll's Delight" Together with a Chronicle of the Bards and Genealogies of the Bard Kinship* (Chambersburg, PA: Kittochtinny Press, 1908), 96–100; Walter Barrett, *The Old Merchants of New York City* (New York: Carleton, 1863), II:283–88; Sharon Ann Murphy, *Investing in Life: Insurance in Antebellum America* (Baltimore: Johns Hopkins University Press, 2010), 13–14; John M'Vickar, *A Domestic Narrative of the Life of Samuel Bard, M.D., LL.D., Late President of the College of Physicians and Surgeons of the University of the State of New-York, &c.* (New York: At the Literary Rooms, 1822), 73–74. Professor John McVickar explained the medicinal use of opium in his children's reader, *First Lessons in Political Economy, for the Use of Primary and Common Schools* (Albany, NY: Common School Depository, 1837), 43. See also "The 150th Anniversary of the Foundation of King's College," *To Dragma of Alpha Omicron Pi*, January 1905, 23.

35. The Royall Professorship is still an active chair at Harvard. Charles Tufts, the Boston businessman, donated about one hundred acres of land and considerable money for Tufts University, a Universalist college in Medford, Massachusetts. *Harvard University Quinquennial Catalogue of the Officers and Graduates, 1636–1930* (Cambridge, MA: By the University, 1930), 24–25; Myrtle Parnell, Report on Isaac Royall House, compiled May 1962, "Medford—Royall, Isaac" vertical files, Medford Public Library; Alexandra A. Chan, *Slavery in the Age of Reason: Archaeology at a New England Farm* (Knoxville: University of Tennessee Press, 2007), 1–6, 19–95; William Richard Cutter, ed., *Historic Homes and Places, and Genealogies and Personal Memoirs Relating to the Families of Middlesex County, Massachusetts* (New York: Lewis Historical Publishing, 1908), II:785–88; Josiah Quincy, *An Address Delivered at the Dedication of Dane Law College in Harvard University, October 23, 1832* (Cambridge, MA: E. W. Metcalf, 1832); Quincy, *History of Harvard University*, II:317–19, 425–27; *Annual Reports of the President and Treasurer of Harvard College, 1860–61* (Cambridge, MA: Welch, Bigelow, 1862), 45.

36. Hofstadter, *Academic Freedom in the Age of the College*, 129–30; Peter Dobkin Hall, "What the Merchants Did with Their Money: Charitable and Testamentary Trusts in Massachusetts, 1780–1880," in Conrad Edick Wright and Katheryn P. Viens, eds., *Entrepreneurs: The Boston Business Community, 1700–1850* (Boston: Massachusetts Historical Society, 1997), 400–01; Massachusetts General Hospital, *Address of the Board of Trustees of the Massachusetts General Hospital to the Public* (Boston: J. Belcher, 1814); *Harvard University Quinquennial Catalogue*, 30; L. Vernon Briggs, *History and Genealogy of the Cabot Family, 1475–1927* (Boston: Charles E. Goodspeed, 1927), I:340–41, II:483–503.

37. Lease between John Bard and Lucas and Ann Lazeire, 8 October 1765, Bard Family Papers, Box 1, Folder 8, Bard Collection; "Petition of Belinda, an aged African slave asking for an allowance from the estate of Isaac Royal, a Absentee," and the General Court's "Resolve," *Acts and Resolves of the General Court*, vol. 239: 11–14, Massachusetts State Archives; "The Petition of Belinda, Servant of Isaac Royall, Esq.," *Royall House Reporter*, April 1967; Chan, *Slavery in the Age of Reason*, 47–95. The lineage of Fortune Howard, who likely was also enslaved at Ten Hills, is available in Franklin A. Dorman, *Twenty Families of Color in Massachusetts, 1742–1998* (Boston: New England Historic Genealogical Society, 1998), 143–92.

38. In 1807, the year Preston died, John Revere, the son of Paul Revere, graduated from Harvard. He stayed to study medicine under James Jackson, a professor at Harvard Medical School and a founder of the Massachusetts General Hospital. Revere continued his education at the University of Edinburgh, graduating in 1811. He went on to a distinguished teaching career at Jefferson College in Philadelphia, and the University of the City

of New York. William Preston, *A Letter to Bryan Edwards, Esquire, Containing Observations on Some of the Passages of His History of the West Indies* (London: J. Johnson, 1795), 5; Bryan Edwards, *The History, Civil and Commercial, of the British Colonies in the West Indies* (London: J. Stockdale, 1793–94); Christopher Preston, "Life and Writings of William Preston 1753–1807," *Studies: An Irish Quarterly Review*, September 1942, 377–86; Valentine Mott, *A Biographical Memoir of the Late John Revere, M.D., Professor of the Theory and Practice of Medicine in the University of New York* (New York: Joseph H. Jennings, 1847), esp. 16–20; E. Digby Baltzell, *Puritan Boston and Quaker Philadelphia* (New Brunswick, NJ: Transaction, 1979), 355.

39. Sloan, *Scottish Enlightenment and the American College Ideal*, 13–15.

40. Ibid.; Roger L. Emerson, "The Philosophical Society of Edinburgh, 1768–1783," *British Journal for the History of Science*, November 1985; William Brown, *An Address to Students, Delivered in the Hall of the Royal Medical Society on 16th December 1852, at the First of a Series of Meetings Conducted by the Medical Missionary Society* (Edinburgh: John Greig and Son, 1854), 5–17; *List of Members, Laws, and Library Catalogue, of the Medical Society of Edinburgh*, appendices; James Ramsay, *An Essay on the Treatment and Conversion of African Slaves in the British Sugar Colonies* (London: James Phillips, 1784), esp. 199–210; Iain Whyte, *Scotland and the Abolition of Black Slavery, 1756–1838* (Edinburgh: Edinburgh University Press, 2006), 108–10.

41. A Pennsylvanian [Benjamin Rush], *An Address to the Inhabitants of the British Settlements, on the Slavery of the Negroes in America*, 2nd ed. (Philadelphia: John Dunlap, 1773), 3; A Pennsylvanian [Benjamin Rush], *A Vindication of the Address, to the Inhabitants of the British Settlements, on the Slavery of the Negroes in America, in Answer to a Pamphlet Entitled, "Slavery Not Forbidden by Scripture; Or a Defence of the West-India Planters from the Aspersions Thrown Out Against Them by the Author of the Address"* (Philadelphia: John Dunlap, 1773), 5.

42. On the influence of Christian teleology on Rush's view of medicine, see D'Elia, "Dr. Benjamin Rush and the American Medical Revolution." Vogt made this assertion at midcentury, when science, including his own research, was fully engaged in the project of categorizing the peoples living outside the narrow cultural and historical pathways of western and northern Europe into species. Vogt's comment on theology followed his methodical anthropological dissection and comparison of what he determined to be the superior Germanic type and the primitive Negro form. Carl Vogt, *Lectures on Man: His Place in Creation, and in the History of the Earth*, ed. James Hunt (London: For the Anthropological Society of Paris, 1864), 171–202, 403.

43. [Rush], *Address to the Inhabitants of the British Settlements, on the Slavery of the Negroes in America*, 3, 15, 26.

44. The Medical Society of South Carolina was founded in 1789. David Ramsay, *An Eulogium upon Benjamin Rush, M.D., Professor of the Institutes and Practice of Medicine and of Clinical Practice in the University of Pennsylvania. Who Departed This Life April 19, 1813, in the Sixty-Ninth Year of His Age. Written at the Request of the Medical Society of South Carolina, and Delivered Before Them and Others, in the Circular Church of Charleston, on the 10th of June, 1813, and Published at Their Request* (Philadelphia: Bradford and Inskeep, 1813), esp. 9. Also see David Hosack, *An Introductory Discourse, to a Course of Lectures on the Theory and Practice of Physic: Containing Observation on the Inductive System of Prosecuting Medical Inquiries; and a Tribute to the Memory of the Late Dr. Benjamin Rush. Delivered at the College of Physicians and Surgeons, on the Third of November, 1813* (New York: C. S. Van Winkle, 1813).

45. Thomas G. Dyer, *The University of Georgia: A Bicentennial History, 1785–1985* (Athens: University of Georgia Press, 1985), 64–65; William S. Powell, *The First State University: A Pictorial History of the University of North Carolina* (Chapel Hill: University of North Carolina Press, 1972), 33; William Gaston, *Address Delivered before the Philanthropic and Dialectic Societies at Chapel-Hill, June 20, 1832* (Raleigh, NC: Jos. Gales, 1832).

46. David F. Ericson, *The Debate over Slavery: Antislavery and Proslavery Liberalism in Antebellum America* (New York: New York University Press, 2000), 96–107; Drew Gilpin Faust, ed., *The Ideology of Slavery: Proslavery Thought in the Antebellum South, 1830–1860* (Baton Rouge: Louisiana State University Press, 1981), 21–77; Daniel Walker Hollis, *University of South Carolina* (Columbia: University of South Carolina Press, 1951–56), I:102–3, 164; Michael Sugrue, "'We Desire Our Future Rulers to Be Educated Men': South Carolina College, the Defense of Slavery, and the Development of Secessionist Politics," *History of Higher Education Annual*, 1994; James H. Thornwell, *The Rights and the Duties of Masters: A Sermon Preached at the Dedication of a Church Erected in Charleston, S.C., for the Benefit and Instruction of the Coloured Population* (Charleston, SC: Walker and James, 1850); Presbyterian Church of the United States [James H. Thornwell], *Report on the Subject of Slavery, Presented to the Synod of South Carolina, at Their Sessions in Winnsborough, November 6, 1851; Adopted by Them, and Published by Their Order* (Columbia, SC: A. S. Johnston, 1852).

47. The "Rogers Brothers" are best known for their contributions to nineteenth century science. James Blythe taught chemistry at several schools, including Washington Medical College in Baltimore, and the universities of Cincinnati and Pennsylvania. Robert Empie became professor of chemistry at the University of Virginia, and then succeeded his brother at Pennsylvania, where he also served as dean of the faculty. Henry Darwin and William Barton opened a school in Windsor, Maryland. Henry Darwin then held professorships in natural philosophy and geology at

Dickinson College and the University of Pennsylvania. In 1835 William Barton left William and Mary for a professorship in natural philosophy at Virginia, where he later served as chair of the faculty.

Report card for James and William Barton Rogers from William and Mary, 23 February 1820; William Barton Rogers to James Rogers, 19 January 1822; and William Barton Rogers to Thomas Jefferson, 14 March 1824, William Barton Rogers Papers, Box 1, Folders 2–4, Institute Archives and Special Collections, Massachusetts Institute of Technology. James P. Munroe, *William Barton Rogers: Founder of the Massachusetts Institute of Technology* (Boston: George H. Ellis, 1904), 4–31; William Barton Rogers to Uncle James Rogers, 22 February 1833, in Emma Savage Rogers, ed., *Life and Letters of William Barton Rogers* (Boston: Houghton Mifflin, 1896), esp. I:1–12, 102–3; "A Statute for the Government of the Steward, and Regulation of the College Table, Passed July 6th, 1830," *Laws and Regulations of the College of William and Mary, in Virginia* (Richmond: Thomas W. White, 1830), 5–6; Thomas R. Dew, *Review of the Debate in the Virginia Legislature of 1831 and 1832* (Richmond: T. W. White, 1832); Larry A. Witham, *Where Darwin Meets the Bible: Creationists and Evolutionists in America* (New York: Oxford University Press, 2002), 14–18.

48. John McCardell, *The Idea of a Southern Nation: Southern Nationalists and Southern Nationalism, 1830–1860* (New York: Norton, 1979), 177–226.

49. John Fulton, *Memoirs of Frederick A. P. Barnard: Tenth President of Columbia College in the City of New York* (New York: Macmillan for Columbia University Press, 1896), 246–59; David G. Sansing, *The University of Mississippi: A Sesquicentennial History* (Oxford: University of Mississippi Press, 1999), esp. 75; J. S. Newberry, *President F. A. P. Barnard, LL.D., S.T.D., L.H.D.* (New York: Privately printed, 1889); Nicholas L. Syrett, *The Company He Keeps: A History of White College Fraternities* (Chapel Hill: University of North Carolina Press, 2009), 74; Don H. Doyle, *Faulkner's County: The Historical Roots of Yoknapatawpha* (Chapel Hill: University of North Carolina Press, 2001), 177–78.

50. Fulton, *Memoirs of Frederick A. P. Barnard*, 251–60; Sansing, *University of Mississippi*, esp. 75; Doyle, *Faulkner's County*, 177–78; "A Great Educator," *The Literary World*, 22 August 1896, 260–61; Newberry, *President F. A. P. Barnard*; *Proceedings at the Inauguration of Frederick A. P. Barnard, S.T.D., LL.D., as President of Columbia College, on Monday, October 3, 1864* (New York: Hurd and Houghton, 1865). On the presence of northerners in the academies of the South and the intellectual course of this era, see Alfred L. Brophy, "'The Law of the Descent of Thought': Law, History, and Civilization in Antebellum Literary Addresses," *Law & Literature*, 2008, 343–402.

51. Virginius Dabney, *Mr. Jefferson's University: A History* (Charlottesville: University Press of Virginia, 1981), 9–26; Bertram Wyatt-Brown, *Southern Honor: Ethics and Behavior in the Old South* (New York: Oxford, 1982), 279;

William Barton Rogers to his brothers, 16 November 1840, in Rogers, ed., *Life and Letters of William Barton Rogers*, I:176–78.

52. John Duffy, "A Note on the Ante-Bellum Southern Nationalism and Medical Practice," *Journal of Southern History*, May 1968, 266–76; Samuel A. Cartwright, "Diseases and Peculiarities of the Negro Race," in Paul F. Paskoff and Daniel J. Wilson, eds., *The Cause of the South: Selections from DeBow's Review, 1846–1867* (Baton Rouge: Louisiana State University Press, 1982), 26–43.

53. Wyatt-Brown, *Southern Honor*, 97; David Greene Haskins, *A Brief Account of the University of the South* (New York: E. P. Dutton, 1877), 5–7; John Henry Hopkins, *Extract from the American Citizen, His Rights and Duties in Reference to Slavery* (New York: Pudney and Ressell, 1860); John Henry Hopkins, *Bible View of Slavery* (New York: Society for the Diffusion of Political Knowledge, 1863); George R. Fairbanks, *History of the University of the South, at Sewanee, Tennessee, from Its Founding by the Southern Bishops, Clergy and Laity of the Episcopal Church in 1857 to the Year 1905* (Jacksonville, FL: H. and W. B. Drew, 1905), 1–44.

54. J. H. Van Evrie, *Negroes and Negro "Slavery": The First an Inferior Race; The Latter Its Normal Condition* (New York: Van Evrie, Horton, 1861), 143–67.

CHAPTER 8: "COULD THEY BE SENT BACK TO AFRICA"

1. John Haskell Hewitt, *Williams College and Foreign Missions: Biographical Sketches of Williams College Men Who Have Rendered Special Service to the Cause of Foreign Missions* (Boston: Pilgrim, 1914), 35–42; Ashbel Green, D.D., L.L.D., President of the College, *A Report to the Trustees of the College of New Jersey: Relative to A Revival of Religion Among the Students of Said College, in the Winter and Spring of the Year 1815* (Philadelphia: Benjamin B. Hopkins, 1815), 6.

2. "Reverend Edward D. Griffin, D.D., President of Williams College, Williamstown, Massachusetts, Jan 20, 1832," in William B. Sprague, ed., *Lectures on Revivals of Religion* (Albany, NY: Packard and Van Benthuysen, 1832), 156; William B. Sprague, comp., *Memoir of the Rev. Edward D. Griffin, D.D.* (New York: Taylor and Dodd, 1839), 90–94; "Extract of a Letter from the Rev. Edward D. Griffin, of Newark, N. Jersey, to the Rev. Dr. Green, of Philadelphia," *Evangelical Intelligencer*, April 1808; Ansel Nash, "Memoir of the Rev. Edward Dorr Griffin, D.D.," *American Quarterly Register*, May 1841.

3. "Professor Stowe on Colonization," *African Repository and Colonial Journal*, December 1834.

4. *Catalogue of the Governors, Trustees and Officers, and of the Alumni and Other Graduates, of Columbia College (Originally King's College), in the City of New York, from 1754 to 1882* (New York: Printed for the College, 1882), 10–12; see the report of the founding meeting, 25 January 1785, "Standing Committee Minutes," vol. V, Records of the New York Manumission Society, New-York Historical Society.

5. See the preface and report of the founding meeting, 25 January 1785, "Standing Committee Minutes," vol. V., Records of the New York Manumission Society; George E. Brooks Jr., "The Providence African Society's Sierra Leone Emigration Scheme, 1794–1795: Prologue to the African Colonization Movement," *The International Journal of African Historical Studies* (1974), 184–87.

6. Franklin Bowditch Dexter, ed., *The Literary Diary of Ezra Stiles, D.D., LL.D., President of Yale College* (New York: Charles Scribner's Sons, 1901), I:39, 204, 213–14, 247–48, 355, III:78, 82, 102, 104, 400; Abiel Holmes, *The Life of Ezra Stiles, D.D., LL.D.: A Fellow of the American Philosophical Society; of the American Academy of Arts and Sciences; of the Connecticut Society of Arts and Sciences; a Corresponding Member of the Massachusetts Historical Society; Professor of Ecclesiastical History; and President of Yale College* (Boston: Thomas and Andrews, 1798), 157–58; "The Constitution of the Connecticut Society for the Promotion of Freedom, and for the Relief of Persons Unlawfully Holden in Bondage" (New Haven, 1790).

7. Ashbel Green, *The Life of Ashbel Green, V.D.M., Begun to be Written by Himself in His Eighty-Second Year and Continued to His Eighty-Fourth* (New York, 1849), 417, 449–52; David C. Humphrey, *From King's College to Columbia, 1746–1800* (New York: Columbia University Press, 1976), 298–302; Milton Halsey Thomas, comp., *Columbia University Officers and Alumni, 1754–1857* (New York: Columbia University Press, 1936), 282–83; John Howard Raven, comp., *Catalogue of the Officers and Alumni of Rutgers College (Originally Queen's College) in New Brunswick, N. J., 1766–1916* (Trenton, NJ: State Gazette Publishing, 1916), 11; *The American Quarterly Register*, May 1836; Thomas Clap, *The Annals or History of Yale-College, in New-Haven, in the Colony of Connecticut, from the First Founding thereof, in the Year 1700, to the Year 1766: with an Appendix, Containing the Present State of the College, the Method of Instruction and Government, with the Officers, Benefactors and Graduates* (New Haven, John Hotchkiss and B. Mecom, 1766), 117; Jonathan Edwards, *The Injustice and Impolicy of the Slave Trade, and of the Slavery of the Africans: Illustrated in a Sermon Preached Before the Connecticut Society for the Promotion of Freedom, and for the Relief of Persons Unlawfully Holden in Bondage, at Their Annual Meeting in New-Haven, September 15, 1791* (New Haven: Thomas and Samuel Green, 1791).

8. The College of Rhode Island did, however, confer honorary degrees to friends in Britain, particularly the wealthy Baptist merchants of Bristol.

Report of the Standing Committee, 9 November 1786, Records of the New York Manumission Society; "An Oration Delivered the Evening Previous to the Commencement 1786," Wells Family Papers, 1738–1953, Box 5, MC 727, Special Collections and University Archives, Alexander Library, Rutgers University; posted in *Daily Advertiser*, 6 January 1787; see Rev. Thomas Clarkson, *An Essay on the Impolicy of the African Slave Trade, in Two Parts* (London: J. Phillips, 1788); Moses Brown to Samuel Hopkins, 20 January 1786, and Samuel Hopkins to Moses Brown, 7 March 1787, Moses Brown Papers, Rhode Island Historical Society; James T. Campbell et al., *Slavery and Justice: Report of the Brown University Steering Committee on Slavery and Justice* (Providence: Brown University, October 2006), 23–24; Hywel Davies, *Transatlantic Brethren: Rev. Samuel Jones (1735–1814) and His Friends, Baptists in Wales, Pennsylvania, and Beyond* (Cranbury, NJ: Associated University Presses, 1995), 127.

9. Samuel Skudder's parents contributed $25, and Griffin promised to free the child after a decade. Rev. Griffin carefully secured his interests in the bargain. Samuel would have to serve faithfully for ten years, adding any time missed for illness or neglect to his term and compensating the reverend for medical costs, clothing beyond what he had when purchased, and other costs. His emancipation was also conditional: he had to provide surety of his independence to protect Griffin from being held liable for him. Reverend Griffin maintained the option of vacating the agreement for any cause. "If the said Samuel should become uneasy and wish to be sold, of if he should behave so as to render it necessary for me to sell him," warned the pastor, "I shall sell him as I bought him, a slave for life." In an amendment to the record, Griffin emphasized his and his heirs' right to sell Samuel for his remaining term if they ever needed money. The minister also agreed to repay Samuel's parents if any funds remained after he or his heirs recovered their investment.

Rev. Griffin assumed the presidency of Williams College during the tumult of 1821. Just before Griffin's arrival, a group of faculty and students divided and organized themselves across the Connecticut River as Amherst College.

Green, *The Life of Ashbel Green*, 326, 411; Harry B. Yoshpe, "Record of Slave Manumissions in New York During the Colonial and Early National Periods," *Journal of Negro History*, January 1941, 91; Henry Rutgers's manumission record for Thomas Boston, 12 June 1817, Records of the New York Manumission Society; Certification from the Overseers of the Poor and Justices of the Peace of the Township of Franklin, New Jersey, dated 27 September 1821, Wells Family Papers, 1738–1953, Box 5. See "Articles of Agreement made this 22nd day of April 1807 between Edward D. Griffin of the one part and Samuel Skudder by black boy, and now my property, of the other part," vol. III, Records of the New York Manumission

Society; John R. Fitzmier, *New England's Moral Legislator: Timothy Dwight, 1752–1817* (Bloomington: Indiana University Press, 1998), 43–44; Sprague, *Memoir of the Rev. Edward D. Griffin*, 6, 90–94; "Extract of a Letter from the Rev. Edward D. Griffin, of Newark, N. Jersey, to the Rev. Dr. Green, of Philadelphia," *Evangelical Intelligencer*, April 1808; Nash, "Memoir of the Rev. Edward Dorr Griffin, D.D."

10. American Board of Commissioners for Foreign Missions, *Instructions to the Missionaries About to Embark for the Sandwich Island: And to the Rev. Messrs. William Goodell and Isaac Bird, Attached to the Palestine Mission* (Boston: Crocker and Brewster, 1823); James Madison, "Notes for a Speech to Indian Tribes," 1812, General Correspondence, James Madison Papers, Library of Congress; John A. Andrew III, *From Revivals to Removal: Jeremiah Evarts, the Cherokee Nation, and the Search for the Soul of America* (Athens: University of Georgia Press, 1992), 99–100, 113–25; *A Narrative of Five Youth from the Sandwich Islands, Now Receiving an Education in This Country* (New York: J. Seymour, 1816), 7–29; L. Vernon Briggs, *History and Genealogy of the Cabot Family, 1475–1927* (Boston: Charles E. Goodspeed, 1927), II:525; William Elliot Griffis, *A Maker of the New Orient: Samuel Robbins Brown, Pioneer Educator in China, America, and Japan: The Story of His Life and Work* (New York: Fleming H. Revell, 1902), 57–62; Yung Wing, *My Life in China and America* (New York: Henry Holt, 1909); also see Amy Bangerter, "The New Englandization of Yung Wing: Family, Nation, Region," in Monica Chiu, ed., *Asian Americans in New England: Culture and Community* (Lebanon: University of New Hampshire Press, 2009), 42–60; Bernd C. Peyer, *The Tutor'd Mind: Indian Missionary-Writers in Antebellum America* (Amherst: University of Massachusetts Press, 1997), 177–79; Constance K. Escher, "She Calls Herself Betsey Stockton," *Princeton History*, 1991, 98–102; "Betsey Stockton" clipping file, New York State Historical Association.

11. The society's formal name was the "American Society for Colonizing the Free People of Color in the United States." Douglas Egerton has persuasively argued that Charles Fenton Mercer was the originator of the African colonization plan. Jared Sparks, *A Historical Outline of the American Colonization Society, and Remarks on the Advantages and Practicability of Colonizing in Africa the Free People of Color from the United States* (Boston: O. Everett, 1824), 5–6; Rev. Isaac V. Brown, A.M., *Memoirs of the Rev. Robert Finley, D.D., Late Pastor of the Presbyterian Congregation at Basking Ridge, New Jersey, and President of Franklin College, Located at Athens, in the State of Georgia, with Brief Sketches of Some of His Contemporaries, and Numerous Notes* (New Brunswick, NJ: Terhune and Letson, 1819), 75–77; "Address of the American Colonization Society to the People of the United States," *Christian Herald*, 13 September 1817; General Charles Fenton Mercer's history of the origins of the ACS, *African Repository and Colonial Journal*,

November 1833; Douglas R. Egerton, "'Its Origin Is Not a Little Curious': A New Look at the American Colonization Society," *Journal of the Early Republic*, Winter 1985, 463–480; Lacy K. Ford, *Deliver Us from Evil: The Slavery Question in the Old South* (New York: Oxford University Press, 2009), 70–72; Hampton Lawrence Carson, *The History of the Supreme Court of the United States; with Biographies of All the Chief and Associate Justices* (Philadelphia: P. W. Ziegler, 1891–92), II:630–31.

    Liberia would be America's Sierra Leone. About 1786 men of rank in London, frustrated with what they saw as the growing presence and poverty of black people in the city, launched a campaign to colonize Africa. In its initial phase it brought four hundred black Britons to the African coast along with about sixty white English, mostly women of poor health and "bad character." Grants of land were secured from the neighboring chiefs and a captain in the Royal Navy transported the settlers. Slaving wars threatened the original encampment and caused the colonists to flee. A year later, only sixty-four settlers remained. While this first venture failed, the commitment to removing black people survived. *Substance of the Report of the Court of Directors of the Sierra Leone Company to the General Court, Held at London on Wednesday the 19th of October, 1791* (London: James Phillips, 1791), 3–8; *Reasons Against Giving a Territorial Grant to a Company of Merchants, to Colonize and Cultivate the Peninsula of Sierra Leona, on the Coast of Africa* [a handwritten note on the title page gives the author's name as "Mr. Campbel"] (London, 1791), 2–7, collection of the British Library.

12. Donna L. Akers, *Living in the Land of Death: The Choctaw Nation, 1830–1860* (East Lansing: Michigan State University Press, 2004), 10–22; Peyer, *Tutor'd Mind*, 173–74; Anthony F. C. Wallace, *The Long, Bitter Trail: Andrew Jackson and the Indians* (New York: Hill and Wang, 1993), 5–11; James Monroe, Second Inaugural Address, 5 March 1821.

13. "Message of the President of the United States, to Both Houses of Congress, at the Commencement of the Second Session of the Twenty-first Congress," 7 December 1830; Ronald N. Satz, *Tennessee's Indian Peoples from White Contact to Removal, 1540–1840* (Knoxville: University of Tennessee Press, 1979), 36–43; Theda Perdue and Michael D. Green, *The Cherokee Nation and the Trail of Tears* (New York: Penguin, 2007), 42–68.

14. "An Act to Provide for an Exchange of Lands with the Indians Residing in Any of the States or Territories, and for Their Removal West of the River Mississippi," 28 May 1830; Perdue and Green, *The Cherokee Nation and the Trail of Tears*, 44; *The Cherokee Nation vs. the State of Georgia*, Supreme Court of the United States, 18 March 1831; Wallace, *Long, Bitter Trail*, 50–56. On Jackson's history with Indian warfare, land policy, and removal, also see Robert V. Remini, *Andrew Jackson and His Indian Wars* (New York: Viking, 2001).

15. "Miscellanies," *The Missionary Herald*, August 1824; *First Report of the New-York Colonization Society* (New York: J. Seymour, 1823); Andrew, *Revivals to Removal*, 113–25.

16. *Speech of Mr. Frelinghuysen, of New Jersey, Delivered in the Senate of the United States, April 6, 1830, on the Bill for an Exchange of Lands with the Indians Residing in Any of the States or Territories, and for Their Removal West of the Mississippi* (Washington, DC: Office of the National Journal, 1830), 3–15.

17. Josiah Quincy, "Remarks on the Visit of President Andrew Jackson to Harvard University, 1834," Papers of Josiah Quincy, Box 6, Harvard University Archives; Ronald N. Satz, *American Indian Policy in the Jacksonian Era* (Lincoln: University of Nebraska Press, 1975), 97–115; Michael Paul Rogin, *Fathers and Children: Andrew Jackson and the Subjugation of the American Indian* (New Brunswick, NJ: Transaction, 1991), 206–48; Ronald N. Satz, "Rhetoric Versus Reality: The Indian Policy of Andrew Jackson," in William L. Anderson, ed., *Cherokee Removal: Before and After* (Athens: University of Georgia Press, 1991), 36–44; Tim Alan Garrison, *The Legal Ideology of Removal: The Southern Judiciary and the Sovereignty of Native American Nations* (Athens: University of Georgia Press, 2002), 1–13; Gary E. Moulton, *John Ross, Cherokee Chief* (Athens: University of Georgia Press, 1978), 42–44.

18. *Speech of Mr. Frelinghuysen, of New Jersey . . . April 6, 1830*, 4–13; *Speech of Mr. Everett, of Massachusetts, in the House of Representatives, on the 14th and 21st of February, 1831, on the Execution of the Laws and Treaties in Favor of the Indian Tribes* (Washington, DC, 1831), 18–19.

19. Everett's signed copy is in the collection at Widener Library, Harvard University. *Speech of Mr. Everett, of Massachusetts . . . on the 14th and 21st of February, 1831*, 1–8; *Speech of Mr. Frelinghuysen, of New Jersey . . . April 6, 1830*, 23–24; Louis P. Masur, *1831: Year of Eclipse* (New York: Hill and Wang, 2001), 118–19.

20. *Speech of Mr. Frelinghuysen, of New Jersey . . . April 6, 1830*, 7, 23–25; *Speech of Mr. Everett, of Massachusetts . . . on the 14th and 21st of February, 1831*, 9.

21. The inscription reads: "Hon. Josiah Quincy with the best respects of his obliged friend, Elliott Cresson, Phila June 1830." See *Report of the Board of Managers of the Pennsylvania Colonization Society, with an Appendix* (Philadelphia: Thomas Kite, 1830), 47, Widener Library, Harvard University; *African Repository and Colonial Journal*, January 1834, March 1836.

22. W.L.G., "To the Hon. Theodore Frelinghuysen: On Reading His Eloquent Speech in Defence of Indian Rights," *Genius of Universal Emancipation*, July 1830; *Nile's Weekly Register*, 19 February 1831; *The Religious Intelligencer*, 24 April 1830, 8 May 1830; *Liberator*, 25 December 1840; "Congressional Temperance Society," *New York Observer and Chronicle*, 9 March 1833; "First Anniversary of the New York Prison Association," *Rural Repository*, 17 December 1845; *Episcopal Recorder*, 28 May 1831. On Garrison's

relationship to the ACS, see William Lloyd Garrison, *Thoughts on African Colonization: Or an Impartial Exhibition of the Doctrines, Principles, and Purposes of the American Colonization Society. Together with the Resolutions, Addresses and Remonstrances of the Free People of Color* (Boston: Garrison and Knapp, 1832); Henry Mayer, *All on Fire: William Lloyd Garrison and the Abolition of Slavery* (New York: St. Martin's, 1998).

23. Theodore Frelinghuysen, *An Oration: Delivered at Princeton, New Jersey, Nov. 16, 1824, Before the New-Jersey Colonization Society, by the Honourable Theodore Frelinghuysen* (Princeton: D. A. Borrenstein, 1824), 6–14.

24. Frelinghuysen, *An Oration: Delivered at Princeton, New Jersey, Nov. 16, 1824*, 8–9; County Tax Ratables, Somerset County, Eastern Precinct, 1784–1796, New Jersey State Archives; Richard A. Harrison, *Princetonians, 1769–1775: A Biographical Dictionary* (Princeton: Princeton University Press, 1980), 78–83.

25. Frelinghuysen, *An Oration: Delivered at Princeton, New Jersey, Nov. 16, 1824*, 9; "Unauthorized Transformation," *African Repository and Colonial Journal*, May 1835; *Liberator*, 11 April 1835; Samuel E. Cornish and Theodore S. Wright, *The Colonization Scheme Considered, in Its Rejection by the Colored People—in Its Tendency to Uphold Caste—in Its Unfitness for Christianizing and Civilizing the Aborigines of Africa, and for Putting a Stop to the African Slave Trade: In a Letter to the Hon. Theodore Frelinghuysen and the Hon Benjamin F. Butler; by Samuel E. Cornish and Theodore S. Wright, Pastors of the Colored Presbyterian Churches in the Cities of Newark and New York* (Newark: Aaron Guest, 1840); *Letter of the Honorable William Jay, to the Hon. Theo. Frelinghuysen* (New York, 1844), 3.

26. Henry Watson Jr., "Notes of Lectures on Ancient History by Charles Follen . . . 1829," in Henry Watson Jr. Lecture Notes, 1829, I:192–94, Rare Books and Special Collections, Neilson Library, Smith College.

27. Malcolm H. Stern, *First American Jewish Families: 600 Genealogies, 1654–1977* (Cincinnati: American Jewish Archives, 1978), 175; Thomas, *Columbia University Officers and Alumni, 1754–1857*, 200; Peter August Jay to the president of the American Society for Ameliorating the Condition of the Jews, 10 November 1822, Jay Family Papers, New-York Historical Society; *Catalogue of the Governors, Trustees and Officers, and of the Alumni and Other Graduates, of Columbia College (Originally King's College) in the City of New York*, 14; Cadwallader D. Colden's address for the New York Manumission Society, *Genius of Universal Emancipation*, 25 November 1826; Jacob Rutsen Van Rens[s]elaer to John R. Murray, 7 May 1823, and Hezekiah B. Pierpont to John R. Murray and R. Milford Blatchford, 19 May 1823, in "Lands Offered for Sale to the American Society for Ameliorating the Condition of the Jews—1823," Misc. Mss. Jews, New-York Historical Society.

In 1823 Annibale della Genga became the spiritual leader of the Roman Catholic Church and, as Pope Leo XII, ordered Jews to return to the ghettos. Leo sought to end what he viewed as unsavory interactions between Jews and Christians in the Papal States by reviving medieval restrictions on the economic, social, and physical mobility of Jews. Leo reestablished compulsory sermons aimed at convincing Jews of the spiritual danger of their faith and the corruption of their religious leaders. The Jewish origin of the Christian savior, David Kertzer explains, prevented Catholic theologians from asserting the racial inferiority of Jews, but the church could and did affirm the central accusations against Jews and embrace core biological images that grounded modern anti-Semitism.

　　　David I. Kertzer, *The Popes Against the Jews: The Vatican's Role in the Rise of Modern Anti-Semitism* (New York: Knopf, 2001), 60–85, 205–12; Joshua Trachtenberg, *The Devil and the Jews: The Medieval Conception of the Jew and Its Relation to Modern Antisemitism* (New Haven: Yale University Press, 1943), 11–52; Albert S. Lindemann, *Esau's Tears: Modern Anti-Semitism and the Rise of the Jews* (Cambridge: Cambridge University Press, 1997), 74–96.

28. *The Constitution of the Portland Society for Promoting Christianity Among the Jews; with an Address to the Christian Public; and a Collection of Interesting Facts Relative to the Conversion of the Jews* (Portland, ME: Arthur Shirley, 1823), 3–18; A Presbyter of the Church of England, *Obligations of Christians to Attempt the Conversion of the Jews* (Salem: Warwick Palfray, 1822), 19–20.

29. *Speech of Mr. Frelinghuysen, of New Jersey . . . April 6, 1830*, 9; *Liberator*, 12 March 1831, 2 July 1831, 5 November 1831, 17 March 1832; *African Repository and Colonial Journal*, February 1835, October 1835, 1 March 1841.

30. David Daggett to Jabez W. Huntington, 15 March 1830, Miscellaneous Manuscripts (arranged alphabetically by writer), Connecticut Historical Society.

31. Rev. Griffin led the effort to establish the New York and New Jersey Synod's school for black youth. Arguing the irrationality of treating a majority of the world's population as unsuited to Christian uplift and intended only for slavery, the synod looked to extend the blessings of Christianity to Africans and other benighted peoples. The effort rested on a rather sober accounting of the rewards that slavery and the slave trade had provided the Americas. The synod judged the United States in "arrears" to Africa for the slave trade. The school was a step in its incremental move toward colonization as the solution to slavery. The burden of evangelizing Africa, the officers noted, rested on the Americas because the Americas housed the victims of the slave trade. Redemption was, however, in reach: "Africa will yet boast of her poets and orators."

　　　Philip Milledoler, *Address, Delivered to the Graduates of Rutgers College, at Commencement Held in the Reformed Dutch Church, New Brunswick, N.J., July 20, 1831* (New York: Rutgers Press, 1831), 8–15; Frelinghuysen, *An Oration: Delivered at Princeton, New Jersey, Nov. 16, 1824*, 12; "Unauthorized

Transformation," *African Repository and Colonial Journal*, May 1835; James Richards and Edward D. Griffin, "African Seminary," *Christian Herald*, 9 November 1816; James Richards and Edward D. Griffin, "An Address to the Public," *Religious Remembrancer*, 28 December 1816; Elias Boudinot to Rev. Edward Dorr Griffin, 21 July 1804, Elias Boudinot Papers, Box 2, MMC 721, Library of Congress.

As the foreign secretary of the United Foreign Missionary Society, Philip Milledoler had governed missions to the Osage in Missouri for more than a decade, and advised Indian policy in Washington, D.C. An Osage child was named for him. See "New Osage Mission," *Religious Intelligencer*, 14 October 1820; "Osage Mission," *Religious Remembrancer*, 4 November 1820, 2 August 1823; "Second Mission to the Osages," *Missionary Herald*, January 1821; "United Foreign Missionary Society," *Boston Recorder*, 1 March 1823.

32. "Speech of the Hon. William W. Ellsworth, Representative of Connecticut, Delivered in the House of Representatives, Sitting as in Committee of the Whole, on the Bill for the Removal of the Indians, Monday, May 17, 1830," in Jeremiah Evarts, ed., *Speeches on the Passage of the Bill for the Removal of the Indians, Delivered in the Congress of the United States, April and May 1830* (Boston: Perkins and Marvin, 1830), 138.

33. Leslie M. Harris, *In the Shadow of Slavery: African Americans in New York City, 1626–1863* (Chicago: University of Chicago Press, 2003); Graham Russell Hodges, *Root and Branch: African Americans in New York and East Jersey, 1613–1863* (Chapel Hill: University of North Carolina Press, 1999); Julie Winch, *Philadelphia's Black Elite: Activism, Accommodation, and the Struggle for Autonomy, 1787–1848* (Philadelphia: Temple University Press, 1988); Gary B. Nash, *Forging Freedom: The Formation of Philadelphia's Black Community, 1720–1840* (Cambridge, MA: Harvard University Press, 1988); Stephen David Kantrowitz, *More than Freedom: Fighting for Black Citizenship in a White Republic, 1829–1889* (New York: Penguin, 2012); Adelaide M. Cromwell, *The Other Brahmins: Boston's Black Upper Class, 1750–1950* (Fayetteville: University of Arkansas Press, 1994); Robert J. Cottrol, *The Afro-Yankees: Providence's Black Community in the Antebellum Era* (Westport, CT: Greenwood, 1982); William D. Piersen, *Black Yankees: The Development of an Afro-American Subculture in Eighteenth Century New England* (Amherst: University of Massachusetts Press, 1988).

34. *Minutes of the Proceedings of the First Annual Convention of the People of Color . . . from the Sixth to the Eleventh of June, Inclusive, 1831* (Philadelphia: For the Convention, 1831), in Howard Holman Bell, ed., *Minutes of the Proceedings of the National Negro Conventions, 1830–1864* (New York: Arno, 1969).

35. *African Repository and Colonial Journal*, April 1836; Sparks, *Historical Outline of the American Colonization Society*. On Milledoler, see note 31.

36. Sparks, *Historical Outline of the American Colonization*, esp. 52–53.

37. *African Repository and Colonial Journal*, March 1835; Edward Everett, *Address of the Hon. Edward Everett, Secretary of State, at the Anniversary of the Am. Col. Society, 18th Jan., 1853*, 4–8.

38. "Professor Stowe on Colonization," *African Repository and Colonial Journal*, December 1834; Harriet Beecher Stowe, *Uncle Tom's Cabin* (Boston: John P. Jewett, 1852), II:251, 300–22; Harriet Beecher Stowe, *A Key to Uncle Tom's Cabin: Presenting the Original Facts and Documents upon Which the Story Is Founded* (London: Samson Low and Son, 1853), 361.

39. *Proceedings of a Meeting Held at Princeton, New-Jersey, July 14, 1824, to Form a Society in the State of New-Jersey, to Cooperate with the American Colonization Society* (Princeton: D. A. Borrenstein, 1824), 39–40, New-York Historical Society; Passenger log from the schooner *Alligator*, MG 49, Ship Logs, 1732–1861, New Jersey Historical Society; Rev. Daniel Coker, "Journal of Daniel Coker, 1821," 9, Manuscripts Division, Library of Congress.

40. Sean Wilentz, "Princeton and the Controversy over Slavery," *Journal of Presbyterian History*, Fall/Winter 2007; *Catalogue of All Who Have Held Office in or Have Received Degrees from the College of New Jersey at Princeton in the State of New Jersey* (Princeton: Princeton University Press, 1896); *African Repository and Colonial Journal*, February 1831, October 1845, December 1846, March 1848, February 1849; Theodore Ledyard Cuyler, *Recollections of a Long Life: An Autobiography* (New York: Baker and Taylor, 1902), 9.

41. *Proceedings of a Meeting Held at Princeton, New-Jersey, July 14, 1824*, 12–26.

42. Frelinghuysen, *An Oration: Delivered at Princeton, New Jersey, Nov. 16, 1824*, 6–14; *Literary and Theological Review*, January 1834; "Address of the Honorable Theodore Frelinghuysen Before the New Jersey Colonization Society, at Princeton," *Western New York Baptist Magazine*, February 1825.

43. *Liberator*, 12 March 1831; Everett, *Address of the Hon. Edward Everett, Secretary of State, at the Anniversary of the Am. Col. Society, 18th Jan., 1853*, 7–8; Edward Everett to John Thornton Kirkland, 30 November 1818 and 1 December 1818, and Edward Everett to Johann Friedrich Blumenbach, 22 December 1818, with inserted letter following Blumenbach's death, dated 15 March 1840, "Edward Everett Letterbook, 1818–1819," Special Collections, Houghton Library, Harvard College; Edward Everett to the Earl of Aberdeen, 30 December 1843, *African Repository and Colonial Journal*, June 1844; "William Lincoln, Notes, 1821, B[ook] II, Mr. Everetts Greek Lectures," esp. 34–41, Lincoln Family Papers, 1667–1937, American Antiquarian Society.

44. The Ivy League is an athletic conference organized in the early twentieth century. It includes Cornell University (1865) in New York State, which is not included here. The institutional and individual affiliations were checked against the records and periodicals of the ACS and its auxiliaries. Frederick Rudolph, *Curriculum: A History of the American Undergraduate Course of Study, Since 1636* (San Francisco: Jossey-Bass, 1977), 29. "Statistics

of Colleges and Theological Seminaries in the United States," *The American*, August 1840; Joseph Caldwell, University of North Carolina, 15 April 1831, American Colonization Society Papers, reel 10, Manuscripts Division, Library of Congress; Donald G. Tewksbury, *The Founding of American Colleges and Universities Before the Civil War, with Particular Reference to the Religious Influences Bearing upon the College Movement* (New York: Teachers College, 1932), 32–42; *Memorial of the Semi-Centennial Anniversary of the American Colonization Society, Celebrated at Washington, January 15, 1867* (Washington, DC: Colonization Society Building, 1867), 182–90; Jeffrey B. Allen, "'All of Us Are Highly Pleased with the Country': Black and White Kentuckians on Liberian Colonization," *Phylon*, Summer 1982, 109.

45. *Abridgment of the Debates of Congress, from 1789 to 1856, from Gales and Seaton's Annals of Congress, from Their Register of Debates, and from the Official Reported Debates, by John C. Rives. By the Author of the Thirty Years' View* (New York: D. Appleton, 1857), IV:112; Alice Dana Adams, *The Neglected Period of Anti-Slavery in America (1808–1831)* (Cambridge, MA: Radcliffe College, 1908), 140–41; *Genius of Universal Emancipation*, 1 July 1826, 27 January 1827, 13 September 1828; *African Repository and Colonial Journal*, September 1827, November 1829, October 1832.

46. Edward Hitchcock, *Reminiscences of Amherst College, Historical, Scientific, Biographical, and Autobiographical; Also, of Other Wider Life Experiences* (Northampton, MA: Bridgman and Childs, 1863), 29; *African Repository and Colonial Journal*, July 1829, March 1830, March 1831, October 1832, January 1833, March 1839, July 1844; Claude Moore Fuess, *Amherst: The Story of a New England College* (Boston: Little, Brown, 1935), 110.

47. Ralph Randolph Gurley, Boston, to Joseph Gales, treasurer, ACS, Washington, DC, 3 October 1835, and Gurley's travel and lecture information, American Colonization Society Papers, reel 24, Library of Congress.

48. As on many campuses, abolition could take root without black people being welcomed. In 1835 John Brown's father, Owen Brown, became a trustee of Oberlin College. He had left the board of Western Reserve when the college refused admission to a black student. Several years later the theology school admitted a black scholar, who later became a compatriot of John Brown.

Several of Lane's southern students began Sunday schools for local black communities. James Thome, a student from a slaveholding family in Kentucky, was dispatched to represent Lane at the American Anti-Slavery Society meeting in New York City. In the final debate, the attendees overwhelmingly decided that Christians could not support the ACS; only one person dissented.

John Greenleaf Whittier, "To the Memory of Charles B. Storrs, Late President of Western Reserve College," *Anti-Slavery Reporter*, November

1833; "Anti-Slavery Society in Oneida Institute," *The Abolitionist: or Record of the New England Anti-Slavery Society*, August 1833; Milton C. Sernett, *Abolition's Axe: Beriah Green, Oneida Institute, and the Black Freedom Struggle* (Syracuse, NY: Syracuse University Press, 1986), 47; *Debate at the Lane Seminary, Cincinnati: Speech of James A. Thome, of Kentucky, Delivered at the Annual Meeting of the American Anti-Slavery Society, May 6, 1834. Letter of the Rev. Dr. Samuel H. Cox, Against the American Colonization Society* (Boston: Garrison and Knapp, 1834), 3–16; "Western Reserve Anti-Slavery Society," *Liberator*, 21 September 1833; "Light in the West!" *The Abolitionist: or Record of the New England Anti-Slavery Society*, February 1833, October 1833; Oswald Garrison Villard, *John Brown, 1800–1859: A Biography Fifty Years After* (Boston: Houghton Mifflin, 1910), 46; Asaph Whittlesey to the Rev. R. R. Gurley, 19 July 1833, *African Repository and Colonial Journal*, August 1833; Arnold Buffum to the New England Anti-Slavery Society, *Liberator*, 14 September 1833.

49. "Value of Young Men," *Liberator*, 26 May 1837; "Education and Slavery," *Western Monthly Magazine, and Literary Journal*, May 1834.

50. Fuess, *Amherst*, 110–11; W. S. Tyler, *History of Amherst College During Its First Half Century, 1821–1871* (Springfield, MA: Clark W. Bryan, 1873), 86–87; "Anti-Slavery Society at Amherst College," *The Abolitionist: or Record of the New England Anti-Slavery Society*, July 1833, August 1833.

51. Arnold Buffum to the Board of Managers of the New England Anti-Slavery Society, in *Liberator*, 14 September 1833; Fuess, *Amherst*, 110–11; *New York Evangelist*, 17 January 1835.

52. *Philanthropist*, 1 April 1836, 8 April 1836.

53. *New York Evangelist*, 17 January 1835, 14 November 1835, 3 June 1837; Fuess, *Amherst*, 110–11.

54. The class that entered Dartmouth in the fall of 1835 included fourteen students who had formed an antislavery society at Phillips Academy in Andover, Massachusetts.

"To the Honourable Board of Trustees of Waterville College," 23 September 1833, Colby College Special Collections, Maine Memory Network; "Union College A.S. Society," *Liberator*, 23 July 1836; William F[rederick] Wallis to Lewis Sawyer, 17 October 1838, #838554, Rauner Library, Dartmouth College; see the constitution of the Dartmouth Anti-Slavery Society, *Herald of Freedom*, 2 April 1836; John King Lord, *A History of Dartmouth College, 1815–1909.* (Concord, NH: Rumford Press, 1913), 251–52, 315–32; Lewis Tappan to John Scoble, Esqr., 1 March 1843, in Annie Heloise Abel and Frank J. Klingberg, eds., *A Side-Light on Anglo-American Relations, 1839–1858: Furnished by the Correspondence of Lewis Tappan and Others with the British and Foreign Anti-Slavery Society* (Lancaster, PA: Association for the Study of Negro Life and History, 1927), 113–21.

55. Promissory note from the American Colonization Society to Chief Justice Marshall, 1 April 1834, American Colonization Society Papers, reel 251, Library of Congress; Early Lee Fox, "The American Colonization Society 1817–1840," Ph.D. diss., Johns Hopkins University, 1917, 50–51, 73; "Meeting of the Connecticut Colonization Society," *Connecticut Courant*, 26 May 1829; "American Colonization Society," *Colonizationist and Journal of Freedom*, March 1834; *African Repository and Colonial Journal*, May 1827, April 1833, May 1838.

56. John Duer, his grandfather, was a British councilor to Antigua, where William Alexander Duer's father, Colonel William Duer, was born. His grandmother, Frances Frye, was the daughter of the island's president. Both families were tied to the Royal African Company, owned large plantations in Dominica and Antigua, and traded slaves. The colonel inherited the Dominica estate and then settled in New York, purchasing land along the Hudson, competing for lumber contacts for the British Navy, and opening a Bronx cotton mill that was among the first in the United States. He created a large investment firm built on wildly speculative bank and land schemes that collapsed in 1792, helping to usher in a general financial panic and leading to his own imprisonment.

   New-York Commercial Advertiser, 10 July 1834; Paul A. Gilje, *The Road to Mobocracy: Popular Disorder in New York City, 1763–1834* (Chapel Hill: University of North Carolina Press, 1987), 162–70; Leonard L. Richards, *"Gentlemen of Property and Standing": Anti-Abolitionist Mobs in Jacksonian America* (New York: Oxford University Press, 1970), 20–81; Amos J. Beyan, *The American Colonization Society and the Creation of the Liberian State: A Historical Perspective, 1822–1900* (Lanham, MD: University Press of America, 1991), 79; *Christian Advocate and Journal and Zion's Herald*, 7 January 1831; *African Repository and Colonial Journal*, April 1832; William A. Duer, "Address," *The Religious Intelligencer*, 1 March 1834; William A. Duer, "New York Colonization Society," *Colonizationist and Journal of Freedom*, March 1834; Edwin G. Burrows and Mike Wallace, *Gotham: A History of New York City to 1898* (New York: Oxford University Press, 1999), 556–60. William Alexander Duer, Biographical Account of Col. William Duer, Duer Family Papers, Box 1, Folder 26, Rare Books and Manuscript Library, Columbia University; William A. Duer, *Reminiscences of an Old Yorker* (New York: W. L. Andrews, 1867), 78–81; "Colonel William Duer," *The Knickerbocker; or New York Monthly Magazine*, August 1852; Elizabeth Donnan, ed., *Documents Illustrative of the History of the Slave Trade to America* (Washington, DC: Carnegie Institution, 1930–35) II:36, 39, 126–27.

57. Craig Steven Wilder, "'Driven . . . from the School of the Prophets': The

Colonizationist Ascendance at General Theological Seminary," *New York History*, Summer 2012.

58. Three years later, Sylvester Hovey, professor of mathematics and natural philosophy at Amherst and a former professor and tutor at Williams and Yale, respectively, finished the final notes on a report to the American Union for the Relief and Improvement of the Colored Race. From 1835 to 1837 Hovey traveled through the Caribbean pursuing his interest in emancipation policy. Taking advantage of his tour, the American Union deputized him to document the condition of free, apprenticed, and enslaved black people in the West Indies and to report on the results of various emancipation processes. The Amherst campus was still in turmoil when Professor Hovey returned. Fuess, *Amherst*, 111; R. R. Gurley (from Portland, Maine) to Joseph Gates, 18 September 1835, American Colonization Society Papers, reel 24, Library of Congress; Edward Everett, *An Address Delivered Before the Literary Societies of Amherst College, August 25, 1835* (Boston: Russell, Shattuck, and Williams, 1835), esp. 35; Sylvester Hovey, *Letters from the West Indies: Relating Especially to the Danish Island St. Croix, and to the British Islands Antigua, Barbadoes and Jamaica* (New York: Gould and Newman, 1838); James Brewer Stewart, *Holy Warriors: The Abolitionists and American Slavery* (New York: Hill and Wang, 1976), 72; *Liberator*, 9 February 1838, 16 February 1838, 30 October 1840.

59. Benjamin Silliman, "Some Causes of the National Anxiety: An Address Delivered in the Centre Church in New Haven, July 4th, 1832," *African Repository and Colonial Journal*, August 1832.

EPILOGUE: COTTON COMES TO HARVARD

1. "Burning of the Lexington," *Christian Reflector*, 22 January 1840; "Remarks on the Death of Dr. Follen," Massachusetts Anti-Slavery Society Annual Meeting, *Liberator*, 7 February 1840.

2. Edmund Spevack, *Charles Follen's Search for Nationality and Freedom: Germany and America, 1796–1840* (Cambridge, MA: Harvard University Press, 1997), 46–165; Eliza Lee Cabot Follen, *The Life of Charles Follen* (Boston: Thomas H. Webb, 1844), 44–104; *A Memoir of Charles Louis Sand; Including a Narrative of the Circumstances Attending the Death of Augustus Von Kotzebue: Also, a Defence of the German Universities* (London: G. and W. B. Whittaker, 1819), esp. 3–34; William E. Channing, *A Discourse Occasioned by the Death of the Rev. Dr. Follen* (Cambridge: Metcalf, Torry, and Ballou, 1840); Alexandre Dumas, *Celebrated Crimes*, trans. I. G. Burnham (London: H. S. Nichols, 1895), III:71–150.

3. Follen, *Life of Charles Follen*, 91–97; George Ticknor, *Outlines of*

the Principal Events in the Life of General Lafayette (Boston: Cummings, Hilliard, 1825); Samuel J. May, *Some Recollections of Our Antislavery Conflict* (Boston: Fields, Osgood, 1869), 248–54; Samuel J. May, *Discourse on the Life and Character of the Rev. Charles Follen, L.L.D. Who Perished, Jan. 13, 1840, in the Conflagration of the Lexington. Delivered Before the Massachusetts Anti-Slavery Society, in the Marlborough Chapel, Boston, April 17, 1840* (Boston: Henry L. Devereux, 1840), 7–22; "Biographical Notices of the Late Dr. Charles Follen," *Monthly Miscellany of Religion and Letters*, February 1840.

4. Charles Follen, Cyrus Pitt Grosvenor, John G. Whittier, D. Helps, and Joshua V. Himes, "Address to the People of the United States," in *Proceedings of the New-England Anti-Slavery Convention, Held in Boston on the 27th, 28th, and 29th of May, 1834* (Boston: Garrison and Knapp, 1834), 59–72.

5. Andrew Preston Peabody, *Harvard Reminiscences* (Boston: Ticknor, 1888), 119–23; May, *Discourse on the Life and Character of the Rev. Charles Follen*, 9–10; Henry Watson Jr., "Notes of Lectures on Ancient History by Charles Follen . . . 1829" in Henry Watson Lecture Notes, 1829, I:206–7, Rare Books and Special Collections, Neilson Library, Smith College; Thomas Wigglesworth, "Student Notes, 1830–1832," vol. 1, Harvard University Archives.

6. Josiah Quincy, "Address Illustrative of the Nature and Power of the Slave States, and the Duties of the Free States; Delivered at the Request of the Inhabitants of the Town of Quincy, Mass., on Thursday, June 5, 1856" (Boston: Ticknor and Fields, 1856), 4; "Proceedings of the New England Anti-Slavery Convention," *Liberator*, 21 June 1850; Follen, *Life of Charles Follen*, 256–70; May, *Some Recollections of Our Antislavery Conflict*, 254–55.

7. Spevack, *Charles Follen's Search for Nationality and Freedom*, 145, 160–61; L. Vernon Briggs, *History and Genealogy of the Cabot Family, 1475–1927* (Boston: Charles E. Goodspeed, 1927), II:466–594; Carl Seaburg and Stanley Paterson, *Merchant Prince of Boston: Colonel T. H. Perkins, 1764–1854* (Cambridge, MA: Harvard University Press, 1971); Claude Moore Fuess, *An Old New England School: A History of Phillips Academy Andover* (Boston: Houghton Mifflin, 1917), 188; *Other Merchants and Sea Captains of Old Boston* (Boston: State Street Trust Company, 1919), 38; William Richard Cutter, ed., *Genealogical and Personal Memoirs Relating to the Families of the State of Massachusetts* (New York: Lewis Historical Publishing, 1910), IV:2191–94; Josiah Quincy, *The History of Harvard University* (Cambridge, MA: J. Owen, 1840), II:384–85.

8. Entries for 10 February, 25 March, and 7 May 1835, in the "Meeting Minutes, 1825–1847," Josiah Quincy Papers, Box 6, Harvard University Archives; John A. Walz, "The Early Days of the German Department," *Harvard Alumni Bulletin*, 20 May 1914, 528–30; George Washington Spindler, *The Life of Karl Follen: A Study in German-American Cultural*

Relations (Chicago: University of Chicago Press, 1917), 110–11; George Ticknor, *Life, Letters, and Journals of George Ticknor* (Boston: James R. Osgood, 1876), I:400–401.

9. Edmund Quincy, *Life of Josiah Quincy of Massachusetts* (Boston: Ticknor and Fields, 1867), 360; Briggs, *History and Genealogy of the Cabot Family*, II:595–96; Donnarae MacCann, *White Supremacy in Children's Literature: Characterizations of African Americans, 1830–1900* (New York: Routledge, 2001), 56–57; Eliza Lee Cabot Follen, *The Skeptic* (Cambridge: J. Munroe, 1835); Eliza Lee Cabot Follen, *Sketches of Married Life* (Boston: Hilliard Gray, 1838).

10. Channing also directed an open letter on slavery to the merchant Jonathan Phillips—a second cousin of Wendell Phillips—one of the donors to Follen's professorship. Samuel Eliot Morison, *Three Centuries of Harvard, 1636–1936* (Cambridge, MA: Harvard University Press, 1936), 254–55; Follen, *Life of Charles Follen*, 104–10; William Ellery Channing, *On the Evils of Slavery* (Richmond, IN: Central Book and Tract Committee of Friends, n.d.); William Ellery Channing, *Slavery* (Boston, 1835); William Ellery Channing, "Remarks on the Slavery Question, in a Letter to Jonathan Phillips, Esq.," *The Works of William E. Channing, D.D.* (Boston: American Unitarian Association, 1875), 782–820; George Willis Cooke, *Unitarianism in America: A History of Its Origin and Development* (Boston: American Unitarian Association, 1902), esp. 359; *Proceedings of the Massachusetts Anti-Slavery Society, at Its Seventh Annual Meeting, Held in Boston, January 23, 1838*, printed in the *Seventh Annual Report of the Board of Managers of the Mass[achusetts]. Anti-Slavery Society. Presented January 24, 1839* (Boston: Isaac Knapp, 1839).

11. Briggs, *History and Genealogy of the Cabot Family*, esp. I:342, II:489–90; David Richardson, ed., *Bristol, Africa and the Eighteenth Century Slave Trade to America* (Bristol: Bristol Record Society, 1986–1996), II:128, 141, III:14, 18; Elizabeth Donnan, ed., *Documents Illustrative of the History of the Slave Trade to America* (Washington, DC: Carnegie Institution, 1930–35), III:88, 99n–100n, IV:631; Frank Edward Manuel and Fritzie P. Manuel, *James Bowdoin and the Patriot Philosophers* (Philadelphia: American Philosophical Society, 2004), 240.

12. Emphasis added. May, *Discourse on the Life and Character of the Rev. Charles Follen*, 17.

13. William B. Weeden, *Economic and Social History of New England, 1620–1789* (New York: Hillary House, 1963), esp. II:466–72, 607–9.

14. Joseph C. and Owen Lovejoy, *Memoir of the Rev. Elijah P. Lovejoy; Who Was Murdered in Defence of the Liberty of the Press, at Alton, Illinois, Nov. 7, 1837*, with an introduction by John Quincy Adams (New York: John S. Taylor, 1838); Eliza Wigham, *The Anti-Slavery Cause in America and Its Martyrs* (London: A. W. Bennett, 1863), 37–45; James Brewer Stewart,

Holy Warriors: The Abolitionists and American Slavery (New York: Hill and Wang, 1976), 72; John Langdon Sibley, *Biographical Sketches of Graduates of Harvard University, in Cambridge, Massachusetts* (Cambridge, MA: Charles William Sever, 1873–), I:221–27; *Liberator*, 9 February 1838, 16 February 1838, 30 October 1840.

15. Quincy, "Address Illustrative of the Nature and Power of the Slave States," 2–6, 8.

16. Josiah Quincy, *A Municipal History of the Town and City of Boston, During Two Centuries. From September 17, 1630, to September 17, 1830* (Boston: Charles C. Little and James Brown, 1852), 354; Carol Bundy, *The Nature of Sacrifice: A Biography of Charles Russell Lowell, Jr., 1835–1864* (New York: Farrar, Straus and Giroux, 2005), 68; Jared Sparks, *The Life of Gouverneur Morris: With Selections from His Correspondence and Miscellaneous Papers, Detailing Events in the American Revolution, the French Revolution, and the Political History of the United States* (Boston: Gray and Bowen, 1832); Jared Sparks, ed., *The Writings of George Washington: Being His Correspondence, Addresses, Messages, and Other Papers, Official and Private, Selected and Published from the Original Manuscripts* (Boston: Ferdinand Andrews, 1839); Paul A. Varg, *Edward Everett: The Intellectual in the Turmoil of Politics* (Selinsgrove, PA: Susquehanna University Press; Cranbury, NJ: Associated University Presses, 1992), 23–24; Ashbel Green, *A Historical Sketch or Compendious View of Domestic and Foreign Missions in the Presbyterian Church of the United States of America* (Philadelphia: William S. Martien, 1838); John Maclean, *A History of the College of New Jersey, from Its Origin in 1746 to the Commencement of 1854* (Philadelphia: Lippincott, 1877); Archibald Alexander, *A History of Colonization on the Western Coast of Africa* (1846; New York: Negro Universities Press, 1969), 48–59; William Alexander Duer, *The Life of William Alexander, Earl of Stirling, Major-General in the Army of the United States During the Revolution, with Selections from His Correspondence, by His Grandson* (New York: Wiley and Putnam, 1847); William Alexander Duer, *New-York as It Was During the Latter Part of the Last Century: An Anniversary Address Delivered before the St. Nicholas Society, of the City of New York, December 1st, 1848* (New York: Stanford and Swords, 1849).

17. See the records from the Cuba plantations and operations, DeWolfe Papers, Box 8, Folders 1 and 2, Papers of the American Slave Trade, Series A, Part 2, Reel 11, Rhode Island Historical Society; James Coughtry, *The Notorious Triangle: Rhode Island and the African Slave Trade* (Philadelphia: Temple University Press, 1981), esp. 31–49, 94, 236; James A. McMillin, *The Final Victims: Foreign Slave Trade to North America, 1783–1810* (Columbia: University of South Carolina Press, 2004), 37, 88–89; Quincy, *History of Harvard*, II:412–13, 542–45, 596–97; William Coolidge Lane, ed., *Library of Harvard University: Bibliographical Contributions* (Cambridge,

MA: Library of Harvard University, 1903), 28; *Charles G. Loring vs. Israel Thorndike & Others*, November 1862, in Charles Allen, *Reports of Cases Argued and Determined in the Supreme Judicial Court of Massachusetts* (Boston: Little, Brown, 1863), V:257–70; Gordon M. Stewart, "Christoph Daniel Ebeling: America's Friend in Eighteenth Century Germany," *Monatshefte*, Summer 1976, 151–61; Charles Horatio Gates, *Memorials of the Class of 1835, Harvard University* (Boston: David Clapp and Son, 1886), 7–8; Stuart George McCook, *States of Nature: Science, Agriculture, and Environment in the Spanish Caribbean, 1760–1940* (Austin: University of Texas Press, 2002), esp. 56–60; Rebecca J. Scott, *Degrees of Freedom: Louisiana and Cuba after Slavery* (Cambridge, MA: Harvard University Press, 2005), 111–19; Richard P. Tucker, *Insatiable Appetite: The United States and the Ecological Degradation of the Tropical World* (Berkeley: University of California Press, 2000), esp. 38–42; César J. Ayala, *American Sugar Kingdom: The Plantation Economy of the Spanish Caribbean, 1898–1934* (Chapel Hill: University of North Carolina Press, 1999), 89–94.

18. Robert F. Dalzell, *Enterprising Elite: The Boston Associates and the World They Made* (Cambridge, MA: Harvard University Press, 1987); Thomas H. O'Connor, *The Athens of America: Boston 1825–1845* (Amherst: University of Massachusetts Press, 2006), 15–20; Harriette Knight Smith, *The History of Lowell Institute* (Boston: Lamson, Wolfe, 1898), 1–15, 49.

19. "Abbott Lawrence," *American Journal of Education and College Review*, January 1856, 205–15; William R. Lawrence, ed., *Extracts from the Diary and Correspondence of the Late Amos Lawrence; with a Brief Account of Some of the Incidents of His Life* (Boston: D. Lothrop, 1855), 244–45; Dalzell, *Enterprising Elite*, 65–78, 150; Mary Ann James, "Engineering an Environment for Change: Bigelow, Peirce, and Early Nineteenth-Century Practical Education at Harvard," in Clark A. Elliott and Margaret W. Rossiter, eds., *Science at Harvard University: Historical Perspectives* (Cranbury, NJ: Associated University Presses, 1992), 55–56; Morison, *Three Centuries of Harvard*, 279–80.

20. Henry B. Nason, ed., *Biographical Record of the Officers and Graduates of the Rensselaer Polytechnic Institute, 1824–1886* (Troy, NY: William H. Young, 1887); Julius A. Stratton and Loretta H. Mannix, *Mind and Hand: The Birth of MIT* (Cambridge, MA: Massachusetts Institute of Technology Press, 2005), 17–20, 47–48; A. J. Angulo, *William Barton Rogers and the Idea of MIT* (Baltimore: Johns Hopkins University Press, 2009), 80–88; 43–47; Henry R. Stiles, *The Civil, Political, Professional and Ecclesiastical History and Commercial and Industrial Record of the County of Kings and the City of Brooklyn, N.Y., from 1683 to 1884* (New York: W. W. Munsell, 1884), I:598–99, 673–74, II:953, 1320; Craig Steven Wilder, *A Covenant with Color: Race and Social Power in Brooklyn* (New York: Columbia University Press, 2000), 53–58; F. A. P. Barnard, "On Improvements

Practicable in American Colleges," *American Journal of Education and College Review*, January 1856, 174; *Charter, Trust Deed, and By-Laws of the Cooper Union for the Advancement of Science and Art: With the Letter of Peter Cooper, Accompanying the Trust Deed* (New York: Wm. C. Bryant, 1859).

21. "Biographical Notices of the Late Dr. Charles Follen."

Index

colleges, British
American students at, 182–87
influence on European science, 185–87
as instruments of colonial rule, 21–22, 25
colleges, colonial. *See also specific
institutions*
campus culture, slaveholders and, 77
founding of, slave trade profits and,
48–50, 67–75
graduates of
as colonial administrators, 17
as planters and slave traders, 31
and Indian dispossession, 156
and Indians, study of, 6
influence of slave-trading families on,
77, 86–88
efforts to avoid, 93–95
as instruments of colonial rule, 6, 17, 18,
20–22, 33, 45
involvement in slavery, 1, 2–3
pandering to wealthy slave owners by, 87
slavery as precondition of, 114
southward migration of graduates
from, 8
and Western migrants, civilization of,
157–58, 159
colleges, early American
antislavery movement and, 244–45
charters and founding of, 314n–15n
collections of Indian remains, 193–94
and racial science, development of,
190–95
and status of races in new nation, as
issue, 242–44, 248–49
colleges, southern
northern scholars at, tensions with,
236–37
and racial science
regionally specific knowledge, claims
of, 237–39
similarity to Northern forms, 231–32
and slavery
hardening of support for, 235
open debate on, before sectional
tensions, 234–35
Colman, Benjamin, 84–86, 87, 92
colonies, early, as militarized outposts,
33–36
Colonization Society of the City of New
York, 271
Columbia College. *See also* King's College
(New York City)
antislavery movement at, 243, 244, 245
medical school
and cadaver dissections, 203–4, 205–6
merger with College of Physicians
and Surgeons, 206

reopening of King's College as, 243
and slavery connection, efforts to hide,
283–84
trustees, support for Jewish removals, 257
Columbia University Law School,
origins of, 294n
Comecho, Job, 221
*Commissioners of the Almshouse v. Alexander
Whistelo, a Black Man* (New York
City, 1808), 211–20
and contemporary scientific knowledge,
223–25
decision in, 220
defense argument in, 219–20
expert witnesses in, 211–12, 213–19,
222–25, 226, 228, 238
facts of case, 212–13
morality of slavery as issue in, 221–22
and politicization of science, 212
slaveholders among participants in, 225
and transition to civil jurisdiction, 220–22
Compagnie de la Nouvelle France, 19
Company of Merchants Trading to Africa,
52
Conestoga Massacre, 149–50
Connecticut
American Colonization Society in, 2
emancipation of slaves in, 134
restrictions on Indian gun ownership, 38
and slavery, laws regulating, 32
Connecticut Colonization Society, 259
Connecticut Society for the Promotion of
Freedom, 244
Connecticut Yankee in King Arthur's Court,
295n
Cooper, Myles, 97, 97, 131, 136, 142, 170
Cooper, Peter, 287
Cooper Union, 287
Copland, Patrick, 22, 30
Corporation for the Propagation of the
Gospel in New England, 24–25,
35–36, 41
cotton, and the funding of northern
colleges, 285–86
Cotton, John, 92
Creek Indians, 91, 116, 250, 252, 259
Cromwell, Oliver, 24
Cruger family, 47–48, 52–53, 57, 60, 67, 96,
229
Cuba, plantations in, 285
Cullen, William, 99, 184, 187
curse of Ham, as justification for slavery,
177–78, 226
Curwen, Samuel, 140
Custis, John "Jacky," 136
Cuvier, Georges, 223, 226
Cuyler family, 60

A Note on the Author

CRAIG STEVEN WILDER is a professor of American history and head of history faculty at the Massachusetts Institute of Technology, and has taught at Williams College and Dartmouth College. Columbia University awarded him the University Medal of Excellence during its 250th Anniversary Commencement in 2004. He is also the author of *A Covenant with Color* and *In the Company of Black Men*, and he has advised and appeared in many historical documentaries including the History Channel series *FDR: A Presidency Revealed* and the award-winning PBS series, *New York: A Documentary Film*. He lives in Cambridge, Massachusetts.